PENGUIN REFERENCE

The Penguin Pocket D

David Pickering graduated in English from St Peter's College, Oxford. An experienced reference books compiler, he has contributed to (and often been sole author and editor of) some 150 reference books, mostly in the areas of the arts, language, local history and popular interest. These include a *Dictionary of Theatre* (1988), an *Encyclopedia of Pantomime* (1993), *Brewer's Twentieth-Century Music* (1994; 1997), a *Dictionary of Superstitions* (1995) and a *Dictionary of Witchcraft* (1996). He lives in Buckingham with his wife and two sons.

THE PENGUIN POCKET DICTIONARY OF BABIES' NAMES

David Pickering

PENGUIN BOOKS

PENGUIN BOOKS

Published by the Penguin Group
Penguin Books Ltd, 80 Strand, London WC2R ORL, England
Penguin Group (USA) Inc., 375 Hudson Street, New York, New York 10014, USA
Penguin Group (Canada), 10 Alcorn Avenue, Toronto, Ontario, Canada M4V 3B2
(a division of Pearson Penguin Canada Inc.)
Penguin Ireland, 25 St Stephen's Green, Dublin 2, Ireland
(a division of Penguin Books Ltd)
Penguin Group (Australia), 250 Camberwell Road,
Camberwell, Victoria 3124, Australia (a division of Pearson Australia Group Pty Ltd)
Penguin Books India Pvt Ltd, 11 Community Centre,
Panchsheel Park, New Delhi – 110 017, India
Penguin Group (NZ), cnr Airborne and Rosedale Roads, Albany,
Auckland 1310, New Zealand (a division of Pearson New Zealand Ltd)
Penguin Books (South Africa) (Pty) Ltd, 24 Sturdee Avenue,
Rosebank 2196, South Africa

Penguin Books Ltd, Registered Offices: 80 Strand, London WC2R ORL, England

www.penguin.com

The Penguin Dictionary of First Names first published 1999
Revised edition published 2004
This abridged edition published as
The Penguin Pocket Dictionary of Babies' Names 2005
6

Set in 7.75/9 pt ITC Stone
Typeset by Rowland Phototypesetting Ltd, Bury St Edmunds, Suffolk
Printed in England by Clays Ltd, St Ives plc

ISBN-13: 978-0-141-01976-5

www.greenpenguin.co.uk

Penguin Books is committed to a sustainable future
for our business, our readers and our planet.
The book in your hands is made from paper
certified by the Forest Stewardship Council.

CONTENTS

INTRODUCTION

Choosing a name for a baby is a matter most new parents naturally take very seriously. After all, a person's name can affect their whole life and career, and an inappropriate choice may cause lasting embarrassment or difficulty whatever that person's age or other qualities. A fanciful or frivolous name, for example, may suggest a likeable, cheerful nature but is not likely to promote a person's chances of being taken seriously, while a plainer, monosyllabic name might.

A person's name is a stamp of their individuality, though in reality it may well say more about the parents' prejudices, class background or social pretensions than it does about the bearer. People tend to make instant judgements about strangers based on names, although these judgements may be modified later. Children in particular may focus on unusual names in order to emphasize their own unique personality or make fun of others. Some names 'fit in' in certain regions or communities, but would look out of place elsewhere. Others change with fashion, being in vogue with one generation, but old-fashioned to the next (although they may well come back into fashion years later).

Examination of the lists of newly registered first names published by various government agencies around the English-speaking world each year reveals much about trends and changing tastes in the naming of children. Even the most cursory study of these records shows how contemporary parents continue to be divided between traditional choices that have been popular for generations and newer coinages, typically ones that have been promoted in various branches of the media. Thus, lists of the most popular names over the past few years have been dominated not only by such well-established choices as Jack, James, Charlotte and Emma but also by such new or rediscovered names as Callum, Oliver, Chloe and Jessica.

Modern parents seem to be more conservative in naming their sons than they are in naming their daughters. According to the records for the year 2002 some 2,430 different boys' names were registered, considerably fewer than the 3,089 names selected for girls. Many of the choices themselves have, however, been far from conservative. Several long-standing favourites for both sexes, which might have been expected to remain top choices for years to come, have recently gone into substantial decline, notable amongst them such examples as David (ending some 50 years as one of the top 10 favourite choices) and Sarah. Also languishing in the lower reaches of the tables are such former staples as Robert, Andrew, John, Susan and Alexandra. Other names that were briefly at a peak a decade ago (among them Jason, Kylie, Chelsea and Imogen) have returned to relative obscurity. Only time will tell if a similar fate awaits Ethan, Tyler, Maisie, Willow and the other recently emerged choices that have taken their place.

Parents continue to range widely for inspiration. While names from the Bible (Joshua, Matthew, Rebecca, etc) continue to play a significant role, many of the other names in the lists appear to reflect the influence of contemporary society, with bursts of interest in names borne by top sports players, film stars, fictional characters and so forth. In the last couple of years television has provided several popular choices, including the girls' name Chardonnay, as featured in the drama series *Foot-ballers' Wives*, and Alfie, familiar from the BBC soap opera *EastEnders*, while the cinema has suggested, among others, Angelina (after actress Angelina Jolie), Erin (from the film *Erin Brockovich*) and Maximus (after the name of the hero in *Gladiator*). Children's literature has inspired a renewal of interest in the old favourite Harry (as a result of the success of the *Harry Potter* stories) and in politics the birth of the prime minister's son Leo Blair focused the spotlight on another previously neglected name.

Imitation being the sincerest form of flattery, many people have followed the lead of various celebrities in taking up the names the famous select for their own children. Highlights in this category have included Brooklyn and Romeo (as bestowed upon David and Victoria Beckham's two sons), Dylan (the name of Catherine Zeta-Jones's first child) and Mia (the name of Kate Winslet's daughter).

A natural conservatism has, however, continued to exert itself with regard to more outlandish choices and parents seem to have been on the whole reluctant to accept the baton proffered by the late Paula Yates, who named her four daughters Fifi Trixibelle, Peaches, Pixie and Heavenly Hiraani Tiger Lily. Other recently recorded names that seem destined to remain unique include those of three Brazilian sisters who were called Xerox, Photocopier and Authenticated (reportedly because their birth resulted from a romp on a photocopying machine) and the British baby girl born in the 1990s with the name Room 21A (named apparently for similar reasons).

Lists of the most popular first names from different parts of the English-speaking world reveal the extent to which first names appear to be becoming increasingly universal, perhaps through the influence of the international media. There remain, however, some regional favourites, examples including Cameron, Ryan and Caitlin in Scotland,

Brandon and Taylor in the USA and Lachlan and Liam in Australia. If richness of choice is to be preserved through the new century such divergences are only to be welcomed.

Unlike some other countries, for example Denmark, the UK does not have a formal list of names from which new parents must choose. It should be noted, however, that the authorities may suggest parents reconsider if they find the proposed names particularly provocative or offensive. Births must be registered with the local register office within 42 days (21 in Scotland), although it is possible to delay for a whole year before notifying the authorities of the child's actual name.

The aim of this book is to expand the number of possibilities available to parents seeking names for their children. To inform their choices, each entry includes brief information about the gender of each name, its meaning and history, its origins and equivalents and diminutive forms, as well as any alternative spellings, abbreviated forms and (where appropriate) a guide to pronunciation. It concludes with an appendix listing the most popular current names.

Finally, it may be reassuring to know that if a baby grows up hating his or her name there remains the option of changing it, for a small fee (currently £39), by deed poll at a Registrar's Office.

Abdullah (m) Arabic name meaning 'servant of Allah'. One of the most popular of all Arabic names, it has special significance in the Islamic world as the name of Muhammad's father.

Abe *See* ABEL; ABNER; ABRAHAM.

Abel (m) Biblical name of uncertain origin. One theory claims that it comes from the Hebrew Hebel, itself derived from *hevel* ('breath' or 'vapour'), while another suggests it comes from the Assyrian for 'son'. It appears in the Bible as the name of Adam and Eve's younger son, famously murdered by his jealous brother Cain, and was consequently taken up by English Puritans after the Reformation. Sometimes abbreviated to **Abe**.

Abigail (f) Biblical name derived from the Hebrew Abigayil, meaning 'my father rejoices' or 'father's joy'. It appears in the Bible as the name of both King David's sister and his wife and was consequently taken up by English Puritans in the 17th century. Familiar forms of the name include **Abbie**, **Abby**, **Gale** and **Gayle**. *See also* ABBEY; GAIL.

Abilene (f) English name derived ultimately from a Hebrew place name thought originally to have meant 'grass'. It appears in the Bible and was consequently adopted as a name for various settlements in the USA, including a city in Kansas. It is unclear to what extent the development of Abilene as a first name resulted

Aaron (m) Biblical name of obscure origin, possibly Egyptian or else derived from the Hebrew Aharon, variously interpreted as meaning 'bright' or 'high mountain'. It appears in the Bible as the name of the brother of Moses and was consequently taken up by English Puritans in the 17th century. Also encountered as **Arn**.

Abbey (f) English name that was taken up as a diminutive of ABIGAIL. It appeared with increasing regularity during the 19th century. Also encountered as **Abbie** or **Abby**.

Abbie/Abby *See* ABBEY.

from its use as a place name or from the influence of ABBEY and relatively commonplace '-lene' feminine endings.

Abner (m) Biblical name derived from the Hebrew for 'father of light'. It appears in the Bible as the name of Saul's cousin and was consequently taken up by English Puritans in the 16th century. Since the early 19th century the name has been more common in the USA than elsewhere. Commonly abbreviated to **Ab** or **Abe**.

Abraham (m) Biblical name derived from the Hebrew Avraham, itself from the Hebrew *av hamon* ('father of a multitude' or 'father of many nations'). It appears in the Bible as the name of the father of the Hebrew nation and was consequently among the biblical names adopted by the Puritans in the 17th century. It continued to appear with some regularity into the early 20th century. Diminutive forms of the name include **Abe**, **Ham** and **Bram**.

Absalom (m) Biblical name derived from the Hebrew Abshalom, meaning 'father of peace'. It appears in the Bible as the name of King David's favourite son and was consequently in use among English-speakers as early as the 12th century. It continued in irregular use into the 19th century.

Achilles (m) Greek name supposedly derived from the Greek *a-* ('without') and *kheile* ('lips'), thus

meaning 'lipless', or else based on the name of the River Akheloos. It was borne in Greek mythology by the hero Achilles, whose name reflected the tradition that he was never suckled. The name has made rare appearances as a first name among English-speakers in relatively recent times.

Ada (f) English name possibly derived from the Old German *adal* ('noble') under the influence of the biblical Adah. It appeared with increasing regularity among English-speakers from the late 18th century, when it appears to have been imported from Germany, but is now rare. **Ad**, **Addie** and **Adie** are diminutive forms of the name. *See also* ADELAIDE.

Adair (m) Irish name meaning 'dweller by the oak wood'. A reference to the druids who attended sacred oaks in Celtic folklore, it also appears in Scotland as a variant of EDGAR.

Adam (m) Biblical name derived from the Hebrew *adama* ('earth') and meaning 'human being' or 'man'. It is sometimes traced back to the Hebrew for 'red' (a reference either to the colour of human skin or to the red colour of the clay from which God fashioned the first man). The Jews have never considered it suitable for use as a first name, but English-speakers adopted it with enthusiasm during the medieval period and it was among the most popular names in England in the

13th century. It has remained in regular use ever since. Diminutive forms of the name include the Scottish **Adie**. **Adamina** is a rare feminine equivalent. **Adamnan** is a related Irish name meaning 'little Adam'.

Adamina/Adamnan *See* ADAM.

Adan *See* AIDAN.

Addi *See* ADELINE.

Addie *See* ADA; ADELAIDE; ADRIAN.

Addy *See* ADELINE.

Ade *See* ADRIAN.

Adela (f) English and German name derived from the Old German *adal* ('noble'). It came to England with the Normans in the 11th century, being borne by William the Conqueror's daughter Adela (1062–1137) among others. The name enjoyed a peak in popularity among English-speakers in the late 19th century. Also encountered as **Adella**, **Adele**, **Adelle** or the French **Adèle** (as generally preferred by English-speakers in recent decades). *See also* DELLA.

Adelaide (f) English name derived from the Old German *adal* ('noble') and *heit* ('kind', 'state' or 'condition') and thus meaning 'woman of noble estate'. English-speakers took up the name during the 18th century after it became well known through William IV's popular German-born wife Queen Adelaide (1792–1849). Commonly abbreviated to **Addie**. Also encountered in the form **Adelia**. *See also* ALICE; HEIDI.

Adele/Adèle *See* ADELA.

Adeline (f) French name that developed as a variant of ADELA and has been in occasional use among English-speakers since the 11th century. It came to England with the Normans and enjoyed a modest vogue towards the end of the 19th century, but is rare today. **Addi**, **Addy** and **Aline** are diminutive forms of the name.

Adella/Adelle *See* ADELA.

Aden *See* AIDAN.

Adie *See* ADA; ADAM; ADRIAN; AIDAN.

Adlai (m) Biblical name derived via Aramaic from the Hebrew Adaliah, meaning 'God is just' or alternatively 'my ornament'. It appears in the Bible and was taken up by English-speakers in the 19th century but has never been common.

Adolf *See* ADOLPH.

Adolph (m) German name descended from the Old German Adalwolf, itself from the Old German *adal* ('noble') and *wolf* ('wolf'). It was introduced to England by the Normans, replacing the Old English equivalent Aethulwulf, and was revived in the wake of the Hanoverian Succession in the 18th century but was dropped when it became identified with the German Nazi dictator Adolf Hitler (1889–1945) – **Adolf** being the usual modern German form of the name.

Adonis (m) Greek name derived from the Phoenician *adon* ('lord').

It appears in Greek mythology as the name of a beautiful youth who captivated Aphrodite.

Adria See ADRIAN.

Adrian (m) English name derived from the Roman Hadrian, itself from the Latin for 'man of Adria' (a reference to a town in northern Italy). It made relatively few appearances between its first appearance in the late 12th century and the middle of the 20th century, when it suddenly came into vogue, enjoying a peak in popularity during the 1960s. **Ade**, **Addie** and **Adie** are diminutive forms of the name. **Adria** is a rare feminine equivalent. *See also* ADRIENNE.

Adriana/Adriane/Adrianna/ Adrianne See ADRIENNE.

Adrienne (f) French name taken up by English-speakers as a feminine version of ADRIAN. It appears to have made its debut among English-speakers in the early 20th century. Among diminutives are **Drena** and **Drina**. Variants include **Adriane**, **Adrianne**, **Adrianna** and **Adriana**.

Aed (m) Scottish and Irish name (pronounced 'aigh') meaning 'fiery one'. It was borne by several early Irish kings.

Aelwyn (m) Welsh name meaning 'fair-browed'. **Aelwen** is a feminine equivalent.

Aeronwy (f) Welsh name meaning 'berry stream'. The name refers to the River Aeron in Ceredigion. Also encountered as **Aeronwen**.

Afra See APHRA.

Africa (f) English name derived from that of the continent. It has enjoyed modest popularity in relatively recent times as a first name among US Blacks eager to demonstrate their African origins.

Agatha (f) English name derived ultimately from the Greek Agathe, itself from the Greek *agathos* ('good'). It was introduced to England by the Normans and was in widespread use throughout medieval times. It was revived in the 19th century, but has since become rare. Commonly abbreviated to **Aggie**.

Aggie See AGATHA; AGNES.

Agnes (f) English, German, Dutch and Scandinavian name descended from the Greek Hagne, itself derived from *hagnos* ('chaste' or 'pure'). Its popularity may also owe something to the influence of the Latin *agnus* ('lamb'), with its Christian connotations. The name was common in medieval England, but declined after the Reformation. It was among the medieval names revived in the 19th century. Commonly abbreviated to **Aggie**. Other diminutives include **Nessie** and **Nesta** (or **Nest**). *See also* ANNIS.

Ahmad See AHMED.

Ahmed (m) Arabic name derived from the Arabic *hamida* ('to praise') and thus meaning 'more praiseworthy'. Also encountered as **Ahmad** or **Ahmet**.

Ahmet See AHMED.

Aidan (m) English version of the Irish Aodan, itself a diminutive of Aodh (the name of a Celtic sun god, meaning 'fire'). The Anglicized form succeeded the Irish form in Ireland early in the 20th century and the name subsequently became popular elsewhere towards the end of the century. **Adie** is a diminutive form of the name. Occasionally also encountered as **Adan**, **Aden** or **Edan**. **Ethne** is a feminine equivalent. *See also* HAYDN.

Ailbhe *See* ELVIS.

Aileen *See* EILEEN.

Ailie *See* AILSA.

Ailsa (f) Scottish name derived from a place name (from the isle of Ailsa Craig in the Firth of Clyde), presumably under the influence of ELSA and similar names. The original place name came from the Old Norse Alfsigesey (meaning 'island of Alfsigr'). Pronounced 'eyela', it remains confined largely to Scotland. **Ailie** is a diminutive form.

Aimée/Aimi *See* AMY.

Ainsley (m/f) English name derived from a place name (common to Nottinghamshire and Warwickshire) based on the Old English *an* ('one') and *leah* ('clearing' or 'wood') and meaning 'lonely clearing' or 'my meadow'. Occasionally spelled **Ainslee** or **Ainslie**.

Aisha (f) Arabic name (pronounced 'eye-eesha') meaning 'alive'. It was borne by Muhammad's third and favourite wife and consequently became a favourite choice of name in the Arabic world. Also encountered as **Ayesha** – as in the H. Rider Haggard novel *Ayesha* (1905) – and as **Asia**.

Aisling (f) Irish first name (pronounced 'ashling') derived from the Gaelic for 'dream' or 'vision'. It became popular in Ireland in the 1960s. Also found as **Aislinn**, **Ashling** or **Isleen**.

Aithne *See* EITHNE.

Al (m/f) Diminutive form of such masculine names as ALAN, ALASTAIR, ALBERT, ALEXANDER, ALFRED and ALVIN and of the feminine ALICE and ALISON. It entered general usage in the USA in the 19th century. Famous bearers of the name have included the US singer and film actor Al Jolson (Asa Yoelson; 1886–1950) and the US film actor Al Pacino (b.1939). **Allie** and **Ally** are diminutive forms.

Alan (m) English and Scottish name of Celtic origin, supposedly from the Celtic *alun* ('concord' or 'harmony') or otherwise interpreted as meaning 'rock'. It was introduced to England by the Normans in the 11th century and became a fairly frequent choice during the medieval period. It was revived, along with other medieval names, in the 19th century. Commonly abbreviated to AL. Variants include **Allan**, **Allen**, the Welsh **Alun** and the Scottish

Gaelic **Ailean**. **Alana** is a feminine form.

Alana *See* ALAN.

Alasdair *See* ALASTAIR.

Alastair (m) English name derived from the Scottish Gaelic **Alasdair**, itself a variant of ALEXANDER. Having established itself among the Scots, it began to appear more widely among English-speakers during the 19th century but has been less frequent since the 1950s. Sometimes abbreviated to **Aly**. Also encountered in the variant forms **Alistair** or **Alister**.

Alban (m) English name possibly derived from the Roman place name Alba Longa (a district of Rome), itself from the Latin *albus* ('white'), or else from the Celtic *alp* ('rock' or 'crag'), and interpreted as meaning 'white hill'. It was in fairly common use during the medieval period and was briefly revived in the 19th century. Commonly abbreviated to **Albie** or **Alby**. Also found as **Albany** or **Albin**. **Albina** and **Albinia** are rare feminine forms.

Albany *See* ALBAN.

Albert (m) English and French name derived from the Old German Adalbert, itself from the Old German *adal* ('noble') and *beraht* ('bright' or 'famous') and thus meaning 'nobly famous'. Although records of its use among English-speakers go back to the Norman Conquest, it did not become popular until the 19th century, promoted by Queen Victoria's German-born husband Prince Albert of Saxe-Coburg-Gotha (1819–61). It has since become uncommon. Diminutive forms of the name include AL and BERT (or BERTIE). *See also* ALBERTA.

Alberta (f) English name that developed as a feminine equivalent of ALBERT. It enjoyed a minor vogue among English-speakers during the 19th century but has been rare since the beginning of the 20th century. Variants include **Albertina** and **Albertine**.

Albertina/Albertine *See* ALBERTA.

Albie/Albina/Albinia *See* ALBAN.

Aldo *See* ALDOUS.

Aldous (m) English name apparently derived from the Old German **Aldo**, itself from the Old German *ald* ('old'). It was a fairly frequent choice in eastern England during the 13th century but has never been in common general use, despite a minor resurgence in the 19th century. The most famous bearer of the name to date has been the British novelist Aldous Huxley (1894–1963). Variants include **Aldus**.

Alec (m) English name that developed as a diminutive of ALEXANDER around the middle of the 19th century, proving especially popular in Scotland. It enjoyed a peak in popularity in the first half of the 20th century but has since suffered a marked decline, in part because of the rise of the rival ALEX. Commonly abbreviated to **Lec**. Variants include **Alic**, **Alick** and **Aleck**.

Aled (m) Welsh name meaning 'offspring'. It enjoyed considerable exposure outside Wales in the 1980s through the Welsh soprano boy-singer Aled Jones (b.1971). **Aledwen** is a feminine equivalent.

Aleta/Aletha *See* ALETHEA.

Alethea (f) English name derived from the Greek *aletheia* ('truth'). It seems to have made its first appearances among English-speakers in the 17th century, perhaps in response to the Puritan enthusiasm for 'virtue' names. Also rendered as ALTHEA, although the two names are otherwise unconnected. **Letty** is a diminutive form. Also encountered as **Aleta** or **Aletha**.

Alex (m/f) English name that developed as a diminutive of the masculine ALEXANDER and also of the feminine ALEXANDRA or ALEXIS. It appears to have been an early 20th-century introduction that has steadily increased in frequency over the decades. **Lex** and **Lexie** are diminutive forms of the name. Also encountered as **Alix**. *See also* ALEC.

Alexa *See* ALEXANDRA; ALEXIS.

Alexander (m) Greek name derived from the Greek *alexein* ('to defend') and *aner* ('man') and thus meaning 'defender of men'. Famous as the name of Alexander the Great, King of Macedon (356–323 BC), it was popular during the medieval period, becoming especially common in Scotland, and has remained in regular use ever since. Among the many diminutive forms of the name are ALEC, ALEX, **Sandy** and SASHA. *See also* ALASTAIR; ALEXANDRA.

Alexandra (f) Feminine version of ALEXANDER. It was in frequent use during the medieval period and was among the medieval names revived in the 19th century. Variants include **Alexandria** and **Alexandrina**. Among common diminutive forms of the name are ALEX, SANDRA and SASHA. Less frequent diminutives include **Alexa**, **Alexia** and **Zandra**. *See also* ALEXIS.

Alexandria/Alexandrina *See* ALEXANDRA.

Alexia/Alexie/Alexina *See* ALEXIS.

Alexis (m/f) English and Russian name descended from the Greek Alexios, itself like ALEXANDER and ALEXANDRA derived from the Greek *alexein* ('to defend'). It has appeared with decreasing frequency as a masculine name in recent times as it has become more common as a feminine name. **Alexa**, **Alexia** and **Alexie** are relatively rare variants. **Lexie** and **Lexy** are diminutive forms. Variants include the Scottish **Alexina**.

Alf/Alfie *See* ALFRED.

Alfred (m) English name descended from the Old English Aelfraed, itself derived from the Old English *aelf* ('elf') and *raed* ('counsel') and interpreted as meaning 'inspired advice'.

Another derivation links the name with the Old English Ealdfrith, meaning 'old peace'. It was well established before the Norman Conquest, becoming widely known through Alfred the Great, King of Wessex (849–99). It was common during the early medieval period and was among the medieval names revived in the 19th century, but is now rare. Diminutive forms of the name include AL, **Alf**, **Alfie** and FRED. *See also* ALFREDA; AVERY.

Alfreda (f) English name descended from the Old English Elfreda, meaning 'elf strength', but now generally regarded as a feminine equivalent of ALFRED. It enjoyed a modest peak in popularity towards the end of the 19th century. FREDA is a diminutive form of the name.

Alger (m) English name (pronounced 'aljer') derived ultimately from the Old English Aelfgar, itself from the Old English *aelf* ('elf') and *gar* ('spear'). As **Algar**, it was fairly common during the medieval period but subsequently fell from favour, with a minor revival in the 19th century. The name received renewed exposure in the 1930s through Alger Hiss (1904–96), a US government agent accused of being a Soviet spy.

Algernon (m) English name derived from the Norman French *als gernons* ('with whiskers'). It was employed originally as a nickname for anyone with a moustache or whiskers. Having come to

England with the Normans, it became particularly identified with the powerful Percy family and acquired a reputation as an aristocratic name. Commonly abbreviated to **Algie** or **Algy**.

Algie/Algy *See* ALGERNON.

Ali (m) Arabic name meaning 'elevated' or 'sublime'. As the name of Muhammad's cousin and the first Islamic convert, it is a traditional favourite throughout the Islamic world. *See also* ALICE; ALISON.

Alice (f) English and French name derived from the Old German Adalheit, meaning 'noble woman'. It was in common currency among English-speakers during the medieval period, but fell from favour in the 17th century. It was revived in the 19th century, when it became well known from Lewis Carroll's stories *Alice's Adventures in Wonderland* (1865) and *Through the Looking-Glass* (1872). Commonly abbreviated to **Al** or **Ali**. Variants include the Welsh **Alys** and the Irish **Alis**, **Ailis** or **Ailish**. *See also* ALICIA; ALISON.

Alicia (f) English name that was taken up as a Latinized variant of ALICE in the 19th century. It has continued to appear alongside other forms of the name up to the present. Variant forms include **Alisa**, **Alissa** and **Alyssa** and the diminutive **Lyssa**.

Alick *See* ALEC.

Aline *See* ADELINE.

Alis *See* ALICE.

Alisa See ALICIA.

Alison (f) English and French name that developed as a Norman French diminutive of ALICE. It was taken up during the medieval period, but seems to have fallen out of favour outside Scotland after the 15th century. It enjoyed a substantial revival throughout the English-speaking world from the 1920s. Commonly abbreviated to **Al**, **Ali**, **Allie** or **Ally**. Also spelled **Allison**.

Alissa See ALICIA.

Alistair/Alister See ALASTAIR.

Alix See ALEX.

Allan See ALAN.

Allegra (f) English and Italian name derived from the Italian *allegro* ('happy', 'lively' or 'merry'). It is possible that the name was actually invented by the British poet Lord Byron, who bestowed it upon his illegitimate daughter Allegra Byron (1817–22).

Allen See ALAN.

Allie See AL; ALISON.

Allison See ALISON.

Ally See AL; ALISON.

Alma (f) English name of obscure origin, possibly derived from the Latin *alma* ('kind'), but often associated with the Italian *alma* ('soul'). It was only taken up with enthusiasm among English-speakers around the middle of the 19th century with reference to the British Army's victory at the Battle of Alma (1854) during the Crimean War. It is now rare.

Almira (f) English name probably derived from the Arabic *amiri* ('princess'). It made early appearances among English-speakers in the 19th century, but has been in only sporadic use since then, chiefly confined to the USA.

Aloisia/Aloisie See ALOYSIUS.

Aloysius (m) English, German, French and Dutch name (pronounced 'alo-ishus') representing a fanciful Latinized variant of LOUIS. It was in common currency in medieval Italy and subsequently became a favourite choice among Roman Catholics around Europe from the 17th century. **Aloisia**, **Aloysia** and **Aloisie** are rare feminine forms of the name.

Alpha (m/f) English name derived from the first letter of the Greek alphabet and thus suggesting excellence or prime importance. Its use as a first name in the English-speaking world goes back to the 19th century. Also spelled **Alfa**. *See also* OMEGA.

Alphonse (m) French name derived from the Old German *adal* ('noble') and *funs* ('ready' or 'prompt'), or else *ala* ('all') and *hadu* ('struggle') or *hild* ('battle'), that has made occasional appearances among English-speakers since the 19th century. **Fonsie** and **Fonzie** are diminutive forms of the name. A feminine variant is **Alphonsine**.

Alphonsine *See* ALPHONSE.

Althea (f) English name descended from the Greek Althaia, itself derived from the Greek *althein* ('to heal') and thus meaning 'wholesome'. It appeared in Greek mythology and was consequently taken up as a poetic name by English-speakers in the 17th century. *See also* ALETHEA.

Alun *See* ALAN.

Alva (m/f) English name derived from the Hebrew Alvah, meaning 'height' or 'exalted', but also in use as a feminine equivalent of ALVIN. It appears in the Bible and was taken up on a very limited scale by English-speakers in the 19th century. Famous bearers of the name have included the US scientist and inventor Thomas Alva Edison (1847–1931).

Alvar (m) English name descended from the Old English Aelfhere, itself derived from *aelf* ('elf') and *here* ('army' or 'warrior'), but also occasionally encountered in use as an Anglicized form of the Spanish Alvaro. Records of its use among English-speakers go back to the Norman Conquest.

Alvie *See* ALVIN.

Alvin (m) English name descended from the Old English Aelfwine, itself derived from the Old English *aelf* ('elf') and *wine* ('friend') and thus 'elf friend'. It made rare appearances among English-speakers before the 20th century, when it began to appear with more frequency, chiefly in the USA. Commonly abbreviated to AL or **Alvie**. **Alwyn** and **Aylwin** are variants of the name. *See also* ALVA.

Alwyn *See* ALVIN.

Aly *See* ALISON.

Alyssa *See* ALICIA.

Amabel (f) English name derived from the Latin *amabilis* ('lovable'). It made early appearances among English-speakers during the medieval period and was the subject of a minor revival in the 19th century but is rare today. *See also* ANNABEL; MABEL.

Amalia *See* AMELIA.

Amanda (f) English name derived ultimately from the Latin *amanda* ('lovable'), apparently under the influence of MIRANDA. There are suggestions that the name was in occasional use in the English-speaking world during the medieval period, but otherwise its first appearance appears to have been as the name of a character in the Colley Cibber play *Love's Last Shift* (1696). Commonly abbreviated to **Manda** or **Mandy** (or **Mandi**).

Amaryllis (f) Greek name possibly derived from the Greek *amaryssein* ('to sparkle') and thus a reference to sparkling eyes. The name appeared in both Virgil and Ovid and was subsequently taken up by English poets in the 17th century. It was revived in the 19th century, partly because it is also used as a flower name.

Amber (f) English name derived from that of the gemstone. It was taken up along with other jewel names towards the end of the 19th century. **Ambretta** is a rare variant.

Ambrose (m) English name descended from the Roman Ambrosius, itself from the Greek *ambrosios* ('immortal' or 'divine'). It has been in regular use among English-speakers since at least the 11th century, particularly among Irish Roman Catholics. It enjoyed a resurgence in popularity in the 19th century but is now uncommon. **Ambrosina** and **Ambrosine** are rare feminine forms. *See also* EMRYS.

Amelia (f) English name descended from the Roman Aemilius under the influence of the Old German *amal* ('labour'). It became popular among English-speakers in the 18th century through the first name of William IV's wife Queen Adelaide (1792–1849) and subsequently as that of Princess Amelia (1783–1810), the youngest daughter of George III. **Millie** and **Milly** are diminutive forms. Variants include **Amalia**. *See also* EMILIA.

Amethyst (f) English name derived from that of the semi-precious stone.

Amias *See* AMYAS.

Amie *See* AMY.

Amita *See* AMITY.

Amity (f) English name derived from the Latin *amitia* ('friend-

ship'). Variants include **Amita**, a relatively modern version of the name.

Amory *See* EMERY.

Amos (m) Hebrew name possibly meaning 'borne' or 'carried' and usually interpreted as meaning 'borne by God'. Another derivation suggests it comes from the Hebrew for 'strong' or 'courageous'. It appears in the Bible as the name of an Old Testament prophet and was taken up by English Puritans after the Reformation. It remained in fairly regular use until the end of the 19th century.

Amy (f) English name derived from the Old French *amee* ('beloved'), itself descended from the Latin *amare* ('to love'). It was taken up by English-speakers in the 18th century and has remained in use ever since, with a recent peak in popularity in the 1980s and 1990s. Variants of the name include **Aimi**, **Amey**, **Amie** and the French **Aimée**.

Amyas (m) English name derived either from the Roman Amatus, from the Latin for 'loved', or alternatively from a French surname meaning 'person from Amiens'. It has made occasional appearances among English-speakers since the 16th century. Also spelled **Amias**.

Anaïs (f) French name derived from the Greek for 'fruitful'. Famous bearers of the name in the English-speaking world have included the writer Anaïs Nin (1903–77).

Anastasia (f) English and Russian name descended from the Greek Anastasios, itself from the Greek *anastasis* ('resurrection'). Because of its meaning the name was popular among early Christians, although it was not adopted by English-speakers until the 19th century. Today the name is often associated with Princess Anastasia (1901–18), the youngest daughter of Czar Nicholas II. Diminutive forms include STACEY. *See also* TANSY.

Anatole (m) French name descended from the Roman Anatolius, itself derived from the Greek *anatole* ('sunrise' or 'east'). It was a popular choice among early Christians but was not taken up by English-speakers until the 19th century, and even then only on a very modest scale.

Andi/Andie *See* ANDREA; ANDREW.

Andrea (f) English name that developed as a variant of the masculine ANDREW, possibly under the influence of the original Greek Andreas. It seems to have made its first appearances as early as the 17th century but it was not until after the Second World War that the name began to appear with any regularity. **Andie** and **Andi** are diminutive forms.

Andrew (m) English, Russian and Greek name derived from the Greek Andreas, itself from the Greek *andreia* ('manliness')

and thus meaning 'manly' or 'brave'. It appears in the Bible as the name of one of the apostles, subsequently adopted as the patron saint of Scotland, Greece and Russia – hence the name's popularity in those countries. It was in regular use among English-speakers by medieval times. The most common diminutive forms include **Andy**, **Andie**, **Andi** and the Scottish DREW. **Andrine**, **Andrene**, **Andrena** and **Andreana** are rare feminine forms. *See also* DANDY.

Andy *See* ANDREW.

Aneira/Aneirin *See* ANEURIN.

Aneka *See* ANNEKA.

Aneurin (m) Welsh name of obscure origin, possibly derived from the Welsh *an* ('all') and *eur* ('gold') and interpreted as 'precious one'. Attempts have also been made to trace it back to the Roman Honorius, meaning 'honourable'. Usually pronounced 'an-eye-rin', it was in use in Wales by the medieval period. Also spelled **Aneirin**. It is often abbreviated to **Nye**. **Aneira** is a rare feminine form.

Ange *See* ANGEL; ANGELA.

Angel (m/f) English name derived via Latin from the Greek *angelos* ('messenger') and meaning 'messenger of God' or simply 'angel'. It seems to have been adopted as early as the 17th century and has continued to make rare reappearances ever since. Famous bearers of the name have included Angel Clare in the Thomas Hardy novel

Tess of the D'Urbervilles (1891).
Ange and **Angie** are diminutive forms of the name. *See also* ANGELA.

Angela (f) English and Italian name that developed as a feminine equivalent of the masculine ANGEL. It was taken up by English-speakers in the 18th century but has been less common since the 1960s. In its early history it was often reserved for children born on 29 September, the feast of St Michael and All Angels. Commonly abbreviated to **Ange**, **Angie** or **Angy**. *See also* ANGELICA.

Angelica (f) English and Italian name derived from the Latin *angelicus* ('angelic') but often regarded as a variant of ANGELA. It was imported to England from Italy in the 17th century but has tailed off significantly since the 1950s. Commonly abbreviated to **Ange** or **Angie**. Variants of the name include **Anjelica**, **Angelina**, **Angeline** and **Angelita**.

Angelina/Angeline/Angelita
See ANGELICA.

Angharad (f) Welsh name (pronounced 'anharad') derived from the Welsh *an* ('more') and *car* ('love') and meaning 'much loved'. Its history among Welsh-speakers goes back at least to the 12th century. It has generally remained confined to Wales, although it became more widely familiar in the 1970s through Welsh actress Angharad Rees (b.1949).

Angie *See* ANGEL; ANGELA; ANGELICA.

Angus (m) English version of the Scottish Gaelic **Aonghas** (or **Aonghus**), itself derived from the Gaelic *aon* ('one') and *ghus* ('choice') and thus meaning 'sole choice'. The name's history in Scotland goes back to at least the 15th century, when it was particularly associated with the clan McDonnell. It retains its distinctive Scottish character. Commonly abbreviated to GUS. **Angusina** is a rare feminine version.

Angy *See* ANGEL; ANGELA; ANGELICA.

Anis *See* ANNIS.

Anita (f) Spanish name that evolved as a diminutive form of ANNE. It was taken up by English-speakers in the 19th century, initially in the USA, but has since spread throughout the English-speaking world. **Nita** is a diminutive form.

Anjelica *See* ANGELICA.

Ann (f) English name that developed as a variant of the Hebrew HANNAH and thus means 'grace' or 'favour'. It became a popular choice of name among English-speakers during the medieval period, although it has been eclipsed in recent decades by the French form of the name, ANNE. Diminutives of the name include ANNIE, **Nan**, **Nana**, NANCY and NINA.

Anna (f) English, French, Dutch, German, Italian, Scandinavian and Russian name that began life as the Greek or Latin form of HANNAH and thus interpreted as meaning 'grace' or 'favour'. It was taken up by English-speakers in the 19th century, alongside ANN and other variants of the same name, and has remained current ever since. **Anya** is a variant form.

Annabel (f) English name that came about through the combination of ANN or ANNA with the French *belle* ('beautiful'), possibly under the influence of AMABEL. It made its first appearances in Scotland as early as the 12th century, but was not taken up more widely among English-speakers until the 19th century. Commonly abbreviated to **Bel** or **Belle**. Also encountered as **Annabella** or **Annabelle**.

Annabella/Annabelle *See* ANNABEL.

Annalisa (f) English version of the German and Scandinavian Anneliese, which resulted from the combination of ANNE and Liese (a diminutive of ELIZABETH).

Anne (f) French name that was taken up by English-speakers as a variant of ANN during the medieval period. It has remained in regular use ever since and established itself as the most common form of the name around the middle of the 20th century. Diminutives of the name include ANNIE, **Nan**, **Nana** and NANCY. Variants include ANNETTE, ANITA and ANNEKA. It is also found in combination with various other names, as in **Mary Anne** or **Anne-Marie**.

Anneka (f) Swedish variant of ANNE that was adopted by English-speakers in the 1950s. Commonly abbreviated to ANNIE. Other forms of the name include **Aneka** and **Annika**.

Annette (f) French diminutive of ANNE that has been in use as a first name among English-speakers since the 19th century. It enjoyed a peak in popularity around the middle of the 20th century. Diminutives include **Netta** and **Nettie**. Also encountered as **Annetta** or **Annett**.

Annie (f) Diminutive form of the English first names ANN, ANNE and their many variants. It was taken up by English-speakers around the middle of the 19th century, popularized by the Scottish song 'Annie Laurie' (1838), and has remained in regular use ever since. **Anny** is a rare variant, confined largely to Ireland.

Annika *See* ANNEKA.

Annis (f) English name that was taken up during the medieval period as a variant of AGNES. Although rare, it is still in occasional use among English-speakers today. Also encountered as **Anis**, **Annys** or **Annice**.

Anona (f) English name of uncertain origin, derived either from the Latin for 'harvest' or else the result of the combination of ANN and FIONA or similar names. It has made infrequent appearances among English-speakers since the early 20th century.

Anouska (f) Russian name that developed as a variant of ANN. It has made occasional appearances among English-speakers since the early 20th century. Also encountered as **Anushka**.

Anselm (m) English name derived from the Old German Anshelm, itself from the Old German *ans* ('god') and *helm* ('helmet') and thus meaning 'protected by God'. It has made occasional appearances among English Roman Catholics over the centuries, with a minor revival in the 19th century. **Ansel** and **Ansell** are related forms of the name. **Anselma** is a rare feminine equivalent.

Anselma *See* ANSELM.

Anthea (f) English name descended from the Greek Antheia, itself derived from the Greek *antheios* ('flowery') and borne in Greek mythology as a title of the goddess Hera. It made early appearances in 17th-century English literature, but was not taken up as a first name on a significant scale until the 20th century.

Anthony (m) English name descended from the Roman Antonius, popularly (although mistakenly) derived ultimately from the Greek *anthos* ('flower') but otherwise of obscure (possibly Etruscan) origin. It was borne by several early saints and was in use among English-speakers by the 12th century. It appeared in its modern spelling from the 17th century and subsequently en-

joyed a peak in popularity in the 1950s. Commonly abbreviated (since the 17th century) to **Tony**. Also rendered as **Antony** (the usual form of the name before the Reformation). Variants in other languages include the German and Russian **Anton**. *See also* ANTOINETTE; ANTONIA.

Antoinette (f) French name that developed as a feminine diminutive of Antoine (*see* ANTHONY). It is usually associated with the French queen Marie-Antoinette (1755–93) and has been in occasional use among English-speakers since the middle of the 19th century. Sometimes abbreviated to **Toni** or **Toinette**.

Anton *See* ANTHONY.

Antonia (f) Feminine form of ANTHONY. It was already long established as a first name in Continental Europe before English-speakers took it up in the early 20th century. Commonly abbreviated to **Toni** and less commonly to **Tonia** or **Tonya**. Variants include **Antonina**.

Antony *See* ANTHONY.

Anushka *See* ANOUSKA.

Anwen (f) Welsh first name meaning 'very beautiful'.

Anya *See* ANNA.

Aodh *See* AIDAN; EGAN; EUGENE; HUGH; IAGAN; MADOC.

Aonghas/Aonghus *See* ANGUS; ENOS; INNES.

Aphra (f) English name that may have evolved from an ancient

Irish name or else from the Roman **Afra** (denoting a woman from Africa), a name that was applied to people with dark hair or swarthy colouring. It appears in the Bible as a place name derived from the Hebrew for 'dust' and it might have been a misinterpretation of the phrase 'the house of Aphrah' that led to it being taken up as a personal name. A rare variant is **Affery**.

April (f) English name derived from the name of the month, presumably inspired by its associations with the spring and new growth. It does not appear to have been taken up with much enthusiasm until the 20th century. Variants include the French AVRIL.

Arabella (f) English name that is thought to have evolved as a variant of Annabella (*see* ANNABEL) or else from the Latin *orabilis* ('entreatable', 'obliging' or 'yielding to prayer'). It was taken up by English-speakers during medieval times, becoming particularly well established in Scotland, and became a popular choice of the English aristocracy in the 18th century. It is now rare. Commonly abbreviated to BELLA or **Belle**. Variants of the name include **Arabel** and **Arabelle**.

Araminta (f) English name of obscure origin, possibly the result of the combination of ARABELLA and the older Aminta or Amynta, derived from the Greek for 'protector'. It has enjoyed modest popularity among English-speakers

since the 17th century. Familiar forms of the name include **Minta** and **Minty**.

Archibald (m) English name that evolved from the Norman French Archambault, itself from the Old German *ercan* ('genuine') and *bald* ('bold') and thus interpreted as 'truly brave'. It was taken up by English-speakers during the 12th century and subsequently became well-established in Scotland, where it was considered an Anglicized form of GILLESPIE. The most common diminutive form is **Archie** (or **Archy**). **Baldie** is a less familiar variant.

Archie/Archy *See* ARCHIBALD.

Ardal (m) Irish name meaning 'high valour'.

Ardan (m) Irish name derived from the Irish Gaelic word for 'pride'. It appears in Irish mythology as the name of the brother of Deirdre's lover Naoise.

Aretha (f) English name descended from the Greek Arete, itself derived from the Greek *arete* ('excellence'). It became widely known in the latter half of the 20th century as the name of US soul singer Aretha Franklin (b.1942).

Ariadne (f) Greek name possibly derived from the Greek *ari* ('more') and *agnos* ('chaste' or 'pure') and thus meaning 'very holy'. It appears in Greek mythology as the name of the daughter of King Minos who shows Theseus how to escape the Labyrinth. It has made irregular appearances among English-speakers over the centuries but is rare today. Variants include the French **Arianne** and the Italian **Arianna**.

Ariane *See* ORIANA.

Arianna/Arianne *See* ARIADNE.

Arianrhod (f) Welsh name meaning 'silver disc'. The allusion is to the moon and the name appears in the *Mabinogion* as that of the moon goddess.

Ariel (m) Jewish name derived from the Hebrew for 'lion of God'. It appears in the Bible and was consequently taken up by English Puritans after the Reformation. It is most famous today as the name of the sprite in William Shakespeare's last play, *The Tempest* (1611).

Arlan (m) Cornish name possibly derived from Allen or Elwin. It was borne by a saint in early Cornish legend.

Arleen/Arlena *See* ARLENE.

Arlene (f) English name that appears to have evolved as a diminutive of such names as CHARLENE and MARLENE. A 20th-century introduction that was taken up initially in the USA, it has also made appearances in such variant forms as **Arline**, **Arleen** and **Arlena**.

Arline *See* ARLENE.

Arn *See* AARON; ARNOLD.

Arnie *See* ARNOLD.

Arnold (m) English and German name derived from the Old

German Arinwalt, itself from the Old German *arn* ('eagle') and *wald* ('ruler') and thus meaning 'eagle ruler'. It was brought to England by the Normans but became rare towards the end of the medieval period. It enjoyed a revival alongside other medieval names in the 19th century. Commonly abbreviated to **Arn** or **Arnie**.

Art (m) English name that evolved as a diminutive of ARTHUR. It was taken up towards the end of the 19th century, chiefly in the USA, and has become peculiarly associated with the jazz world, being borne by such luminaries as the pianist Art Tatum (1909–56) and the saxophonist Art Pepper (1925–82).

Artair *See* ARTHUR.

Artemus (m) Greek name that is thought to have evolved from the feminine Artemis, which appears in Greek mythology as the name of the virgin goddess of the moon and the hunt. It appears in the New Testament and was taken up by English Puritans in the 17th century but remains rare. Variants include the feminine **Artemisia**.

Arthur (m) English name of obscure Celtic origin, possibly derived from the Celtic *artos* ('bear') or the Irish *art* ('stone') or else descended from the Roman clan name Artorius. It is famous in the English-speaking world (and beyond) as the name of the legendary English King Arthur. It was revived in the 18th century. Commonly abbreviated to **Art**.

Variants in other languages include the Scottish Gaelic **Artair**.

Asa (m) Jewish name derived from the Hebrew for 'healer' or 'doctor'. It appears in the Bible as the name of a king of Judah and was consequently adopted by English Puritans in the 17th century.

Ash *See* ASHLEY.

Asher (m) Jewish name derived from the Hebrew for 'fortunate' or 'happy'. It appears in the Bible as the name of one of Jacob's sons and was consequently taken up on a limited scale by English Puritans in the 17th century.

Ashley (m/f) English name derived from a place name based on the Old English *aesc* ('ash') and *leah* ('clearing' or 'wood'). It enjoyed a considerable boost following the success of the film *Gone with the Wind* (1939), based on the novel by Margaret Mitchell, in which the name appears. Its use as a feminine name appears to date from the 1940s. Commonly abbreviated to **Ash**. Also encountered (when in use as a name for females) as **Ashleigh**, **Ashlee** or **Ashlea**.

Ashling *See* AISLING.

Asia *See* AISHA.

Aspasia (f) Greek name meaning 'welcome one'. It appears in classical history as the name of the lover of the 5th-century Athenian statesman Pericles and was taken up centuries later by English-speakers in response to a contemporary interest in classical culture.

Asta *See* ASTRID.

Astra (f) English name derived ultimately from the Greek *aster* ('star') but often considered to be a variant of ESTHER, STELLA or other names sharing the same source. It has made rare appearances among English-speakers since the end of the 19th century.

Astrid (f) English and Scandinavian name derived from the Old Norse Astrithr, itself from the Norse *ans* ('god') and *frithr* ('fair') and thus meaning 'divinely beautiful'. It has been in occasional use among English-speakers since the early 20th century. **Asta** and **Sassa** are diminutive forms.

Athelstan (m) English name descended from the Old English Aethelstan, itself derived from the Old English *aethel* ('noble') and *stan* ('stone') and thus meaning 'nobly strong'. It was in fairly common use prior to the Norman Conquest, but fell from use during the medieval period. It was among the historical names revived in the 19th century.

Aub *See* AUBREY.

Auberon (m) English name of obscure origin, possibly a variant of AUBREY. It has made occasional appearances among English-speakers since the 19th century and is sometimes associated with **Oberon**, the name borne by the king of the fairies in Shakespeare's *A Midsummer Night's Dream*

(1595–6). Sometimes abbreviated to **Bron**.

Aubrey (m/f) English and French name derived from the Old German Alberic, itself from the Old German *alb* ('elf') and *richi* ('riches' or 'power') and thus interpreted as meaning 'elf ruler' or 'supernaturally powerful'. It came to England with the Normans and remained in use throughout the medieval period, when it was regarded as a masculine name. When it was revived towards the end of the 19th century, it was also adopted for girls. Sometimes abbreviated to **Aub**. *See also* AUBERON.

Aud/Audi/Audie/Audra *See* AUDREY.

Audrey (f) English name descended from the Old English Aethelthryth, itself derived from the Old English *aethel* ('noble') and *thryth* ('strength') and thus meaning 'noble strength'. It fell from favour during the medieval period and it was not until the early 20th century that the name became popular in its modern form. Also spelled **Audrie** or **Audry**. Among the name's diminutive forms are **Aud**, **Audi** and **Audie**. **Audra** and **Audrina** are rare variants.

Audrie/Audrina/Audry *See* AUDREY.

Augie/August *See* AUGUSTUS.

Augusta (f) English and German feminine equivalent of AUGUSTUS. Roman emperors traditionally styled themselves *Augustus* and the feminine form of the title was consequently bestowed upon female members of their families. English-speakers took up the name after it became widely known through Frederick, Prince of Wales's wife Princess Augusta of Saxe-Coburg-Gotha (1719–72), the mother of George III. It is now rare. Familiar forms include GUS and **Gussie**. Among variant forms are **Augustina** and AUGUSTINE.

Augustine (m/f) English name descended from the Roman Augustinus, a diminutive of AUGUSTUS. Famous as the name of St Augustine of Hippo (354–430) and of St Augustine (d.604), the first Archbishop of Canterbury, it was in limited use among English-speakers during the medieval period and enjoyed a modest revival in the 19th century. It retains its ecclesiastical associations. Commonly abbreviated to GUS or **Gussie**. *See also* AUSTIN.

Augustus (m) Roman name derived from the Latin *augustus* ('august', 'great' or 'magnificent') that has been in use among English-speakers since the 18th century. It was first adopted as a title by the Roman Emperor Octavian in 27 BC and was later introduced to Britain from Germany as a consequence of the Hanoverian Succession. It is now rare. Diminutive forms include GUS, **Gussie** and **Augie**. *See also* AUGUSTA; AUGUSTINE; AUSTIN.

Aulay *See* OLAF.

Aurelia (f) English name that developed as a feminine equivalent of the Roman Aurelius, itself derived from the Latin *aurum* ('gold') and thus sometimes meaning 'golden-haired'. It was taken up by English-speakers in the 17th century and remained in occasional use until the end of the 19th century.

Auriol (f) English name derived from the Latin *aureus* ('golden'), although also associated with the Roman clan name Aurelius. It was taken up by English-speakers in the 19th century. Also spelled **Auriel** or **Auriole**. **Aurie** and **Aury** are familiar forms of the name. *See also* ORIEL.

Aurora (f) English, German and French name derived from the Latin *aurora* ('dawn'). It appears in Roman mythology as the name of the goddess of the dawn and was revived throughout Europe during the Renaissance. It was taken up with some enthusiasm by English poets in the 19th century.

Austen *See* AUSTIN.

Austin (m) English name that developed as a variant of AUGUSTINE. It was taken up by English-speakers in the medieval period and has remained in occasional use ever since. Also encountered as **Austen**.

Ava (f) English name that is thought to have evolved as a variant of EVE, although it is often assumed to have links with the Latin *avis* ('bird'). It appears to

have fallen into disuse before the end of the medieval period but was revived among English-speakers around the middle of the 20th century, promoted by the fame of the US film actress Ava Gardner (Lucy Johnson; 1922–90).

Avaril *See* AVERIL.

Aveline (f) French name derived from the Old German Avila, itself a variant of AVIS. It came to England with the Normans in the 11th century and was subsequently among the many historical names revived in the 19th century.

Averell *See* AVERIL.

Averil (f) English name that evolved either as a variant of AVRIL or else from the Old English Eoforhild (or Everild), itself derived from the Old English *eofor* ('boar') and *hild* ('battle') and thus meaning 'boarlike in battle'. It enjoyed a modest revival as a first name in the early 20th century. Variants include **Avaril**, **Averill** and **Averell**.

Avery (m) English name, derived from ALFRED in medieval times, that has been in occasional use since the end of the 19th century.

Avice *See* AVIS.

Avis (f) English name of obscure origin, possibly related to the German Hedwig (meaning 'struggle') or else derived from the Latin *avis* ('bird'). Recorded in use among English-speakers in medieval times, it entered more frequent use from the early 20th century, although it has never been very common. Variants include **Avice**.

Avril (f) English name derived from the French *avril* ('April'), or otherwise descended from the Old English Eoforhild, itself derived from the Old English *eofor* ('boar') and *hild* ('battle') and thus meaning 'boarlike in battle'. It was adopted by English-speakers early in the 20th century, often being reserved for girls born in the month of April. *See also* APRIL; AVERIL.

Axel (m) Scandinavian variant of ABSALOM that has also been in occasional use among English-speakers – chiefly in the USA, where it was introduced by Scandinavian immigrants. **Acke** is a familiar form of the name. Also found occasionally as the feminine variant **Axelle**.

Ayesha *See* AISHA.

Aylmer (m) English name descended from the Old English Aethelmaer, itself derived from the Old English *aethel* ('noble') and *maere* ('famous') and thus meaning 'nobly famous'. The Old English form of the name was in use before the Norman Conquest. The name fell from favour after the medieval period but had a modest revival in the 19th century. *See also* ELMER.

Aylwin *See* ALVIN.

Azalea (f) English flower name that was taken up as a first name among English-speakers towards the end of the 19th century.

Azaria (m) Biblical name derived from the Hebrew Azaryah, meaning 'helped by God'. It appears in the Bible and has consequently been in occasional use as a first name among English-speakers since the 17th century. Also spelled **Azariah**.

Flanders around the 12th century and was the subject of a modest revival in the 19th century. Variants include the Welsh MALDWYN.

Balthasar *See* BALTHAZAR.

Balthazar (m) English version of the biblical Belshazzar, which was itself derived from the Babylonian Belsharrausur (meaning 'Baal protect the king'). The name appears in the Bible as that of one of the Three Wise Men and was later made use of by Shakespeare. Also encountered as **Balthasar**.

Baptist (m) English name derived ultimately from the Greek *batistes* ('baptist'). Because of its biblical associations with John the Baptist the name has a long history in the Christian world.

Barbara (f) English, German and Polish name derived ultimately from the Greek *barbaros* ('strange' or 'foreign') and thus interpreted as meaning 'foreign woman'. It is thought that the Greek word imitated the stammering of foreigners unable to speak Greek with any fluency. English-speakers took up the name during the medieval period and it was revived in the early 20th century. Diminutive forms include **Bab, Babs, Bar, Barb, Barbie** and **Bobbie**. Also rendered as **Barbra**.

Barbie/Barbra *See* BARBARA.

Barclay *See* BERKELEY.

Barnabas (m) English name derived ultimately from the Aramaic for 'son of consolation'.

Bab/Babs *See* BARBARA.

Baldie *See* ARCHIBALD.

Baldric (m) English name derived from the Old German *balda* ('bold') and *ricja* ('rule'). It came to England with the Normans in the 11th century and became familiar to British television audiences in the 1990s through a character of the name in the historical comedy series *Blackadder*.

Baldwin (m) English name derived from the Old German *bald* ('bold' or 'brave') and *wine* ('friend') and thus interpreted as meaning 'brave friend'. It was introduced as a first name from

It appears in the Bible as the name of one of St Paul's companions and was taken up by English-speakers during the medieval period. It was eventually eclipsed by BARNABY. **Barney** (or **Barny**) is a diminutive form.

Barnaby (m) English name that developed as a variant of BARNABAS and established itself as the dominant form of the name in the 19th century. Often encountered today in the diminutive form **Barney**.

Barnard See BERNARD.

Barney See BARNABAS; BARNABY.

Barrie See BARRY.

Barry (m) English name derived either from the Gaelic *bearach* ('spear') or else from the Irish **Barra**, a diminutive of **Fionnbarr** (*see* FINBAR). It entered general usage among English-speakers around the middle of the 19th century and was at its most frequent in the 1950s. The variant form **Barrie** did not emerge until the 1920s. **Bas**, **Baz** and **Bazza** are common diminutive forms of the name.

Bart See BARTHOLOMEW.

Bartholomew (m) Biblical name derived from the Aramaic for 'son of Talmai' (Talmai meaning 'abounding in furrows'). It appears in the New Testament as a name borne by one of the apostles (possibly Nathaniel) and has been in occasional use among English-speakers since medieval times. Commonly abbreviated to **Bart**

or **Barty** and less commonly to **Bat** or **Tolly**.

Bas See BARRY; BASIL.

Basil (m) English name derived from the Greek *basileus* ('king') and thus meaning 'royal'. It made occasional appearances among English-speakers in medieval times, having been imported with returning Crusaders. It was the subject of a significant revival in the 19th century but has been less common since the 1920s. Commonly shortened to **Bas** (or **Baz**).

Bastian See SEBASTIAN.

Bat See BARTHOLOMEW.

Bathsheba (f) Hebrew name variously interpreted as meaning 'seventh daughter' or 'daughter of the oath'. It appears in the Bible as the name of the wife of King David and was taken up by English Puritans in the 17th century. **Sheba** is a diminutive form of the name.

Baz See BARRY; BASIL; SEBASTIAN.

Bazza See BARRY; SEBASTIAN.

Bea See BEATRICE.

Beatrice (f) Italian, French and English name derived from the Latin *beatus* ('blessed' or 'lucky'). It was fairly common in medieval Italy and became lastingly famous through Beatrice Portinari (1266–90), the model for Beatrice in Dante's *Divine Comedy*. The name was taken up with enthusiasm by English-speakers in the

19th century after Queen Victoria chose it for her youngest daughter, Princess Beatrice (1857–1944). Familiar forms of the name include **Bee**, **Bea**, **Beattie** (or **Beatty**), **Tris** and **Trissie**. Versions in other languages include the Welsh **Betrys** or **Bettrys**. *See also* BEATRIX.

Beatrix (f) English, German and Dutch first name derived like BEATRICE from the Latin *beatus* ('happy' or 'blessed'). Records of the name's use among English-speakers go back to the Norman Conquest, but it has become rare since the early 20th century. Diminutive forms of the name include **Trix** and **Trixie**.

Beattie/Beatty *See* BEATRICE.

Beau (m) English name derived from the French *beau* ('handsome'). It became well known as the adopted first name of the British dandies Beau Nash (Richard Nash; 1674–1762) and Beau Brummell (George Bryan Brummell; 1778–1840). Notable bearers of the name in recent times have included the US film actor Beau Bridges (b.1941).

Beavis *See* BEVIS.

Becca/Becky *See* REBECCA.

Bee *See* BEATRICE.

Bel *See* ANNABEL; BELINDA; ISABEL.

Belinda (f) English name derived either from the Italian *bella* ('beautiful') or possibly from the Old German *lint* ('snake') and thus suggestive of a cunning nature.

Today it is often assumed to have resulted from the combination of BELLA and LINDA. It does not appear to have been taken up by English-speakers before the 17th century. Commonly abbreviated to **Bel**. Other diminutives include **Bindy**, **Linda** or **Lindy**.

Bella (f) English and Italian name that developed as a diminutive of such names as ARABELLA and ISABELLA, apparently promoted through association with the French and Italian *bella* ('beautiful'). It emerged in general use among English-speakers in the 18th century. Variants in other languages include the French **Belle**.

Belle *See* BELLA.

Ben (m) English name that developed as a diminutive form of BENEDICT or BENJAMIN. Although occasional records of this diminutive form go back as far as the medieval period, it was not until the 19th century that it began to appear on a significant scale among English-speakers.

Benedict (m) English name derived from the Latin *benedictus* ('blessed'). Borne by the 6th-century St Benedict who founded the Benedictine order of monks, it became a popular name among English Roman Catholics and was a common choice during the medieval period, when variant forms included **Benedick** and **Bennett**. It has enjoyed a resurgence in popularity since the 1980s. Commonly abbreviated to **Ben**. **Benedicta**

is a rare feminine version of the name.

Benedicta *See* BENEDICT.

Benjamin (m) English name derived from a Hebrew name variously interpreted as meaning 'son of the right hand', 'son of the south' or 'son of my old age' but often interpreted as meaning 'favourite'. It appears in the Bible as the name of the youngest of the sons of Jacob and Rachel. It made occasional appearances in medieval times, often being reserved for children whose mothers had died in childbirth (as the biblical Rachel did). It was taken up with renewed enthusiasm by Puritans in the 17th century. Commonly shortened to **Ben**, **Benny** or **Benjie** (or **Benjy**).

Benjie/Benjy *See* BENJAMIN.

Bennett *See* BENEDICT.

Benny (m) English name that developed as a diminutive of BENJAMIN. It began to appear with increasing frequency from the early 20th century. Also encountered as **Bennie**. *See also* BEN.

Bentley (m) English name derived from a place name (occurring in several counties of England) based on the Old English *beonet* ('bent grass') and *leah* ('wood' or 'clearing') and thus interpreted as meaning 'place of coarse grass'.

Berenice *See* BERNICE.

Berkeley (m) English name derived from a place name (from Gloucestershire) based on the Old English *beorc* ('birch') and *leah* ('wood'). It is pronounced 'barklee' in Britain and 'burklee' in the USA. Variants of the name include **Barclay** and **Berkley**.

Bernadetta *See* BERNADETTE.

Bernadette (f) Feminine equivalent of BERNARD that was taken up by English-speakers in the 19th century. Borne by the French St Bernadette of Lourdes (Marie-Bernarde Soubirous; 1844–79), whose visions made Lourdes a celebrated place of pilgrimage, it became popular among Roman Catholics, especially in Ireland. Sometimes abbreviated to **Bernie** or **Detta**. Variants include **Bernardine** and the Italian **Bernadetta**.

Bernard (m) English and French name derived either from the Old English *beorn* ('man' or 'warrior') and *heard* ('brave'), or else from the Old German *ber* ('bear') and *hart* ('bold') and thus interpreted as meaning 'brave as a bear'. It came to England at the time of the Norman Conquest, but has become less common since the middle of the 20th century. Commonly abbreviated to **Bernie** and, less frequently, to **Bunny**. Also encountered in the form **Barnard**.

Bernardine *See* BERNADETTE.

Bernice (f) English and Italian name derived ultimately from the Greek Pherenike, meaning 'victory bringer'. It appears in the Bible and was taken up by English-speakers after the Reformation, enjoying a modest peak in popularity in the late 19th and early 20th centuries. Diminutive forms of the name include **Bernie**, **Berry**, BINNIE and **Bunny**. Also encountered occasionally in the older form **Berenice**.

Bernie *See* BERNARD; BERNICE.

Berry (f) English name derived from the ordinary vocabulary word 'berry' that enjoyed modest popularity among English-speakers towards the end of the 19th century. It fell from favour early in the 20th century and is now rare. *See also* BERNICE; BERYL.

Bert (m) English name that developed as a diminutive of such names as ALBERT, BERTRAM and HERBERT. It appeared with increasing frequency among English-speakers from the 19th century and remained a common choice until the middle of the 20th century. Also encountered as **Burt**. *See also* BERTIE.

Bertha (f) English and German name derived from the Old German *beraht* ('bright' or 'famous'). Early records of the name's use among English-speakers go back to the 11th century, although it fell into neglect after the 14th century. It appeared with increasing frequency during the 19th century but is now rare. Familiar forms of the name include **Bert** and **Bertie**.

Bertie (m) English name that developed as a diminutive of such

names as ALBERT and BERTRAM (*see also* BERT). It emerged towards the end of the 19th century and was in regular use until the 1940s, since when it has largely fallen out of favour. *See also* BERTHA.

Bertram (m) English name derived from the Old German *beraht* ('bright' or 'famous') and *hramn* ('raven') and thus interpreted as meaning 'famous raven' or more loosely – because ravens were symbols of wisdom in Germanic mythology – 'wise person'. It was fairly common in medieval times and enjoyed a significant revival in the 19th century, although it was eclipsed by BERT (or **Burt**) and BERTIE from the early 20th century. Variants include **Bartram** and **Bertrand**, although this can also be traced back to the Old German for 'bright shield'.

Bertrand *See* BERTRAM.

Beryl (f) English name derived from that of the precious gem. It was among the many jewel names that were adopted by English-speakers towards the end of the 19th century but has been in decline since the middle of the 20th century. **Berry** is a diminutive form.

Bess (f) English name that developed as a diminutive of ELIZABETH. Queen Elizabeth I was nicknamed 'Good Queen Bess' but the name did not establish itself as a particular favourite until the 17th century. It remained in fairly regular use until the end of the

19th century, but is now rare. Also encountered as **Bessie** (or **Bessy**).

Bessie/Bessy See BESS.

Bet See BETH; BETSY; ELIZABETH.

Beth (f) English name that developed as a diminutive of ELIZABETH or BETHANY. It appeared with increasing frequency in the 19th century and has continued in fairly regular use ever since, with a recent peak in popularity in the 1990s. Sometimes abbreviated to **Bet**. Also found in combination with various other names, as in **JoBeth** and **Mary Beth**. Variants include the Welsh **Bethan**.

Bethan See BETH.

Bethany (f) English name derived from a Hebrew place name meaning 'house of figs'. It appears in the New Testament as the name of the village near Jerusalem that Christ passed through shortly before his Crucifixion and also as the name of Mary of Bethany, sister of Martha and Lazarus, as a result of which it has been a traditional favourite among Roman Catholics. Sometimes abbreviated to **Beth**.

Bethia (f) English name derived from the Hebrew *bith-yah* ('daughter of God'), or alternatively from the Gaelic *beath* ('life'). It appears in the Old Testament and was taken up among English-speakers in the 17th century, becoming modestly popular in Scotland. Sometimes abbreviated to **Beth**.

Betrys See BEATRICE.

Betsy (f) English name that developed as a diminutive of ELIZABETH, apparently through the combination of **Bet** and **Bessie**. It was in fairly widespread use by the middle of the 19th century but has been rare since the early 20th century. Also encountered as **Betsey**.

Bette (f) English name (variously pronounced 'bet' or 'bettee') that developed as a diminutive of ELIZABETH (*see also* BETTY). Originally French, it is today often associated with the US film actress Bette Davis (Ruth Elizabeth Davis; 1908–89).

Bettina See BETTY.

Bettrys See BEATRICE.

Betty (f) English name that developed as a diminutive of ELIZABETH. It appeared with increasing frequency among English-speakers from the 18th century, but has become rare since a peak in popularity in the 1920s. Variants include the Italian and Spanish **Bettina**, which enjoyed some popularity in the English-speaking world in the 1960s. *See also* BETTE.

Beulah (f) Hebrew name for Israel, meaning 'she who is married', that was taken up as a first name among English-speakers in the 17th century, becoming particularly popular within the Black community in the USA. The original Hebrew 'land of Beulah' is also sometimes interpreted to be a reference to heaven.

Bev *See* BEVAN; BEVERLEY; BEVERLY.

Bevan (m) Welsh name derived from the Welsh *ap Evan* ('son of Evan'). Commonly abbreviated to Bev.

Beverley (m) English name derived from a place name (from Humberside) based on the Old English *beofor* ('beaver') and *leac* ('stream'). It became a modestly popular choice of first name in the 19th century but has become rare since the 1950s, largely through competition from the feminine form of the name, BEVERLY. Commonly abbreviated to **Bev**.

Beverly (f) English name that developed as a feminine equivalent of BEVERLEY and is now more widespread than the original from which it evolved. It first became popular in the USA in the early years of the 20th century. Often abbreviated to **Bev**. Occasionally also encountered as **Beverley**.

Bevis (m) English name possibly derived from the French *beau fils* ('handsome son'), or else from the French place name Beauvais. The name came to England with the Normans and enjoyed a revival towards the end of the 19th century. Variants include **Beavis**.

Bianca (f) Italian name derived from the Italian *bianca* ('white' or 'pure'). English-speakers adopted the name in the 16th century, when it also appeared in the plays of William Shakespeare. *See also* BLANCHE; CANDIDA.

Biddy/Bidelia *See* BRIDGET.

Bijay *See* VIJAY.

Bill/Billie/Billy *See* WILLIAM.

Bina *See* SADHBH.

Bindy *See* BELINDA.

Bing (m) English name of obscure origin. It may have been adopted originally as an abbreviated form of **Bingo**, the name of a well-known cartoon character, and subsequently enjoyed a boost as the stage name of the US singer and film actor Bing Crosby (Harry Lillis Crosby; 1901–77).

Bingo *See* BING.

Binnie (f) English name that developed as a diminutive of BERNICE or any longer name ending '-bina' but may also be encountered as a familiar form of several other names with no apparent connection. It was a fairly common choice around the middle of the 19th century but has since become rare.

Blaine (m) Scottish name of obscure origin that has been in occasional use among English-speakers since the early 20th century. It would appear to be a modern reworking of the much older **Blane**.

Blair (m/f) Scottish name derived from a place name based on the Gaelic *blar* ('field' or 'plain'). It has enjoyed a modest revival since the middle of the 20th century, chiefly in Canada and the USA.

Blaise (m) English and French name derived from the Roman Blasius, itself from the Latin *blaesus* ('lisping' or 'stammering'). A long-established favourite in France, the name has made only infrequent appearances among English-speakers since the medieval period. Also encountered as **Blase** or **Blaze**.

Blake (m) English name derived either from the Old English *blaec* ('black') or conversely *blac* ('pale' or 'white'). The name has sometimes been bestowed in honour of the English admiral Robert Blake (1599–1657) or in tribute to the British poet William Blake (1757–1827).

Blanche (f) English and French name derived from the French *blanc* ('white' or 'pure') and originally normally bestowed upon blondes. English-speakers used the name in medieval times and it was briefly revived towards the end of the 19th century. *See also* BIANCA.

Blane *See* BLAINE.

Blase/Blaze *See* BLAISE.

Blod *See* BLODWEN.

Blodwen (f) Welsh name derived from the Welsh *blodau* ('flowers') and *gwyn* ('white') and possibly first taken up under the influence of the French Blanchefleur. It was fairly common in medieval times and enjoyed a significant revival in the late 19th century, although still confined chiefly to Wales. Commonly abbreviated to **Blod**. Also encountered as **Blodwyn**.

Blondie (f) English name that evolved as a nickname for anyone

with blond hair. It appears to have been a relatively recent introduction that probably made its first appearances in the 1920s.

Blossom (f) English name derived from the ordinary vocabulary word 'blossom'. It was among the various flower names and related terms that were adopted as first names among English-speakers towards the end of the 19th century.

Bluebell (f) English name derived from that of the bluebell flower. It has made rare appearances among English-speakers since the late 19th century.

Blythe (f) English name probably derived from the ordinary vocabulary word 'blithe' that has made occasional appearances since the 1940s.

Boaz (m) Hebrew name of uncertain origin, possibly meaning 'swiftness' or perhaps 'man of strength'. It appears in the Bible as the name of Ruth's husband and was consequently taken up on a rather modest scale by English-speakers in the 17th and 18th centuries, generally confined to the Jewish community. Also spelled **Boas**.

Bob (m) English name that developed as a diminutive of ROBERT. This form of the name was in use among English-speakers by at least the early 18th century, appearing with increasing frequency from around the middle of the 19th century. *See also* BOBBIE; BOBBY.

Bobbie (f) English name that developed as a diminutive of ROBERTA. It is sometimes also encountered as a diminutive of BARBARA or as a feminine version of BOBBY.

Bobby (m) English name that developed as a diminutive of ROBERT. It seems to have become established early in the 18th century and has remained in use ever since. Sometimes encountered in combination with other names, as in **Bobby Joe**. *See also* BOB; BOBBIE.

Boniface (m) English name derived ultimately from the Latin *bonum* ('good') and *fatum* ('fate') or alternatively *bonum* ('good') and *facere* ('to do') and thus interpreted as meaning either 'good fate' or 'well-doer'. It was a fairly frequent choice among English-speakers during the medieval period, but has become infrequent since the Reformation.

Bonita (f) English name derived from the Spanish *bonito* ('pretty'). The name does not appear to have originated in Spain itself, having made its first appearances among English-speakers in the USA in the 1920s. *See also* BONNIE.

Bonnie (f) English name derived from the Scottish 'bonny' (meaning 'pretty' or 'fine'), itself ultimately from the Latin *bonus* ('good'). It is also in occasional use as a diminutive of BONITA. It was taken up by English-speakers on

both sides of the Atlantic early in the 20th century. Also encountered as **Bonny**.

Booth (m) English name derived from a surname originally based on the Old Norse for 'hut' or 'shed'.

Boris (m) Russian name derived either from the Old Slavonic *bor* ('fight' or 'struggle') or more likely from the Tartar nickname Bogoris, meaning 'small'. It was taken up by English-speakers in the 19th century and has continued in irregular use into modern times.

Boyce (m) English name derived from the French *bois* ('wood'). It has made occasional appearances as a first name since the early 20th century.

Boyd (m) Scottish name derived from the Gaelic *buidhe* ('yellow'). Its history as a first name among the Scots goes back several hundred years, having been reserved initially for people with blond hair (although another derivation suggests it evolved as a reference to people from the island of Bute).

Brad *See* BRADFORD; BRADLEY.

Bradford (m) English name derived from a place name (from northern England) based on the Old English *brad* ('broad') and *ford* ('ford'). **Brad** is the usual diminutive form of the name.

Bradley (m) English name derived from a place name based on the Old English *brad* ('broad') and *leah* ('wood' or 'clearing'). Its modern use is largely confined to the USA.

Commonly abbreviated to **Brad** –
as borne by the US film actor Brad
Pitt (b.1965).

Brady (m) Irish name possibly
derived ultimately from the
Gaelic *bragha* ('chest' or 'throat'),
and thus interpreted as meaning
'large-chested'.

Bram *See* ABRAHAM.

Bramwell (m) English name
derived from a place name (from
Derbyshire) meaning 'place of
brambles'. Variants include
Branwell – as borne by Patrick
Branwell Brontë (1817–48), the
artist-brother of the celebrated
Brontë sisters.

Brandon (m) English name
derived from a place name based
on the Old English *brom* ('broom'
or 'gorse') and *dun* ('hill'). It was
taken up as a first name in the
19th century, chiefly in the USA,
apparently under the influence of
the Irish BRENDAN. Sometimes
abbreviated to **Brandy**. Variants
include **Branton**.

Brandy *See* BRANDON.

Branwell *See* BRAMWELL.

Branwen (f) Welsh name derived
from the Welsh *bran* ('raven') and
gwyn ('white' or 'blessed'), but
also in existence as a variant of
BRONWEN. It appears in the *Mabinogion* as the name of the beautiful
sister of King Bran and is still in
occasional use in Wales.

Bren *See* BRENDA.

Brenda (f) English name derived
from the Old Norse *brandr*

('sword' or 'torch'), but also sometimes regarded as a feminine
equivalent of the Irish BRENDAN.
It was taken up initially as a first
name in the Shetland Isles but subsequently became more widespread, although it has become
less frequent since the middle of
the 20th century. Commonly
shortened to **Bren**.

Brendan (m) Irish name derived
from the Gaelic Breanainn, meaning 'prince' – although alternative derivations suggest it means
'stinking hair' or 'dweller by the
beacon'. It appeared with increasing frequency among English-
speakers from the early 20th century and had become one of the
top fifty names in Australia by the
1970s. Variants include **Brandan**,
Brandon and the Irish Gaelic
Breandan.

Brent (m) English name derived
from a place name (from Devon
and Somerset) apparently derived
from the Old English word for
'hill'. Popular chiefly in Canada
and the USA, it enjoyed a peak in
popularity in the 1970s and 1980s.

Brett (m) English name originally
bestowed upon Breton settlers in
medieval England that has been
in increasing use as a first name
since the middle of the 20th century, chiefly in the USA. Also
encountered as **Bret**.

Brian (m) English and Irish name
derived ultimately from the Irish
Gaelic *brigh* ('strength' or 'power').
It appears in Irish mythology as
the name of the 10th-century king

Brian Boru but came to England with the Bretons who arrived with William the Conqueror. It was in fairly regular use during the medieval period and was subsequently revived in England in the 18th century. Also encountered as **Brien** or **Bryan**. Sometimes abbreviated to **Bri**. **Brianna** is a rare feminine version of the name. *See also* BRYONY.

Brice *See* BRYCE.

Bride *See* BRIDGET.

Bridget (f) English name derived from the Gaelic Brighid, itself from the Celtic *brigh* ('strength' or 'power'). In its original Gaelic form it was the name of a Celtic fire goddess and consequently became popular in Ireland and Scotland, although it has appeared with increasing regularity elsewhere in the English-speaking world since the 18th century. Diminutive forms of the name include **Gita**, **Bride**, **Bridie** and **Biddy**. Also encountered as **Brigit** or **Brigid**. **Bidelia** is a rather fanciful elaboration of the name.

Bridie *See* BRIDGET.

Brien *See* BRIAN.

Brigham (m) English name derived from a place name (from Cumbria and North Yorkshire) derived from the Old English *brycg* ('bridge') and *ham* ('homestead'). In the USA the name is usually associated with the US Mormon leader Brigham Young (1801–77).

Brigid/Brigit *See* BRIDGET.

Brin *See* BRYN.

Briony *See* BRYONY.

Britney (f) English name that may have evolved from BRITTANY. Its popularity has been promoted in recent years through the US pop singer Britney Spears (b.1981).

Britt *See* BRIDGET.

Brittany (f) English name derived from that of the province of Bretagne (Anglicized as Brittany). It has enjoyed modest popularity among English-speakers since the middle of the 20th century.

Broderick (m) English name meaning 'son of Roderick' that has made occasional appearances as a first name in relatively recent times, apparently under the influence of RODERICK.

Brodie (m) Scottish name derived from the Scots Gaelic for 'ditch'. Also encountered as **Brody**.

Bron *See* AUBERON; BRONWEN.

Bronwen (f) Welsh name derived from the Welsh *bron* ('breast') and *gwyn* ('white') and thus meaning 'fair-bosomed'. It has long been a favourite in Wales but has also made occasional appearances among English-speakers elsewhere since the end of the 19th century. Also encountered as **Bronwyn** and sometimes confused with the otherwise unrelated BRANWEN. Commonly abbreviated to **Bron**.

Brook (m) English name derived from the ordinary vocabulary word 'brook'. It was adopted initially by Black Americans in the USA but has since made sporadic appearances throughout the English-speaking world. The more frequently encountered feminine form is **Brooke**, as borne by the US film actress Brooke Shields (b.1965).

Brooke See BROOK.

Brooklyn (m/f) English name derived from the Brooklyn district of New York City. Also found as **Brooklynn** or **Brooklynne**, it enjoyed a significant boost in 1999 when it was chosen by English footballer David Beckham and pop singer Victoria Beckham for their newborn son.

Bruce (m) Scottish name adopted throughout the English-speaking world from the late 19th century. It was originally imported as the Norman French baronial name de Brus, itself from an unidentified place name in northern France. The name has largely lost its uniquely Scottish character and today ranks among the most popular names in Australia, to the extent that it is used there as a generic name for any adult male. **Brucie** is a fairly common diminutive form of the name.

Bruno (m) English and German name derived from the Old German *brun* ('brown') and originally usually reserved for people with brown hair, brown eyes or a swarthy complexion. It was in use among English-speakers in medieval times and was subsequently revived towards the end of the 19th century.

Bryan See BRIAN.

Bryce (m) English name of obscure Celtic origin. Also encountered as **Brice**.

Bryn (m) Welsh name derived from the Welsh *bryn* ('hill') but also in use as a diminutive form of BRYNMOR. It appears to have been an early 20th-century introduction. Also encountered as **Brin**.

Brynmor (m) Welsh name derived from a place name (from Gwynedd) based on the Welsh *bryn* ('hill') and *mawr* ('large'). Sometimes abbreviated to **Bryn**.

Bryony (f) English name derived from that of the wild hedgerow plant, although also in occasional use as a feminine equivalent of BRIAN. It appears to have been taken up by English-speakers towards the middle of the 20th century. Also encountered as **Briony**.

Buck (m) English name derived from the ordinary vocabulary word 'buck' (denoting a male deer or goat) and thus suggesting a lively, spirited young man. It emerged as a popular choice of name in the USA in the early 20th century.

Bud See BUDDY.

Buddy (m) English name that developed as a nickname meaning 'friend' or 'pal', possibly originally as a variant of 'brother'. It has been in fairly regular use in the USA since the early 20th century. **Bud** is a diminutive form of the name.

Bunny *See* BERNARD; BERNICE.

Buntie *See* BUNTY.

Bunty (f) English name of uncertain origin, possibly with its roots in a nickname derived from a dialect term for a lamb. It became fairly common in the UK in the wake of the popular play *Bunty Pulls the Strings* (1911). Also encountered as **Buntie**.

Burl (m) English name derived from the Germanic for 'cup bearer'. Confined chiefly to the USA, it became well known through the US singer and actor Burl Ives (1909–95).

Burt *See* BERT.

Buster (m) English name that developed as a nickname presumably derived from the verb 'bust' and thus suggesting a person given to breaking or smashing things. It was taken up by English-speakers in the USA towards the end of the 19th century. Famous bearers of the name have included the US silent film comedian Buster Keaton (Joseph Francis Keaton; 1895–1966).

Byron (m) English name derived from the Old English *aet thaem byrum* ('at the byres') that has made rare appearances as a first name in relatively recent times. The name is usually associated with the celebrated British poet Lord Byron (George Gordon, 6th Baron Byron; 1784–1824).

Peters featuring the detective monk Brother Cadfael.

Cadwalader (f) Welsh name derived from the Welsh *cad* ('battle') and *gwaladr* ('disposer') and thus interpreted as 'general' or 'commander'. Borne by a 7th-century saint who died fighting the Saxons and by several other Welsh kings and princes, it remains a uniquely Welsh name. Also spelled **Cadwallader** or **Cadwaladr**.

Caerwyn (m) Welsh name derived from *caer* ('fort') and *gwyn* ('white'). Also spelled CARWYN.

Caesar (m) Roman name possibly derived from the Latin *caesaries* ('head of hair') or otherwise from *caedere* ('to cut') that has made occasional appearances as a first name among English-speakers since the 18th century. Variants include **Cesar**.

Cahal *See* CAROL.

Cai *See* CAIUS.

Caitlin *See* CATHERINE; KATHLEEN.

Caius (m) Roman name derived from the Latin for 'rejoice' that has continued in irregular use among English-speakers into modern times. Sometimes abbreviated to **Cai**, although this form of the name can also be traced as a Welsh name (*see* KAY). Also encountered as **Gaius**.

Cal *See* CALUM; CALVIN; CATHAL.

Caleb (m) Biblical name derived from the Hebrew Kaleb, variously interpreted as meaning 'intrepid',

Caddy *See* CANDICE; CAROLINE.

Cade (m) English name derived ultimately from a traditional nickname meaning 'round'. It enjoyed some popularity among English-speakers after appearing in the Margaret Mitchell novel *Gone with the Wind* (1936).

Cadell (m) Welsh name derived from the Old Welsh *cad* ('battle'). Also encountered as **Cadel**.

Cadfael (m) Welsh name (pronounced 'cadful') meaning 'battle metal'. It was popularized in the late 20th century through the medieval mystery novels of Ellis 'bold' or 'dog' (suggesting a dog-like devotion to God). It appears in the Bible as the name of one of Moses' companions and was consequently taken up by Puritans after the Reformation, becoming especially popular in the USA.

Calista *See* CALLISTA.

Calliope (f) Greek name (pronounced 'kaleeopee') meaning 'beautiful face'. Borne by the ancient Greek muse of epic poetry, it has made occasional reappearances among English-speakers over the centuries. Sometimes abbreviated to **Cally**.

Callista (f) Feminine equivalent of the Italian Callisto, itself descended from the Roman Callistus, which came from the Greek *kalos* ('fair' or 'good'). In the altered form **Calista** it became widely known in the late 1990s through the US actress Calista Flockhart (b.1964), star of the US television series *Ally McBeal*.

Callum *See* CALUM.

Calum (m) Scottish name derived from the Roman Columba, meaning 'dove'. Although it has a long history as a Scottish name, it has enjoyed increasing acceptance among English-speakers since the middle of the 20th century. Also spelled **Callum**. Commonly shortened to **Cal**, **Cally** or **Caley**. **Calumina** is a rare feminine version of the name.

Calvin (m) French name derived via the Old French *chauve* from the Latin *calvus* ('bald'), and thus

meaning 'little bald one', that was taken up in the 16th century in tribute to the French Protestant theologian Jean Calvin (1509–64). It became especially popular among Protestants in the USA. Famous bearers of the name have included US President Calvin Coolidge (John Calvin Coolidge; 1872–1933). Commonly shortened to **Cal**.

Calypso (f) Greek name meaning 'concealer'. In Greek myth, Calypso was a sea nymph who kept Odysseus prisoner for seven years.

Cameron (m/f) Scottish name derived from the Gaelic *cam shron* ('crooked nose') that has been in occasional use as a first name among English-speakers since the beginning of the 20th century. It has retained its strong Scottish connections, being well known as a clan name. Its use as a feminine name, as borne by US film actress Cameron Diaz (b.1972), is a relatively recent phenomenon.

Camilla (f) Feminine version of the Roman Camillus, thought to mean 'attendant at a sacrifice', that has been in use as a first name among English-speakers since the 13th century. Also spelled **Camellia**, it was regarded initially as a literary name. Among diminutive forms of the name are **Cam**, **Cammie**, **Millie** and **Milly**.

Campbell (m) Scottish name derived from the Gaelic *cam beul* ('crooked mouth') that has been in occasional use over the centuries, chiefly in Scotland. It is best known as the surname of one of the Scottish clans, historically the sworn enemies of the MacDonalds.

Candace *See* CANDICE.

Candi *See* CANDIDA; CANDY.

Candice (f) English name of uncertain origin. It represents a modern variant of Candace, in which form the name appears in the Bible as that of a queen of Ethiopia. Records of Candace as a first name among English-speakers go back to the 17th century. As Candice it was adopted early in the 20th century, becoming particularly popular in the USA. Commonly abbreviated to **Caddy** or CANDY. Variants include **Candis**.

Candida (f) Roman name derived from the Latin *candidus* ('white') that has been in use among English-speakers since the medieval period. It has remained in irregular use into modern times, enjoying a minor peak in popularity in the early 20th century, promoted by the George Bernard Shaw play *Candida* (1894). Familiar forms of the name include **Candi**, **Candia**, **Candie** and CANDY.

Candie *See* CANDIDA.

Candis *See* CANDICE.

Candy (f) Diminutive form of CANDICE and CANDIDA, possibly influenced by the ordinary vocabulary word 'candy' (a word of Indian origin). Also spelled **Candi**.

Caprice (f) English name appar-

ently derived from the ordinary vocabulary word meaning 'whim'. It has become widely familiar through the US glamour model Caprice Bourret (b.1971).

Cara (f) English name derived from the Latin or Italian *cara* ('dear'). It is also possible to trace the name back to the Irish *cara* ('friend' or 'dear one'). It was taken up by English-speakers in the early 20th century and enjoyed a brief revival in the 1970s. Variants include **Kara** and **Carita**. *See also* CARINA.

Caradoc (m) Welsh name derived from the Welsh *car* ('love') and thus meaning 'amiable'. As Caradog or Caractacus, it was borne by a famous 1st-century British chieftain who led the resistance against the Romans. It has been in irregular use among the Welsh since the medieval period.

Cardew (m) English name derived from the Welsh for 'black fort'.

Careen (f) English name of uncertain origin. It appears to have been created by the US novelist Margaret Mitchell in her novel *Gone with the Wind* (1936), perhaps under the influence of CARA or CARINA.

Carey (m/f) English name that developed as a variant of CARY in the 19th century. In Irish use it may have evolved from the Gaelic O Ciardha ('descendant of the dark one'). The Welsh may trace it back to the place name Carew. It was used initially as a boys' name but since the 1950s has been reserved almost exclusively for girls.

Cari *See* CERI.

Carina (f) Scandinavian, German and English name derived from CARA. It appears to have made its debut towards the end of the 19th century. Variants include **Karina** and **Karine**.

Carita *See* CARA.

Carl (m) English name derived from the Old English *ceorl* ('man'), or otherwise encountered as a diminutive of CARLTON. It was taken up by English-speakers around the middle of the 19th century and has continued in modest use ever since. Sometimes encountered in the German form **Karl**. *See also* CARLA; CARLENE; CHARLES.

Carla (f) English, German and Italian name that evolved as a feminine form of CARL. It was taken up by English-speakers in the 1940s and enjoyed a peak in popularity in the 1980s. Familiar forms of the name include **Carly** – as borne by US pop singer Carly Simon (b.1945) – and **Karly**.

Carlene (f) English name that developed as a variant form of CARL under the influence of such names as CHARLENE and DARLENE. Famous bearers of the name have included the US singer-songwriter Carlene Carter (b.1955). Also spelled **Carleen**.

Carleton *See* CARLTON.

Carlie/Carley *See* CARLA.

Carlton (m) English name derived from a place name based on the Old English *ceorl* ('man') and *tun* ('settlement'). Its history as a first name began in the late 19th century. Commonly shortened to **Carl**. Also spelled **Carleton**. *See also* CHARLTON.

Carly *See* CARLA.

Carlyn *See* CAROLINE.

Carmel (f) Hebrew place name meaning 'vineyard' or 'garden' that has made occasional appearances as a first name among English-speakers since the end of the 19th century. It appears in the Bible as the name of the sacred Mount Carmel in Israel. It was taken up as a first name by English-speaking Roman Catholics in the late 19th century. Variants of the name include **Carmela**, **Carmelina** and **Carmelita**. *See also* CARMEN.

Carmela/Carmelina/Carmelita *See* CARMEL.

Carmen (f) Spanish equivalent of CARMEL that is often associated with the Latin *carmen* ('song'). The huge success of Bizet's opera *Carmen* (1873–4) made the name popular among English-speakers in the 19th century.

Caro *See* CAROLINE.

Carol (m/f) English name that developed as a diminutive of CAROLINE, although it is also associated with the ordinary vocabulary word 'carol' and has thus often been reserved for children born at Christmas. It appeared with increasing frequency towards the end of the 19th century and enjoyed a peak in popularity in the 1950s. As a masculine name, it is (now rarely) used as an Anglicized form of the Roman Carolus. Variants of the feminine version include CAROLE, **Carroll** and CARYL. Masculine variants include **Carroll**. See also CEARBHALL.

Carole (f) English and French name that evolved as a variant of CAROL. English-speakers adopted the name from the French around the middle of the 20th century, but it has since declined.

Carolina See CAROLINE.

Caroline (f) English name derived from the Italian **Carolina**, itself a feminine equivalent of Carlo (*see* CHARLES). It came to England with George II's wife Queen Caroline of Ansbach (1683–1737) and has remained in common currency ever since. Its popularity in the USA reflects its use as the name of the states of North and South Carolina, which were named in honour of Charles I. Among the name's diminutive forms are **Caddy**, **Carlyn**, **Caro** and LINA. Also encountered (since the early 20th century) as **Carolyn** or, more rarely, **Carolyne**. *See also* CARRIE.

Carolyn/Carolyne See CAROLINE.

Caron (f) Welsh name derived from the Welsh *caru* ('to love') but also in use as a variant of KAREN, perhaps under the influence of CAROL. It was taken up by English-speakers in the 1950s.

Carrie (f) English name that emerged as a diminutive form of CAROLINE in the 19th century. Interest in the name reached a peak in the USA during the 1970s, possibly under the influence of the Stephen King horror novel *Carrie* (1974). Also found as **Carri** or **Carry**. Sometimes combined with other names, as in **Carrie-Ann**.

Carroll *See* CAROL; CEARBHALL.

Carry *See* CARRIE.

Carson (m/f) English name that has been in occasional use since the 19th century. Records of its use go back to the 13th century, when it may have been based on an unidentified place name. As a first name, it is associated primarily with people with Irish or Scottish connections. Famous bearers of the name have included the US novelist Carson McCullers (Lula Carson McCullers; 1917–67).

Carter (m) English name denoting a person who transports goods by cart. In Scotland it is sometimes treated as an Anglicization of the Gaelic Mac Artair, meaning 'son of Artair'.

Carver (m) English name derived from the Cornish Gaelic for 'great rock'. It appears in R. D. Blackmore's classic romance *Lorna Doone* (1869).

Carwyn (m) Welsh name derived from the Welsh *car* ('love') and *gwyn* ('white' or 'blessed'). *See also* CAERWYN.

Cary (m/f) English name derived

from a place name (taken from the River Clary in the counties of Devon and Somerset) that has been in occasional use since the 19th century. It enjoyed a peak in popularity in the 1940s and 1950s when it became well known through British-born US film star Cary Grant (Alexander Archibald Leach; 1904–86). *See also* CAREY.

Caryl (f) Variant of CAROL, possibly influenced by BERYL and other similar names. It was taken up by English-speakers in the 19th century.

Caryn *See* KAREN.

Carys (f) Welsh name derived from the Welsh *car* ('love') that developed under the influence of such names as GLADYS. **Cerys** is a variant form.

Casey (m/f) English name that can be traced back to an Irish surname meaning 'vigilant in war'. It is often associated with the US folk hero and engine-driver Casey Jones (John Luther Jones; 1863–1900), who lost his life saving his passengers on the 'Cannonball Express' and who was himself named after his birthplace Cayce, in Kentucky. Also spelled **Kasey**.

Caspar (m) English version of the Dutch JASPER that was adopted by English-speakers in the 19th century. Traditionally identified as the name of one of the biblical Three Wise Men (who are not actually named in the Bible), it may also be spelled **Casper**.

Cass *See* CASSANDRA; CASSIUS.

Cassandra (f) Greek name meaning 'ensnaring men' that has been in occasional use among English-speakers since the medieval period. It appears in Greek mythology as the name of a celebrated prophetess, whose prophecies were fated never to be believed. Common diminutives of the name include **Cass** and **Cassie**. *See also* SANDRA.

Cassia *See* KEZIA.

Cassidy (m/f) English name derived from the Irish O Caiside. A relatively recent introduction, it is confined largely to the USA.

Cassie *See* CASSANDRA; CASSIUS.

Cassius (m) Roman name of uncertain meaning, possibly derived from the Latin *cassus* ('empty'), that has made occasional appearances among English-speakers since the 19th century. Well-known bearers of the name in modern times have included the US boxer Muhammad Ali (Cassius Clay; b.1942). Commonly abbreviated to **Cass** or **Cassie**.

Cat (m/f) English name that evolved initially as a nickname for anyone with a tempestuous character or as an abbreviation of CATHERINE. It has appeared in generally informal use among English-speakers since the early 20th century, enjoying particular popularity among jazz musicians.

Cath/Catha *See* CATHERINE.

Cathal (m) Irish name derived from the Gaelic *cath* ('battle') and *val* ('rule'). Notable bearers of the name have included a 7th-century Irish saint. Occasionally abbreviated to **Cal**. Also found as **Cahal**.

Catharine *See* CATHERINE.

Catherine (f) English name derived from the Greek Aikaterina, which is itself of unknown meaning. The link with the St Catherine of Alexandria, who was tortured on a spiked wheel before being beheaded, has led to the name being popularly associated with the Greek *aikia* ('torture'), although it has also been linked with the Greek *katharos* ('pure'), hence the alternate spellings **Katherine**, **Katharine** and **Catharine**. English-speakers took up the name during the medieval period. Among the name's many diminutives are CAT, **Cath** (or **Kath**), **Catha**, KATE, **Katie** (or **Katy**), **Cathy** (or **Kathy**), KAY, **Kit** and KITTY. Other variants include **Kathryn** (or **Cathryn**), KATRINA (or **Catrina**), the Welsh **Catrin** and the Irish **Caitlin** (from which KATHLEEN and **Cathleen** evolved). *See also* CATRIONA; KAREN.

Cathleen *See* CATHERINE; KATHLEEN.

Cathryn/Cathy/Catrin *See* CATHERINE.

Catrina *See* CATHERINE; CATRIONA.

Catriona (f) Scottish and Irish name that developed as a variant of CATHERINE. Usually pronounced 'catreena', it was adopted more widely throughout the English-speaking world in the 19th century. Sometimes abbreviated to **Trina** or, chiefly among the Irish,

to **Riona**. Also encountered as **Catrina**, **Catrine** or KATRINA.

Ceallagh *See* KELLY.

Cearbhall (m) Irish name (pronounced 'keerval' or 'kurval') of uncertain meaning, possibly from the Gaelic *cearbh* ('hacking'). It was fairly frequent in Ireland during the medieval period and in the 20th century became more widely known as that of Irish President Cearbhall O Dalaigh (1911–78). Sometimes Anglicized as **Carroll** or CHARLES.

Cecil (m) English name derived either from the Roman Caecilius, itself from the Latin *caecus* ('blind'), or else from the Welsh Seissylt, ultimately from the Latin *sextus* ('sixth'). It became well known in England as the surname of the powerful Cecil family, but was not adopted as a first name until around the middle of the 19th century. It is now rare. *See also* CECILIA.

Cécile *See* CECILIA.

Cecilia (f) English name derived from the Roman Caecilia, itself from the Latin *caecus* ('blind'). English-speakers took up the name during the medieval period and it was the subject of a strong revival towards the end of the 19th century. **Cecil**, **Ciss** (or **Sis**), CISSIE (or **Cissy**) and **Sissie** (or **Sissy**) are diminutive forms. Variants include **Cicely** and **Cecily** (or **Cecilie**) as well as the French **Cécile**. Other less well-known variants include **Sisley**. *See also* CELIA.

Cecilie/Cecily *See* CECILIA.

Cedric (m) English name derived from the Old English Cerdic, itself of uncertain meaning, or alternatively from the Welsh Cedrych, derived from *ced* ('bounty'). Although the Scottish novelist Sir Walter Scott may have had the Welsh form of the name in mind, it is traditionally believed that the modern form of the name resulted from an inaccurate rendering of the Old English name in his historical novel *Ivanhoe* (1819).

Ceinwen (f) Welsh name (pronounced 'kainwen') derived from *cain* ('fair') and *gwyn* ('white' or 'blessed') and sometimes interpreted as meaning 'beautiful gems'.

Celeste (f) English name derived via the masculine French name Céleste from the Roman Caelestis, itself from the Latin *caelestis* ('heavenly'). It was taken up by English-speakers in the 20th century, though only as a name for girls. Variants include **Celestina** and **Celestine**.

Celestina/Celestine *See* CELESTE.

Celia (f) English and Italian name derived from the Roman Caelia, itself probably from the Latin *caelum* ('heaven'), but often also treated as a diminutive of CECILIA. Although records of the name go back to the 16th century, it became popular among English-speakers only in the 19th century. *See also* CÉLINE; SHEILA.

Celina *See* CÉLINE; SELINA.

Céline (f) French name derived from the Roman Caelina, itself probably from the Latin *caelum* ('heaven'). Often treated as an elaboration of CELIA. Variants include **Celina**. *See also* SELINA.

Cenydd *See* KENNETH.

Cera (f) Irish name (pronounced 'keera') of obscure meaning. It was borne by a queen of ancient Irish legend and by three Irish saints. Also spelled **Ceara**.

Ceri (f) Welsh name derived from the Welsh *caru* ('to love'), and thus meaning 'loved one', but also often encountered as a diminutive form of CERIDWEN or as a variant of KERRY. It is a relatively recent introduction that does not appear to have been in use before the 1940s. Still largely confined to the Welsh community.

Ceridwen (f) Welsh name derived from the Welsh *cerdd* ('poetry') and *gwyn* ('white' or 'blessed') and thus interpreted as meaning 'poetically fair'. It was borne by the Celtic goddess of poetical inspiration and is still in occasional use today, although rare outside Wales itself. Sometimes abbreviated to **Ceri**.

Cerys *See* CARYS.

Cesar *See* CAESAR.

Chad (m) English name derived from the Old English Ceadda, possibly based on the Celtic *cad* ('battle' or 'warrior'). Borne by the 7th-century St Chad, Archbishop of York, it enjoyed a modest peak in popularity as a first name during the 1970s, chiefly in the USA.

Chae *See* CHARLES.

Chaim (m) Jewish name (pronounced 'hyim') derived from the Hebrew Hyam, itself from the Hebrew *hayyim* ('life'). It is in fairly common use within Jewish communities around the world, especially in the USA. Variants include the feminine equivalent **Chaya**.

Chance (m) English name derived from the ordinary vocabulary word denoting fortune or luck.

Chandler (m) English name denoting a maker of candles that has made occasional appearances in recent times. It enjoyed a boost in the late 1990s as the name of one of the flatmates in the popular US television series *Friends*.

Chantal (f) French name derived from the Old Provençal *cantal* ('stone' or 'boulder') but popularly associated with the French *chant* ('song'). English-speakers took up the name in the 20th century and it may be encountered today within English-speaking communities all over the world. Variants include **Chantale**, **Chantalle**, **Chantelle**, **Shantel** and **Shantelle**.

Chantale/Chantalle/Chantelle *See* CHANTAL.

Chapman (m) English name denoting a merchant or pedlar that has been in occasional use over the years. Notable bearers of the name have included the British journalist and novelist Chapman Pincher (Henry Chapman Pincher; b.1914).

Chardonnay (f) English name alluding to Chardonnay wine. It became widely known in 2001 through the popular television series *Footballers' Wives*, which featured a character of the name. Also found as **Chardonay**.

Charis (f) English first name (pronounced 'kariss') derived from the Greek *kharis* ('grace'). Borne in classical mythology by one of the three Graces, it was taken up by English-speakers in the 17th century alongside numerous other 'virtue' names. In the variant form **Charissa** (possibly influenced by CLARISSA) it made an early appearance in Edmund Spenser's epic *The Faerie Queen* (1590).

Charissa *See* CHARIS.

Charity (f) English name derived from the ordinary vocabulary word 'charity'. It was among the many 'virtue' names taken up by English Puritans after the Reformation. CHERRY and **Chattie** are diminutive forms of the name.

Charlene (f) English name (pronounced 'sharleen') that developed as a feminine variant of CHARLES. It is a relatively recent coinage, dating only to the middle of the 20th century. Commonly abbreviated to **Charlie**, **Charley** or **Charly**. Variants include **Charleen**, **Charline** and **Sharlene**.

Charles (m) English and French name derived ultimately from the

Old German *karl* ('free man'). Also encountered in Ireland as an Anglicization of CEARBHALL. It was in occasional use among English-speakers during the medieval period but did not become generally popular until the 16th century when Mary Queen of Scots imported the name from France, giving it to her son Charles James Stuart. Among familiar forms of the name are **Charlie**, **Chas**, **Chaz**, CHUCK and CHICK. Variants in other languages include the Scottish **Chae** or **Chay**. *See also* CAROL.

Charley *See* CHARLENE; CHARLOTTE.

Charlie *See* CHARLENE; CHARLES; CHARLOTTE.

Charline *See* CHARLENE.

Charlotte (f) English and French name (pronounced 'sharlot') derived from the Italian Carlotta, itself a feminine variant of Carlo (the Italian equivalent of CHARLES). English-speakers took up the name as early as the 17th century and it became frequent in the 18th and 19th centuries. Diminutive forms of the name include **Charley**, **Charlie**, **Charly**, **Chattie**, **Lotta**, **Lottie**, **Lotty**, **Tottie** and **Totty**. Among variants are **Charlotta** and the rare **Sharlott**.

Charlton (m) English name derived from a place name based on the Old English *ceorl* ('free man') and *tun* ('settlement'), and thus meaning 'settlement of free men'. The most famous bearer of the name to date has been the US film actor Charlton Heston (John

Charlton Carter; b.1924). *See also* CARLTON.

Charly *See* CHARLENE; CHARLOTTE.

Charmaine (f) English first name (pronounced 'sharmain') that is thought to have evolved either as a variant of CHARMIAN or else from the ordinary vocabulary word 'charm'. It became fairly popular among English-speakers around the middle of the 20th century, promoted by the popular song 'Charmaine' (1926). Variants include **Charmain**, **Sharmain**, **Sharmaine** and **Sharmane**.

Charmian (f) English name derived from the Greek Kharmion, itself from the Greek *kharma* ('joy' or 'delight'). It was in use among English-speakers by the 16th century, when it became more widely known as the name of Cleopatra's lady-in-waiting in William Shakespeare's *Antony and Cleopatra* (1606–7). *See also* CHARMAINE.

Chas *See* CHARLES.

Chase (m) English name popular chiefly in the USA. It came originally from the ordinary vocabulary word 'chase' and was in use in medieval times as a nickname for a hunter.

Chastity (f) English name derived from the ordinary vocabulary word. It was among the 'virtue' names adoped in the 17th century, but has never been common.

Chattie *See* CHARITY; CHARLOTTE.

Chauncey (m) English name of uncertain Norman French origin that has been in occasional use among English-speakers since the 13th century. Today it is found chiefly in the USA. Also spelled **Chauncy**.

Chay *See* CHARLES.

Chaya *See* CHAIM.

Chaz *See* CHARLES.

Chelle *See* MICHELLE.

Chelsea (f) English name derived from a place name (from central London) meaning 'landing-place for limestone'. It emerged as a first name in the 1950s, initially in Australia and the USA but later more widely. It enjoyed renewed exposure in the 1990s through Chelsea Clinton (b.1980), daughter of US President Bill Clinton. Also encountered as **Chelsie**.

Chelsie *See* CHELSEA.

Cher (f) French name derived from the French *chère* ('dear'), but sometimes also employed as a diminutive form of such names as CHERRY and CHERYL. It enjoyed a boost in the 1960s through the US pop singer and film actress Cher (Cherilyn Sarkasian LaPierre; b.1946).

Cheralyn/Cherelle *See* CHERYL.

Cherida (f) English name that appears to have resulted from the combination of CHERYL and **Phillida** (*see* PHYLLIDA). It is a relatively recent coinage, possibly influenced by the Spanish *querida* ('dear').

Cherie (f) French name (pronounced 'sheree') derived from the French *chérie* ('dear one' or 'darling'). It was taken up by English-speakers in the 1950s. Also spelled **Sheree**, **Sheri**, **Sherie** or **Sherry**. *See also* CHER; CHERRY; CHERYL.

Cherill/Cherilyn *See* CHERYL.

Cherish (f) English name derived from the ordinary vocabulary word 'cherish'. As a first name it is a relatively recent introduction.

Cherry (f) English name that developed as a diminutive form of such names as CHARITY, CHERIE and CHERYL but is also associated with the fruit of the same name. It appeared with increasing regularity among English-speakers from the middle of the 19th century but is now rare. Variants include **Cherrie** and the fairly uncommon **Cherelle**.

Cheryl (f) English name (pronounced 'sherril') that is thought to have resulted from the combination of CHERRY and BERYL (or other similar names) perhaps under the influence of CHERIE. It seems to have made its debut among English-speakers in the early 20th century but did not become frequent until the 1940s. Variants include **Cheryll**, **Cherill**, **Sherill** and **Sheryl**. Among the name's diminutives are various combinations with LYNN, including **Cheralyn**, **Cherilyn** and **Sherilyn**.

Chesney (m) English name that has been in occasional use since the beginning of the 20th century.

Commonly abbreviated to **Ches** or **Chet** – as borne by the US jazz musician Chet Baker (Chesney Baker; 1929–88).

Chester (m) English name derived from a place name (from the city of Chester in Cheshire), itself from the Latin *castra* ('camp' or 'fort'). Sometimes abbreviated to **Chet**.

Chet *See* CHESNEY; CHESTER.

Chevonne *See* SIOBHAN.

Chick (m) English name that is sometimes regarded as a diminutive form of CHARLES or otherwise as a nickname for a youth or person of small build. It appeared with increasing frequency among English-speakers from the 19th century, mainly in the USA.

Chip *See* CHRISTOPHER.

Chloe (f) English name derived from the Greek Khloe, meaning 'young green shoot'. It appeared in Greek mythology as an alternative name for the goddess of agriculture Demeter and in the legend of Daphnis and Chloe, but owed its adoption in post-Reformation England to its appearance in the Bible as the name of a convert of St Paul. The name became increasingly popular in the 20th century. Sometimes abbreviated to **Clo**. Also spelled **Chloë**.

Chloris (f) Greek name derived from *khloros* ('green' or 'fresh'). Representing fertility, it appears in the poetry of the Roman poet Horace and was consequently taken up by English poets in the 17th and 18th centuries. Also spelled **Cloris**.

Chris (m/f) Diminutive form of various longer names, including the masculine CHRISTOPHER and CHRISTIAN and the feminine CHRISTINE, CHRISTABEL and CRYSTAL. This shortened version of the name appeared with increasing regularity from the end of the 19th century. Sometimes spelled **Kris**. Variants of the feminine form of the name include **Chrissie** and **Chrissy**.

Chrissie/Chrissy *See* CHRIS.

Christa *See* CHRISTINA; CHRISTINE.

Christabel (f) English name derived from the Latin *Christus* ('Christ') and *bella* ('beautiful') and thus 'beautiful Christian'. It made its first appearance among English-speakers as early as the 16th century and became popular on the publication of Samuel Taylor Coleridge's poem *Christabel* (1797). Commonly abbreviated to CHRIS, **Chrissie**, **Chrissy**, **Christie**, **Christy**, BELLA or **Belle**. Variants include **Christobel**, **Christabelle** and **Christabella**.

Christelle *See* CRYSTAL.

Christian (m) English name derived from the Roman Christianus, itself from the Latin for 'Christian'. It was taken up by English-speakers in the 17th century, since when it has continued in irregular use. Its adoption was promoted through Christian, the allegorical central character in John Bunyan's *The Pilgrim's*

Progress (1678, 1684). Sometimes abbreviated to CHRIS. *See also* CHRISTIANA.

Christiana (f) Feminine equivalent of CHRISTIAN. It seems to have made its first appearances among English-speakers in the 17th century. It is now rare, under pressure from CHRISTINE. Commonly abbreviated to CHRIS or Christie (or Christy). Variants include **Christiania** and **Christianna**. *See also* CHRISTINA.

Christie *See* CHRISTABEL; CHRISTIANA; CHRISTINE.

Christina (f) English name that developed as a variant of CHRISTIANA. It was taken up alongside the older form of the name as early as the 18th century and is still in use today, alongside CHRISTINE. Diminutive forms of the name include CHRIS, **Christa**, KIRSTY and TINA.

Christine (f) English and French name derived via CHRISTINA from CHRISTIANA. This modern variant of the name established itself among English-speakers towards the end of the 19th century. It reached a peak in frequency in the 1950s. Commonly abbreviated to CHRIS, **Chrissie**, **Chrissy**, **Christa**, **Christie**, **Christy** or KIRSTY. Variants include the Welsh **Crystin**.

Christmas (m) English name, based on the name of the festival, that has made rare appearances as a first name since the 13th century, usually reserved for children born on Christmas Day itself. *See also* CAROL; NATALIE; NOËL.

Christobel *See* CHRISTABEL.

Christopher (m) English name derived from the Greek Khristophoros, itself from the Greek *Khristos* ('Christ') and *pherein* ('to bear') and thus meaning 'bearing Christ' – a reference to the legend of St Christopher, who carried the boy Jesus over a stream and thus became the patron saint of travellers. Popular among early Christians, the name was taken up by English-speakers around the 13th century. Familiar forms of the name include CHRIS, **Christy**, **Kit** and **Chip**. *See also* KESTER.

Christy *See* CHRISTINE; CHRISTOPHER.

Chrystal/Chrystalla *See* CRYSTAL.

Chuck (m) Diminutive form of CHARLES that is also used informally as a term of endearment. It can be traced back to the Old English *chukken* (to cluck). It has been in common use among English-speakers in the USA since the 19th century. Variants include **Chuckie**.

Ciabhan (m) Irish name (pronounced 'keevan') derived from the Irish Gaelic for 'full-haired'. It is sometimes Anglicized as **Keevan**.

Cian (m) Irish name (pronounced 'kain' or 'kee-ern') derived from the Gaelic for 'ancient'. It appears in Irish mythology as the name of the son-in-law of Brian Boru. Also encountered as **Kean** or **Keane**.

Ciannait is a feminine form of the name.

Ciannait *See* CIAN.

Ciara/Ciaran *See* KIERAN.

Cicely *See* CECILIA.

Cilla (f) Diminutive form of PRISCILLA and of the less frequent DRUSILLA. It seems to have made its first appearances among English-speakers around the middle of the 20th century. It has become particularly well known in the UK through British pop singer and television presenter Cilla Black (Priscilla White; b.1943).

Cillian *See* KILLIAN.

Cimmie *See* CYNTHIA.

Cinderella (f) English version of the French Cendrillon, meaning 'little cinders'. Best known from the classic fairy tale *Cinderella*, it has made occasional appearances as a first name, usually reserved for children with rather dull surnames. **Cindy** is a diminutive form.

Cindy (f) Diminutive form of such names as CYNTHIA, LUCINDA and even CINDERELLA, which is now often encountered as a name in its own right. It began to appear with increasing frequency among English-speakers in the 1950s and is now fairly common. Variants include **Cindie**, **Cindi**, **Cyndi** and **Sindy**.

Cis/Ciss *See* CISSIE.

Cissie (f) English name that developed as a diminutive form of CECILIA and its variants. English-speakers began to use the name in the 19th century but it has become rare since the 1930s. Commonly abbreviated to **Cis** or **Ciss**. Also found as **Cissy**, **Sissie** or **Sissy**.

Cissy *See* CECILIA; CISSIE.

Claire (f) English and French name derived from the Roman Clara, itself from the Latin *clarus* ('clear' or 'pure'). It came to England with the Normans but remained infrequent among English-speakers until the 19th century, during which time it usually appeared as **Clare**. In the French form Claire, the name was at its most common in the 1970s. Also found as **Clair** or, more rarely, **Clarette** or **Claretta**. *See also* CLARA.

Clancey *See* CLANCY.

Clancy (m) English and Irish name that developed variously from the Irish surname Mac Fhlannchaidh ('son of Flannchadh') or else as a diminutive of CLARENCE. It was taken up by English-speakers in the 19th century, chiefly in the USA. Also spelled **Clancey**.

Clara (f) English, German and Italian name derived from the Latin *clarus* ('clear' or 'pure') that was taken up in the English-speaking world as a Latinized version of the already accepted **Clare** (*see* CLAIRE). In Scotland it is sometimes considered to be an Anglicized form of SORCHA. It became popular among English-speakers in the 19th century. **Clarrie** is a diminutive form of the name. *See also* CLARIBEL; CLARICE; CLARINDA.

Clare *See* CLAIRE.

Clarence (m) English name meaning 'of Clare' that was adopted in the 14th century as a ducal title and appeared as a first name from the 19th century. Its use among English-speakers owed much to Edward VII's son Albert Victor, Duke of Clarence (1864–92), whose premature death attracted public sympathy. The name is more popular in the USA than elsewhere. Commonly abbreviated to **Clarrie** and less frequently to CLANCY. *See also* SINCLAIR.

Claretta *See* CLAIRE.

Claribel (f) English name that resulted from the combination of CLARA and such names as ANNABEL and ISABEL. It was adopted as a literary name in the 16th century, but is rare today.

Clarice (f) English and French name derived from the Roman Claritia, itself from the Latin *clara* ('clear' or 'pure') or else from *clarus* ('famous' or 'renowned'). It was taken up by English-speakers in medieval times and was revived in the late 19th century but has since become rare. *See also* CLARISSA.

Clarinda (f) English name that appears to have resulted from the combination of CLARA and BELINDA, LUCINDA or other similar names. It emerged in the late 16th century, appearing possibly for the first time in Edmund Spenser's epic poem *The Faerie Queene* (1590, 1596). Spenser's choice of name may have been influenced by the already extant **Clorinda**. It enjoyed a peak in popularity in the 18th century but is now rare.

Clarissa (f) English name derived from CLARICE. The name was recorded in medieval times and became well known in the 18th century through the Samuel Richardson novel *Clarissa* (1748). It has remained in occasional use ever since. Sometimes abbreviated to **Clarrie**, **Clarry** or **Claris**.

Clark (m) English name denoting a clerk or secretary that has been in occasional use as a first name since the late 19th century, chiefly in the USA. Well-known bearers of the name have included the US film actor Clark Gable (William Clark Gable; 1901–60). Also spelled **Clarke**.

Clarke *See* CLARK.

Clarrie *See* CLARA; CLARENCE; CLARISSA.

Clarry *See* CLARISSA.

Claud *See* CLAUDE.

Claude (m) English and French name descended from the Roman Claudius, itself derived from the Latin *claudus* ('lame'). It was taken up by English-speakers during the 16th century and was at its most frequent towards the end of the 19th century but fell from favour around the middle of the 20th century. Also spelled **Claud**.

Claudette *See* CLAUDIA.

Claudia (f) English, French and German name descended from the Roman Claudius, itself derived from the Latin *claudus* ('lame'). It seems to have made its first appearances among English-speakers during the 16th century. It has remained in irregular use ever since. In Wales it is sometimes treated as an equivalent of GLADYS. Variants include the French **Claudette** (in use among English-speakers since the early 20th century) and **Claudine**. *See also* CLODAGH.

Claudine *See* CLAUDIA.

Clay *See* CLAYTON.

Clayton (m) English name derived from a place name (from north and central England) that has been in use since the early 19th century. The original place name came from the Old English *claeg* ('clay') and *tun* ('settlement'). **Clay** is a diminutive form.

Cledwyn (m) Welsh name derived from the Welsh *caled* ('hard' or 'rough') and *gwyn* ('white' or 'blessed').

Clelia (f) English and Italian name descended from the Roman Cloelia. It appears in Roman mythology as the name of a legendary heroine who escaped capture by the Etruscans.

Clem *See* CLEMENT; CLEMENTINA.

Clement (m) English name derived from the Latin *clemens* ('merciful'). It was in common

currency among English-speakers during the medieval period but had become rare by the late 20th century. Commonly abbreviated to **Clem**. Variants include **Clemence**. *See also* CLEMENTINA.

Clementina (f) Feminine version of CLEMENT. It seems to have made its first appearances among English-speakers in the 17th century but has become rare since the early 20th century. The French variant **Clementine** has also made occasional appearances among English-speakers and is best known through Lady Clementine Spencer-Churchill (1885–1977), wife of the British Prime Minister Winston Churchill. Diminutive forms of the name include **Clem**, **Clemmie**, **Clemmy** and **Cleo**.

Clementine/Clemmie/Clemmy *See* CLEMENTINA.

Cleo *See* CLEMENTINA; CLEOPATRA.

Cleopatra (f) English version of the Greek Kleopatra, derived from the Greek *kleos* ('glory') and *pater* ('father') and thus meaning 'father's glory', which has made occasional appearances over the centuries. Universally associated with the historical queen of Egypt famed for her liaisons with Julius Caesar and Mark Antony, it is in occasional use today. Commonly abbreviated to **Cleo** or CLIO.

Cliff (m) Diminutive of CLIFFORD or CLIFTON. It was taken up by English-speakers early in the 20th century and enjoyed a peak in popularity in the late 1950s and

1960s, largely in response to the popularity of the British pop singer Cliff Richard (Harold Webb; b.1940).

Clifford (m) English name derived from a place name (common to the counties of Gloucestershire, Herefordshire and Yorkshire) based on the Old English *clif* ('cliff' or 'riverbank') and *ford* ('ford') and thus meaning 'ford by a slope'. It enjoyed a peak in popularity in the first half of the 20th century, especially in the USA. Commonly abbreviated to CLIFF.

Clifton (m) English name derived from a place name (common to several English counties) based on the Old English *clif* ('cliff' or 'riverbank') and *tun* ('settlement') and thus meaning 'town on a cliff'. It is popular chiefly in the USA. Sometimes abbreviated to CLIFF.

Clint (m) Diminutive form of CLINTON. Today it is usually identified with the US film actor and director Clint Eastwood (b.1930), whose popularity in the 'spaghetti westerns' of the 1960s and 1970s brought the name new exposure.

Clinton (m) English name derived, like CLIFTON, from a place name based on the Old English *clif* ('cliff' or 'riverbank') and *tun* ('settlement') and thus meaning 'town on a cliff'. It was adopted initially by English-speakers in the USA in tribute to the notable Clinton family, which produced two early governors of New York. *See also* CLINT.

Clio (f) English first name descended from the Greek Kleio, itself derived from the Greek *kleos* ('glory' or 'praise'). Borne in classical mythology by one of the Muses, it is sometimes encountered today as a variant of **Cleo** and thus regarded as a diminutive form of CLEOPATRA.

Cliona (f) Irish name derived from the Gaelic Cliodhna (or Clidna). Borne in Irish legend by a beautiful fairy princess, it was taken up with some enthusiasm as a first name in the 20th century, although chiefly confined to the Irish community.

Clitus (m) English name descended from the Greek Kleitos, which may itself have come from the Greek *kleos* ('glory'). Borne by one of Alexander the Great's generals, it has made occasional appearances as a first name in modern times, chiefly in the USA.

Clive (m) English name derived from a place name (common to several English counties) based on the Old English *clif* ('cliff' or 'riverbank'). Perhaps the earliest bearer of the name was the fictional Clive Newcombe in the William Makepeace Thackeray novel *The Newcomes* (1853–5), who was apparently named after the British soldier and colonial administrator Robert Clive (1725–74). It enjoyed a peak in popularity in the 1950s.

Clo *See* CHLOE; CLODAGH.

Clodagh (f) Irish name (pronounced 'cloda') derived from that of a river in County Tipperary, Ireland. A relatively recent introduction that appears to have begun with the bestowal of the name upon the daughter of the Marquis of Waterford early in the 20th century, it is sometimes treated as an Irish equivalent of CLAUDIA. It has retained its essentially Irish associations. Sometimes abbreviated to **Clo**.

Clorinda See CLARINDA.

Cloris See CHLORIS.

Clotilda (f) English version of the French Clothilde, which was itself derived from the Old German *hlod* ('famous' or 'loud') and *hild* ('battle'). It enjoyed a modest peak in popularity among English-speakers in the 19th century. Variants include **Clotilde**.

Clotilde See CLOTILDA.

Clova See CLOVER.

Clover (f) English name derived from that of the wild flower. A relatively rare choice of first name, it enjoyed some exposure in the 19th century as the name of a character in the *Katy* books of the US children's writer Susan Coolidge (Sarah Chauncy Woolsey; 1835–1905). Also spelled **Clova**.

Clovis (m) English name that was taken up as a Latinized version of the French LOUIS in the 19th century. It enjoyed renewed exposure through the collection of short stories entitled *The Chronicles of Clovis* (1911), written by the British author Saki (Hector Hugh Monro; 1870–1916).

Clyde (m) Scottish name derived from that of the River Clyde in south-west Scotland, which can be interpreted as meaning 'the washer'. It established itself early on as a popular choice among Black Americans (perhaps because many US plantation owners were of Scottish descent).

Cody (m/f) English name that is thought to have evolved from an Irish surname meaning 'descendant of a helpful person'. Although rare in the UK, it has enjoyed some popularity in the USA and elsewhere, perhaps through association with the celebrated Wild West hero Buffalo Bill Cody (William Frederick Cody; 1846–1917). Also spelled **Codey** or **Kody**.

Coinneach (m) Scottish name (pronounced 'kooinock') derived from the Gaelic for 'handsome' or 'fair'. It continues in occasional use in Scotland but elsewhere has given way to KENNETH.

Colan See COLIN.

Colbert (m) English name derived from the Old German *col* (of uncertain meaning) and *berht* ('bright' or 'famous'). It was in common use during the medieval period and has made occasional reappearances into modern times.

Cole (m) English name of uncertain origin that may have evolved originally from the Old English *cola* ('swarthy') or else as a variant of NICHOLAS or as an abbreviated form of **Coleman** (*see* COLMAN). It is best known today as the name of the celebrated US songwriter Cole Porter (1891–1964).

Coleen/Colene *See* COLLEEN.

Coleman *See* COLMAN.

Colette (f) French name derived from Nicolette (a French equivalent of NICOLA). Borne by a 15th-century French saint, it was taken up with increasing regularity among English-speakers in the early 20th century, partly in response to the popularity of the French novelist Colette (Sidonie Gabrielle Colette; 1873–1954). Also spelled **Collette**.

Colin (m) English name that developed via the medieval diminutive Col from NICHOLAS but is now widely regarded as an independent name. In Scotland it is sometimes considered to be an Anglicization of the Gaelic Cailean, meaning 'puppy' or 'whelp'. It was established among the English by at least the 12th century and remained in common use until the 16th century, by which time it was thought of as a predominantly rural name. It enjoyed a revival in the 20th century. Variants include **Collin**, **Colyn**, the Welsh **Collwyn** and the Irish **Colan**. **Colina**, **Colene**, **Coletta** and **Colinette** are rare feminine versions.

Colina/Colinette *See* COLIN.

Coll (m) Scottish name derived from the Gaelic Colla, itself from the Old Celtic for 'high'.

Sometimes encountered in use as a diminutive of COLIN.

Colleen (f) Irish name derived from the Gaelic *cailin* ('girl'). Sometimes considered to be a feminine form of COLIN, it was adopted by English-speakers in the 19th century, becoming particularly popular in Australia, Canada and the USA from the 1940s. Despite its strong Irish connections it is not very common in Ireland itself. Variants include **Coleen** and **Colene**.

Collette *See* COLETTE.

Colley (m) Irish name meaning 'swarthy' that has been in occasional use over the centuries. Famous bearers of the name have included the English actor and playwright Colley Cibber (1671–1757).

Collin/Collwyn *See* COLIN.

Colm *See* COLUM.

Colman (m) Irish name that developed like COLUM out of the Roman Columba, itself from the Latin for 'dove'. It was borne by several early Irish saints.

Colom *See* COLUM.

Colum (m) Irish name derived from the Roman Columba, itself from the Latin for 'dove'. Its popularity in Ireland can be traced back to St Columba (521–97), who brought Christianity to the country. Variants include **Colm** and **Colom**.

Columbine (f) English and French version of the Italian Columbina, itself descended from the Roman Columba, from the Latin for 'dove'. It became well known in France and England as the name of Harlequin's lover in traditional harlequinade entertainments. The name was promoted among English-speakers in the 19th century through its association with the flower columbine.

Comfort (m/f) English name that enjoyed some popularity among English-speakers after the Reformation. It continued to make rare appearances among both sexes into the 19th century.

Con *See* CONNOR; CONRAD; CONSTANCE; CONSTANTINE.

Conal (m) Irish name derived from the Irish Gaelic for 'wolf' and 'strong' or otherwise meaning 'high mighty'. Notable bearers of the name have included several famous Irish warriors and chieftains. Also spelled **Conall** or, in Scotland, **Comhnall**.

Conan (m) Irish name derived from the Irish Gaelic *cu* ('hound' or 'wolf', or otherwise 'high') that was fairly common among English-speakers between the 12th and 15th centuries and has remained in currency throughout the English-speaking world since a revival in the 19th century. In the USA the name is usually pronounced with a long 'o', whereas the Irish generally prefer a short 'o' (as in 'Connan').

Conn *See* CONNOR.

Connee *See* CONNIE.

Connie (f) English name that evolved as a diminutive of CONSTANCE. It seems to have made its first appearance towards the end of the 19th century. Commonly abbreviated to **Con**. Also spelled **Connee**.

Connor (m) Irish name derived from the Gaelic Conchobar or Conchobhar, itself thought to mean 'hound lover' or 'wolf lover' and thus usually bestowed originally upon hunters. It appears in mythology as the name of a legendary Irish king. Commonly abbreviated to **Con** or **Conn** (which is, however, sometimes traced back to a different origin and interpreted as meaning 'wisdom'). **Conor** is a modern variant of the name.

Conor *See* CONNOR.

Conrad (m) English version of the German Konrad, itself derived from the Old German *kuon* ('bold') and *rad* ('counsel') and thus meaning 'bold counsel'. It was taken up by English-speakers during the medieval period and has continued in modest use ever since, with a marked revival in the 19th century. Commonly abbreviated to **Con**.

Conroy (m) English name derived from the Gaelic for 'wise'.

Constance (f) English and French name derived from the Roman Constantia, meaning 'constancy' or 'perseverance'. Borne by a daughter of William the Conqueror, it was fairly common among English-speakers in the medieval period and enjoyed renewed popularity in the 17th century when the Puritans included it among their favourite 'virtue' names. It has become less common since the early 20th century. Commonly abbreviated to **Con** or CONNIE. Variants include **Constancy** and **Constantina**.

Constancy *See* CONSTANCE.

Constant (m) English and French name descended from the Roman Constans, itself from the Latin *constantis* ('constant' or 'steadfast'). Recorded in use during medieval times, it was among the 'virtue' names taken up by Puritans after the Reformation, but is now rare. Sometimes shortened to **Con** or CONNIE.

Constantine (m) English and French version of the Roman Constantinus, itself from the Latin *constantis* ('constant' or 'steadfast'). It was taken up by English-speakers in the 19th century in response to renewed interest in classical history but has never been common.

Cooper (m) English name meaning 'barrel maker'. Sometimes abbreviated to **Coop**.

Cora (f) English name derived from the Greek *kore* ('girl'). In the Greek form Kore, it appeared in classical mythology as an alternative name for Persephone, goddess of the underworld. It became fairly popular in its modern form in the 19th century but is now

uncommon. Variants include **Coretta**. *See also* CORALIE; CORINNE.

Coral (f) English name that appears to have been adopted as a result of the fashion for coral jewellery in the late 19th century. It is sometimes suggested, however, that the name can be considered a variant of CORA. **Cory** is a diminutive form. *See also* CORALIE.

Coralie (f) French name of uncertain meaning that has also made occasional appearances as a first name among English-speakers. It was one of a range of new names that enjoyed some popularity in France in the years immediately following the Revolution of 1789. It is sometimes regarded as a variant of CORA or CORAL (both of which it apparently predates).

Corbin (m) English name derived from the Old French for 'black-haired' or 'raucous'.

Cordelia (f) English name of obscure origin, possibly a variant of the Celtic Cordula, itself derived from the Latin *cor* ('heart'). Best known from Cordelia, the daughter of the king in William Shakespeare's tragedy *King Lear* (1604–5). Diminutive forms of the name include **Cordy** and DELIA.

Coretta *See* CORA.

Corey (m) English name of uncertain origin that has made occasional appearances since the 1960s, chiefly within the Black community in the USA. Also found as **Cory**.

Corin (m) French name descended from the Roman Quirinus, which may have evolved ultimately from the Sabine *quiris* ('spear'). It was borne by a number of early Christian martyrs and has made irregular appearances among English-speakers in recent times.

Corinna *See* CORINNE.

Corinne (f) English and French name derived ultimately from the Greek Korinna, itself probably from the Greek *kore* ('girl'). It was adopted by English-speakers in the late 19th century, when it was often considered a variant of CORA. The variant **Corinna** became well known from Robert Herrick's poem 'Corinna's going a-Maying' (1648).

Cormac (m) Irish name derived from the Gaelic *corb* ('defilement') and *mac* ('son') or otherwise interpreted as meaning 'charioteer'. It was borne by many notable figures in early Irish history and has remained in common currency to the present day. Variants include **Cormick** and the Scottish **Cormag**.

Cormag/Cormick *See* CORMAC.

Cornel *See* CORNELL.

Cornelia (f) English, German and Dutch name that developed as a feminine version of the Roman CORNELIUS. It was adopted by English-speakers in the 19th century and has remained in limited currency ever since. Diminutive forms of the name include **Cornie**, **Corrie** and **Nellie**.

Cornelius (m) Biblical name of uncertain origin, possibly derived from the Latin *cornu* ('horn'). It appears in the Bible and was imported to the English-speaking world from the Netherlands around the 15th century. Familiar forms of the name include **Cornie**, **Corney** and **Corny**. *See also* CORNELIA.

Cornell (m) English name that has been in occasional use since the 19th century, chiefly in the USA. It is thought that it may have begun originally as a medieval diminutive of CORNELIUS. **Cornel** is a variant form.

Corney/Cornie/Corny *See* CORNELIUS.

Corrie *See* CORNELIA.

Cory *See* CORAL; COREY.

Cosima *See* COSMO.

Cosmo (m) English, German and Italian name derived from the Greek Kosmas, itself from the Greek *kosmos* ('order', 'harmony' or 'beauty'). It was introduced to the English-speaking world by the Scottish dukes of Gordon in the 18th century, who encountered it in Tuscany in the Italian form Cosimo. **Cosima** is a feminine form of the name.

Courtenay/Courteney *See* COURTNEY.

Courtney (m/f) English name that has been in use as a masculine first name since the middle of the 19th century, chiefly in the USA. The original surname came from the Norman French place name Courtenay (meaning 'domain of Curtius'), although it was also a nickname based on the French *court nez* ('short nose'). As a name for girls it appears to have been adopted around the middle of the 20th century. Variants include **Courtenay** and **Courteney**.

Coy (m) English name of uncertain origin, possibly taken from the ordinary vocabulary word 'coy'. Mostly confined to the USA.

Craig (m) Scottish name derived from a place name based on the Gaelic *creag* ('crag'). It has largely lost its uniquely Scottish character and is now in fairly widespread use throughout the English-speaking world. It enjoyed a peak in popularity in the 1970s.

Crawford (m) Scottish name derived from a place name meaning 'ford where the crows gather'.

Creighton (m) Scottish name (pronounced 'cryton') derived from a place name based on the Gaelic *crioch* ('border' or 'boundary') and the Old English *tun* ('settlement').

Cressida (f) English version of the Greek Khryseis, derived from the Greek *khrysos* ('gold'). It is well known in the English-speaking world from the legend of Troilus and Cressida, as related by Chaucer and Shakespeare. Chaucer's source was the Italian poet Boccaccio, who gave the name as Criseida through an apparent misreading of Briseida (meaning 'daughter of Brisis'). In

its modern form the name was taken up among English-speakers in the 20th century. Sometimes abbreviated to **Cressy**.

Cressy *See* CRESSIDA.

Crispin (m) English version of the Roman Crispinus, meaning 'curly-haired'. It was taken up by English-speakers in the 17th century and remained fairly common until the 20th century.

Crystal (f) English name derived from the ordinary vocabulary word 'crystal'. It was taken up by English-speakers towards the end of the 19th century. Commonly abbreviated to CHRIS or **Chrissie**. Also encountered as **Chrystal**, **Christel**, **Cristal**, **Crystle**, **Krystle** or **Krystal** and, more rarely, as **Christelle** or **Chrystalla**.

Cuddie/Cuddy *See* CUTHBERT.

Cullan (m) Scottish and Irish name derived from the Gaelic for 'at the back of the river'. Also spelled **Cullen**.

Cullen *See* CULLAN.

Curt *See* CURTIS; KURT.

Curtis (m) English name derived from the Old French *curteis* ('courteous') that has been in use as an occasional first name since the 11th century, when it was borne by the eldest son of William the Conqueror. Early in its history it acquired a new derivation, from the Middle English *curt* ('short') and *hose* ('leggings'). Sometimes abbreviated to **Curt**.

Cuthbert (m) English name

derived from the Old English Cuthbeorht, itself from *cuth* ('known') and *beorht* ('bright' or 'famous') and thus meaning 'well known'. It became famous as the name of the 7th-century English St Cuthbert, Bishop of Lindisfarne, and continued in fairly common currency right up until the 1930s. Diminutives include BERT and the Scottish **Cuddie** or **Cuddy**.

Cy *See* CYRUS.

Cybill *See* SYBIL.

Cyndi *See* CINDY.

Cynthia (f) English version of the Greek Kynthia, a name borne in mythology by the goddess Artemis, whose birthplace was supposed to have been Mount Kynthos (a name of obscure origin) on the island of Delos. The name was taken up by English-speakers in the 16th century, notably as a poetical name for Elizabeth I. It has remained in currency ever since, but is now rare.

Diminutives include **Cimmie** and CINDY.

Cyra *See* CYRUS.

Cyril (m) English name derived from the Greek Kyrillos, itself from the Greek *kurios* ('lord'). It was borne by several early saints and became popular among English-speakers towards the end of the 19th century. It has been in decline since the 1920s. **Cyrilla** is a rare feminine form.

Cyrilla *See* CYRIL.

Cyrus (m) Biblical name derived from the Greek Kyros, which may have evolved from the Greek *kurios* ('lord'), although it may equally have come from Persian words meaning 'sun' or 'throne'. It made irregular appearances among English-speakers from the 17th century and enjoyed a modest peak in popularity in the USA in the 19th century. The diminutive form **Cy** has been in use, chiefly in the USA, since the early 20th century. **Cyra** is a rare feminine version.

Dacre (m) English name (pronounced 'dayker') derived from a place name (from Cumbria), meaning 'trickling stream'. A strongly aristocratic name, it is now rare.

Daff *See* DAFFODIL; DAPHNE.

Daffodil (f) English name derived from that of the flower. Like other flower names it made its first appearances towards the end of the 19th century. **Daff** and **Dilly** are diminutive forms of the name.

Daffy *See* DAPHNE.

Dafydd *See* DAVID.

Dahlia (f) English name (pronounced 'dayleea') taken up towards the end of the 19th century. The flower itself was named in honour of the celebrated Swedish botanist Anders Dahl (1751–89). Also spelled **Dalia** or **Dalya**.

Dai (m) Welsh first name (pronounced 'die') derived originally from the Old Celtic *dei* ('to shine') but often considered to be a diminutive form of DAVID. Since the 19th century it has become established as one of the most characteristic of all Welsh names.

Daibhidh *See* DAVID.

Daisy (f) English name derived from that of the flower, itself from the Old English *daegeseage* ('day's eye') – so called because it opens its petals at daybreak. Through association with the French *margeurite*, the French name for the daisy, it came to be regarded as a familiar form of MARGARET. It was taken up by English-speakers in the 19th century.

Dale (m/f) English name, originally borne by people living in a dale or valley. It was employed initially as a boys' name, in which role it enjoyed a peak in popularity in the 1960s. As a name for girls it appears to have made early appearances in the first decade of the 20th century. It is confined chiefly to the USA.

Daley (m) Irish name derived from the Gaelic for 'descendant of Dalach'. Sometimes encountered as **Daly**.

Dalia *See* DAHLIA.

Dallas (m) English name derived from a place name meaning 'dweller in the dale'. Its use in the USA has been promoted through association with Dallas, Texas.

Daly See DALEY.

Dalya See DAHLIA.

Damian (m) English name derived from the Greek Damianos, itself from the Greek *daman* ('to subdue' or 'to rule') and thus meaning 'tamer'. It was known among English-speakers as early as the 13th century but did not appear with any regularity until the 20th century. Also found as **Damien** (the usual French version of the name). *See also* DAMON.

Damon (m) English variant of DAMIAN that emerged around the middle of the 19th century. It features in Greek mythology in the legend of the two devoted friends Damon and Pythias.

Dan (m) English name derived from the Hebrew Dan, meaning 'judge', but more often in use today as a diminutive of DANIEL or other similar names. It appears in the Bible as the name of a son of Jacob. *See also* DANNY.

Dana (m/f) English name that evolved as a diminutive form of DANIEL in the 19th century. Today it is unusual to find it in use as a masculine name and is more often bestowed upon girls, in which case it developed as a variant of such names as DANIELLE.

Dandy (m/f) English name derived from the ordinary vocabu- lary word 'dandy', but also in use as a familiar form of such names as DANIELLE. It has made occasional appearances in both sexes since the early 20th century.

Dane (m) English name that is thought to have developed as a variant of DEAN. It has appeared with increasing frequency since the early 20th century, but is now rare outside the USA.

Danette See DANIEL.

Daniel (m) English, French and German name derived from the Hebrew for 'God is my judge' or 'God has judged'. In Ireland, where it has long been popular, it is also regarded as an Anglicized form of Domhnall. In Wales it may be treated as an Anglicization of Deiniol, meaning 'attractive' or 'charming'. It appears in the Bible as the name of an Old Testament prophet and made early appear- ances among English-speakers before the Norman Conquest. It has remained in currency ever since. Commonly shortened to DAN or DANNY (or **Dannie**). Among feminine equivalents are DANIELLE, **Danette** and **Danita**. *See also* DANA.

Daniella See DANIELLE.

Danielle (f) French equivalent of DANIEL that has become popular among English-speakers since the 1940s. It enjoyed a peak in popu- larity in the 1980s. Diminutive forms of the name are **Dan**, **Danny**, **Dannie** and **Dani**. Variants include **Daniella**.

Danita See DANIEL.

Dannie *See* DANIEL; DANNY.

Danny (m) English name that was taken up as a diminutive form of DANIEL early in the 20th century. Like Daniel, it has strong Irish associations, as celebrated in the song 'Danny Boy' (1913). Commonly abbreviated to DAN. Also encountered as **Dannie**.

Daph *See* DAPHNE.

Daphne (f) Greek name meaning 'laurel tree'. Borne in Greek mythology by a nymph who was transformed by her father into a laurel tree when pursued by Apollo, it was taken up among English-speakers in the 18th century. It has become much less frequent since the 1950s. Sometimes shortened to **Daff**, **Daffy** or **Daph**.

Dara (m/f) Irish name derived from the Gaelic Mac Dara. The name is also familiar, as a girls' name, among the world's Jewish communities, in which context it is traced back to the Hebrew for 'pearl of wisdom' (although when it appears in the Old Testament it is given as a boys' name). Also encountered as **Darach**.

Darby (m) English name derived from the place name Derby that has been in occasional use as a first name since the medieval period. The original place name came from the Old Norse *diur* ('deer') and *byr* ('settlement'), thus meaning 'deer park'. Sometimes used in Ireland as an Anglicization of DERMOT. Also encountered as **Derby**.

Darcey (f) Feminine equivalent of the masculine DARCY. It has made irregular appearances among English-speakers since the early 20th century, primarily in the USA. Famous bearers of the name have included the British ballerina Darcey Bussell (b.1969).

Darcy (m) English name, derived from the town of Arcy in France, that has been in occasional use among English-speakers since the 19th century. The popularity of the name was promoted by the stern but handsome aristocrat Fitzwilliam Darcy in the Jane Austen novel *Pride and Prejudice* (1813). Also spelled **D'Arcy**.

Darel/Darell *See* DARRYL.

Daria (f) English, Italian and Polish name that evolved originally as a feminine equivalent of the Roman DARIUS. It has made irregular appearances among English-speakers into modern times.

Darina (f) Irish name derived from the Irish Gaelic *daireann* ('fruitful'). Also found as **Daireann**, **Doirend** or **Doirenn**.

Darius (m) Roman name derived from the Persian *daraya* ('to hold' or 'to possess') and *vahu* ('good' or 'well') and thus meaning 'protector' or 'wealthy'. It has made occasional appearances among English-speakers into modern times. *See also* DARIA.

Darlene (f) English name that is thought to have evolved from the ordinary vocabulary word 'darling' under the influence of such similar coinages as CHARLENE. It became fairly popular in the USA in the 1950s and has remained in occasional use ever since. Also found as **Darleen** or **Darline**.

Darran See DARREN.

Darrell See DARRYL.

Darren (m) English name that is thought to have developed as a variant of DARRYL. It seems to have made its first appearance among English-speakers in the USA in the 1920s and enjoyed a peak in popularity in the 1960s and 1970s. Also found as **Darran** or **Darrin**. **Darrene** is a rare feminine form of the name.

Darrene/Darrin See DARREN.

Darryl (m/f) English name derived ultimately from the Norman baronial surname d'Airelle (referring to Airelle in Calvados). An alternative derivation traces the name back to the Old English *deorling* ('darling'). In such variant forms as **Darel**, **Darell** or **Darrell**, it made early appearances among English-speakers in the late 19th century. Also rendered as **Daryl** (the usual form when the name is bestowed upon females).

Daryl See DARRYL.

Dave/Davey See DAVID.

David (m) English name derived from the Hebrew for 'favourite', 'beloved' or 'darling'. It appears in the Bible as the name of the greatest of the kings of the Israelites.

The name was taken up by English-speakers during the medieval period and has remained one of the most popular of all boys' names ever since. It became especially well established in Wales and Scotland. **Dave**, **Davie**, **Davey** and **Davy** are well-known diminutive forms. Feminine equivalents include DAVINA, **Davida** and **Davinia**. Among variants in other languages are the Gaelic **Daibhidh** and the Welsh **Dafydd** or DEWI. See *also* DAI; TAFFY.

Davida/Davie See DAVID.

Davina (f) Scottish feminine variant of DAVID. It appears to be a fairly recent introduction of early 20th-century coinage. Sometimes abbreviated to **Vina**. Variants include **Davida**, **Davena** and **Davinia**. See *also* DIVINA.

Davinia See DAVINA; DIVINA.

Davis (m) English name meaning 'David's son'.

Davy See DAVID.

Dawn (f) English name derived from the ordinary vocabulary word 'dawn'. It seems to have made its first appearances among English-speakers in the 1920s and was at its most frequent in the 1960s. See *also* AURORA.

Dean (m) English name that can be traced back either to the Old English *denu* ('valley') or to the ecclesiastical rank 'dean'. It seems to have made its debut as a first name in the USA but has since been taken up throughout the English-speaking world, enjoying a peak in popularity in the 1980s. Variant forms are **Deane** and **Dene**. *See also* DEANNA.

Deanna (f) English name that evolved as a variant of DIANA in the early 20th century but is also occasionally encountered as a feminine equivalent of DEAN. Famous bearers of the name have included the Canadian-born US film actress and singer Deanna Durbin (Edna Mae Durbin; b.1921).

Deanne *See* DIANE.

Dearbhail *See* DERVLA.

Deb *See* DEBORAH.

Debbie (f) Diminutive form of DEBORAH that is sometimes treated as a name in its own right. It became widely heard in the 1950s and enjoyed a peak in popularity in the 1960s and 1970s. Also found as **Debby**.

Debby *See* DEBBIE.

Deborah (f) English name derived from the Hebrew for 'bee' and thus suggestive of a diligent, industrious nature. It appears in the Bible and was consequently taken up with some enthusiasm by Puritans in the 17th century. It enjoyed a peak in popularity in the 1960s. Commonly shortened to **Deb**, **Debs** or DEBBIE (or **Debby**). **Debra** is a variant form of the name.

Debra/Debs *See* DEBORAH.

Declan (m) English version of the Irish Deaglan, of uncertain meaning. It became popular as a first name among the Irish in the 1940s and was subsequently taken up more widely in the English-speaking world from the 1980s.

Dee (f) English name that evolved as a diminutive form of various names beginning with the letter 'D', including DEIRDRE and DOROTHY. Variants include **DeeDee** (or **Didi**).

Deforest (m) English name that has made occasional appearances since the 19th century, chiefly in the USA, sometimes in reference to US novelist John DeForest (1826–1906). Variously rendered as Deforest, **Deforrest** or **DeForrest**.

Deidre *See* DEIRDRE.

Deiniol *See* DANIEL.

Deirbhile *See* DERVLA.

Deirdre (f) Irish name derived from the Irish *deardan* ('storm') and thus meaning 'raging' or 'tempestuous'. The name has featured prominently in Irish literature through retellings of the tragic legend of the beautiful Deirdre of the Sorrows. It was adopted more widely in the English-speaking world from the 1930s. Also encountered as **Deidre**, **Diedre** or **Deidra**.

Del *See* DELBERT; DELROY; DEREK.

Delbert (m) English name that is thought to have evolved in parallel with DELMAR and DELROY and other similar names. It appears to have been a relatively recent introduction that made its first appearances among English-speakers in the early 20th century.

Delfina *See* DELPHINE.

Delia (f) English name derived ultimately from that of the Greek island of Delos, which in Greek mythology was identified as the home of Artemis and Apollo. It is occasionally encountered as a diminutive form of such names as CORDELIA. It was taken up by English-speakers towards the end of the 16th century, when it became established as a favourite literary name. Sometimes abbreviated to **Dee**. **Della** is a variant form.

Delicia (f) English name derived from the Roman Delicius, itself from the Latin *deliciae* ('delight'). Variants include **Delys**.

Delight (f) English name derived from the ordinary vocabulary word denoting 'joy' or 'pleasure'.

Delilah (f) Hebrew name meaning 'delight', possibly from the Arabic *dalla* ('to flirt' or 'to tease'). It appears in the Bible as the name of Samson's deceitful lover and the cause of his downfall, but despite this connection was taken up with some enthusiasm by English Puritans in the 17th century. It is rare today. **Delila** is a variant form.

Dell *See* DELLA.

Della (f) Diminutive form of ADELA and DELIA among other names. It made its first appearances towards the end of the 19th century. Commonly abbreviated to **Dell**.

Delmar (m) English name of uncertain origin, possibly a variant of ELMER. It has enjoyed some

popularity in the USA since the middle of the 20th century.

Delores *See* DOLORES.

Delphine (f) French name derived from the Roman Delphina, meaning 'woman of Delphi'. Madame de Staël's use of the name in her epistolary novel *Delphine* (1802) undoubtedly promoted awareness of the name and English-speakers were using it by the end of the 19th century. Also encountered in the variant forms **Delfina**, **Delphina** and **Delvene**.

Delroy (m) English name that is thought to have evolved as a variant of LEROY. It has enjoyed some popularity in the UK since the middle of the 20th century.

Delwyn (m) Welsh name derived from the Welsh *del* ('pretty' or 'neat') and *gwyn* ('white' or 'blessed'). It made its first appearances among the Welsh early in the 20th century. Also encountered as **Delwen**.

Delys *See* DELICIA.

Delyth (f) Welsh name (pronounced 'dellith') derived from the Welsh *del* ('pretty' or 'neat'). It remains confined largely to Wales itself.

Demelza (f) English name that enjoyed some popularity among English-speakers from the 1950s. Although it purported to be a traditional Cornish name, it was in fact the name of a Cornish village, meaning 'hill-fort of Maeldaf', that was selected by the British novelist Winston Graham for a character in his *Poldark* series of novels set in historical Cornwall, beginning with *Demelza* (1946).

Demi (f) English name that evolved as a diminutive of the Roman Demetra, itself descended from Demeter, the name of the goddess of the harvest in Greek mythology. It has become well known in recent years through the US film actress Demi Moore (b.1962).

Dempsey (m) English name derived from the Gaelic for 'proud descendant'.

Den *See* DENNIS.

Dene *See* DEAN.

Deneice *See* DENISE.

Denholm (m) English name derived from a place name based on the Old English *denu* ('valley') and *holm* ('island'). Famous bearers of the name have included the British actor Denholm Elliott (1922–92). Variants include **Denham**, meaning 'home in a valley'.

Denice/Deniece *See* DENISE.

Denis *See* DENNIS.

Denise (f) French name that developed as a feminine version of Denis (*see* DENNIS). It was taken up by English-speakers in the 1920s and enjoyed a peak in popularity in the 1950s and 1960s. **Dennie** is a familiar form of the name. Variants include **Deneice**, **Denice** and **Deniece**.

Dennie *See* DENISE.

Dennis (m) English name derived from the Greek Dionysios, denoting a devotee of the Greek god of wine Dionysos. It came to England with the Normans but fell from favour in the 17th century. It was revived in the early 20th century but is now less common. Also rendered as **Denys** or **Denis** (the French spelling of the name). Commonly abbreviated to **Den** or, more rarely, **Denny**. *See also* DENISE.

Denny *See* DENNIS.

Denton (m) English name derived from a place name based on the Old English *denu* ('valley') and *tun* ('settlement').

Denys *See* DENNIS.

Denzel *See* DENZIL.

Denzil (m) English name derived from the Cornish place name Denzell, alternatively interpreted as meaning 'fort' or 'fertile upland'. Records of its use go back to the 16th century, when it was borne by the English statesman Denzil Holles (1599–1680). Also encountered as **Denzel** or **Denzyl**.

Derby *See* DARBY.

Derek (m) English name derived from the Old German Theodoric, meaning 'ruler of the people'. It is thought to have come to England with Flemish immigrants in the 15th century but remained rare until the end of the 19th century and has never been common in the USA. **Del** and **Derry** are common diminutive forms of the name. Also rendered as **Deryck** or

Deryk. Variants from other languages include the Dutch **Dirk**. *See also* KERMIT.

Dermot (m) English version of the Irish Diarmaid or Diarmuid, possibly derived from the Gaelic *di* ('without') and *airmait* ('envy'). As Diarmaid it was the name of a legendary king of Tara. As Dermot, it made its first appearances in Ireland in the 19th century and has since been encountered elsewhere, usually among people with strong Irish connections. Variants include **Diarmid**, **Dermid** and the Scottish **Diarmad**.

Derry *See* DEREK.

Dervla (f) Irish name possibly derived from the Irish *dear* ('daughter') and *file* ('poet') or *Fal* ('Ireland') and meaning 'daughter of Ireland'. Variants include **Dearbhail**, **Deirbhile** and **Dervila**.

Derwent (m) English name derived from a place name meaning 'river that flows through oak woods'.

Deryck/Deryk *See* DEREK.

Deryn (f) Welsh name possibly derived from *aderyn* ('bird'). It seems to have made its first appearance in Wales around the middle of the 20th century.

Des *See* DESMOND.

Desdemona (f) English name apparently derived from the Greek *dusaimon* ('ill-fated'). It is famous as the name of the doomed wife of the central character in William Shakespeare's tragedy *Othello* (1602–4).

Desi *See* DESMOND.

Désirée (f) French name meaning 'desired'. It can be traced back ultimately to the Roman Desiderata, meaning 'desired' in Latin. It became fairly well known among English-speakers in the 1950s, chiefly in the USA. Often rendered without the accents.

Desmond (m) English name derived from the Irish Gaelic surname Deas-Mhumhan, meaning 'someone from south Munster'. It appears to have come to England from Ireland towards the end of the 19th century, assuming its present form under the influence of ESMOND, and remained fairly frequent until the middle of the 20th century. Commonly abbreviated to **Des** or **Desi** (also rendered as **Desy** or **Dezi**).

Desy *See* DESMOND.

Detta *See* BERNADETTE.

Deverell (m) Celtic name derived from a place name meaning 'fertile river bank'. Also spelled **Deverill**.

Devereux (m) English name derived from the French *d'Evreux* ('of Evreux') that has made occasional appearances since medieval times. Its modern use as a first name is confined chiefly to the USA.

Devlin (m) Irish name derived from the Irish Gaelic for 'fiercely brave'.

Devon (m) English name derived from that of the county of Devon. It has made rare appearances, chiefly in the USA, since the middle of the 20th century. Well-known bearers of the name have included the Jamaican-born British cricketer Devon Malcolm (b.1963).

Dewey *See* DEWI.

Dewi (m) Welsh variant of DAVID. Of ancient origins, it enjoyed a revival in Wales in the 20th century. **Dewey** is a variant of the name in the USA.

Dex *See* DEXTER.

Dexter (m) English name derived from the Old English *deag* ('dye') and thus meaning 'dyer' that has been in occasional use among English-speakers since the 1930s. It is sometimes associated with the Latin *dexter*, meaning 'right-handed' or 'auspicious'. Commonly shortened to **Dex**.

Dezi *See* DESMOND.

Di *See* DIANA; DIANE; DINAH.

Diamond (f) English name derived from that of the gemstone. It was among the various jewel names that enjoyed some popularity in the 19th century.

Diana (f) English name derived from that of the Roman goddess of the moon and the hunt. Despite its pagan associations, it was taken up by English-speakers after the Reformation and subsequently enjoyed a peak in popularity around the middle of the

20th century. Notable bearers of the name have included Diana, Princess of Wales (1961–97). Commonly shortened to **Di**. *See also* DEANNA; DIANE; DINAH.

Diane (f) French version of the English DIANA that was taken up alongside the existing form of the name by English-speakers in the 1930s. Commonly abbreviated to **Di**. Variants include **Dian**, **Dianne**, **Deanne**, **Diahann** and **Dyan** (or **Dyanne**). *See also* DION.

Dianne *See* DIANE.

Diarmaid/Diarmuid *See* DERMOT.

Dick (m) Diminutive form of RICHARD. It has been suggested that the name evolved via **Rick** as a result of the difficulty English-speakers experienced in pronouncing the initial 'R' in the rolled Norman French manner. It was in widespread use among English-speakers by the 17th century. **Dickie** and **Dicky** are diminutive forms of 19th-century origin.

Dickie/Dicky *See* DICK.

Diedre *See* DEIRDRE.

Digby (m) English name derived from a place name (from Digby in Lincolnshire) derived from the Old Norse *diki* ('ditch') and *byr* ('settlement'), and thus meaning 'farm by a ditch'. Its use as a first name dates from the 19th century.

Diggory (m) English name of uncertain origin, but possibly derived from the French *l'esgaré* ('the lost one' or 'astray'). The name may have been popularized by the 14th-century romance *Sir Degaré* but it was not until the 16th century that the name began to appear with any regularity among English-speakers, most frequently in Cornwall. Also encountered as **Digory**.

Dil/Dill *See* DILYS.

Dillon *See* DYLAN.

Dilly *See* DILWEN; DILYS.

Dilwen (f) Welsh name that is thought to have resulted from the combination of DILYS and *gwyn* ('white') and meaning 'fair' or 'holy'. It appears to be an introduction of 20th-century origin. **Dilly** is a diminutive form of the name. Also encountered as **Dilwyn**.

Dilwyn *See* DILWEN.

Dilys (f) Welsh name derived from *dilys* ('genuine', 'steadfast' or 'sincere'). It appears to have been a 19th-century introduction that soon found favour beyond Welsh borders. **Dylis** and **Dyllis** are variant forms of the name. Diminutives include **Dil**, **Dill** and **Dilly**.

Dina *See* DINAH.

Dinah (f) Hebrew name derived from *din* ('judgement' or 'lawsuit') and interpreted as meaning 'vindicated'. It often appears as a variant of DIANA, despite the fact that the two names have distinct origins. It appears in the Bible and was taken up by English Puritans after the Reformation. Commonly shortened to **Di**. **Dina** is a variant form of the name.

Dinsdale (m) English name derived from a place name meaning 'settlement by a moat'.

Dion (m) English name derived via the Roman Dionysius from the Greek Dionysios or some other similar Greek source. It was taken up by English-speakers in the 16th century and has remained in irregular use ever since, chiefly in the USA. **Dionne**, **Dione** and **Dionna** are feminine variants.

Dione/Dionna/Dionne *See* DION.

Dirk *See* DEREK.

Divina (f) English name that developed as a variant of DAVINA, possibly under the influence of the ordinary vocabulary word 'divine'. It has appeared irregularly since the early 20th century. Variants include **Davinia**, which may reflect the influence of LAVINIA.

Dixie (f) English name derived from the French *dix* ('ten'). It is popular chiefly in the USA, where it is best known as the nickname of the southern states of the USA. Also found as **Dixee**.

Dod/Dodie/Dodo *See* DOROTHY.

Doireann *See* DOREAN.

Doll *See* DOLLY.

Dolly (f) English name that evolved as a diminutive of DOROTHY or DOLORES and is sometimes presumed (inaccurately) to have been inspired by the ordinary vocabulary word 'doll' (which is, however, a later coinage dating from the 17th century). It appears to have been taken up by English-speakers in the 16th century. Commonly abbreviated to **Doll**. Also spelled **Dolley**, chiefly in the USA.

Dolores (f) Spanish first name meaning 'sorrows' and thus referring to the title *Maria de los Dolores* ('Mary of the Sorrows') borne by the Virgin Mary. It became popular in the 20th century, when it spread with Spanish emigrants to many parts of the English-speaking world, especially the USA. Also spelled **Delores**. *See also* DOLLY; LOLA; LOLITA.

Dom *See* DOMINIC.

Dominic (m) English name descended from the Roman Dominicus, itself derived from the Latin *dominus* ('lord'). Borne in the 13th century by St Dominic, founder of the Dominican order of monks, it was popular among English-speakers in medieval times and remained a favourite choice of Roman Catholics. In Ireland it is sometimes treated as an Anglicization of Domhnall. Commonly abbreviated to **Dom**. **Dominica** is a rare feminine version. *See also* DOMINIQUE.

Dominica *See* DOMINIC.

Dominique (m/f) French equivalent of the male DOMINIC. The French originally applied the name to both sexes but today regard it as a name for girls. It has always been employed as a girls' name among English-speakers,

who first took up the name in this French incarnation in the 1960s.

Don (m) Diminutive form of DONALD and DONOVAN. It won acceptance as a name in its own right from the 19th century and remained a fairly popular choice among English-speakers until the middle of the 20th century. **Donny** is a diminutive form of the name.

Donal *See* DONALD.

Donald (m) English version of the Gaelic Domhnall, itself from the Celtic *dubno* ('world') and *val* ('rule' or 'mighty') and thus meaning 'world mighty' or 'world ruler'. The final 'd' came either through attempts by English-speakers to pronounce the Gaelic name in an authentic manner or through the influence of such Germanic names as RONALD. It has strong Scottish associations, but was taken up widely elsewhere from the 1920s. Commonly abbreviated to DON and less frequently to **Donny**. An Irish form of the name is **Donal. Donalda**, **Donaldina** and **Donella** are feminine equivalents.

Donalda/Donaldina/Donella *See* DONALD.

Donna (f) English name derived from the Italian *donna* ('lady'). It was taken up by English-speakers in the 1920s, initially in the USA but later throughout the English-speaking world. It was at its most frequent in the 1960s and again in the 1980s. *See also* MADONNA.

Donny *See* DONALD; DONOVAN.

Donovan (m) Irish name derived from the Gaelic *donn* ('brown') and *dubh* ('black' or 'dark'), and thus meaning 'dark brown' (referring to the colour of a person's hair, eyes or complexion). It was taken up by English-speakers early in the 20th century. Commonly shortened to DON or **Donny**.

Dora (f) English name that developed as a diminutive of such names as **Dorothea** (*see* DOROTHY), ISADORA and THEODORA, which all share common origins in the Greek word *doron* ('gift'). It was adopted by English-speakers in the 19th century but is now rare. Familiar forms of the name include **Dorry** and **Dory**. **Doria**, **Doretta**, **Dorette** and **Dorita** are rare variants.

Doran (m) English name derived from an Irish Gaelic surname meaning 'descendant of Deoradhan' (Deoradhan itself meaning 'exile' or 'wanderer').

Dorcas (f) English name derived from the Greek *dorkas* ('doe' or 'gazelle'). It appears in the Bible as an interpretation of the Aramaic TABITHA. English Puritans adopted it as a first name after the Reformation and it has continued in irregular use. In Scotland it is sometimes employed as an Anglicization of Deoiridh.

Dorean (f) Irish name that developed as an Anglicization of the Gaelic Doireann, itself resulting from the combination of the Gaelic *der* ('daughter') and the name of the legendary Irish hero Finn. It emerged as a popular choice of name among Irish-speakers in the 20th century, perhaps in response to the popularity of the English DOREEN.

Doreen (f) English name that resulted from the combination of such names as DORA, KATHLEEN and MAUREEN. English-speakers took up the name towards the end of the 19th century and it was subsequently at its most frequent in the 1930s. Variants include **Dorene** and **Dorine**. *See also* DOREAN.

Doretta/Dorette/Doria *See* DORA.

Dorian (m) English name derived from the Greek Dorieus, meaning 'person from Doris' (Doris being a region in ancient Greece). It is well known from the Oscar Wilde novel *The Picture of Dorian Gray* (1891), in which it may have made its first appearance. **Dorien** and **Dorrien** are variant forms. The feminine equivalents **Dorianne** and **Doriana** have also made occasional appearances.

Dorinda (f) English name that resulted from the combination of DORA and the suffix '-inda', as found in such names as BELINDA and CLARINDA. It made appearances as a literary name in the 17th century.

Doris (f) English name derived from the Greek for 'bountiful' or else 'person from Doris' (Doris being a region in ancient Greece), but also treated as a combination of DOROTHY and PHYLLIS. It appears in mythology as the name of a minor goddess and was adopted by English-speakers towards the end of the 19th century. **Dorrie** is a diminutive form.

Dorita *See* DORA.

Dorothea *See* DOROTHY.

Dorothy (f) English name derived via **Dorothea** from the Greek *doron* ('gift') and *theos* ('god') and thus meaning 'gift of God'. As Dorothea, it was taken up by English-speakers in the 16th century and became fairly common in the 19th century before falling from favour. As Dorothy, it made its first appearance as early as the 16th century and gradually eclipsed Dorothea from the late 19th century. Diminutive forms include **Thea, Dee, Dot, Dottie** (or **Dotty**), **Dod, Dodo** and **Dodie**. *See also* DOLLY; DORA.

Dorrie *See* DORA; DORIS.

Dorrien *See* DORIAN.

Dory *See* DORA.

Dot/Dottie/Dotty *See* DOROTHY.

Doug *See* DOUGAL; DOUGLAS.

Dougal (m) English version of the Gaelic Dubhgall or Dughall, derived from the Gaelic *dubh* ('black') and *gall* ('stranger'). It was applied originally to the dark-haired Danes who settled in Ireland early in that country's history. The Scottish then took up the name and it began to appear more widely in the English-

speaking world from the early 20th century. Commonly abbreviated to **Doug** (or **Dug**) and **Dougie** (or **Duggie**). Variants include **Dugald** and **Doyle**.

Dougie *See* DOUGAL; DOUGLAS.

Douglas (m) Scottish name derived from a place name based on the Gaelic *dubh* ('black') and *glas* ('stream'). Well known in Scotland from the earls of Douglas, it was applied initially to children of either sex, although it has been reserved exclusively for boys since the 17th century. Commonly shortened to **Doug** (or **Dug**) and **Dougie** (or **Duggie**).

Doyle *See* DOUGAL.

Drake (m) English name meaning 'dragon'.

Dreda *See* ETHELDREDA.

Drena *See* ADRIENNE.

Drew (m/f) English name that evolved as a diminutive of ANDREW or otherwise as a derivation of DROGO. It established itself in Scotland before winning acceptance elsewhere in the English-speaking world from the 1940s, usually as a name for boys. Famous bearers of the name have included the US film actress Drew Barrymore (b.1975).

Drina *See* ADRIENNE.

Driscoll (m) English name derived from the Irish Gaelic for 'interpreter'. Also spelled **Driscol**.

Drogo (m) English name of uncertain meaning, possibly derived from the Old Saxon *drog* ('ghost') or Old German *tragan* ('to bear' or 'to carry') or, more likely, from the Slavonic *dorogo* ('dear'). It was brought to England by the Normans and remained in currency until the late 17th century. It enjoyed a limited revival among English-speakers in the 19th century. *See also* DREW.

Drummond (m) Scottish name derived from a place name. Still largely confined to Scotland.

Drusilla (f) English name derived ultimately from the Roman Drusus, itself supposedly from the Greek *drosos* ('dew') and meaning 'fruitful' or 'dewy-eyed'. It appears in the Bible and was taken up by English-speakers in the 17th century. It is still encountered occasionally today, chiefly in the USA. Also found as **Drucilla** or **Druscilla**. *See also* CILLA.

Duane (m) English version of the Gaelic Dubhan, itself derived from *dubh* ('black') and meaning 'little dark one'. It became popular among English-speakers in the 1940s and reached a peak in frequency in the 1970s. Also spelled **Dwayne** or **Dwane**.

Dubhghall *See* DOUGAL.

Dud *See* DUDLEY.

Dudley (m) English name derived from a place name based on the Old English for 'wood or clearing of Dudda'. It is also encountered in Ireland as an Anglicization of Dubhdara or DARA. It became well known as the surname of Elizabeth I's favourite Robert Dudley, Earl of

Leicester (c.1532–88). Commonly shortened to **Dud**.

Duff (m) Scottish name derived from the Gaelic *dubh* ('dark' or 'black') and originally bestowed upon people with dark hair or complexion. Famous bearers of the name have included the British politician Sir Alfred Duff Cooper, 1st Viscount Norwich (1890–1954).

Dug *See* DOUGAL; DOUGLAS.

Dugald *See* DOUGAL.

Duggie *See* DOUGAL; DOUGLAS.

Duke (m) English name derived either from the title 'duke' or else as a diminutive of MARMADUKE. It was taken up by English-speakers early in the 20th century, chiefly in the USA, where it was further popularized as the nickname of the popular US film actor John Wayne (1907–79).

Dulce *See* DULCIE.

Dulcie (f) English name derived from the Latin *dulcis* ('sweet'). Recorded in use among English-speakers in medieval times in such forms as Duce or Dowse, it was revived in its modern form towards the end of the 19th century. **Dulce** is a diminutive form.

Duncan (m) English version of the Gaelic Donnchadh, derived from the Old Celtic *donn* ('dark') and *cath* ('battle') and thus meaning 'dark warrior'. It has a long history as a Scottish name, having been borne by three 11th-century Scottish kings. It was taken up throughout the English-speaking world in the 20th century. Commonly abbreviated to **Dunk**, **Dunkie** or **Dunky**.

Dunk/Dunkie/Dunky *See* DUNCAN.

Dunstan (m) English name derived from a place name based on the Old English *dun* ('dark') and *stan* ('stone') and meaning 'stony hill'. Popular chiefly among Roman Catholics, it is best known as the name of the 10th-century English St Dunstan, Archbishop of Canterbury.

Durand (m) French and English name derived from the Latin *durans* ('enduring'). It came to England with the Normans and remained in fairly common currency until the end of the medieval period. It has made rare reappearances in succeeding centuries.

Dustin (m) English name of uncertain origin that has made occasional appearances among English-speakers since the early 20th century. It has been suggested that the name evolved as a Norman version of the Old Norse Thurstan, meaning 'Thor's stone', or else from the Old German for 'brave fighter'. The most famous bearer of the name to date has been the US actor Dustin Hoffman (b.1937). *See also* DUSTY.

Dusty (m/f) English name that emerged either as a feminine equivalent of the masculine DUSTIN or else as a borrowing of the ordi-

nary vocabulary word 'dusty' (referring to the colour of a person's hair or complexion). It has made occasional appearances as a first name since the 1950s.

Dwane/Dwayne *See* DUANE.

Dwight (m) English name possibly derived from the medieval French Diot that has made irregular appearances since the end of the 19th century, chiefly in the USA. It has been suggested that the medieval form of the name can be traced back ultimately to the Roman Dionysius (*see* DENNIS). Its popularity in the USA reflects the fame of the US President Dwight D. Eisenhower (1890–1969).

Dyan/Dyanne *See* DIANE.

Dylan (m) Welsh name that may have evolved via the Welsh *dylif* ('flood') from the Celtic word for 'sea'. Attempts to interpret the name more exactly have included 'son of the wave' and 'influence'. Long established in Wales, it was taken up by English-speakers in the 1950s. The most famous bearer of the name to date has been the Welsh poet Dylan Thomas (1914–53). **Dillon** is a variant spelling.

Dylis/Dyllis *See* DILYS.

Dymphna (f) Irish name that is thought to have evolved from the Gaelic Damhnait, itself from *damh* ('fawn' or 'stag') and *damh* ('poet'). It is little known outside Ireland itself. **Dympna** is a variant form.

Ee

Eachann (m) Scottish name derived from the Gaelic *each* ('horse') and *donn* ('brown'). Sometimes considered to be a Gaelic equivalent of HECTOR.

Eadan (m) Irish name derived from the Old Irish Etain, possibly based on the Old Irish *et* ('jealousy'). Usually pronounced 'aidan' or 'adan', it features in Irish legend as the name of a sun goddess. Also encountered as **Etan**.

Eamon (m) Irish equivalent of the English EDMUND, pronounced 'aimon'. Also encountered as **Eamonn**.

Earl (m) English name derived from the aristocratic rank, itself from the Old English *eorl* ('nobleman' or 'chieftain'). It was often bestowed upon those who worked as servants in the households of English earls. Records of the name go back as far as the 12th century. Also encountered as **Earle** or **Erle**. *See also* DUKE; EARLENE; ERROL; KING; PRINCE.

Earlena *See* EARLENE.

Earlene (f) Feminine equivalent of EARL. Variants include **Earlena**, **Erlean**, **Erleen** and **Erlinda**.

Earnest *See* ERNEST.

Eartha (f) English name derived from the ordinary vocabulary word 'earth'. It made irregular appearances among English-speakers through the 20th century. Famous bearers of the name have included the US jazz singer and actress Eartha Kitt (b.1928). Variants include **Ertha** and **Erthel**.

Eben *See* EBENEZER.

Ebenezer (m) English name derived from the Hebrew *eben-haezer* ('stone of help'). It appears in the Bible and was consequently taken up as a first name by Puritans in the 17th century. Sometimes shortened to **Eb** or **Eben**.

Ebo *See* EBONY.

Ebony (f) English name derived from the name of the black wood ebony. It was taken up chiefly among Black Americans in the 1970s and by the 1980s ranked among the top three most popular names among female members of the Black community in the USA. Commonly abbreviated to **Ebo**.

Echo (f) English name derived from the ordinary vocabulary word 'echo'. In Greek legend, Echo was a nymph whose unceasing chatter irritated the goddess Hera, who robbed her of the power of independent speech and allowed her only to repeat the last fragment of what others said.

Ed (m) English name that developed as a diminutive of such names as EDGAR, EDMUND, EDWARD and EDWIN. It became more frequent among English-speakers around the beginning of the 20th century. **Eddie** and **Eddy** are diminutive forms that emerged at much the same time.

Eda See ADA.

Edan See AIDAN.

Eddie/Eddy See ED.

Ede See EDITH.

Eden (m/f) English name variously derived from the Old English **Edun** or **Edon**, which came in turn from the Old English *ead* ('riches') and *hun* ('bear cub'), or from the name of the biblical Paradise, itself from the Hebrew *eden* ('delight' or 'paradise'). It was taken up as a first name by Puritans in the 17th century.

Edgar (m) English name derived from the Old English Eadgar, itself based on the Old English *ead* ('riches') and *gar* ('spear') and thus

interpreted as meaning 'rich in spears' or 'owner of many spears'. The modern form of the name was in common use among English-speakers during the medieval period and was revived towards the end of the 19th century. Commonly abbreviated to **Ed** or **Eddie**. Variants include **Adair**.

Edie See EDITH.

Edina See EDNA; EDWINA.

Edith (f) English, French, German and Scandinavian name derived from the Old English Eadgyth, itself based on the Old English *ead* ('riches') and *gyth* ('strife') and thus interpreted as meaning 'rich in war'. It was popular among English-speakers in medieval times and was revived towards the end of the 19th century. It is now rare. Sometimes shortened to **Edie** or **Eda**.

Edmé See ESMÉ.

Edmund (m) English name derived from the Old English Eadmund, itself based on the Old English *ead* ('riches') and *mund* ('protector') and thus meaning 'protector of wealth' or 'happy protection'. The modern form of the name has been in regular use since the medieval period, although it has become less common since the early 20th century. Diminutive forms of the name include **Ed**, **Eddie** (or **Eddy**), **Ned**, **Neddie** (or **Neddy**), **Ted** and **Teddie** (or **Teddy**). See also EAMON.

Edna (f) English name possibly derived from the Hebrew *ednah* ('rejuvenation' or 'pleasure') or more likely from the Irish EITHNE, itself from the Irish Gaelic for 'kernel'. It appears in the Apocrypha as the name of Sarah's mother. Sometimes considered a feminine equivalent of EDEN, it was taken up by English-speakers in the 18th century. Variants include **Edina**.

Edsel (m) English equivalent of the German Etzel, derived either from the Old German *adal* ('noble') or from the nickname *Atta* ('father'). The most famous bearer of the name to date has been Edsel Ford (1893–1943), son of the US industrialist Henry Ford.

Edward (m) English name derived from the Old English Eadweard, itself from the Old English *ead* ('riches') and *weard* ('guard') and thus meaning 'guardian of riches', 'fortunate guardian' or 'wealth guardian'. Recorded as early as the 9th century, it was familiar in medieval times and was later revived in the 19th century. Famous bearers of the name have included eight kings of England. Commonly abbreviated to **Ed**, **Eddie**, **Eddy**, **Ned**, **Neddie**, **Neddy**, **Ted**, **Teddie** or **Teddy**.

Edweena/Edwena *See* EDWINA.

Edwin (m) English name derived from the Old English Eadwine, itself based on the Old English *ead* ('riches') and *wine* ('friend') and thus interpreted to mean 'friend of riches' or 'rich friend'. It was in fairly regular use among English-speakers during the medieval period and was subsequently among the historical names revived in the 19th century. It is now rare. **Ed** and **Eddie** are common diminutives of the name. *See also* EDWINA.

Edwina (f) Feminine form of EDWIN. It does not seem to have been in use in medieval times and probably made its first appearances in the 19th century when Edwin was revived. Today it is more common in Scotland than elsewhere. Variants include **Edweena** and **Edwena**.

Effie *See also* EPHRAIM; EUPHEMIA.

Egan (m) Irish name derived from the Gaelic Aogan, itself a variant of Aodh, meaning 'fire'.

Egbert (m) English name derived from the Old English Ecgbeorht, from the Old English *ecg* ('edge') and *beorht* ('bright' or 'famous') and thus meaning 'bright sword' or 'famed swordsman'. It was common in Anglo-Saxon England prior to the Norman Conquest, but appears to have fallen into disuse following the medieval period. It was briefly revived in the 19th century.

Eglantine (f) English flower name based on that of the plant usually identified as sweetbrier (which has the French name *aiglent*), but often confused with honeysuckle. The name was in use among English-speakers during the medieval period and was revived on a modest scale in the 19th century.

Variants include **Eglantina**, **Eglantyne** and **Eglentyne**.

Eibhlin *See* EILEEN.

Eileen (f) English first name derived from the Irish **Eibhlin**, an Irish equivalent of AVELINE or EVELYN, but also often treated as an Irish form of HELEN. It was taken up by English-speakers towards the end of the 19th century (when it was exported widely by Irish emigrants). **Eily** is a familiar form of the name. Variants include **Aileen** (a Scottish variant), **Eilean**, **Eilene** and **Ileen**.

Eilwen (f) Welsh name meaning 'fair brow'.

Eily *See* EILEEN.

Eira (f) Welsh name (pronounced 'eera' or 'ighra') meaning 'snow'. It is a relatively recent introduction that has yet to win acceptance outside Wales.

Eirian (f) Welsh name (pronounced 'evan' or 'ighreean') meaning 'bright', 'beautiful' or 'silver'. Apparently dating back to around the middle of the 20th century, it has remained confined to Wales. Variants include **Eireen**, **Arian** and **Ariane**.

Eirlys (f) Welsh name (pronounced 'airlees' or 'igherliss') meaning 'snowdrop'. It made its first appearances towards the end of the 19th century but still appears to be in exclusively Welsh use.

Eithne (f) Irish name probably derived from the Gaelic *eithne*

('kernel'), although often treated as a feminine version of AIDAN. Borne by an Irish goddess, several Irish queens and nine saints, the name remains rare outside Ireland. English-speakers pronounce the name as 'ethnee', whereas the Irish know it as 'eenya' – hence the Irish variant **Enya**. Other variants include **Ethna**, **Ethne**, **Etna** and **Aithne**. *See also* ENA.

Elain (f) Welsh name meaning 'fawn' or 'hind'. Sometimes confused with the otherwise unrelated ELAINE.

Elaine (f) English name derived via Old French from HELEN. It appeared with increasing frequency among English-speakers from the late 19th century following its appearance in Alfred, Lord Tennyson's *Idylls of the King* (1859). Variants include **Elayne**.

Eldred (m) English name derived from the Old English Ealdred, itself from the Old English *eald* ('old') and *raed* ('counsel') and thus meaning 'long-established counsel'. Common in medieval times and earlier, it is now rare. Variants include the feminine **Eldreda** (sometimes shortened to **Dreda**).

Eldreda *See* ELDRED.

Eleanor (f) English name of disputed origin. It probably evolved as a French version of HELEN, itself derived from the Old German *al* ('all'). The name came to England with Henry II's wife Eleanor of

Aquitaine (1122–1204) and has remained in use ever since. **Ellie**, NELL, **Nellie**, **Nelly**, NORA and **Norah** are diminutive forms. Alternative versions of the name include **Eleanora**, **Elenora**, **Eleonora**, **Eleonore**, **Lenore** and **Elinor**.

Eleanora *See* ELEANOR.

Electra (f) English version of the Italian Elettra, itself derived from the Greek *elektor* ('brilliant'). It is usually associated with the legend of Orestes and Electra, the children of Agamemnon who avenged their father's murder.

Elen (m) Welsh equivalent of HELEN. The name may have developed not directly from Helen but perhaps from the Welsh *elen* ('nymph'). Variants include **Elin**.

Elena *See* HELEN.

Elenora/Eleonora/Eleonore *See* ELEANOR.

Eleri (f) Welsh name of uncertain meaning. It appears in Welsh mythology as the name of the daughter of Brychan.

Eli (m) Hebrew name meaning 'high', 'elevated' or 'exalted'. It appears in the Bible and was consequently adopted as a first name by English-speakers in the 17th century. It has been rare since the middle of the 20th century. **Ely** is a variant form.

Elias (m) Greek version of the biblical ELIJAH. It was taken up by English Puritans in the 17th century but became infrequent after

the 19th century. Variants include ELLIS.

Elihu (m) Hebrew name meaning 'God is he' or 'the Lord is Yah'. It appears in the Old Testament and was consequently taken up by English Puritans after the Reformation.

Elijah (m) Biblical name derived from the Hebrew Eliyahu, meaning 'God is Yah' (Yah being another name for Jehovah). It was the name of a biblical prophet and was also borne by John the Baptist. Adopted by Puritans in the 17th century, it was not until the 19th century that it appeared with any regularity. It is now largely confined to the USA. *See also* ELIAS.

Elinor *See* ELEANOR.

Eliot/Eliott *See* ELLIOTT.

Elisabeth *See* ELIZABETH.

Elisha (m) Hebrew name derived from *el* ('God') and *sha* ('to help' or 'to save') and thus meaning 'God is salvation'. It appears in the Bible as the name of a revered Old Testament prophet and was consequently taken up by English Puritans in the 17th century. It has appeared only infrequently since then.

Elita (f) English name derived from the French *élite* ('chosen').

Eliza (f) English first name that evolved as a diminutive form of ELIZABETH. It was taken up by English-speakers in the 16th century and enjoyed a peak in

popularity in the 18th century. It
has become rare since the end of
the 19th century. *See also* LISA.

Elizabeth (f) English name
derived from the Hebrew Elisheba,
meaning 'oath of God' or 'God
has sworn'. It was the name of
John the Baptist's mother and
became popular among English-
speakers during the medieval
period. In 1600 around one in five
females born in England were
given the name. Also encountered
as **Elisabeth**. Diminutive forms
include **Lib**, **Libby**, LISA, **Lisbeth**,
Liz, **Liza**, **Lizzie**, **Lizzy** and **Tetty**.
Variants in other languages
include the Welsh **Bethan**. *See also*
BESS; BETH; BETSY; BETTY; ELIZA; ELSA;
ELSIE; ELSPETH; ISABEL; LISA.

Elkanah (m) Hebrew name meaning 'God has created' or 'the Lord
is possessing'. It appears in the
Bible and was taken up by
English-speakers in the 17th
century.

Elke (f) Jewish name derived from
the Hebrew *elkahan* ('possessed by
God'), although it is also regarded
as a Yiddish version of ELAINE or as
a German equivalent of ALICE. Also
found as **Elkie**.

Ella (f) English name derived via
French from the Old German Alia,
itself from the German *al* ('all'). It
is also used as a diminutive form
of such names as ELEANOR and
ELLEN. It came to England with the
Normans but it was not until the
19th century that it became
common. **Ellie** is a common diminutive form.

Ellar (f) Scottish name that
developed as an Anglicization of
the Gaelic Eallair, itself from the
Latin *cella* ('cellar'). The name
was originally borne by butlers or
stewards in monasteries.

Ellen (f) English name that was
taken up as a variant of HELEN in
the 16th century. Popular towards
the end of the 19th century, it was
still fairly common 100 years later.
Variants include **Ellie**, NELL, **Nellie**
and **Nelly**.

Ellery (m) English name that has
made occasional appearances
since the early 20th century.
Occasionally spelled **Ellerie**, in
which form it is also sometimes
bestowed upon females.

Ellie *See* ELEANOR; ELLA; ELLEN; ELSA;
HELEN.

Elliott (m) English name that
made its first appearances among
English-speakers in the 16th century. It came originally from a
Norman French variant of ELIAS.
Also encountered as **Eliot**, it
enjoyed a recent peak in popularity in the 1990s. Other variants
include **Eliott** and **Elliot**.

Ellis (f) English name that evolved
either from the identical surname,
derived from ELIAS, or else as a
variant of ISABEL or ALICE or as an
Anglicization of the Irish Eilis or
the Welsh Elisud, itself from *elus*
('kind').

Elly *See* ELEANOR; ELLA; ELLEN; HELEN.

Elma (f) English name that is
thought to have evolved through
the combination of ELIZABETH and

MARY. Largely confined to the USA, it is also found as a diminutive form of WILHELMINA and names ending '-elma' and occasionally as a feminine equivalent of ELMER.

Elmer (m) English name derived from the Old English *aethel* ('noble') and *maer* ('famous') that was taken up in the 19th century, chiefly in the USA. The name's popularity in the USA may be traced back to the brothers Ebenezer and Jonathan Elmer, who were prominent figures during the American War of Independence. **Elm** and **Elmy** are diminutive forms of the name. *See also* AYLMER.

Elmo (m) Italian name derived ultimately from the Old German *helm* ('helmet' or 'protection') that has made irregular appearances among English-speakers since the 19th century. Also encountered as a familiar form of ERASMUS.

Elmore (m) English name derived from a place name meaning 'river banks with elms'.

Eloisa *See* ÉLOISE.

Éloise (f) French name of uncertain Germanic origin that has made irregular appearances (usually without the accent) among English-speakers over the centuries. It may come from the Old German for 'hale' or 'wide'. It came to England with the Normans, possibly as a feminine equivalent of LOUIS. Also encountered as **Eloisa**.

Elroy (m) English name that developed as a variant of LEROY. It has proved particularly popular among Black Americans since the 19th century.

Elsa (f) English, German and Swedish name derived from ELIZABETH. It became popular among English-speakers in the 19th century. **Ellie** is a familiar form of the name. *See also* AILSA.

Elsdon (m) English name derived from a place name (from Northumbria) based on the Old English for 'Elli's valley'. It is popular today chiefly in the USA.

Else *See* ELSIE.

Elsie (f) English name that developed via **Elspie** as a diminutive form of ELSPETH, although it is also sometimes encountered as an abbreviated form of ELIZABETH. It was popular among English-speakers in the 18th and 19th centuries, particularly in Scotland. Sometimes abbreviated to **Else**.

Elspeth (f) English and Scottish name that developed as a diminutive form of ELIZABETH in the 19th century. **Elspie** is a familiar form of the name. *See also* ELSIE.

Elspie *See* ELSPETH.

Elton (m) English name derived from a place name based on the Old English for 'Ella's settlement'. It made its debut as a first name in the 20th century.

Eluned (f) Welsh name that is thought to have evolved out of the earlier Luned or Lunet, names which may have evolved out of the Welsh *eilun* ('idol'). Rarely found outside Wales. Also encountered in the forms **Eiluned** or **Elined**.

Elvie/Elvin/Elvina *See* ALVIN.

Elvira (f) Spanish name of uncertain origin, possibly derived from the Old German Alwara, itself from the Old German *al* ('all') and *wer* ('true') and thus meaning 'true to all'. It was not taken up by English-speakers until the 19th century.

Elvis (m) English name that is thought to have evolved from the surname Elwes, which had its origins in ÉLOISE, or alternatively from the Irish Ailbhe. Today it is universally associated with the US rock and roll singer Elvis Presley (1935–77), who inherited the name from his father Vernon Elvis Presley.

Elwin *See* ELWYN.

Elwyn (m) Welsh name that is thought to have evolved from the Welsh for 'fair brow' or 'elf friend'. It has also been suggested that it may have come about as a variant of ALVIN. Other versions of the name include **Elwin**.

Ely *See* ELI.

Elysia (f) English name derived from the Greek for 'blissful'. It evolved as a feminine version of Elysium, the name of heaven in Greek mythology.

Em *See* EMILY; EMMA; EMMELINE.

Emanuel (m) Biblical name derived from the Hebrew

Immanuel, meaning 'God with us'. It appears in the Bible and was consequently taken up by English-speakers in the 17th century. Often spelled **Emmanuel** or found, in the USA, in the Spanish variant **Manuel**. Familiar forms of the name include **Man** and **Manny**. **Emanuelle** and **Manuela** are feminine equivalents of the name.

Emanuelle *See* EMANUEL.

Emblem/Emblin/Emblyn/ Emeline/Emelyn *See* EMMELINE.

Emer (f) Irish name of uncertain origin. It is famous in Irish mythology as the name of the hero Cuchulain's beloved, who was depicted as the personification of all female qualities. **Emir** is a rare variant form.

Emerald (f) English name derived from the name of the gem. Like other jewel names, it enjoyed some popularity among English-speakers towards the end of the 19th century. Occasionally encountered as a familiar form of ESMERALDA.

Emerson (m) English name meaning 'son of Emery' that has made occasional appearances as a first name in relatively recent times. **Emmerson** is a rare variant.

Emery (m) English name derived from the Old German Emmerich or Amalric, itself from the Old German *amal* ('labour') and *ric* ('ruler') and meaning 'powerful noble'. It came to England with the Normans and until the 18th century was borne by both sexes but is now reserved exclusively for males. Occasionally encountered as **Emory**.

Emil *See* EMILE.

Emile (m) French name descended, possibly via French Huguenots, from the Roman Aemilius, itself from the Latin for 'striving' or 'eager'. Usually rendered in France as **Émile**, it has made irregular appearances among English-speakers since the middle of the 19th century.

Emilia (f) English name derived from AMELIA. It emerged during medieval times and is still in use today, although it has never been common. Well-known bearers of the name have included three characters in the plays of William Shakespeare.

Emily (f) English first name derived from the Roman Aemilia, itself from the Latin for 'striving' or 'eager'. It was adopted by English-speakers in the 18th century and has enjoyed a marked revival since the 1970s. **Em**, **Emmie**, **Emmy** and **Milly** (or **Millie**) are diminutive forms of the name. *See also* AMELIA.

Emir *See* EMER.

Emlyn (m) Welsh name sometimes traced back to the Roman Aemilius, itself from the Latin for 'striving' or 'eager', or else from unknown Celtic roots. It has retained its strong Welsh associations and is today rarely found outside Wales itself.

Emma (f) English name derived

from the Old German *ermen* ('entire' or 'universal'). It was in use among English-speakers during medieval times and was at its most frequent in the 19th century. It has remained in regular use ever since, with a recent peak in popularity in the 1980s. **Em**, **Emmie** and **Emmy** are diminutive forms of the name.

Emmanuel *See* EMANUEL.

Emmeline (f) English name that developed as a variant of EMMA but can also be traced back via the Old French Ameline to the Old German *amal* ('labour'). It was taken up by English-speakers in medieval times and was revived in the 18th century, since when it has continued to make rare appearances, often as a variant of EMILIA or EMILY. Diminutive forms include **Emeline** and **Emelyn** as well as the rarer **Emblem**, **Emblin** and **Emblyn**.

Emmerson *See* EMERSON.

Emmet (m) English name derived from EMMA. It is sometimes bestowed in Ireland in honour of the Irish rebel Robert Emmet (1778–1803).

Emmie/Emmy *See* EMILY; EMMA; EMMELINE.

Emory *See* EMERY.

Emrys (m) Welsh name that developed as a variant of AMBROSE. Apparently a 20th-century introduction, it is still largely confined to Wales.

Ena (f) English version of the Irish

EITHNE that is also encountered as a diminutive of **Eugenia** (*see* EUGENIE), HELENA and various other names with similar endings. It became popular towards the end of the 19th century after it was bestowed upon Queen Victoria's granddaughter Princess Ena (Victoria Eugénie Julia Ena; 1887–1969). Sometimes encountered as INA.

Engelbert (m) German name derived from the Old German *Angil* ('Angle') and *berht* ('famous' or 'bright'). A notable bearer of the name in modern times is British singer Engelbert Humperdinck (Arnold George Dorsey; b.1936). Also found as **Englebert**.

Enid (f) English name that may have developed out of the Welsh *enaid* ('soul' or 'life') or possibly from *enit* ('woodlark'). It became popular among English-speakers towards the end of the 19th century in reference to the Arthurian legend of Enid and Geraint, in which Enid proves her innocence against charges of infidelity. It is now rare.

Enoch (m) English name derived from the Hebrew Hanok, thought to mean 'dedicated', 'trained' or 'experienced'. It appears in the Bible and was consequently taken up by English Puritans in the 17th century.

Enola (f) English name of uncertain meaning. A late 19th-century introduction, it acquired some notoriety through the 'Enola Gay', the nickname of the US Super-fortress bomber used to drop the first atomic bomb on Hiroshima on 6 August 1945.

Enos (m) Biblical name derived from the Hebrew for 'mankind'. It is sometimes encountered in Ireland as an Anglicization of the Gaelic Aonghus (*see* ANGUS). It was taken up by English-speakers in the 19th century.

Enya *See* EITHNE.

Eoan *See* EUGENE.

Eoghan (m) Irish and Scottish name of uncertain origin. It may have evolved from the Gaelic words for 'yew' and 'born' and may mean 'born of the yew'. It is sometimes encountered in Ireland as an Anglicization of EUGENE or OWEN and in Scotland of EWAN, EVAN or HUGH.

Ephraim (m) Biblical name derived from the Hebrew Ephrayim, meaning 'fruitful'. It appears in the Bible as the name of Joseph's second son but it was not until the 18th century that it appeared with any frequency among English-speakers. **Effie** and **Eph** are familiar forms of the name.

Eppie *See* EUPHEMIA; HEPHZIBAH.

Erasmus (m) English name derived via Latin from the Greek Erasmos, itself from *eran* ('to love') and thus meaning 'beloved', 'desired' or 'longed for'. It was taken up by English-speakers in the 17th century and remained current until the end of the 19th century. *See also* ELMO.

Erastus (m) English name derived from the Greek Erastos, meaning 'beloved' or 'dear one'. It was taken up on a limited basis by English-speakers in the 18th century. Today it is equally familiar in its diminutive form **Rastus**.

Eric (m) English name derived from the Old Norse Eyrekr, itself from *ei* ('ever' or 'always') or *einn* ('one') and *rikr* ('ruler') and thus meaning 'ever-ruling' or possibly 'island ruler'. It would appear that the name came to England with Danish settlers before the Norman Conquest. It was not, however, until the middle of the 19th century that the name began to be adopted regularly by English-speakers. Variants include **Rick** and **Ricky** (or **Rikki**). *See also* ERICA.

Erica (f) English name that developed as a feminine equivalent of ERIC. It may have been influenced by *erica*, the Latin name for the plant heather. In Scotland it is sometimes treated as an Anglicization of the Gaelic **Oighrig**. It made early appearances among English-speakers towards the end of the 18th century. **Rica**, **Ricki**, **Rika** and **Rikki** are diminutive forms of the name.

Erin (f) Irish name derived from *Eire*, the traditional Gaelic name for Ireland itself. It has made occasional appearances as a first name since the end of the 19th century, not only in Ireland but also in Australia, the USA and elsewhere. **Errin** and **Eryn** are variant forms.

Erle *See* EARL.

Erlean/Erleen/Erlinda *See* EARLENE.

Erma *See* IRMA.

Ermintrude (f) English, French and German name derived from the Old German *ermen* ('entire' or 'universal') and *traut* ('beloved') and thus meaning 'wholly beloved'. It came to England with the Normans but is today effectively defunct. Sometimes shortened to **Trudie**, **Trudi** OR TRUDY.

Ern *See* ERNEST.

Erna (f) English name that developed as a diminutive form of **Ernesta** and **Ernestine** (*see* ERNEST). It was taken up by English-speakers in the 19th century.

Ernest (m) English name derived from the Old German *eornost* ('earnestness' or 'seriousness'). It made its first appearances among English-speakers at the time of accession of the Hanoverian George I and remained popular until the early 20th century. Commonly shortened to **Ern** or **Ernie**. Occasionally found as **Earnest** through confusion with the ordinary vocabulary word. **Ernesta**, **Ernestina** and **Ernestine** are feminine versions. *See also* ERNA.

Ernesta/Ernestina/Ernestine/ Ernie *See* ERNEST.

Errin *See* ERIN.

Errol (m) Scottish name derived from a place name that was taken up by English-speakers in the late

19th century. Sometimes associated with EARL, from which it may have evolved, or HAROLD, it proved especially popular among Black Americans in the 20th century.

Erskine (m) Scottish name derived from a place name (from Erskine, near Glasgow) that was subsequently taken up among English-speakers from the 19th century.

Eryn *See* ERIN.

Esau (m) Biblical name derived from the Hebrew Esaw, meaning 'hairy'. It appears in the Bible as the name of one of Isaac and Rebecca's twin sons, who was born covered with red hair, and enjoyed some popularity among English-speakers after the Reformation.

Esmaralda *See* ESMERALDA.

Esmé (m/f) French name derived from the Old French *esme* ('loved' or 'esteemed'). It seems to have been imported to England as early as the 16th century. It has continued to make occasional reappearances ever since, originally borne by both sexes. As a name for girls, also spelled **Esmée**, it was taken up by English-speakers in the 18th century and now appears to be in exclusively feminine use. Sometimes treated as an abbreviated form of ESMERALDA. *See also* AMY.

Esmée *See* ESMÉ.

Esmeralda (f) English name derived from the Spanish *esmeralda* ('emerald'). Borne by the

gypsy girl in Victor Hugo's *The Hunchback of Notre Dame* (1831), it was taken up by English-speakers in the 19th century but has never been common. Sometimes shortened to ESMÉ. Also rendered as **Esmerelda** or **Esmaralda**. *See also* EMERALD.

Esmond (m) English name derived from the Old German *est* ('favour' or 'grace') and *mund* ('protection') and thus meaning 'favoured protector'. It disappeared from use after the 14th century but was revived among English-speakers in the 19th century. Occasionally rendered as **Esmund**.

Esmund *See* ESMOND.

Essa *See* ESTHER.

Essie *See* ESTELLE; ESTHER.

Esta *See* ESTHER; HESTER.

Estella *See* ESTELLE.

Estelle (f) French name derived from STELLA and thus meaning 'star'. It was taken up by English-speakers in the 19th century. Before Estelle became the dominant form of the name in the 20th century it was usually encountered as **Estella**. Diminutive forms of the name include **Essie**.

Esther (f) Biblical name that may have had its roots in the Persian *stara* ('star') but is otherwise associated with the Hebrew Hadassah, meaning 'myrtle' or 'bride'. Another theory suggests it is a Hebrew version of Ishtar, the name of the Babylonian-Assyrian goddess of love. It was taken up by English-speakers in the 17th century. **Ess, Essa, Esta, Ettie, Etty, Hester** and **Hetty** are all diminutive forms.

Etan *See* EADAN.

Eth *See* ETHEL.

Ethan (m) Biblical name derived from the Hebrew Eythan, meaning 'constant', 'firm', 'strong' or alternatively 'long-lived'. It appears in the Bible and was taken up by Puritans from the 17th century and increased a little in frequency during the 19th century, proving most popular in the USA. **Etan** is a Jewish variant.

Ethel (f) English name derived ultimately from the Old German *ethel* ('noble'). It is thought to represent a shortened version of a range of Anglo-Saxon names such as Ethelburga and Ethelthryth. Because of its historical associations it was taken up by English-speakers in the 19th century. It is now virtually defunct. Commonly shortened to **Eth** and, more rarely, to **Thel**.

Ethelbert (m) English name derived from the Old English *aethel* ('noble') and *beorht* ('bright'). Borne by the brother of Alfred the Great, it continued in irregular use after the Norman Conquest and enjoyed a brief resurgence in popularity in the 19th century. A rare feminine equivalent is **Ethelberta**. *See also* ALBERT.

Etheldreda (f) English first name derived from the Old English *aethel* ('noble') and *thryth* ('strength'). It was borne by a 7th-century English saint and remained in occasional use through medieval times before giving way to the related AUDREY around the 16th century. **Dreda** is an accepted derivative of the name.

Ethelred (m) English name derived from the Old English *aethel* ('noble') and *raed* ('counsel') and thus meaning 'noble counsel'. It was common in England before the Norman Conquest but fell from favour after the 19th century.

Ethna/Ethne/Etna *See* EITHNE.

Etta/Ettie *See* HENRIETTA.

Etty *See* ESTHER; HENRIETTA.

Euan *See* EWAN.

Eudora (f) Greek name derived from *eu* ('good') and *doron* ('gift') and thus meaning 'good gift'. It enjoyed some popularity among English-speakers towards the end of the 19th century. Commonly shortened to **Dora**.

Eugene (m) English name derived via French from the Greek Eugenios, meaning 'noble' or 'well-born'. It was borne by several early Christian saints and popes. In Ireland it became accepted as an Anglicization of **Aodh**, EOGHAN or **Eoan**. English-speakers took up the name in the 19th century and it has remained in irregular use ever since, especially in the USA. Commonly shortened to GENE. *See also* EWAN; OWEN.

Eugenia *See* EUGENIE.

Eugenie (f) French name (Eugénie) adopted as a feminine equivalent of EUGENE. Famous from Napoleon III's wife the Empress Eugénie (1826–1920), who spent much of her life in England, it was taken up by English-speakers in the 19th century. Notable bearers of the name in more recent times have included Princess Eugenie (b.1990), the daughter of Prince Andrew and Sarah, Duchess of York. Commonly abbreviated to **Gene** or **Genie**. The variant **Eugenia** is now rare. *See also* ENA.

Eulalia (f) English, Italian and Spanish name derived from the Greek *eu* ('good') and *lalein* ('chatter' or 'talk') and thus meaning 'sweetly speaking'. It was a popular choice of name in medieval times but is now uncommon. **Lalla**, **Lallie** and **Lally** are diminutive forms.

Eunice (f) Biblical name (pronounced 'yoonis') derived from the Greek *eu* ('good') and *nike* ('victory') and thus meaning 'good victory'. It was taken up by English Puritans in the 17th century (then pronounced 'yooneesee'). It enjoyed a peak in popularity in the 1920s. Also rendered as **Unice**.

Euphemia (f) Greek name derived from *eu* ('well') and *phenai* ('to speak') and thus meaning 'well spoken of', 'well regarded' or 'of good repute'. It seems to have made its first appearances among English-speakers in the 12th century and enjoyed a modest peak in popularity in the 19th century, particularly in Scotland. **Effie**, **Eppie**, **Phemie** and **Fanny** are diminutive forms of the name.

Eustace (m) English name derived via French from the Greek Eustakhios, from the Greek *eu* ('good') and *stakhus* ('ear of corn' or 'grapes') and thus interpreted as meaning 'fruitful'. It was brought to England by the Normans and was revived in the 19th century. **Stacy** is an established diminutive form of the name. *See also* EUSTACIA.

Eustacia (f) Feminine equivalent of EUSTACE. Sometimes shortened to **Stacey** or **Stacy**.

Eva (f) Roman name derived from the Hebrew Havvah, meaning 'living'. The usual form of the English EVE in many non-English-speaking cultures, it was taken up by English-speakers as an alternative form of the name around the middle of the 19th century. *See also* AVA; EVANGELINE.

Evadne (f) Greek name derived from *eu* ('well') in combination with another unknown root. It appears in Greek mythology and has made occasional appearances among English-speakers since the 17th century.

Evaline/Evalyn *See* EVELYN.

Evan (m) Welsh name derived from Iefan or Ieuan, a Welsh variant of the English JOHN. It seems to have made its first appearance among the Welsh around 1500 and became a popular choice of first name throughout Wales in the 19th century. Also found as **Ifan**.

Evander (m) Roman name derived from the Greek Euandros, from the Greek *eu* ('good') and *aner* ('man'). It appears in Roman legend as the name of a hero who founded a city on the site of modern Rome. It was subsequently taken up by English-speakers, enjoying special popularity among the Scottish, who sometimes treated it as an Anglicization of the Gaelic Iomhair.

Evangelina *See* EVANGELINE.

Evangeline (f) English name derived ultimately from the Latin *evangelium* ('gospel'). It appears to have been popularized through Henry Wadsworth Longfellow's narrative poem *Evangeline* (1847). Also found as **Evangelina**. Diminutive forms of the name include **Eva** and **Evie**.

Eve (f) English and French name derived via Latin from the Hebrew Havvah, based on the Hebrew *hayya* ('living'). As the name of the female companion of the biblical Adam, the name has always had special religious significance among Christians. It was in use among English-speakers by the medieval period and has remained modestly popular ever since. **Evie** is a familiar form of the name. *See also* EVA; EVELYN.

Eveleen/Evelina/Eveline *See* EVELYN.

Evelyn (m/f) English name bestowed upon both sexes. As a masculine name it appears to have made its first appearance early in the 20th century. As a name for girls, possibly a combination of EVE and LYNN or influenced by the French AVELINE, it was in use among English-speakers by the late 19th century. Commonly abbreviated to **Evie** or EVE. Variants include **Evalina**, **Evaline**, **Evalyn**, **Evelyne**, **Eveline**, **Eveleen** and **Eibhlin**.

Everard (m) English name derived from the Old German *eber* ('boar') and *hart* ('brave' or 'strong') and thus meaning 'fierce as a boar'. The name is recorded among English-speakers in medieval times and was revived in the 19th century.

Everett (m) English name that was taken up on an occasional basis towards the end of the 19th century. It is thought to have evolved as a variant of EVERARD. Also encountered as **Everitt**.

Evie *See* EVA; EVANGELINE; EVE; EVELYN.

Evonne *See* YVONNE.

Ewan (m) English version (pronounced 'yoowan') of the Gaelic EOGHAN (also the source of OWEN). Although it is now in modest use throughout the English-speaking world, it has retained its strong Scottish associations. Also spelled **Euan** or **Ewen**.

Ewart (m) English name derived from EDWARD, or else from a place name in Northumbria, that was subsequently taken up as a first name in the 19th century. The name enjoyed modest popularity among English-speakers in tribute to Prime Minister William Ewart Gladstone (1809–98).

Ewen *See* EWAN.

Ezekiel (m) Biblical name derived from the Hebrew Yehezqel, meaning 'God will strengthen'. It appears in the Bible and was consequently taken up by English Puritans in the 17th century. It remained in fairly regular use until the end of the 19th century. **Zeke** is a common diminutive form.

Ezra (m) Hebrew name meaning 'help'. It appears in the Bible as the name of a prophet and was consequently taken up by Puritans in the 17th century. It has been rare since the early 20th century.

Fabia (f) Roman name derived via the masculine Fabianus from the Latin *faba* ('bean'). It was taken up by English-speakers in the 19th century but has never been in frequent use.

Fabian (m) English name descended from the Roman Fabianus, itself derived from the Latin *faba* ('bean') and thus signifying a grower of beans. It is thought to have been introduced to England by the Normans, although there is scant evidence of the name's use among the English before the 16th century.

Fachtna (m) Irish name (pro-

nounced 'fokna') of uncertain origin, though possibly derived from the Gaelic for 'malicious' or 'hostile'.

Fae *See* FAY.

Faith (f) English virtue name that was taken up by the Puritans in the 17th century, initially as a name for either sex. Unlike some of the other virtue names that became popular around the same time, Faith has remained in use into modern times, although it is now reserved exclusively for females. Familiar forms of the name include **Fay** and **Faithie**.

Fan *See* FANNY.

Fancy (f) English name that may have arisen as a variant of FANNY, or possibly under the influence of the ordinary vocabulary word 'fiancée'. It appears to have made its first appearances in the 19th century.

Fannie *See* FANNY.

Fanny (f) English name that developed as a diminutive form of such names as EUPHEMIA, FRANCES and MYFANWY. Also found as **Fannie**, it appeared with considerable frequency among English-speakers from the late 17th century but became rare after the 19th century. Commonly shortened to **Fan**.

Faron *See* FARRAN.

Farquhar (m) Scottish name (pronounced 'farkwah') that developed as an Anglicized form of the Scottish Gaelic Fearchar, derived from the Gaelic for 'man' and 'dear' and thus meaning 'dear one'.

Farrah (f) English name ultimately derived from the Latin for 'iron'. The name became widely known in the 1970s as that of the US actress Farrah Fawcett-Majors (b.1947). **Farrer** is a masculine variant.

Farran (m/f) English name possibly derived from the Old French for 'pilferer' or 'ferret' or else a medieval variant of FERDINAND. Other forms of the name include **Farren** and **Faron**.

Farren See FARRAN.

Fatima (f) Arabic name meaning 'weaning' or 'abstaining', often interpreted to mean 'chaste' or 'motherly'. Borne by the favourite daughter of Muhammad, it has long been a popular choice among Muslims because it implies chastity and other forms of abstention desirable among Muslim women. It has also made occasional appearances among English-speakers since the 20th century.

Faustina See FAUSTINE.

Faustine (f) French name derived from the Latin *faustus* ('fortunate') that has made occasional appearances over the centuries. **Faustina** is a rare English variant. Both versions of the name are closely associated with the Faust legend as recounted in Christopher Marlowe's play *Doctor Faustus* (c.1592).

Fawn (f) English name that evolved either from the ordinary vocabulary word for a young deer or else from the combination of FAY and DAWN or similar names. It made its debut in the 19th century.

Fay (f) English name derived from the traditional name for a fairy. It may also be encountered as a diminutive form of FAITH. It does not seem to have been taken up as a first name until the 19th century, since when it has continued to make infrequent appearances. **Faye** and **Fae** are variant forms of the name.

Faye See FAY.

Fearghal See FERGAL.

Fearghas/Feargus See FERGUS.

Fearne See FERN.

Feichin (m) Irish name derived from the Irish Gaelic *fiach* ('raven').

Felicia See FELICITY.

Felicity (f) English name derived from the ordinary vocabulary word meaning 'good luck' or 'good fortune', ultimately descended from the Latin *felicitas* ('fertility' or 'fortune') and often treated as a feminine equivalent of FELIX. It was among the so-called virtue names adopted by English Puritans in the 17th century and has remained in currency ever since. Familiar forms of the name include **Flick**, **Liss**, **Lissa**, **Lissie**, **Phil** and LUCKY. **Felicia** is a rare variant of 18th-century origin.

Felix (m) Roman name derived

from the Latin *felix* ('happy' or 'lucky') that entered use as a first name among English-speakers in medieval times. It appears in the Bible and has enjoyed a marked resurgence in popularity since the 1990s. Variants in other languages include the Irish **Phelim**.

Femie *See* EUPHEMIA.

Fenella (f) Irish name derived from Fionnuala, from the Gaelic *fionn* ('fair' or 'white') and *guala* ('shoulder') and thus meaning 'fair-shouldered'. In Irish legend Fionnuala is turned into a swan by her wicked stepmother and is only released from the spell when Ireland adopts Christianity. English-speakers took up the name in the 19th century. Commonly shortened to **Nella**, **Nola** or **Nuala**. Variant forms include **Finella**, **Finola** and **Fionola**. *See also* PENELOPE.

Fenton (m) English name derived from a place name from northern England. The original place name came from the Old English *fenn* ('marsh' or 'fen') and *tun* ('settlement').

Ferdie *See* FERDINAND.

Ferdinand (m) German, French and English name derived from the Old German *fridu* ('peace') and *nand* ('bravery') and thus meaning 'peace through bravery'. Another derivation suggests the name developed out of the Old German *farth* ('journey') and *nand* ('prepared'). It came to England with the Normans in the 11th century

and enjoyed a brief period in favour among English-speakers during the 1550s. Sometimes shortened to **Ferd**, **Ferdie**, **Ferdy** or **Nandy**.

Ferdy *See* FERDINAND.

Fergal (m) Anglicized form of the Irish **Fearghal**, itself derived from the Gaelic *fear* ('man') and *gal* ('valour'), thus meaning 'man of valour'.

Fergie *See* FERGUS.

Fergus (m) English version of the Gaelic **Fearghas**, derived from *fear* ('man') and *gus* ('force' or 'strength') and thus meaning 'man of force'. Borne by a legendary Irish hero of Ulster, the name has retained its strong Scottish and Irish associations. Commonly shortened to **Fergie** or **Fergy**. Variant forms of the name include **Feargus**.

Fern (f) English name derived from the name of the plant, itself from the Old English *fearn*. It is thought to have made its first appearance among English-speakers along with other flower and plant names in the 19th century. Also rendered as **Fearne**.

Fernley (m) Cornish first name of unknown meaning.

Fester (m) German diminutive of SYLVESTER. The name became familiar to English-speakers through a character of the name in the popular 1960s US television series (later filmed) *The Addams Family* (based on the Charles Addams cartoons).

Festus (m) Roman name meaning either 'festive' or else 'steadfast'. It appears in the Bible and was taken up occasionally in the medieval period. It enjoyed a minor resurgence in popularity in the 19th century.

Fi *See* FIONA.

Fiachna *See* FIACHRA.

Fiachra (m) Irish name derived from the Gaelic *fiach* ('raven'). It was borne by a 7th-century French saint, the patron saint of gardeners. Also found in the form **Fiachna**, a variant revived in the 20th century.

Fidelia (f) English name derived from the Latin *fidelis* ('faithful'). It was included among the virtue names that were taken up by English Puritans in the 17th century and remained in occasional use for 100 years or more, with very rare revivals since the 18th century.

Fidelma (f) Irish name derived from the Gaelic **Feidhelm** or **Fedelm**, itself of uncertain meaning, although it may have originally meant 'beauty'. It was borne by an early Irish saint who was converted to Christianity by St Patrick. Sometimes shortened to **Delma**. **Fedelma** is a variant form of the name.

Fife (m) Scottish name derived from a place name based on the name of the legendary Pictish hero Fib. Largely confined to people with strong Scottish associ-ations, it also appears in the variant form **Fyfe**.

Fifi (f) French name that developed as a diminutive of JOSEPHINE and various other names incorporating 'fi', such as FIONA and YVONNE.

Fina *See* FIONA; FINLAY.

Finbar (m) Anglicized form of the Irish **Fionnbarr** or **Fionbharr**, itself from the Gaelic *fionn* ('fair' or 'white') and *barr* ('head'). It was borne by several early Irish saints. Also found as **Finnbar**.

Findlay *See* FINLAY.

Finella *See* FENELLA.

Fingal (m) Anglicized form of the Scottish Fionnghall, derived from *fionn* ('fair' or 'white') and *gall* ('stranger'), thus meaning 'pale stranger'. Initially it was borne chiefly by Norse immigrants in Scotland. Also found as **Fingall**.

Finian *See* FINNIAN.

Finlay (m) Scottish name descended from the Gaelic **Fionnlagh**, itself from the Gaelic *fionn* ('fair' or 'white') and *laogh* ('warrior') and thus interpreted to mean 'fair hero'. Also found as **Findlay** or **Finley**.

Finn (m) Irish name derived from the Gaelic *fionn* ('fair' or 'white'). Also found in the form **Fionn**, it was borne by the celebrated legendary hero Finn MacCool.

Finnian (m) Irish name derived from the Gaelic *fionn* ('fair' or 'white'). Also found as **Finian**.

Finola See FENELLA.

Fiona (f) English name derived from the Scottish Gaelic *fionn* ('fair' or 'white'). It became well-known through its appearance in the Ossianic poems of James Macpherson (1736–96), who seems to have been the first person to use the name. Sometimes thought of as an aristocratic name, it enjoyed a peak in popularity in the 1960s. Commonly shortened to **Fi**. Variants of the name include **Fina** and the rare **Tiona**.

Fionn See FINN.

Fionnuala/Fionola See FENELLA.

Fitz See FITZROY.

Fitzgerald (m) English name meaning 'son of Gerald'. Ultimately of Old French origins, it is often encountered in the shortened form **Fitz**.

Fitzroy (m) English name meaning 'son of the king' in use since the middle of the 19th century. It was used initially as a nickname for illegitimate sons of English monarchs. Commonly shortened to **Fitz**.

Flann (m) Irish name that developed as a diminutive form of **Flannan**, itself derived from the Gaelic *flann* ('red' or 'ruddy'). Famous bearers of the name have included the Irish novelist Flann O'Brien (Brian O'Nolan; 1911–66).

Flannan See FLANN.

Flavia (f) Roman name derived from *flavus* ('yellow' or 'golden'), probably a reference to blond hair. Records of its use among English-speakers go back to the 16th century. Sometimes shortened to **Flave** or **Flavie** (also a French variant of the name). See also FULVIA.

Fletcher (m) English name, denoting a maker of arrows, that has been in occasional use as a first name since the 19th century. It developed out of the Old French *fleche* ('arrow') and is perhaps best known through Fletcher Christian (c.1764–94), leader of the infamous 1789 *Bounty* mutiny.

Fleur (f) French name, meaning 'flower', that was taken up by English-speakers in the early 20th century. Recorded in France in medieval times, its adoption in the English-speaking world resulted from the popularity of a character bearing the name in John Galsworthy's *Forsyte Saga* novels (1906–22). Related names include **Flora**, **Flower** and **Blossom**. A diminutive form of the name is **Fleurette**.

Fleurette See FLEUR.

Flick See FELICITY.

Flint (m) English name meaning 'stream'.

Flip See PHILIP.

Flo See FLOELLA; FLORA; FLORENCE.

Floella (f) English name that is thought to have resulted from the combination of FLORA and FLORENCE with ELLA or similar names. It appears to have made its first appearances among English-speakers in the 1950s. Commonly shortened to **Flo**.

Flora (f) Roman name derived from the Latin *flos* ('flower'). The name of the Roman goddess of the spring, it was taken up by English-speakers in the 18th century. It became particularly popular in Scotland in tribute to Flora Macdonald (Fionnaghal Macdonald; 1722–90), the woman who in 1746 helped Bonnie Prince Charlie escape from Scotland. Variants include **Floretta**, **Florette** and **Florinda**. Abbreviated forms of the name include **Flo**, **Florrie**, **Floss** and **Flossie**.

Florence (f) English name derived from the Roman Florentia, itself from the Latin *florens* ('blossoming' or 'flourishing'). It was first taken up by English-speakers in the medieval period (when it was also used as a name for boys) and enjoyed a peak in popularity in the 19th century. Shortened forms of the name include **Flo**, **Florrie**, **Floss**, **Flossie** and **Floy**.

Floretta/Florette See FLORA.

Florian (m) English and German name derived from the Roman Florianus, itself from *flos* ('flower'). It has made irregular appearances among English-speakers since medieval times but has become rare since the end of the 19th century.

Florinda See FLORA.

Florrie/Floss/Flossie See FLORA; FLORENCE.

Flower See FLEUR.

Floy See FLORENCE.

Floyd (m) English name derived from the Welsh LLOYD. It has been in use as a first name since the 19th century, chiefly in the USA.

Flynn (m) Scottish first name derived from the Scots Gaelic for 'son of the red-haired one'. Also encountered as **Flinn**.

Forbes (m) Scottish name derived from the Gaelic *forba* ('field' or 'district').

Ford (m) English name derived from a surname denoting a person living close to a river crossing.

Forrest (m) English name derived from the ordinary vocabulary word 'forest' that has made occasional appearances as a first name since the 19th century. Its popularity in the USA can be traced back to the fame of Confederate commander Nathan Bedford Forrest (1821–77). Also found as **Forest**.

Forrester (m) English name meaning 'forester'. Ultimately of Old French origins, it may also be encountered as **Forster**.

Fortune (f) English name derived from the Latin *fortuna* ('fortune' or 'fate'). It was taken up by English Puritans in the 17th century but is rare today.

Foster (m) English name of obscure origin variously interpreted as meaning 'foster-parent', 'forester', 'shearer' or 'saddle-tree maker'. Famous bearers of the name have included US statesman John Foster Dulles (1888–1959).

Fran *See* FRANCES; FRANCESCA.

France (m) English name derived either from the name of the country or else a diminutive form of FRANCIS. Encountered occasionally in the USA but rare elsewhere.

Frances (f) English name that developed as a feminine form of FRANCIS. It should be noted that the spelling Frances was also formerly used for the masculine form of the name. As a name for girls, it was taken up by English-speakers in the 17th century and went on to enjoy a peak in popularity in the 19th century. Commonly shortened to **Fran**, **Frannie** (or **Franny**), **Francie**, **Frankie** or **Fanny**. Variants of the name include **Francine** (or **Francene**). *See also* FRANCESCA.

Francesca (f) Italian name that developed as a feminine form of the Italian Francesco, which was itself descended from the Roman Franciscus, meaning 'Frenchman'. It has made increasingly frequent appearances as a first name among English-speakers since the middle of the 20th century. Commonly shortened to **Fran** or **Franny**.

Francie/Francine *See* FRANCES.

Francis (m) English name descended from the Roman Franciscus, itself from the Latin for 'Frenchman'. The name is supposed to have had its origin in St Francis of Assisi (1182–1226), who was renamed by his father

following his return from France. It was taken up by English-speakers in the 16th century and remained fairly common until the 20th century. Commonly shortened to FRANK or **Frankie**. *See also* FRANCES.

Frank (m) English name that developed as a diminutive form of FRANCIS or FRANKLIN (and also of the feminine FRANCES and FRANCESCA) but is now frequently considered to be a name in its own right. The name became increasingly common among English-speakers from the middle of the 19th century but has been in decline since the middle of the 20th century. Also found in the diminutive form **Frankie**.

Frankie *See* FRANCES; FRANCESCA; FRANCIS; FRANK.

Franklin (m) English name derived from the Middle English *frankeleyn* ('freeman') that was taken up as a first name in the 19th century. In medieval times the word was used to describe a person who owned land but who was not of noble rank. The name has proved particularly popular in the USA. Commonly shortened to **Frank** or **Frankie**. Also encountered in the variant form **Franklyn**.

Franklyn *See* FRANKLIN.

Frannie/Franny *See* FRANCES; FRANCESCA.

Fraser (m) Scottish name that has been in occasional use as a first name among English-speakers since the 1930s. Ultimately derived from a Norman place name of uncertain meaning, it has retained its strong Scottish links. Also found as **Frazer** or **Frazier**.

Frazer/Frazier *See* FRASER.

Frea *See* FREYA.

Fred (m) English name that developed as a diminutive form of FREDERICK and which is occasionally considered a name in its own right. Variants include **Freddie** and **Freddy**. *See also* ALFRED; FREDA; FREDERICA.

Freda (f) English name that developed as a diminutive form of such names as ALFREDA, FREDERICA and WINIFRED, although it is often treated as a feminine equivalent of FRED or FREDERICK. It was taken up by English-speakers in the 19th century and enjoyed a peak in popularity in the 1920s, but has since become rare. Sometimes encountered as **Frida** or **Frieda**.

Freddie/Freddy *See* FREDERICK.

Frederica (f) English name that evolved as a feminine form of FREDERICK. It made its first appearance among English-speakers in the 19th century. Often shortened to **Fred**, **Freda**, **Freddie**, **Rickie**, **Ricky** or **Rica**. Variant forms include **Fritzi**.

Frederick (m) English name derived from the Old German *fridu* ('peace') and *ric* ('ruler' or 'power') and usually interpreted to mean 'peaceful ruler'. It came to England with the Normans in the

11th century but it was not until the 18th century that the name became widespread. It has been in decline since a peak in the early 20th century. Also encountered as **Frederic** or **Fredric**. Commonly shortened to **Fred**, **Freddie** or **Freddy**. Another variant is the German **Fritz**.

Fredric *See* FREDERICK.

Freeman (m) English name meaning 'free man'.

Freya (f) Scandinavian name derived from that of the Norse goddess of love (after whom Friday was named). It is thought to have come originally from the German *frau* ('woman'). It has made infrequent appearances among English-speakers since the late 19th century, chiefly in Scotland and the Shetland Islands. Variants include the relatively rare **Frea**.

Frida *See* FREDA.

Frieda *See* FREDA.

Fritz *See* FREDERICK.

Fritzi *See* FREDERICA.

Fulton (m) Scottish name, possibly derived from a Scottish place name, that has been in occasional use as a first name since the end of the 19th century.

Fulvia (f) Italian and English name that developed originally as the feminine form of the Roman Fulvius, itself derived from the Latin *fulvus* ('dusky' or 'tawny').

Fyfe *See* FIFE.

developed as a feminine equivalent of GABRIEL. English-speakers adopted the name towards the end of the 19th century. Commonly shortened to **Gab**, **Gabby**, **Gabi** or **Gaby**. Variants include **Gabriella**. *See also* GAY.

Gaby *See* GABRIELLE.

Gae *See* GAY.

Gaea *See* GAIA.

Gaenor *See* GAYNOR.

Gaia (f) Greek name derived from the Greek *ge* ('earth'). In classical mythology it was borne by the goddess of the earth who gave birth to the Titans. The so-called 'Gaia theory' argues that the earth and all life on it should be considered a single living entity. Also encountered as **Gaea**.

Gail (f) English name that evolved as a diminutive form of ABIGAIL. It began to appear among English-speakers during the 1930s and enjoyed a peak in popularity in the 1960s. Also found as **Gale** or **Gayle**.

Gab/Gabby/Gabi *See* GABRIEL; GABRIELLE.

Gabriel (m) Biblical name derived from the Hebrew Gabhriel, meaning 'my strength is God' or 'man of God'. It appears in the Bible as the name of the Archangel Gabriel and was consequently taken up by English-speakers during the medieval period. It remained in fairly frequent use through the 18th and 19th centuries but then became less common. **Gab** and **Gabby** are diminutive forms of the name. *See also* GABRIELLE.

Gabriella *See* GABRIELLE.

Gabrielle (f) French name that

Galahad (m) English name of uncertain origin that has made occasional appearances as a first name over the centuries. It would seem to have been invented by early compilers of Arthurian legend as the name of the most virtuous of King Arthur's knights. Attempts have been made to link the name with the Hebrew Gilead.

Gale *See* GAIL.

Gamaliel (m) Biblical name derived from the Hebrew Gamliel, meaning 'my reward is God' or 'recompense of God'. It appears in the Bible as the name of a teacher of St Paul and was consequently taken up by English Puritans in the 17th century. It was the middle name of the US President Warren G. Harding (1865–1923).

Gardenia (f) English flower name that has made irregular appearances as a first name since the 19th century. The flower itself was named after an 18th-century naturalist called Dr Alexander Garden.

Gareth (m) Welsh name that developed as a variant of GERAINT, although it has also been linked with such names as GARTH, GARY and GERARD and is often interpreted as meaning 'gentle'. Having established itself in Wales, it made its first appearance in England as early as the 16th century. Commonly shortened to **Gaz**.

Garey See GARY.

Garfield (m) English name derived from the Old English *gar* ('spear-shaped area' or 'triangle of land') and *feld* ('open country'), and thus meaning 'field of spears'. It has been in occasional use as a first name, chiefly in the USA, since the end of the 19th century. Diminutive forms of the name include **Garry** and **Gary**.

Garnet (m/f) English name of uncertain meaning taken up as a first name in the 19th century, at a time when many other jewel names came into fashion.

Garret (m) Irish and English name adopted as an occasional first name from the 17th century, becoming particularly popular in Ireland. The name itself seems to have been derived from GERALD or GERARD. Also found as **Garrett**. **Garry** and **Gary** are diminutive forms of the name. *See also* GARRISON.

Garrick (m) English name derived from the Old English *gar* ('spear') and *ric* ('ruler'). Its initial popularity may have been promoted by the fame of the 18th-century British actor David Garrick (1717–79).

Garrison (m) English name derived from a place name (from Garriston in North Yorkshire). Another possibility is that the name evolved simply as 'Garrett's son'. The name was boosted in the USA through admiration for William Lloyd Garrison (1805–79), a noted campaigner against slavery.

Garry See GARFIELD; GARRET; GARY.

Garth (m) English name derived from the Old Norse *garthr* ('enclosure'). Sometimes treated as a variant of GARETH, it enjoyed a peak in popularity in the 1940s. Notable bearers of the name have included the US country singer Garth Brooks (b.1962).

Gary (m) English name that was probably of Norman French origin, perhaps from the Germanic *gar* ('spear'). Often linked to the Welsh GARETH, it was at its most popular between the 1930s and the 1960s. The name became widely known through the US film actor Gary Cooper (Frank James Cooper; 1901–61), who took his pseudonym from Gary, Indiana, where his agent lived. Also found as **Garry** or **Garey**. Sometimes abbreviated to **Gaz**.

Gavin (m) Scottish and English form of the Welsh GAWAIN that has been taken up throughout the English-speaking world since the early 20th century. It enjoyed a peak in popularity in the 1970s and 1980s.

Gawain (m) Welsh name possibly derived from the Welsh *gwalch* ('hawk'). It became relatively well known among English-speakers during the medieval period and is usually associated with Sir Gawain, one of the knights of the Round Table in Arthurian legend. It virtually disappeared from use by the 16th century, but subsequently returned to favour as GAVIN.

Gay (f) English name derived from the French *gai* ('joyful' or 'cheerful'). It became popular among English-speakers in the 1930s, initially in the USA, and in its early history was occasionally borne by men as well as women. It continued in fairly regular use until the 1960s. Variants include **Gaye** and the rarer **Gae**.

Gaye *See* GAY.

Gayle *See* GAIL.

Gaylord (m) English name derived from the French *gaillard* ('dandy') taken up from the 19th century. Often assumed to mean literally 'gay lord', it disappeared from use during the latter half of the 20th century. **Gayelord** is a variant form.

Gaynor (f) English name that evolved in medieval times as a variant of GUINEVERE. It enjoyed a shortlived revival in the 1960s. **Gaenor** is a Welsh variant.

Gaz *See* GARETH; GARY.

Geena *See* GINA.

Gem *See* GEMMA.

Gemma (f) English, Irish and Italian name derived from the Italian for 'gem' or 'jewel'. A long-established favourite in Italy, it has become relatively common in the English-speaking world, perhaps under the influence of EMMA, enjoying a peak in popularity from the 1960s. Sometimes abbreviated to **Gem**. Also found as **Jemma**.

Gena *See* GINA.

Gene (m/f) English name that developed as a diminutive form of EUGENE, EUGENIA and JEAN. It was particularly popular in the USA in the first half of the 20th century.

Genette *See* JEANETTE.

Geneva (f) English name of uncertain origin. It may have been inspired by the name of the city in Switzerland, although it has also been suggested that it developed as a variant of GENEVIEVE or JENNIFER.

Genevieve (f) French name possibly derived from the Old German *geno* ('people' or 'race') and *wefa* ('woman') and thus meaning 'lady of the people' or more simply 'female'. It was adopted by English-speakers (usually without the accent of the French Geneviève) in the 19th century. Sometimes shortened to **Ginny**, **Gina**, **Ginette** or **Veva**.

Genie *See* EUGENIE.

Geoff *See* GEOFFREY.

Geoffrey (m) English name derived from the Old German *gavja* ('territory') and *fridu* ('peace') and thus interpreted as meaning 'peaceful ruler'. Another derivation suggests that it may have evolved from GODFREY. It came to England with the Normans and was in relatively frequent use until the 15th century. It enjoyed a revival in the 19th century. Commonly shortened to **Geoff**. Variants include **Jeffrey** (or **Jeffery**) and its abbreviated form **Jeff**.

Geordie *See* GEORGE.

George (m) English name derived via the Latin Georgius from the Greek Georgios, itself from *georgos* ('farmer'). The name of the patron saint of England, it made irregular appearances in medieval times but became popular only after the accession of George I in 1714. Diminutive forms include **Georgie**, **Georgy** and **Geordie** (commonest in northern England and Scotland). *See also* GEORGETTE; GEORGIA; GEORGIANA; GEORGINA.

Georgene *See* GEORGINA.

Georgette (f) French variant of the masculine GEORGE that was taken up by English-speakers in the early 20th century. Sometimes shortened to **Georgie** or **George**.

Georgia (f) Feminine equivalent of GEORGE, promoted in the USA through association with the state of Georgia. It was taken up towards the end of the 19th century and enjoyed a recent peak in popularity in the 1990s. Diminutive forms include **Georgie** and **George**.

Georgiana (f) English name that developed from GEORGIA or GEORGINA as a feminine version of GEORGE, perhaps under the influence of JULIANA. This Latinate form of the name enjoyed considerable popularity in the 18th century and remained fairly frequent until the end of the 19th century. Sometimes shortened to **Georgie** or **Georgy**.

Georgie *See* GEORGE; GEORGETTE; GEORGIA; GEORGIANA; GEORGINA.

Georgina (f) Feminine version of GEORGE. It was taken up by English-speakers in the 18th century, becoming especially popular in Scotland. It largely replaced GEORGIANA in the 19th century. Commonly shortened to **Georgie**, **George** or **Gina**. The English **Georgene** is a variant form of the name.

Georgy *See* GEORGE; GEORGIANA.

Ger *See* GERALD; GERARD.

Geraint (m) Welsh name (pronounced 'gerighnt') of uncertain meaning, possibly derived via the Roman Gerontius from the Greek *gerontos* ('old man'). The name features in Arthurian legend as that of one of the knights of the Round Table.

Gerald (m) English and Irish name derived from the Old German *ger* ('spear') and *wald* ('rule') and thus meaning 'spear rule'. The name came to England with the Normans but fell from favour after the late 13th century, except in Ireland. It was revived among English-speakers in the 19th century, acquiring a reputation as an aristocratic name. Commonly shortened to **Ger**, **Gerry** or **Jerry**. **Jerrold** is a variant of largely historical interest. Variants in other languages include the Welsh **Gerallt**. *See also* GARRET; GERALDINE.

Geraldine (f) Feminine version of GERALD. Records of its use go back to the 16th century. It entered general usage as a first name in the English-speaking world in the 19th century, partly due to its appearance in Samuel Taylor Coleridge's poem *Christabel* (1816), and subsequently enjoyed a peak in popularity in the 1950s. Diminutive forms of the name include **Gerrie**, **Gerry**, **Jerrie** and **Jerry**.

Gerallt *See* GERALD.

Gerard (m) English, Irish and

Dutch name descended from the Old German *ger* ('spear') and *hardu* ('brave' or 'hardy') and thus meaning 'brave with the spear'. Having been brought to England by the Normans, it remained fairly frequent during the medieval period but became less common from the 17th century. It was revived around the middle of the 19th century. Commonly shortened to **Ger**, **Gerry** or **Jerry**. Variants include **Gerrard** and **Jerrard**. *See also* GARRET.

Germaine (f) English and French name derived from the masculine French name Germain, itself descended from the Roman Germanus, meaning 'brother'. English-speakers began to use the name in the early 20th century. Also found as **Jermaine**.

Gerrard *See* GERARD.

Gerrie *See* GERALDINE.

Gerry (m/f) English name that evolved as a diminutive form of such names as the masculine GERALD and GERARD and the feminine GERALDINE and now often considered a name in its own right. Also found as **Gerrie** or **Jerry**.

Gert/Gertie *See* GERTRUDE.

Gertrude (f) English, French, German and Dutch name derived from the Old German *ger* ('spear') and *traut* ('strength') and thus meaning 'strong with the spear' or 'ruler of the spear'. It was taken up by English-speakers towards the end of the medieval period, perhaps as an import from the

Netherlands, but has become rare since the 19th century. Diminutive forms of the name include **Gert**, **Gertie**, **Trudy**, **Trudi** and **Trudie**.

Gervase (m) English name derived ultimately from the Roman Gervasius, itself from the Greek *geras* ('old age'), or else from the Old German *ger* ('spear') and *vas* ('servant') and thus interpreted to mean 'spear servant'. The name of a 1st-century saint, it was taken up by English Roman Catholics in the 16th century. Also encountered as **Gervaise** or JARVIS.

Gerwyn (m) Welsh name meaning 'fair love'. Also spelled **Gerwen**.

Gethin (m) Welsh name meaning 'dark-skinned'.

Ghislaine (f) French name that developed as a variant of GISELLE. Usually pronounced 'gislane' or 'gilane', it has made occasional appearances as a first name among English-speakers since the 1920s. Sometimes shortened to **Gigi**. Variants include **Ghislane** and **Ghislain**.

Gib *See* GILBERT.

Gid *See* GIDEON.

Gideon (m) Biblical name derived from the Hebrew Gidon, meaning 'hewer' or 'one who cuts down' or alternatively 'having a stump for a hand' but often interpreted as meaning 'great warrior'. It appears in the Bible and was consequently taken up by English-speakers in the 17th century. Today it is more commonly encountered in the

USA than elsewhere. Sometimes shortened to **Gid**.

Gigi (f) French name (pronounced 'jeejee') that developed as a diminutive form of GHISLAINE and other names. In Colette's novel *Gigi* (1958) it is treated as a familiar form of the French Gilberte (*see* GILBERT).

Gil *See* GILBERT; GILCHRIST.

Gilbert (m) English name derived via French from the Old German *gisil* ('pledge' or 'hostage') and *berht* ('bright' or 'famous') and usually interpreted to mean 'bright pledge'. In Scotland it is sometimes encountered as an Anglicized form of the Gaelic Gilbride, meaning 'servant of St Bridget'. It came to England with the Normans and became increasingly frequent from the 17th century, but is now rare. Commonly shortened to **Gib**, **Gibbie**, **Gil**, **Gilly**, **Bert** or **Bertie**. Feminine equivalents of the name include **Gilberta** and **Gilbertine**.

Gilberta/Gilbertine *See* GILBERT.

Gilchrist (m) English name derived from the Gaelic for 'servant of Christ'. It has a fairly long history but seems to have disappeared from use since the 19th century.

Gilda (f) Italian name that may have developed either from an Old German name derived from *hild* or *gild* ('sacrifice') or else from the Gaelic for 'servant of God' or from the Old English for 'golden'. The name was known in

Anglo-Saxon England and continued to make irregular appearances in its modern form until the end of the 19th century, since when it has become rare.

Giles (m) English name derived via French from the Greek Aigidios, itself from the Greek *aigidion* ('kid' or 'young goat'). The name was moderately common among English-speakers of both sexes in medieval times, especially in Scotland, but is now reserved exclusively for males. **Gyles** is a variant form.

Gill *See* GILLIAN.

Gillespie (m) Anglicized form of the Scottish Gaelic Gilleasbaig, meaning 'servant of the bishop'. As a first name it is now rare.

Gillian (f) English name that developed either as an elaboration of JILL or as a feminine version of JULIAN. Another theory suggests it evolved from the Scottish Gaelic for 'servant of St John'. It was popular during the medieval period but fell from fashion after the 17th century. It was taken up by English-speakers once more around the middle of the 20th century. Commonly shortened to **Gill**, **Gillie** or **Gilly**. Also found as **Jillian**, a relatively modern form of the name.

Gillie/Gilly *See* GILLIAN.

Gilroy (m) Irish and Scottish name derived from the Gaelic for 'son of the red-haired lad' that has made occasional appearances

since the beginning of the 20th century.

Gina (f) Italian and English name that developed as a diminutive form of GEORGINA and REGINA. It was taken up by English-speakers in the 1920s. Also found as **Gena** or **Geena** – as borne by the US actress Geena Davis (b.1957). *See also* GENEVIEVE.

Ginette *See* GENEVIEVE.

Ginger (m/f) English name that developed as a nickname for anyone with red hair or a tempestuous character. As a girls' name it is sometimes used as a familiar form of VIRGINIA. It appears to be a 20th-century introduction that was at its most popular between the two world wars.

Gini/Ginnie/Ginny *See* GENEVIEVE; VIRGINIA.

Giselle (f) French and English name derived from the Old German *gisil* ('pledge'). Like other names derived from the same source it may have come about through the medieval practice of handing over children to foreign courts as pledges or guarantees of alliances. It was not until the mid 19th century that English-speakers took up the name, inspired by Adolphe Adam's ballet *Giselle* (1841).

Gita (f) Indian name derived from the Sanskrit *gita* ('song'). Also found as **Geeta**.

Glad *See* GLADYS.

Gladstone (m) Scottish name

derived from a place name based on the Old English *glaed* ('kite') and *stan* ('rock'). It has made irregular appearances as a first name since the late 19th century, initially in tribute to the British Prime Minister William Gladstone (1809–98).

Gladys (f) English name derived from the Welsh Gwladys, itself possibly from the Welsh *gwledig* ('ruler over territory' or 'princess'). It is also encountered as a variant of CLAUDIA. Known in Wales in various forms since before the Norman Conquest, it was taken up by English-speakers elsewhere towards the end of the 19th century. It had virtually disappeared from use by the mid 20th century. Commonly shortened to **Glad**.

Glanville (m) English name derived either from a Norman French place name or else from the Old English for 'clean field'. Variants include **Glenvil** and **Glenville**.

Glen *See* GLENDA; GLENN.

Glenda (f) Welsh name derived from the Welsh *glan* ('clean' or 'holy') and *da* ('good'). English-speakers elsewhere took up the name around the 1930s but it has never been common. The most famous bearer of the name to date has been the British actress and politician Glenda Jackson (b.1936). Sometimes abbreviated to **Glen**.

Glendower (m) Welsh name derived from a place name based on the Welsh *glyn* ('valley') and

dwr ('water'). Its adoption as a first name in relatively recent times was inspired by admiration for the Welsh hero Owen Glendower (c.1359–1416). Also encountered as **Glyndwr**.

Glenice/Glenis *See* GLENYS.

Glenn (m/f) Scottish and English name derived from the Gaelic *gleann* ('valley') that was taken up as a first name for boys towards the end of the 19th century and for girls from the 1940s. Famous bearers have included the US bandleader Glenn Miller (1904–44) and the US film actress Glenn Close (b.1945). **Glen** is a masculine version of the name. **Glenna** is a rare feminine variant. *See also* GLYN.

Glenna *See* GLENN.

Glenys (f) Welsh name that is thought to have evolved relatively recently as a variant of GLYNIS. Other theories suggest that it may have come about through the combination of GLADYS and GLENDA. It was taken up by English-speakers in the 1940s. Sometimes shortened to **Glen**. Also found as **Glenice** or **Glenis**.

Glinys *See* GLYNIS.

Gloria (f) English name derived from the Latin *gloria* ('glory'). It seems to have made its first appearance as the name of a character in the George Bernard Shaw play *You Never Can Tell* (1889). It was at its most frequent in the 1930s, but has since become rare. Sometimes rendered as **Glory**.

Glory *See* GLORIA.

Glyn (m) Welsh name derived from the Welsh *glyn* ('valley'). Its early development in the early 20th century may have been influenced by the similar GLENN and GWYN. Having established itself as a fairly popular choice of name in Wales it began to make appearances elsewhere in the English-speaking world, reaching a peak in popularity during the 1950s and 1960s. Also found as **Glynn**. *See also* GLENN; GLYNIS.

Glyndwr *See* GLENDOWER.

Glynis (f) Welsh name that is thought to have developed from the Welsh *glyn* ('valley') under the influence of GLADYS. It was taken up by English-speakers around the beginning of the 20th century. Commonly shortened to **Glyn**. Sometimes rendered as **Glinys** or **Glynnis**.

Glynn *See* GLYN.

Glynnis *See* GLYNIS.

Godfrey (m) English name derived from the Old German *god* ('god') and *fridu* ('peace') and thus meaning 'god's peace'. It came to England with the Normans and was a popular choice of name through medieval times and beyond, although it is now very rare.

Golda (f) Jewish name derived from a Yiddish nickname meaning 'gold'. Also found as GOLDIE.

Goldie (f) English name of uncertain origin, though usually assumed to be from the ordinary vocabulary word 'gold'. It may have been derived from an identical surname or else have been taken up as a name for anyone with blond hair. First recorded during the 19th century. Famous bearers of the name have included the US film actress Goldie Hawn (b.1945). *See also* GOLDA.

Gomer (m) Hebrew name meaning 'complete'. It appears in the Bible and was consequently taken up by Puritans in the 17th century. It has continued to make rare appearances in the USA into modern times.

Gordon (m) Scottish name derived from a place name possibly based on the Celtic for 'spacious fort'. The name retains its strong Scottish associations, being a famous clan name, but this did not prevent it becoming popular with English-speakers elsewhere from the late 19th century. It has since become rather less frequent.

Goronwy (m) Welsh name of uncertain meaning. It appears in the *Mabinogion* and as a consequence has been taken up on an occasional basis over succeeding centuries.

Grace (f) English virtue name based on the ordinary vocabulary word 'grace'. It was among the many virtue names adopted by Puritans in the 17th century and continued in fairly regular use into the 19th century and beyond, enjoying a recent peak in popularity in the 1990s. Variant forms of the name include **Gracie**. In Ireland the name sometimes appears as an Anglicization of the Gaelic GRAINNE.

Gracie *See* GRACE.

Grady (m) Irish name meaning 'noble'.

Graeme *See* GRAHAM.

Graham (m) English and Scottish name of 12th-century origin, thought to have come from an English place name (Grantham in Lincolnshire), which itself came from the Old English *grand* ('gravel') and *ham* ('homestead'), thus meaning 'gravelly place' or alternatively 'Granta's homestead'. It enjoyed a peak in popularity in the 1950s. A variant form of the name that has enjoyed some popularity since the early 20th century, especially in Scotland, is **Graeme**. Also encountered as **Grahame**.

Grainne (f) Irish name derived from the Gaelic *gran* ('grain') or *grain* ('disgust'), or otherwise from *graidhne* ('love'). The name appears in Irish legend as that of the daughter of King Cormac, who killed herself after her lover Dermot died following a long pursuit by the jealous Finn MacCool. It is sometimes Anglicized as GRACE. Variants include **Grania** and **Granya**.

Granger (m) English name meaning 'farmer' or 'bailiff'.

Grant (m) Scottish surname probably derived from the Norman French *grand* ('large' or 'tall') that

was taken up as a first name throughout the English-speaking world from the 19th century. As a first name it has enjoyed particular popularity in Canada and the USA, where its frequency was promoted by admiration for the US President Ulysses S. Grant (1822–85).

Granville (m) English name derived from a Norman baronial surname. The original Norman surname came from a place name based on *grand* ('large') and *ville* ('settlement'). Also found as **Grenville**.

Greer (f) Scottish name derived from Gregor (*see* GREGORY) that has made occasional appearances as a first name since medieval times. The most famous bearer of the name to date has been the Anglo-Irish actress Greer Garson (1908–96), whose mother bore it as her maiden name. Occasionally encountered as **Grier**.

Greg/Gregg/Gregor *See* GREGORY.

Gregory (m) English name derived via the Roman Gregorius from the Greek Gregorios, itself from *gregorein* ('to watch' or 'be vigilant'). Because St Peter had bid his followers to 'be vigilant' the name was taken up with some enthusiasm by early Christians and has remained in fairly common currency among English-speakers ever since the Norman Conquest. Common diminutive forms of the name include **Greg**, **Gregg** and **Greig**. Variants include the Scottish **Gregor** and the Welsh **Grigor**.

Greig *See* GREGORY.

Grenville *See* GRANVILLE.

Greta (f) Scandinavian and German name that developed as a diminutive form of Margareta (*see* MARGARET). It has made infrequent appearances among English-speakers since the 1920s. The name was made internationally famous through the Swedish film actress Greta Garbo (Greta Lovisa Gustafsson; 1905–90).

Greville (m) English name that has been in occasional use since the 17th century. The surname came in its turn from a Norman French place name. The name has strong aristocratic associations, having been borne as a surname by the earls of Warwick.

Griff *See* GRIFFITH.

Griffin (m) Welsh name derived from the Roman Griffinus. It appears to have developed as a variant of GRIFFITH.

Griffith (m) English version of the Welsh Gruffudd or Gruffydd, derived from the Welsh for 'lord' or 'prince'. Records of its use in Wales go back to at least the 16th century but it has only rarely been adopted outside the principality in succeeding centuries. Sometimes shortened to **Griff**. *See also* GRIFFIN.

Grigor *See* GREGORY.

Griselda (f) German and English name derived from the Old

German *gris* ('grey') and *hild* ('battle') and thus meaning 'grey warrior'. It was reasonably familiar among English-speakers in medieval times. **Grizzie** and **Zelda** are diminutive forms of the name. **Grizel** (or **Grizzel**) is a Scottish variant.

Grizel/Grizzel/Grizzie *See* GRISELDA.

Grover (m) English name derived from a place name based on the Old English *graf* ('grove'). As a first name it is confined largely to the USA, sometimes used in tribute to the US President Stephen Grover Cleveland (1837–1908).

Gruffud/Gruffydd *See* GRIFFITH.

Gudrun (f) German and Scandinavian name derived from *guth* ('battle' or 'god') and *run* ('secret') and thus sometimes interpreted as meaning 'wily in battle'. It has made occasional appearances among English-speakers since the late 19th century, notably as the name of the principal character in D. H. Lawrence's novels *The Rainbow* (1915) and *Women in Love* (1921).

Guenevere *See* GUINEVERE.

Guinevere (f) French and English equivalent of the Welsh Gwenhwyfar, itself from the Welsh *gwyn* ('white' or 'fair') and *hwyfar* ('smooth' or 'soft'). The name is usually associated with King Arthur's faithless wife, who bore the name, but has been superseded long ago by the related JENNIFER. Sometimes shortened to

Gwinny. Guenevere is a variant form. *See also* GAYNOR.

Gus (m) English name that evolved as a diminutive form of such masculine names as ANGUS and AUGUSTUS and also the feminine AUGUSTA. It was taken up by English-speakers in the 19th century. **Gussie** is a familiar form.

Gussie *See* GUS.

Gusta *See* AUGUSTA.

Guy (m) English name derived via French from the Old German Wido, from *wit* ('wide') or *witu* ('wood'). It came to England with the Normans in the 11th century and subsequently became popular through the medieval romance *Guy of Warwick*. It was among the medieval names revived in the 19th century.

Gwen (f) Welsh name derived from the Welsh *gwyn* ('white', 'fair' or 'blessed') or else as a diminutive form of GWENDOLEN or GWYNETH. Although it still has strong Welsh connections, the name was taken up throughout the English-speaking world during the 20th century.

Gwenda (f) Welsh name derived from the Welsh *gwyn* ('white', 'fair' or 'blessed) and *da* ('good') that was occasionally taken up by English-speakers early in the 20th century. Sometimes used as a diminutive form of GWENDOLEN. Often abbreviated to **Gwen**.

Gwendolen (f) Welsh name derived from the Welsh *gwyn* ('white', 'fair' or 'blessed') and *dolen* ('ring' or 'bow') that has become popular throughout the English-speaking world since the middle of the 19th century. Sometimes interpreted as meaning 'white circle' and thus a reference to the moon. It enjoyed a peak in popularity among English-speakers in the 1920s. Variant forms include **Gwendolin**, **Gwendoline** and **Gwendolyn**.

Gweneth *See* GWYNETH.

Gwenllian (f) Welsh first name (pronounced 'gwencleean') derived from the Welsh *gwyn* ('white', 'fair' or 'blessed') and *lliant* ('flood' or 'flow'). Sometimes interpreted to mean 'foamy white' and thus a reference to a pale complexion. Confined largely to Wales itself.

Gwenyth *See* GWYNETH.

Gwilym *See* WILLIAM.

Gwinny *See* GUINEVERE.

Gwladys *See* GLADYS.

Gwyn (m) Welsh name derived from the Welsh *gwyn* ('white', 'fair' or 'blessed'). It has retained its strong Welsh associations although it has made occasional appearances elsewhere in the English-speaking world since the early 20th century. Also found as **Gwynn**. *See also* WYNN.

Gwynedd *See* GWYNETH.

Gwyneth (m) Welsh name derived from the Welsh *gwynaeth* ('luck' or 'happiness'). It has been taken up throughout the English-speaking world since the 19th century. Commonly abbreviated to **Gwen**. Variants include **Gwynedd**, **Gwynneth**, **Gwenyth**, **Gweneth** and **Gwenneth**.

Gwynfor (m) Welsh name derived from the Welsh *gwyn* ('white', 'fair' or 'blessed') and *mawr* ('great' or 'large') and interpreted to mean 'fair lord' or 'fair place'. Apparently an early 20th-century introduction. **Wynfor** is a variant.

Gwynn *See* GWYN.

Gwynneth *See* GWYNETH.

Gyles *See* GILES.

Gypsy (f) English name derived from the ordinary vocabulary word 'gypsy'. It was taken up by English-speakers during the 19th century, found both inside and outside the Romany community. Also found as **Gipsy**.

Hadley (m) English name derived from a place name meaning 'heathery hill'.

Hadyn *See* HAYDN.

Haidee (f) English name derived from the Greek *aidoios* ('modest') or else treated as a variant form of HEIDI. It made irregular appearances as a first name among English-speakers from the 19th century.

Hailey *See* HAYLEY.

Hal *See* HARRY; HENRY.

Hale (m) English name derived from a place name meaning 'nook' or 'recess'.

Haley *See* HAYLEY.

Hall (m) English name derived from the ordinary vocabulary word 'hall' that has made occasional appearances as a first name over the centuries. The name was given originally to servants in the halls of great manor houses.

Hallam (m) English name derived from a place name meaning 'nook' or 'stone'.

Halle (f) English name (pronounced 'halley') that came into prominence in the 1990s through the US film actress Halle Berry (b.1968). She is said to have been named after the US department store Halle Brothers.

Ham *See* ABRAHAM.

Hamilton (m) English name derived from a place name, used chiefly in Scotland and the USA. The original place name referred to the (lost) village of Hamilton or Hameldune in Leicestershire, which itself took its name from the Old English *hamel* ('flat-topped') and *dun* ('hill'). It seems to have made its debut as a first name among English-speakers early in the 19th century.

Hamish (m) Scottish name derived from the Gaelic **Sheumais**, itself a version of **Seumas** (a variant of JAMES). Taken up by English-speakers around the middle of the 19th century, it has retained its Scottish links, but is today encountered across the English-speaking world (usually where the population have Scottish connections).

Hammond (m) Scottish name derived from the Old German *heim* ('house' or 'home') that has been in occasional use among English-speakers since the 19th century. Notable bearers of the name have included the British novelist Hammond Innes (Ralph Hammond Innes; 1913–98).

Hanford (m) English name derived from a place name meaning 'rocky ford'.

Hank (m) English name that developed as a diminutive form of JOHN. Originally Hankin, it is often treated as a diminutive form of HENRY. It established itself during the 19th century, chiefly in the USA.

Hannah (f) Hebrew name meaning 'favour' or 'grace' and sometimes interpreted to mean 'God has favoured me'. It appears in the Bible and was consequently taken up with some enthusiasm by English Puritans during the 17th century. It remained in frequent use until the end of the 19th century. Also encountered as **Hanna**. Diminutive forms of the name include **Han**, **Hannie** (or **Hanny**) and **Nancy**. *See also* ANNA.

Hannibal (m) Italian name derived from the Phoenician *hann* ('grace') and Baal (the name of a god), thus meaning 'grace of Baal', that has made occasional appearances as a first name among English-speakers since the 16th century. It is famous as the name of the 3rd-century BC Carthaginian general who led his army over the Alps to launch a surprise attack on Rome.

Hannie/Hanny *See* HANNAH.

Happy (f) English name derived from the ordinary vocabulary word 'happy'. It does not appear to have been in use prior to the 20th century.

Harcourt (m) English name variously derived from an Old French place name meaning 'from a fortified court' or from the Old English for 'falconer's cottage'.

Harding (m) English name derived from the Old English *heard* ('brave' or 'strong').

Hardy (m) English name of uncertain meaning that has been in occasional use as a first name since the early 20th century. It is possible that the name was based originally on the ordinary vocabulary word 'hardy'.

Harlan (m) English name derived from a place name based on the Old English *hara* ('hare') and *land* ('land'). It is confined largely to the USA, where its initial popularity was promoted by the US judge John Marshall Harlan (1833–1911), a staunch defender of civil rights. **Harland** is a variant form of the name.

Harland *See* HARLAN.

Harley (m) English name that was taken up as a first name in the 19th century.

Harmony (f) English name derived via Latin from the Greek for 'concord' or 'unity'. A relatively rare choice of first name of 20th-century origin, it is occasionally found in the variant forms **Harmonie** or **Harmonia**.

Harold (m) English name derived from the Old English Herefeald, itself from *here* ('army') and *wealdan* ('to rule') and thus meaning 'general'. It was borne by the Saxon King Harold II, whose death at the Battle of Hastings in 1066 signalled the beginning of the Norman Conquest. Because of this royal link the name fell out of use during the Norman period but reappeared in the 19th century. Commonly shortened to **Harry**. *See also* ERROL.

Harper (m/f) English name, denoting someone who plays the harp. It is found chiefly in the USA. Notable bearers of the name have included the US novelist Harper Lee (b.1926).

Harriet (f) English name that developed as a feminine equivalent of HARRY. It was taken up among English-speakers in the 17th century and remained fairly popular until the early 20th century, when it went into a sharp decline. It was revived once more in the 1990s. Commonly shortened to **Harrie**, **Harry**, **Hatty** or **Hattie**. Variant forms include **Harriett**, **Harriette** and **Harrietta**.

Harrison (m) English name meaning 'son of Harry' that has been in irregular use as a first name since the 19th century. Its relative popularity in the USA may have been influenced by the two presidents with the surname Harrison. Other notable bearers of the name have included the US film actor Harrison Ford (b.1942). Commonly shortened to **Harry**.

Harry (m) English name that developed as a diminutive form of HENRY but is now frequently treated as a name in its own right. It was established among English-speakers by medieval times and enjoyed another peak in popularity in the 19th century. **Hal** is a diminutive form. *See also* HARRIET; HARRISON.

Hartley (m) English name derived from a place name (found in several counties of England) usually derived from the Old English *heorot* ('hart') and *leah* ('clearing'). Another derivation suggests it means 'stony meadow'.

Harvey (m) English name that was taken up among English-speakers in the 19th century. The surname was of Breton origin, from *haer* ('battle') and *vy* ('worthy'), and came to England with the Normans. It seems to have disappeared from use after the 14th century but was revived in the 19th century. Commonly shortened to **Harv** or **Harve**. Occasionally rendered in the form **Hervey**.

Hattie/Hatty *See* HARRIET.

Havelock (m) English and Welsh name (pronounced 'haverlok') that has made infrequent appearances as a first name since the 19th century, usually thought to have arisen as a Welsh equivalent of OLIVER.

Haydn (m/f) Welsh name of uncertain origin, though possibly a variant of the English surname Haddon, meaning 'hill with heather'. It may also have evolved as a Welsh version of the Celtic AIDAN. As a Germanic surname it had its roots in the medieval *heiden* ('heathen'). It was initially an exclusively masculine name, but is today also bestowed upon girls, possibly under the influence of HEIDI. Also rendered as **Hadyn**, **Hayden** or **Haydon**.

Hayley (f) English name derived from a place name (from Hailey in Oxfordshire) that was subsequently taken up as a first name from the 1960s. The original place name means 'hay field'. It enjoyed a peak in popularity towards the end of the 1980s. Also found as **Haley**, **Hailey** or **Haylie**.

Hazel (f) English name derived from that of the tree but more often assumed to refer to the nut-brown colour of some people's eyes. It was one of many flower and plant names taken up by English-speakers towards the end of the 19th century. It enjoyed a peak in popularity in the 1930s. Commonly shortened to **Haze**.

Headley *See* HEDLEY.

Heath (m) English name derived from the ordinary vocabulary word 'heath' that has been in occasional use since the 19th century. The most famous bearer of the name to date has been the British cartoonist William Heath Robinson (1872–1944).

Heather (f) English name derived from the name of the moorland plant. It was taken up by English-speakers towards the end of the 19th century, enjoying particular popularity in Scotland, and was at its most frequent around the middle of the 20th century.

Hebe (f) Greek name (pronounced 'heebee') derived from the Greek *hebos* ('young') that made its first appearances among English-speakers towards the end of the 19th century. The name is borne in Greek mythology by a daughter of Zeus.

Heck/Heckie *See* HECTOR.

Hector (m) Greek name derived from *ekhein* ('to hold' or 'to resist') and usually interpreted as meaning 'holding fast'. It was famous in Greek mythology as the name of the Trojan warrior killed by Achilles. It enjoyed a minor resurgence in popularity in the late 19th century. **Heck** and **Heckie** are abbreviated forms of the name in Scotland, where Hector is sometimes connected to the Gaelic EACHANN.

Hedda (f) Scandinavian name derived from the German Hedvig, itself based on the Old German words *hadu* ('contention' or 'struggle') and *wig* ('war').

Universally identified with the Henrik Ibsen play *Hedda Gabler* (1890), the name has made occasional appearances as a first name among English-speakers since the 19th century.

Heddwyn (m) Welsh name derived from *hedd* ('peace') and *gwyn* ('white' or 'blessed'). The name enjoyed some popularity among Welsh-speakers in tribute to the poet Ellis Humphrey Evans (1887–1917), who wrote under the name Hedd Wyn until his death in the First World War.

Hedley (m) English name derived from a place name (from several locations in northern England) based on the Old English *haeth* ('heather') and *leah* ('clearing'). Also found in the variant form **Headley**.

Heidi (f) Swiss name derived from Adelheid (the German equivalent of ADELAIDE). It was taken up with some enthusiasm by English-speakers in the 1960s in response to the popularity of the televisation of the Swiss novelist Johanna Spyri's children's story *Heidi* (1881).

Heilyn (m) Welsh name derived from *heilio* ('to prepare'). The name, which appears twice in the *Mabinogion*, was originally reserved for servants who worked as stewards or wine-pourers in big houses.

Heledd (f) Welsh name of uncertain origin. It was borne by a legendary 7th-century Welsh princess. Also found as **Hyledd**.

Helen (f) English name derived from the Greek *helios* ('sun') and thus meaning 'shining one' or 'bright one'. The name is often linked with Helen of Troy, the beautiful daughter of Zeus over whom the 10-year Trojan War was fought. The name was in use among English-speakers as early as the 16th century. **Lala** is an informal version of the name. *See also* EILEEN; ELAINE; ELEANOR; ELEN; ELLA; ELLEN; HELENA; NELL.

Helena (f) English name that developed as a Latinized form of HELEN. The name became popular among English-speakers during the medieval period and has been in fairly regular use ever since. Variants include LENA and the Italian, Spanish and Portuguese **Elena**.

Helga (f) German and Scandinavian name derived ultimately from the Old Norse *heill* ('hale' or 'hearty'), but later interpreted to mean 'blessed' or 'holy'. The name was recorded in use among English-speakers at the time of the Norman Conquest and has made reappearances since the 20th century.

Hennie/Henny *See* HENRIETTA.

Henrietta (f) English equivalent of the French **Henriette**, itself a feminine version of Henri (*see* HENRY). English-speakers took up the name in the 17th century after it was introduced through

Charles I's French wife Queen Henrietta Maria (Henriette-Marie; 1609–69). Subsequently it was eclipsed by HARRIET but enjoyed a revival in the late 19th century. Among the diminutive forms of the name are **Etta**, **Ettie** (or **Etty**), **Hennie** (or **Henny**), **Hattie**, **Hettie** and **Nettie** (or **Netty**).

Henriette *See* HENRIETTA.

Henry (m) English name derived from the German Heinrich, itself from *heim* ('house' or 'home') and *ric* ('ruler' or 'owner') and thus meaning 'house owner' or 'lord of the manor'. It was taken up by English-speakers in the medieval period and became firmly established as a royal name, although HARRY was the more common form before the 17th century. It enjoyed a limited revival in the 1990s. As well as Harry, other diminutive forms of the name include HANK and **Hal**.

Hephzibah (f) Hebrew name meaning 'in her is my delight'. It appears in the Bible and was consequently taken up by Puritans in the 17th century. Shortened forms of the name include **Eppie**, **Hepsie**, **Hepsey** and **Hepsy**. A variant form is **Hepzibah**.

Hepsey/Hepsie/Hepsy/ Hepzibah *See* HEPHZIBAH.

Herb *See* HERBERT.

Herbert (m) English, German and French name derived from the Old German *heri* or *hari* ('army') and *berht* ('bright') and often interpreted to mean 'famous army'.

The name was relatively common among English-speakers during the medieval period but went out of fashion after the 13th century. It was revived in the 19th and early 20th centuries. Diminutive forms of the name include **Herb** and **Herbie**. *See also* BERT.

Herbie *See* HERBERT.

Hercules (m) Roman equivalent of the Greek Heracles or Herakles that has made occasional appearances as a first name among English-speakers since the 16th century. The name resulted from a combination of the name of the Greek goddess Hera and *kleos* ('glory'), thus meaning 'glory of Hera'. It is sometimes found in Scotland as an Anglicization of the Gaelic **Athairne** and in the Shetlands as an equivalent of the Norse **Hacon**. **Herk** and **Herkie** are shortened forms of the name.

Hereward (m) English name derived from the Old English *here* ('army') and *weard* ('protection'). It became famous as the name of the Anglo-Saxon leader Hereward the Wake, who rebelled against Norman rule in the 11th century. It remains rare.

Herk/Herkie *See* HERCULES.

Herman (m) English name derived from the Old German Hariman, itself from *hari* ('army') and *man* ('man') and thus interpreted to mean 'soldier' or 'warrior'. It was taken up by English-speakers around the middle of the 19th century, chiefly among

German immigrants in the USA. A rare feminine version of the name is **Hermine**.

Hermia (f) English name that developed as a variant of HERMIONE. It was taken up by English-speakers in medieval times and appeared in Shakespeare but is rare today.

Hermine See HERMAN.

Hermione (f) Greek name (pronounced 'hermighohnee') that was adopted as a feminine equivalent of Hermes, the name of the Greek messenger of the gods. It may originally have been derived from the Greek for 'stone'. The name appears in Greek mythology as that of the daughter of Menelaus and Helen and was subsequently taken up by English-speakers during the medieval period.

Hero (f) Greek name of uncertain meaning. It is most familiar in ancient mythology as the name of the lover of LEANDER.

Hervey See HARVEY.

Hesba (f) Greek name derived from *hespera* ('western'). It has made infrequent appearances among English-speakers since the 19th century.

Hesketh (m) English name derived from a place name (from northern England) based on the Old Norse *hestr* ('horse') and *ske-ithr* ('racecourse'). It was probably inspired by the long-established tradition of horse-racing in Scandinavia.

Hester (f) English name that was adopted as a variant form of ESTHER in the 17th century. Shortened forms of the name include **Esta**, **Ester**, **Hettie** and **Hetty**.

Hettie/Hetty See ESTHER; HENRIETTA; HESTER.

Heulwen (f) Welsh name meaning 'sunshine'.

Hew/Hewie See HUGH.

Hezekiah (m) Biblical name derived from the Hebrew Hizqiyah, meaning 'my strength is Yah' or 'Yah is strength' (Yah being an alternative name of Jehovah or God). It appears in the Bible and was subsequently taken up by English-speakers in the 17th century, although it has never been in frequent use.

Hilary (m/f) English name descended ultimately from the Roman Hilarius, itself from the Latin *hilaris* ('cheerful'). It was taken up by English-speakers during the medieval period as a name chiefly for boys. The name fell into disuse after medieval times but was revived during the 19th century as a name for both sexes. Commonly shortened to **Hil** or **Hilly**. **Hillary** is a variant spelling used for both boys and girls. Variants of the name in other languages include the Welsh **Ilar**. See also ELLERY.

Hilda (f) German, Dutch, Scandinavian and English name derived from the Old German *hild* ('battle'). The name appears to have developed as an abbreviated form of HILDEGARD and other similar names. The name was taken up more widely by English-speakers during the medieval period and enjoyed a later peak in the early 20th century, but has since become rare. A variant form of the name is **Hylda**.

Hildebrand (m) German name derived from the Old German *hild* ('battle') and *brand* ('sword'). It fell out of use among English-speakers around the end of the medieval period but enjoyed a minor revival in the 19th century.

Hildegard (f) German, Scandinavian and English name derived from the Old German *hild* ('battle') and *gard* ('enclosure') and interpreted to mean 'comrade in arms'. The name has made occasional appearances among English-speakers of German descent, chiefly in the USA. Sometimes shortened to HILDA. Also found as **Hildegarde**.

Hillary/Hilly *See* HILARY.

Hilton (m) English name derived from a place name meaning 'from the hill farm'. Also found as **Hylton**.

Hiram (m) Hebrew name possibly descended from Ahiram, meaning 'my brother is exalted', or else of unknown Phoenician origin. It appears in the Bible as the name of a king of Tyre and was subsequently taken up by Puritans in the 17th century. It is now con-

fined largely to the USA. Also found as **Hyram**.

Hob *See* ROBERT.

Hobart *See* HUBERT.

Hodge *See* ROGER.

Holden (m) English name derived from a place name meaning 'hollow valley'. As a first name its history goes back as far as the 19th century. Today it is best known through Holden Caulfield, the central character in J. D. Salinger's celebrated novel *The Catcher in the Rye* (1951).

Hollie *See* HOLLY.

Hollis (m/f) English name meaning 'dweller in the holly grove'.

Holly (f) English name that may have developed out of the ordinary vocabulary word 'holy' or else may have come from the name of the evergreen tree. It was in use among English-speakers by the late 19th century and enjoyed a peak in popularity towards the end of the 20th century, often bestowed upon girls born in the Christmas season. The name has also made very rare appearances as a masculine name. Also found as **Hollie**.

Homer (m) Greek name possibly derived from the Greek *homeros* ('hostage'). The name is universally associated with the celebrated 8th-century BC Greek poet, author of the *Odyssey*. It was taken up as a first name among English-speakers in the 19th century, chiefly in the USA.

Honey (f) English name derived from the ordinary vocabulary word 'honey', which has been in use as a term of endearment since medieval times. It may also have developed as a diminutive of **Honoria** (*see* HONOR).

Honor (f) English name derived either from the Roman **Honoria** or else from the ordinary vocabulary word 'honour'. Recorded among English-speakers as early as the Norman Conquest, it was among the virtue names taken up by Puritans in the 17th century. In its early history it was applied to boys as well as girls. Sometimes shortened to NORA. Variants include **Honora**, **Honorine** and the French **Honore**. *See also* ANFLIRIN; HONEY.

Honora/Honoria/Honorine/ Honour *See* HONOR.

Hope (f) English virtue name that was taken up by English Puritans after the Reformation. It was sometimes given to sets of triplets alongside FAITH and CHARITY, occasionally as a name for boys as well as girls. It is now reserved exclusively for girls and is more common in the USA than elsewhere.

Hopkin (m) English and Welsh name derived in medieval times via **Hob** from ROBERT. **Hopcyn** is a Welsh variant.

Horace (m) English and French name derived from the Roman **Horatius**, itself possibly from the Latin *hora* ('hour' or 'time'). Celebrated as the name of the Roman poet Horace (Quintus Horatius Flaccus; 65–8 BC), it was adopted by English-speakers in the 18th century and continued in fairly frequent use until the end of the 19th century. Occasionally shortened to **Horry**. *See also* HORATIO.

Horatia *See* HORATIO.

Horatio (m) English name that developed as a variant of HORACE under the influence of the Roman **Horatius**. It was in occasional use among English-speakers by the 16th century. It became well-known through Admiral Lord Horatio Nelson (1758–1805), who also bestowed the feminine form of the name upon his daughter **Horatia**.

Horatius *See* HORACE; HORATIO.

Horry *See* HORACE.

Hortense (f) French name derived from the Roman **Hortensia**, itself possibly from the Latin *hortus* ('garden'). English-speakers took up the name in the 19th century but it is now rare. The old Roman form of the name is still occasionally encountered.

Hortensia *See* HORTENSE.

Hosanna (m/f) English name derived from the Hebrew *hosanna* ('save now' or 'save pray'). Because of its biblical associations it was taken up by English-speakers early in the 13th century and was used initially for both sexes, although after the 17th century it appears to have been reserved chiefly for girls. Also found as **Hosannah**.

Howard (m) English name that was taken up among English-speakers early in the 19th century. It may have had its origins in a similar Scandinavian name derived from *ha* ('high') and *ward* ('guardian'). Other suggestions link the name with the Old German Huguard, from *hugu* ('heart') and *vardu* ('protection'), or with the Old French Houard, meaning 'worker with a hoe', or the Old English for 'hog-warden'. As a first name its history goes back to the 19th century. **Howie** is a common diminutive form.

Howell (m) English name that was derived either from an English surname or else from the Welsh HYWEL. It made its first appearances among English-speakers around the middle of the 19th century. Also found as **Howel**.

Howie *See* HOWARD.

Hubert (m) English, French and German name derived from the Old German Hugibert, meaning 'bright spirit' or 'inspiration'. It came to England with the Normans in the 11th century and was a popular choice in medieval times. It was revived in the 19th century but is now rare. Commonly shortened to BERT. Variants include **Hobart**.

Hudson (m) English name meaning 'son of Hudd' or 'son of Hugh'. Its popularity in Canada and the USA is a reflection of the early exploration of the area by the English adventurer Henry

Hudson (d.1611), after whom the Hudson Bay was named.

Huey *See* HUGH.

Hugh (m) English and Welsh name derived ultimately from the Old German *hug* ('heart' or 'mind'). It came to England with the Normans in the 11th century. It is also found as an Anglicization of various Gaelic names, including the Irish **Aodh** and the Scottish **Uisdean**. A Welsh variant of the name is **Huw**. In Scotland the name is sometimes rendered in the familiar forms **Shug** or **Shuggie**. A rare feminine version of the name is **Hughina**. Diminutive forms of the name include **Hughie** and **Hewie** (or **Huey**). *See also* HUGO.

Hughie *See* HUGH.

Hugo (m) English name that developed as a diminutive form of HUGH. It emerged as an alternative Latinized form of Hugh around the middle of the 19th century.

Humbert (m) English, French and German name derived from the Old German *hun* ('bear-cub' or 'Hun') and *berht* ('bright' or 'famous'). It came to England with the Normans in the 11th century and has resurfaced from time to time, notably as the name of the fictional Humbert Humbert in the Vladimir Nabokov novel *Lolita* (1955). Sometimes abbreviated to **Hum**.

Humph *See* HUMPHREY.

Humphrey (m) English name derived from the Old German

Hunfred, itself from *hun* ('bear-cub' or 'Hun') and *fridu* ('peace') and thus interpreted as meaning 'peaceful Hun'. It came to England with the Normans in the 11th century and was relatively frequent through the medieval period and beyond, although it has become less common since the 19th century. Commonly shortened to **Humph** or **Huffie**. Also rendered as **Humphry**.

Hunter (m) English and Scottish name derived from the ordinary vocabulary word 'hunter'.

Huw *See* HUGH.

Hy *See* HYACINTH, HYMAN.

Hyacinth (f) English flower name that was among the many flower names taken up by English-speakers towards the end of the 19th century. It was borne in Roman legend by a youth accidentally killed by Apollo. It was employed as a masculine name until the late 19th century, when it began to be regarded as exclu-sively feminine. Sometimes shortened to **Hy** and, in Ireland, to **Sinty**. Variants include **Hyacintha** and **Jacinth**.

Hyacintha *See* HYACINTH.

Hyam *See* HYMAN.

Hylda *See* HILDA.

Hyman (m) Jewish name derived via **Hyam** from the Hebrew *hayyim* ('life'). Sometimes shortened to **Hy**. **Hymie** and **Chaim** are familiar forms of the name.

Hymie *See* HYMAN.

Hypatia (f) Greek name derived from the Greek *hupatos* ('highest') that has made rare appearances as a first name among English speakers since the late 19th century. Sometimes abbreviated to **Patsy**.

Hyram *See* HIRAM.

Hywel (m) Welsh name meaning 'eminent' or 'conspicuous'. It remains rare outside Wales itself despite a resurgence in popularity in the 20th century. *See also* HOWELL.

similarly made its first appearances in the 19th century.

Ianthe (f) Greek name derived
from *ion* ('violet') and *anthos*
('flower'). It was borne in Greek
legend by a sea nymph, daughter
of the sea god Oceanus. The name
enjoyed some popularity as a literary name in the 19th century. Rare
variants include **Iantha**, **Ianthina**,
Janthina and **Janthine**. *See also*
IOLANTHE.

Iarlaith (m) Irish name derived
from the Gaelic *ior* (of unknown
meaning) and *flaith* ('leader' or
'prince'). Sometimes encountered
in the Anglicized form JARLATH.

Ib/Ibbie/Ibby *See* ISABEL.

Ibrahim (m) Arabic version of
ABRAHAM. A revered name in
Islamic tradition, it was borne by
the father of Ismail, also the
builder of the temple of Kaaba in
Mecca and from whom all
Muslims claim descent. Also
encountered as **Ebrahim** or
Ibraheem, it remains one of the
most popular names in the Arab
world today.

Iagan (m) Scottish name rep-
resenting a Gaelic version of
Aodhagan, itself derived from
Aodh, meaning 'fire'.

Iain *See* IAN.

Ian (m) Scottish name that
developed as a variant of the
English JOHN. It emerged as a distinct name in Scotland in the 19th
century and quickly made the
transition to other parts of the
English-speaking world (although
it has never been very popular in
the USA). It enjoyed a peak in
popularity in the 1950s and 1960s.
A variant largely confined to
Scotland is the Gaelic **Iain**, which

Ichabod (m) Biblical name
derived from the Hebrew
Ikhabhodh, meaning 'no glory' or
'where is the glory?'. It appears in
the Bible and was taken up by
Puritans in the 17th century,
although it has never been
common. The most famous bearer
of the name to date has been the
fictional Ichabod Crane in
Washington Irving's classic short

story 'The Legend of Sleepy Hollow' (1820).

Ida (f) English name derived via Norman French from the Old German *id* ('labour' or 'work') or possibly *itis* ('woman'), or else from the name of the Norse goddess Iduna. Some authorities link the name with Mount Ida in Crete, home of the infant Zeus. In Ireland it is sometimes traced back to the Gaelic **Ide** or **Ita**, derived from *ita* ('thirsty'). The name came to England with the Normans and was revived during the 19th century, best known from Gilbert and Sullivan's opera *Princess Ida* (1884)

Ide *See* IDA.

Idonea (f) English name derived from the Old Norse *idh* ('work' or 'labour'), as borne by the Norse goddess Iduna, or else possibly from the Latin *idoneus* ('suitable'). Also found as **Idony**, it was fairly common among English-speakers as early as the 12th century but has been rare since.

Idris (m) Welsh name derived from *iud* ('lord') and *ris* ('ardent', 'fiery' or 'impulsive') and thus meaning 'ardent ruler' or 'fiery lord'. The name appears in Welsh mythology as that of the sorcerer Idris after whom Cader Idris, the second highest mountain in Wales, was named. It was common among Welsh-speakers by medieval times and enjoyed a resurgence in popularity towards the end of the 19th century.

Idwal (m) Welsh name derived from *iud* ('lord' or 'master') and *wal* ('wall').

Iefan *See* EVAN.

Iesha *See* AISHA.

Iestyn *See* JUSTIN.

Ieuan/Ifan *See* EVAN.

Ifor (m) Welsh name of uncertain origin, possibly derived from *iôr* ('lord'). The name was borne by several important figures in Welsh legend and history but as a first name was rare before the early 20th century. It is often confused with IVOR, although the names do not come from the same source.

Ignatius (m) Spanish, Russian and English name derived from the Roman family name Egnatius, the origins of which are obscure – although it later came to be associated with the Latin *ignis* ('fire'). From the 16th century it became popular among Roman Catholics in many countries in tribute to St Ignatius Loyola (1491–1556), the Spanish founder of the Jesuits. *See also* INIGO.

Igor (m) Russian name derived either from IVOR or else from the Scandinavian Ingvarr, which resulted from the combination of Ing (the name of the Norse god of peace and fertility) and *varr* ('careful'), thus meaning 'cared for by Ing'. It has made irregular appearances among English-speakers since the 19th century.

Ike *See* ISAAC.

Ila *See* ISLA.

Ilana (f) Jewish name derived from the Hebrew for 'tree'. A variant form applied to males is **Ilan**.

Ilayne *See* ELAINE.

Ilean/Ileen/Ileene/Ilene *See* EILEEN.

Illtyd (m) Welsh name derived from *il* ('multitude') and *tud* ('land'), thus meaning 'land of the people'. It was borne by a 6th-century Welsh saint but did not make many appearances as a first name among the Welsh until the 19th century. Also found in the variant form **Illtud**.

Ilma *See* WILHELMINA.

Imelda (f) Spanish and Italian name derived from the Old German Irmhilde, itself from *irmin* or *ermin* ('whole' or 'entire') and *hild* ('battle'), thus meaning 'all-conquering'. It became popular among Roman Catholics in tribute to a 14th-century St Imelda, and made occasional appearances among English-speakers from the 20th century, chiefly in Ireland. Famous bearers of the name have included the British actress Imelda Staunton (b.1957).

Immaculata (f) Irish name derived via the Italian Immacolata from a title borne by the Virgin Mary, Maria Immacolata (a reference to the Immaculate Conception). It has made irregular appearances among Roman Catholics over the centuries.

Immy *See* IMOGEN.

Imogen (f) English name that appears to have evolved through a mistaken reading of the Celtic Innogen, itself derived either from the Latin *innocens* ('innocent') or the Irish Gaelic *inghean* ('daughter', 'maiden' or 'girl'). The mistake seems to have been made when William Shakespeare's play *Cymbeline* (1609) was printed for the first time, the 'nn' becoming 'm'. As Imogen, the name came into favour among English-speakers towards the end of the 19th century. Sometimes shortened to **Immy**.

Ina (f) English and Scottish name that evolved as a variant of ENA and also as a diminutive of various longer names ending '-ina', including CHRISTINA, EDWINA and GEORGINA. It was taken up by English-speakers in the 19th century.

India (f) English name derived from the name of the country, itself from that of the River Indus. The name began to be taken up among English-speakers towards the end of the 19th century, when India was the 'jewel of the British Empire'. It was made familiar to a wider audience as the name of a character in the Margaret Mitchell novel (and film) *Gone with the Wind* (1936).

Indiana (m/f) English name of relatively recent invention that developed either as a variant of INDIA or else from the name of the US state Indiana. When it made its first appearance in the early 20th century it was reserved exclusively for girls. The appearance of the name in the *Indiana Jones* movies of the 1980s, however, made it an acceptable name for males. Commonly shortened to **Indy**.

Indy *See* INDIANA.

Ingram (m) English name that is thought to have developed from the Norman Ingelram or Engelram, itself derived from the Germanic name Ingilrammus, from Engel and *hramn* ('raven'). It was in fairly common use among English-speakers from medieval times until the 17th century and enjoyed a revival in the 19th century.

Ingrid (f) Scandinavian and German name derived from Ing (the name of a Norse fertility god) and *frithr* ('fair' or 'beautiful') or *rida* ('to ride') and often interpreted to mean 'Ing's ride'. It made a few appearances among English-speakers in the 13th century but was not taken up on a significant scale in the English-speaking world until around the middle of the 19th century.

Inigo (m) Spanish variant of IGNATIUS, which was subsequently taken up by English-speakers. Records of the name in use in England go back to at least the 16th century, when it was borne by the celebrated English architect Inigo Jones (1573–1652). It enjoyed a resurgence in popularity in the 19th century.

Innes (m/f) Scottish name that

developed as an Anglicization of the Gaelic **Aonghas** (*see* ANGUS).

Iolanthe (f) English name derived from the Greek *iole* ('violet') and *anthos* ('flower'). This appears to have been a relatively recent invention influenced by other flower names popular around the end of the 19th century. It was made more widely known through the Gilbert and Sullivan opera *Iolanthe* (1882). *See also* YOLANDA.

Iolo (m) Welsh name that developed as a diminutive form of IORWERTH, although it is often considered to be a variant of JULIUS. Welsh-speakers had taken up the name by the 18th century. A variant form is **Iolyn**.

Iolyn *See* IOLO.

Iomhar *See* IVOR.

Iona (f) English name derived from that of the Scottish monastery island of Iona (originally Ioua, meaning 'yew-tree island', but supposedly altered to Iona by a misreading) or else possibly descended from the Greek *ion* ('violet'). As a first name Iona has been in irregular use since the 19th century, chiefly among Scots.

Ione (f) Greek name meaning 'violet'. It made irregular appearances among English-speakers in the 19th century, apparently in the belief that it was an authentic ancient Greek coinage (although no classical records exist of the name).

Ior *See* IVOR.

Iorwerth (m) Welsh name derived from the Welsh *iôr* ('lord') and *berth* ('beautiful' or 'handsome'), thus meaning 'handsome lord'. The name appeared in the *Mabinogion* and remains confined to Wales, where it is sometimes considered a variant of the English EDWARD. **Yorath** is a variant form of the name.

Ira (m) Hebrew name meaning 'watchful'. It appears in the Bible and in the 17th century was taken up by English Puritans, who introduced it to America, where it has always been more popular than elsewhere. Famous bearers of the name have included the US lyricist Ira Gershwin (1896–1983).

Irene (f) English name derived from the Greek *eirene* ('peace'). The name of a minor Greek goddess, it was taken up by English-speakers towards the end of the 19th century and enjoyed a peak in popularity in the 1920s, but has since become infrequent. The name was formerly usually pronounced in the Greek manner as 'eyereenee' but is now more commonly rendered as 'eyereen'. Commonly shortened to **Rene** (pronounced 'reenee') or **Renie**.

Irial (m) Irish first name of unknown Gaelic origin. It was revived in the 20th century.

Iris (f) English, German and Dutch name derived from that of the flower, although it may also have been inspired in part by the identical name of the Greek goddess of the rainbow. It was taken up by English-speakers along with other flower names towards the end of the 19th century but became relatively rare after the 1930s.

Irma (f) German name meaning 'whole' that was taken up to a limited extent by English-speakers towards the end of the 19th century. Its popularity in the USA was promoted by the films *My Friend Irma* (1949) and *Irma la Douce* (1963), starring Shirley Maclaine. Also found as **Erma**. *See also* EMMA.

Irvin/Irvine *See* IRVING.

Irving (m) Scottish name that has made rare appearances among English-speakers since the 19th century. The name came originally from a place name in Dumfriesshire. Notable bearers of the name have included the Russian-born US songwriter Irving Berlin (Israel Baline; 1888–1989). Variants include **Irvin** and **Irvine**.

Irwin (m) English name derived from the Old English *eofor* ('boar') and *wine* ('friend'), thus meaning 'boar friend', that has made rare appearances among English-speakers since the middle of the 19th century. It has become less frequent since the middle of the 20th century.

Isa *See* ISABEL.

Isaac (m) Biblical name derived from the Hebrew Yitschaq, possibly meaning 'he laughs' or 'laughter'. It appears in the Bible as the name of the son of Abraham and

Sarah, whose birth brought delight to his elderly parents. It was among the biblical names taken up by the Puritans in the 17th century but is chiefly a Jewish name today, also spelt **Izaak**. Common abbreviated forms of the name include **Ike**, **Zack**, **Zak** and **Zakki**.

Isabel (f) Spanish equivalent of ELIZABETH that was taken up by English-speakers in the medieval period. It ranked among the most popular first names during the 13th and 14th centuries and enjoyed a significant revival in the 19th century and again in the 1990s. Variant forms include ISABELLA, **Ysabel** and the Scottish **Ishbel**, **Isbel** or **Isobel**. Diminutive forms include **Ib**, **Ibbie** (or **Ibby**), **Isa**, **Izzie**, **Izzy**, **Nib**, **Sib** and **Tibbie**. *See also* BELLA, ELLA.

Isabella (f) Italian version of ELIZABETH that made its first appearances among English-speakers in the 12th century. It began to appear more frequently in the English-speaking world towards the end of the 19th century, enjoying particular popularity in Scotland. Variant forms include the French **Isabelle**. *See also* ISABEL.

Isabelle *See* ISABELLA.

Isadora (f) English name that developed as a feminine version of ISIDORE. It made its first appearances among English-speakers in the 19th century. The most celebrated bearer of the name to date has been the US dancer Isadora Duncan (1878–1927). Also found as

Isidora. Familiar forms of the name include **Issy**, **Izzy** and DORA.

Isaiah (m) Biblical name derived from the Hebrew Yeshayah, meaning 'salvation of Yah' (Yah being another name for Jehovah, or God). It features in the Bible as the name of an Old Testament prophet and was consequently taken up by Puritans in the 17th century and became enduringly popular among Jews. It is now rare.

Isbel/Ishbel *See* ISABEL.

Ishmael (m) Biblical name derived from the Hebrew Yishmael, meaning 'God will hearken'. It appears in the Bible as the name of Abraham's son and was consequently taken up by English-speakers in the 19th century. **Ismail** is a popular Arabic form of the name.

Isidora *See* ISADORA.

Isidore (m) English name derived from the Greek Isidoros, itself from the Egyptian Isis (the name of an Egyptian goddess) and the Greek *doron* ('gift'), thus meaning 'gift of Isis'. In ancient times it was sometimes treated as a Christian equivalent of the Jewish ISAIAH. It was taken up by English-speakers in the 19th century. Commonly shortened to **Izzy**.

Isla (f) Scottish name of relatively recent invention, apparently unknown before the 1930s. Pronounced 'eyela', it was based on a Scottish place name, that of the Scottish island of Islay, although it is sometimes considered to be a diminutive form of ISABELLA. Also found as **Ila** or **Islay**.

Isleen *See* AISLING.

Islwyn (m) Welsh name derived from that of a mountain in Gwent, itself from the Welsh *is* ('below') and *llwyn* ('grove').

Ismail *See* ISHMAEL.

Ismay (f) English name of uncertain origin. Recorded in use as early as the 13th century, it is sometimes linked with ESMÉ.

Ismene (f) Greek name of unknown meaning. It is usually associated with the tragic myth of Oedipus, in which the name appears as that of a daughter of Oedipus and Jocasta. Despite this melancholy association, the name has made occasional appearances among English-speakers since the 19th century.

Isobel *See* ISABEL.

Isolda *See* ISOLDE.

Isolde (f) English and French name derived from the Old French Iseult or Yseult, itself from the Celtic for 'fair' or 'beautiful', or from the Old German Isvald, from the words for 'ice' and 'rule'. The name figures prominently in Arthurian legend as that of the Irish princess in the tragic tale of Tristram and Isolde. It was fairly common in medieval times but is rare today. Variant forms include **Isolda**, **Ysolde** and the traditional Welsh **Esyllt** (meaning 'of fair aspect').

Israel (m) Biblical name derived from the Hebrew Yisrael, from *sarah* ('to struggle') and *el* ('God'), thus meaning 'he who struggles with God' or alternatively 'may God prevail'. It features in the Bible as the collective name borne by Jacob's descendants, the source of the name of the modern state of Israel. Because of its biblical connotations the name was taken up by English Puritans in the 17th century, but it has since remained confined largely to the world's Jewish communities. Commonly shortened to **Issy** or **Izzy**.

Issy *See* ISADORA; ISRAEL.

Ithel (m) Welsh name meaning 'generous lord'.

Ivah (f) Biblical name derived from an Old Testament place name.

Ivan (m) Russian equivalent of the English JOHN that has been in occasional use among English-speakers since the end of the 19th century. It fell into disfavour from the 1930s, largely in response to changes in international relations between Russia and the English-speaking world. Commonly shortened to **Van**. Feminine versions of the name include the Czech **Ivana**.

Ivana *See* IVAN.

Ives (m) Cornish equivalent of the French Yves, derived ultimately from the Old Norse *yr* ('yew').

Ivor (m) English version of the Scandinavian Ivarr, derived from *ur* ('yew' or 'bow') and *arr* ('warrior') and thus meaning 'bow-man'. It appeared with increasing frequency among English-speakers during the 19th century, but has become less common since the 1930s. Today it is commonly associated with the Welsh IFOR. A Scottish Gaelic variant is **Iomhar**.

Ivy (f) English plant name that was taken up as a first name alongside other plant and flower names towards the end of the 19th century. It enjoyed a peak in popularity in the 1920s but has since fallen out of favour.

Izaak *See* ISAAC.

Izzie/Izzy *See* ISABEL; ISADORA; ISIDORE; ISRAEL.

Jacaline/Jacalyn *See* JACQUELINE.

Jacinth/Jacintha *See* HYACINTH.

Jack (m) English name that evolved as a diminutive of JOHN. It appeared as Jankin (an elaboration of JAN) and then Jackin before arriving at its modern form, becoming increasingly popular from around the middle of the 19th century. *See also* JACKIE; JACKSON; JAKE; JOCK.

Jackalyn *See* JACQUELINE.

Jackey/Jacki *See* JACKIE.

Jackie (m/f) English diminutive of the boys' name JACK, itself a derivative of JOHN, and also of the girls'

name JACQUELINE. As a name for boys, also found as **Jacky**, it became increasingly common from the end of the 19th century. As a name for girls, also found as **Jackey**, **Jacky**, **Jacqi** or **Jacqui**, it was taken up by English-speakers in the 1930s.

Jackson (m) English name meaning 'son of Jack'. Its popularity in the USA was promoted by admirers of President Andrew Jackson (1767–1845) and the Confederate general Thomas 'Stonewall' Jackson (1824–63). Sometimes shortened to **Jack** or **Jacky**.

Jacky *See* JACKIE; JACKSON.

Jaclyn *See* JACQUELINE.

Jacob (m) Biblical name derived via the Roman Jacobus from the Hebrew Yaakov, meaning 'May God protect'. It was in occasional use as a clerical name among English-speakers before the Norman Conquest and was taken up with new enthusiasm by the Puritans in the 17th century. JAKE is sometimes treated as a diminutive form. **Jacoba**, **Jacobine** and **Jacobina** are rare feminine forms of the name. *See also* JAMES.

Jacoba/Jacobina/Jacobine *See* JACOB.

Jacqueline (f) French diminutive of Jacques, the French equivalent of the English JAMES. The name was exported to England at a relatively early date, being recorded in use in the 13th century, but it was not until the middle of the 20th century that it became widely popular. Commonly shortened to **Jackie**. Variants include **Jacalyn**, **Jacaline**, **Jaclyn**, **Jacklyn**, **Jackalyn**, **Jaqueline** and **Jacquelyn**. *See also* JACQUETTA.

Jacquetta (f) French diminutive of the French Jacques, itself an equivalent of the English JAMES. Early records of the name in use among English-speakers date from medieval times. *See also* JACQUELINE.

Jacqui *See* JACKIE.

Jade (f) English name derived from that of the semi-precious stone. The name of the stone came originally from the Spanish *piedra de ijada* ('stone of the bowels'), which referred to the stone's supposed magical influence upon intestinal disorders. It was taken up by English-speakers towards the end of the 19th century.

Jago (m) English name that evolved as a Cornish version of JAMES. It enjoyed a minor revival in popularity in the 20th century.

Jake (m) English name that developed as a variant of JACK and as a diminutive form of JACOB but which is now often regarded as a name in its own right. It appeared with increasing frequency from the beginning of the 20th century.

Jakki *See* JACKIE.

Jamal (m/f) Arabic and Indian name derived from the Arabic *jamal* ('beauty'). Although not one of the older traditional names of the Islamic world, it is neverthe-

less popular in many countries of the Middle East. In Egypt and several other countries it appears only as a masculine name, whereas in Syria and elsewhere it is generally thought of as a feminine name. Also found as **Gamal**, **Gamil** or **Jamil** and in India as **Jameel**. **Jamila** and the Indian **Jameela** are feminine forms of the name.

Jameel/Jameela *See* JAMAL.

James (m) Biblical name derived from the Roman Iacomus or Jacomus and sharing the same roots as JACOB. It was the name of two disciples and was taken up by English-speakers in the 12th century, when thousands of pilgrims visited the shrine of St James at Compostella. It was popular among Puritans in the 16th and 17th centuries and has remained one of the most enduring of all English first names. Commonly shortened to JIM, **Jimmy** or **Jimmie** and more rarely to JEM or **Jemmy**. **Jamie** is another diminutive form (originally Scottish), which like **Jami** and **Jaime** has also appeared occasionally as a name for girls. Variants in other languages include the Irish SEAMUS. A rare feminine version of the name is **Jamesina** (sometimes shortened to INA). *See also* HAMISH; JAGO; JEMIMA.

Jamesina/Jami/Jamie *See* JAMES.

Jamil/Jamila *See* JAMAL.

Jan (m/f) English name that developed as a diminutive of various masculine and feminine names, including JOHN, JANET, JANICE and JANINE. Alternatively it may also be considered a variant of JANE, JEAN or JOAN or else a borrowing of the Dutch and Scandinavian masculine name Jan (usually pronounced 'yan'). As a Middle English version of John it was in use among English-speakers in medieval times. Since the early 20th century it has been much more common as a name for girls.

Jancis (f) English name that appears to have resulted from the combination of JANE with FRANCES or CICELY. It made its first appearances in the 1920s, possibly invented by the novelist Mary Webb for a character in her book *Precious Bane* (1924).

Jane (f) English name derived via the French Jeanne or Jehane from the Roman Johanna, a feminine variant of Johannes (*see* JOHN). It was taken up by English-speakers in the 16th century and gradually eclipsed the related JEAN and JOAN. During the 19th century it was associated with domestic servants and appeared frequently as the name of housemaids in fiction. It returned to mainstream use in the early 20th century. Sometimes rendered as **Jayne** or used in combination with other names, as in **Sarah-Jane**. Familiar forms of the name include **Janie**, **Janey** and **Jaynie**. *See also* JANELLE; JANET; JANICE; JENNY; SHEENA; SIÂN; SIOBHAN.

Janelle (f) English name that

developed as an elaboration of JANE. Variants include **Janella**.

Janene *See* JANINE.

Janet (f) English name that evolved as a diminutive of JANE. It was in use among English-speakers in medieval times but subsequently fell into disuse except in Scotland until its revival in the 19th century. The name became increasingly widespread in the English-speaking world in the 1950s and 1960s. Commonly shortened to **Jan**. Familiar forms of the name include **Jennie**, JENNY, **Jinty** and **Netta** and (in Scotland) **Jess** and JESSIE. Another variant is the French **Janette**.

Janette *See* JANET; JEANETTE.

Janey *See* JANE.

Janice (f) English name that evolved as a diminutive form of JANE. It may have made its first appearance with the publication of Paul Leicester Ford's novel *Janice Meredith* (1899). The name enjoyed a peak in popularity in the 1950s. Commonly shortened to **Jan**. Also rendered as **Janis** – as borne by the US rock singers Janis Joplin (1943–70) and Janis Ian (b.1951).

Janie *See* JANE.

Janina *See* JANINE.

Janine (f) English version of the French Jeannine, itself an elaboration of the masculine name JEAN. It enjoyed some popularity among English-speakers in the 1930s and again in the late 1960s. Commonly shortened to **Jan**. Also found as **Jannine**, **Janene** and (rarely) **Janina**.

Janis *See* JANICE.

Jannine *See* JANINE.

Janthina/Janthine *See* IANTHE.

Japheth (m) Biblical name derived from the Hebrew Yepheth, meaning 'enlargement' or 'expansion'. It appears in the Bible as the name of Noah's eldest son and was consequently among the biblical names taken up by the Puritans in the 17th century.

Jaqueline *See* JACQUELINE.

Jared (m) Biblical name derived from the Hebrew *yeredh* ('descended' or 'descent', or possibly 'rose'). It features in the Bible as the name of one of Adam's descendants and was consequently taken up by Puritans in the 17th century, although it has never been very common. Also encountered as **Jarred**, **Jarod** or **Jarrod**.

Jarlath (m) English version of the Irish Gaelic IARLAITH. The name is rarely found outside Galway, where it was borne by a local saint.

Jarvis (m) English name derived from GERVASE in use as a first name since the 19th century. There is a character of the name in Charles Dickens's novel *A Tale of Two Cities* (1859). Also encountered as **Jervis**.

Jasmine (f) English name derived from that of the flower jasmin (ultimately from the Persian *yasmin*). It was adopted by English-speakers along with other flower names towards the end of the 19th century. Also found as **Jasmin, Yasmin, Yasmine** or **Yasmina** and more rarely as **Jessamine, Jessamyn** or **Jessamy**.

Jason (m) English name derived from the Greek Iason, itself probably from the Greek *iasthai* ('to heal'). Familiar in Greek legend from the story of Jason and the Argonauts, it also appears in the Bible and in this instance may represent a variant of JOSHUA. It was taken up by English-speakers in the 17th century although it was not until the 1970s that it established itself as a leading favourite.

Jasper (m) English name that may have its origins in the Persian for 'treasurer', although it is usually assumed that it relates to the gemstone jasper. Jasper (or CASPAR) is popularly supposed to have been the name of one of the Three Wise Men and was consequently popular among English-speakers in the 17th century. In Victorian times it was a favourite name for the villains of melodrama and pantomime.

Javier *See* XAVIER.

Jay (m/f) English name that evolved as a diminutive of various names beginning with 'J', including JAMES and JANE, although it is often assumed that it relates to the bird of the same name or that it is distantly descended from the Roman Gaius. As a name for boys it was taken up by English-speakers in the 19th century. It appears to have been applied to girls from the early 20th century. It is more frequent in Canada and the USA. Sometimes found as **Jaye**.

Jaye *See* JAY.

Jayne *See* JANE.

Jean (f) English name derived – like JANE and JOAN – from the Old French Jehane, itself a feminine version of the masculine Jean. All the various forms of the name are descended ultimately from the Roman Johannes (*see* JOHN). It became a favourite in Scotland in medieval times but was taken up more widely throughout the English-speaking world only towards the end of the 19th century. **Jeanie** and **Jeannie** are familiar forms of the name with strong Scottish associations. Diminutive forms include JEANETTE. *See also* GENE; SHEENA.

Jeanette (f) English name that developed as a diminutive of the French Jeanne. It was taken up in Scotland at a relatively early date but did not enter regular usage elsewhere in the English-speaking world until the 20th century. Also encountered as **Jeannette**. A familiar form of the name in Scotland is **Jinty**.

Jeanie *See* JEAN.

Jeannette *See* JEANETTE.

Jeannie *See* JEAN.

Jed *See* JEDIDIAH.

Jedidiah (m) Biblical name meaning 'beloved of God' or 'friend of Yah' ('Yah' being another name for Jehovah, or God). It features in the Bible and was consequently among the names taken up by English Puritans in the 17th century. Today it is more likely to be encountered in its abbreviated form **Jed**.

Jeff *See* GEOFFREY; JEFFERSON.

Jefferson (m) English name meaning 'son of Jeffrey'. The name was adopted by many people in the USA in tribute to the US President Thomas Jefferson (1743–1826) and Confederate President Jefferson Davis (1808–89). Sometimes shortened to **Jeff**.

Jeffery/Jeffrey *See* GEOFFREY.

Jem (m) English name that evolved as a diminutive form of JAMES, although it is now often associated with JEREMY. It was taken up by English-speakers in the 19th century. **Jemmy** is a diminutive form. *See also* JEMIMA; JEREMIAH; JEREMY.

Jemima (f) Biblical name derived from the Hebrew Yemimah, meaning 'wild dove' or possibly 'bright as day'. It was taken up by English Puritans in the 17th century and has remained a relatively popular choice of name in succeeding centuries, being considered by many people a feminine equivalent of the masculine JAMES. **Jem**, **Jemmy** and **Mima** are familiar forms of the name.

Jemma *See* GEMMA.

Jemmy *See* JEM; JEMIMA.

Jen *See* JENNIFER; JENNY.

Jeni *See* JENNY.

Jenifer *See* JENNIFER.

Jenkin (m) English and Welsh name that is thought to have evolved originally from the medieval first name Jankin (*see* JACK). It has a strong Welsh flavour, largely because the surname Jenkins is particularly common among the Welsh.

Jenna (f) English name that developed as a variant of JENNY. It is a relatively recent adoption, making early appearances in the 1970s, when it was promoted through a character of the same name in the US television soap opera *Dallas*.

Jenni/Jennie *See* JENNY.

Jennifer (f) English name that developed initially as a Cornish variant of GUINEVERE, meaning 'white ghost' – the name borne by King Arthur's unfaithful wife in Arthurian legend. It became established among English-speakers in the 18th century but remained relatively uncommon until the early years of the 20th century. Also encountered as **Jenifer**. Commonly shortened to **Jen**, **Jennie** or JENNY.

Jenny (f) English name that is generally thought of as a diminutive form of JANE, JANET and JENNIFER. It seems to have made early appearances during medieval times as a variant of JEAN but had become connected with several other girls' names by the 18th century, being taken up with particular enthusiasm in Scotland. Commonly shortened to **Jen**. Also found as **Jeni**, **Jenni**, **Jennie** or the Latinate JENNA.

Jep *See* JEPSON.

Jephthah (m) Biblical name derived from the Hebrew Yiphtah, meaning 'God opens'. It appears in the Bible and was revived by English-speakers in the 19th century. Also found as **Jephtha** or **Jeptha**.

Jepson (m) English name that evolved originally out of a medieval variant of GEOFFREY. Sometimes shortened to **Jep**.

Jeremiah (m) Biblical name derived from the Hebrew Yirmeyah, meaning 'appointed by God' or 'exalted by Yah' (Yah being an alternative for Jehovah, or God). It appears in the Bible and was taken up by Puritans in the 17th century. It is now rare, although it continues to make occasional appearances in Ireland, where it may also be encountered as a variant of **Diarmaid** (*see* DERMOT). Commonly shortened to **Jerry** or **Jem**.

Jeremy (m) English name that evolved out of the biblical JEREMIAH. It was in use during the medieval period and remained in currency even after the Puritans revived the biblical Jeremiah in the 17th century. In the 1970s it appeared in the top 50 most popular names given to babies born in

Canada and the USA. Commonly shortened to JERRY or **Jerrie** and, less commonly, to JEM.

Jermaine *See* GERMAINE.

Jerome (m) English name descended via Hieronymus from the Greek Hieronymos, itself derived from *hieros* ('holy') and *onoma* ('name') and thus meaning 'one who bears a holy name'. Often confused with the otherwise unconnected JEREMY, it made irregular appearances among English-speakers as early as the 12th century. Other versions of the name were subsequently replaced by the French form Jerome. Commonly shortened to JERRY.

Jerrard *See* GERARD.

Jerrie *See* GERALDINE.

Jerrold *See* GERALD.

Jerry (m) English name that exists as a diminutive of several other names, including JEREMIAH, JEREMY and JEROME. As a variant of GERRY, it may also be found as an abbreviation of GERALD or GERARD. It appears to have made its debut among English-speakers in the 18th century and has remained in wide circulation ever since. *See also* GERALDINE.

Jervis *See* JARVIS.

Jess *See* JANET; JESSE; JESSICA.

Jessamine/Jessamy/Jessamyn *See* JASMINE.

Jesse (m) English name derived from the Hebrew Yishay, meaning 'Jehovah exists' or 'gift of

Jehovah'. It features in the Bible as the name of King David's father and was taken up by English-speakers in the 18th century, becoming particularly popular in the USA. Usually pronounced 'jessee' and accordingly sometimes rendered as JESSIE. Sometimes shortened to **Jess**.

Jessica (f) English name that appears to have been invented by William Shakespeare as the name of Shylock's daughter in his play *The Merchant of Venice* (1596). It seems Shakespeare modelled the name on the Hebrew Iscah or Jesca, meaning 'God beholds', as featured in the Bible. It enjoyed a considerable vogue from the 1990s. Commonly shortened to **Jess** or JESSIE.

Jessie (f) English name that evolved as a diminutive form of JEAN, JANET and JESSICA. It was taken up by English-speakers, especially in Scotland, in the 19th century and was fairly common until the 1920s. Sometimes shortened to **Jess**. Also rendered as **Jessi** or **Jessye**. A Gaelic form of the name is **Teasag**. *See also* JESSE.

Jessye *See* JESSIE.

Jethro (m) English name derived from the Hebrew Yitro or Ithra, meaning 'abundance' or 'excellence'. It appears in the Bible as the name of the father-in-law of Moses and was consequently taken up by English Puritans in the 16th century. It remained fairly common until the end of the 19th century.

Jetta (f) English name derived from the name of the mineral jet. The name of the mineral came ultimately, via the Old French *jaiet*, from the Latin *gagates* ('stone from Gagai').

Jevon *See* EVAN.

Jewel (f) English name derived from the ordinary vocabulary word 'jewel'. It was among the many words connected with gemstones that were taken up by English-speakers as first names in the 19th century.

Jill (f) English name that evolved as a diminutive form of GILLIAN. Jill began to appear as an alternative to **Gill** as the usual shortened form of Gillian from the 17th century and enjoyed peaks in popularity in the 1930s and again since the 1970s. **Jilly** and **Jillie** are diminutive forms of the name.

Jillian *See* GILLIAN.

Jillie/Jilly *See* GILLIAN; JILL; JULIANA.

Jim (m) English name that evolved as a diminutive of JAMES and is now often considered to be a name in its own right. Medieval in origin, it was taken up on a significant scale by English-speakers by the middle of the 19th century and was greatly promoted throughout the English-speaking world by Robert Louis Stevenson's Jim Hawkins, the hero of his adventure novel *Treasure Island* (1883). In recent years Jim has been substantially eclipsed by its diminutive form **Jimmy**. Other variants are **Jimmie** and **Jimi**.

Jimmie/Jimmy *See* JIM.

Jinny *See* VIRGINIA.

Jinty *See* JEANETTE.

Jo (m/f) English name that developed as a diminutive form of various longer names, including the masculine JOHN, JONATHAN and JOSEPH and the feminine JOAN, JOANNA, JOANNE, JODY and JOSEPHINE. It emerged during the 19th century and is today more often encountered in use as a name for females. It is sometimes used in combination with other names, as in **Jobeth**. A rare Scottish variant is **Joina**.

Joan (f) English name derived from the Latin Johanna, itself a feminine version of Johannes (*see* JOHN). Records of the name's use among English-speakers go back to the medieval period, when the name was imported from France in the form Jhone or Johan. The modern spelling of the name seems to have been established by the 14th century. It was one of the top three feminine names among English-speakers in the 16th century and was revived in the 1920s and 1930s. *See also* JOANNA; JOANNE; JONI; SIOBHAN.

Joanna (f) English variant of JOAN derived via Hebrew and Latin from the Greek Ionna and in origin one of several feminine versions of JOHN. In medieval times the name was usually rendered as **Johanna** and it was not until the 18th century that the modern spelling became widely accepted, replacing Joan as the dominant form of the name from the 1930s. Commonly shortened to JO. *See also* JOANNE.

Joanne (f) English name borrowed from Old French and, like JOAN, in origin a feminine equivalent of JOHN. It enjoyed a peak in popularity among English-speakers in the 1970s but has since lost ground. Commonly shortened to JO. Also found as **Jo-Anne** or **Jo Anne**.

Job (m) Biblical name derived from the Hebrew Iyyobh, meaning 'persecuted' or 'hated'. The biblical Job demonstrated his faithfulness to God through a series of trials and misfortunes, as told in the Book of Job, and the name was consequently taken up by English Puritans in the 17th century. It is now rare. **Joby** and **Jobie** are familiar forms of the name.

Jobeth *See* JO.

Jobie/Joby *See* JOB.

Jocasta (f) Greek name of uncertain meaning. According to some authorities, the name comes from the mythical Io (understood to refer to the moon) combined with *kaustikos* ('burning') and thus meaning 'shining moon'. It is most famous from the various literary works based on the myth of Queen Jocasta of Thebes, who committed suicide after unknowingly marrying her own son, Oedipus.

Jocelyn (m/f) English name derived from the Old Norman

Joscelin. The Old Norman name may have come originally from that of a Germanic tribe or else from the Old German names Jodoc or Josse (meaning 'champion'). The name was in regular use in England through the medieval period and was revived in the 19th century. When bestowed upon girls, it is often considered to be a combination of JOYCE and LYNN. Commonly shortened to **Jos** or **Joss**. Variants include **Jocelin**, **Joseline**, **Joscelin**, **Josceline**, **Joselyn** and **Josslyn** (all feminine versions of the name).

Jock (m) Scottish variant of JACK, itself a diminutive of JOHN. It is strongly associated with Scotland, although it is not in fact much used as a name in Scotland itself. **Jocky** (or **Jockey**) is a familiar form of the name. A Gaelic variant is Seoc.

Jodene/Jodi/Jodie *See* JODY.

Jody (m/f) English name that evolved as a diminutive form of the masculine GEORGE, JUDE and JOE and of the feminine JO, JOSEPHINE, **Josie** and JUDITH. As a boys' name, it was heard with increasing frequency among English-speakers during the 19th century. As a girls' name it seems to date from the 1950s, enjoying its greatest popularity in Canada and the USA. Also found as **Jodi** or **Jodie**. Another variant is **Jodene**.

Joe (m) English name that evolved as a diminutive form of such names as JOSEPH, JOHN and JOSHUA. It became common among

English-speakers in the 19th century. Also encountered as **Jo** or **Joey**.

Joel (m) Biblical name derived from the Hebrew Yoel, meaning 'Yah is god' (Yah being another name for Jehovah, or God). It appears around a dozen times in the Bible and was in use in medieval England. The biblical history of the name led to it being taken up by English Puritans in the 16th century. It is also popular among Jews. Since the 19th century it has been confined largely to the USA. A feminine version is **Joelle**.

Joelle See JOEL.

Joey See JOE; JOSEPH; JOSHUA.

Johanna See JOANNA.

John (m) English name derived via the Latin Johannes from the Hebrew Yohanan or Johanan, meaning 'Yah is gracious' or 'Yah is merciful' (Yah being another name for Jehovah, or God). It features in the Bible as the name of John the Baptist, among others, and because of its strong religious associations, ranks among the most enduringly popular of all Christian names. It came to England with the Normans in the 11th century and has been in regular use since the 16th century. Diminutives include JACK, HANK, **Jon** and **Jonny** (also found as **Johnnie** or **Johnny**). Variants in other languages include the Irish SEAN, the Scottish IAN and the Welsh EVAN.

Johnathan/Johnathon See JONATHAN.

Johnnie/Johnny See JOHN.

Jola/Jolana/Jolanda See YOLANDA.

Joleen See JOLENE.

Jolene (f) English name that probably resulted from the combination of JO and MARLENE or another name with a '-lene' ending. It appears to be a name of relatively recent coinage, becoming popular in the USA in the 1940s. Also found in the form **Joleen**.

Jolie (f) English name that evolved as a variant of JULIA, JULIE or JULIANA. It appears to be a relatively recent introduction of the late 20th century.

Jon See JOHN; JONATHAN.

Jonah (m) Biblical name derived from the Hebrew Yonah, meaning 'dove'. It appears in the Bible as the name of a prophet who is swallowed by a whale and was consequently among the biblical names adopted by the Puritans in the 17th century, although later generations tended to avoid the name because it signified bad luck. See also JONAS.

Jonas (m) English name derived from the Greek Ionas, an equivalent of JONAH. It has been in use among English-speakers since the 19th century or earlier and, because it does not carry the same association with misfortune, gradually came to eclipse Jonah across the English-speaking world.

Joney is a familiar form of the name.

Jonathan (m) English name derived from the Hebrew Yahonathan, meaning 'Yah has given' or 'Yah's gift' (Yah being another name for Jehovah, or God). It appears in the Bible and was taken up by English-speakers as early as the 13th century. It has been in regular use since the 17th century, sometimes confused with JOHN. Also encountered as **Jonathon** and occasionally as **Johnathan** or **Johnathon**. Commonly shortened to **Jon**. Diminutive forms of the name include the relatively rare **Jonty**.

Joni (f) English name that developed via **Joani** as a variant of JOAN. It was taken up by English-speakers in the 1950s, becoming popular chiefly in Canada and the USA. Well-known bearers of the name have included Canadian singer-songwriter Joni Mitchell (Roberta Joan Anderson; b.1943). Sometimes shortened to JO.

Jonny See JOHN.

Jonquil (f) English name derived from the French *jonquille*, itself ultimately from the Latin *juncus* ('reed'). One of the less well known of the flower names that were taken up by English-speakers towards the end of the 19th century and early 20th century, it was at its most popular in the 1940s and 1950s.

Jonty See JONATHAN.

Jools See JULES.

Jordan (m/f) English name derived from that of the sacred River Jordan – itself from the Hebrew *hayarden* ('flowing down') – in the Holy Land. Formerly given to children baptized with water brought back from the River Jordan by pilgrims. As a girls' name, it is also found as **Jordana** or **Jordyn**. **Judd** is a shortened masculine version of the name.

Jordana/Jordyn See JORDAN.

Jos See JOCELYN; JOSEPH; JOSIAH.

José (m) Spanish equivalent of JOSEPH that is also occasionally encountered among English-speakers, chiefly in the USA. It is sometimes used as a name for girls in combination with other names, as in **Maria José**. Other feminine variants include **Josiane**.

Joseph (m) English and French name derived from the Hebrew Yoseph, meaning 'Yah may add' or 'Yah added' (in other words, 'God gave this son'). The name appears in the Bible and made irregular appearances among English-speakers in medieval times, becoming increasingly popular after the Reformation and again in the early 20th century. JO, JOE, **Joey** and **Jos** are diminutive forms of the name. *See also* JOSEPHINE.

Josepha/Josephina See JOSEPHINE.

Josephine (f) English equivalent of the French Joséphine, a feminine version of JOSEPH. It appears to have made its debut among English-speakers around the middle of the 19th century. Commonly shortened to JO. Variants include **Josepha** and **Josephina**. Diminutive forms include **Josie**, **Josette** and **Pheeny**. *See also* FIFI; JODY.

Josette *See* JOSEPHINE.

Josh *See* JOSHUA; JOSIAH.

Joshua (m) Biblical name derived from the Hebrew Yehoshua or Hosea, meaning 'Yah saves' or 'Yah is salvation' (Yah being another name for Jehovah, or God). It appears in the Bible as the name of the man who succeeded Moses as the leader of the Israelites and was taken up by English-speakers in the 18th century. It enjoyed a revival in the USA in the 1950s and in the UK in the 1990s. JOE and **Josh** are common diminutives.

Josiah (m) Biblical name derived from the Hebrew Yoshiyah, meaning 'Yah supports' or 'Yah heals' (Yah being another name for Jehovah, or God). It appears in the Bible and was taken up by English-speakers in the 17th century but is now rare. The usual diminutives are **Jos** or **Josh**.

Josiane *See* JOSÉ.

Josie *See* JOSEPHINE.

Joss *See* JOCELYN.

Joy (f) English name derived from the ordinary vocabulary word 'joy', itself from the Old French *joie*. Also encountered as a diminutive form of JOYCE. It was in use in England as early as the 12th cen-

tury and was taken up by English Puritans in the 17th century, who interpreted it as expressive of the 'joy' of religious faith. It has remained in irregular use ever since.

Joyce (m/f) English name descended from the Norman French Josce, meaning 'lord'. Today it is commonly associated with the ordinary vocabulary words 'joy' or 'rejoice'. The name came to England with William the Conqueror in the 11th century, although in those days it was treated as a masculine name. Having vanished from use by the 14th century, it reappeared (chiefly as a name for girls) around the 17th century. Sometimes shortened to JOY.

Judah (m) Biblical name derived from the Hebrew Yehudhah or Yehuda, meaning 'praised' or 'he who is praised'. It appears in the Bible and was consequently taken up by English-speakers in the 17th century. **Yehudi** is a variant form. *See also* JUDE.

Judd *See* JORDAN.

Jude (m) English variant of the biblical Judas. The name is sometimes applied to the apostle Judas Thaddaeus (the patron saint of lost causes) to distinguish him from Judas Iscariot. It was taken up by English-speakers in the 17th century. The best-known bearer of the name is the fictional Jude Fawley in the Thomas Hardy novel *Jude the Obscure* (1895).

Judi *See* JUDITH.

Judith (f) Biblical name derived from the Hebrew Yehudhith, meaning 'Jewess' or 'woman of Judea'. It appears in the Bible and records of its use among English-speakers go back beyond the Norman Conquest. It was not, however, until the 17th century that the name began to appear with any frequency in the English-speaking world. Commonly shortened to **Judi**, **Judie** or **Judy**. The full version of the name may sometimes be encountered as an Anglicization of the Gaelic SIOBHAN. *See also* JODY.

Judy *See* JUDITH.

Jules (m) French name derived either from JULIAN or JULIUS. It was taken up by English-speakers on a limited basis towards the end of the 19th century. A variant form of relatively recent invention is **Jools** – as borne by the British keyboardist and television presenter Jools Holland (Julian Holland; b.1958). *See also* JULIA; JULIE; JULIET.

Julia (f) Roman name that evolved as a feminine equivalent of JULIUS and was subsequently taken up by English-speakers in the 16th century. It enjoyed a resurgence in popularity in the second half of the 20th century. Since 1900, however, it has lost ground to the French form of the name, JULIE.

Julian (m) English name derived from the Roman Julianus, a variant of JULIUS. It made occasional appearances in medieval times, when it was also in use as a variant of the feminine GILLIAN, but was not taken up on a significant scale until the 18th century. It enjoyed a peak in popularity in the 1960s but has since been in decline. A rare variant is **Julyan**. Sometimes shortened to **Jolly** or JULES.

Juliana (f) Feminine version of the Roman Julianus, a variant of JULIUS. It was taken up by English-speakers as early as the 12th century and enjoyed a resurgence in popularity in the 18th century. It is now rare. Occasionally abbreviated to **Jilly** or, more rarely, to LIANA. Variant forms include **Julianna**, **Julianne**, **Julie Ann** and the German **Juliane**.

Juliane/Julianne *See* JULIANA.

Julie (f) French version of the Roman JULIA that was widely taken up among English-speakers around the end of the 19th century. It gradually replaced Julia as the more common version of the name and remains in fairly regular use. Commonly shortened to JULES.

Juliet (f) English name derived from the Italian Giulietta, itself an elaboration of the Italian Giulia (*see* JULIA). Its use among English-speakers was much promoted by William Shakespeare's tragedy *Romeo and Juliet* (1595). The name has been in regular use ever since, with its most recent peak in the 1960s. Sometimes shortened to JULIE or JULES. Variants from other

languages include the French
Juliette.

Juliette *See* JULIET.

Julius (m) Roman family name of
uncertain origin that was subsequently taken up by English-
speakers during the 19th century.
According to legend, the very first
bearer of the name was Iulus, the
son of Aeneas. Some authorities
suggest that the name comes originally from the Greek meaning
'downy' or 'hairy' – a reference to
the first growth of beard in young
men. Occasionally shortened to
JULES.

Julyan *See* JULIAN.

June (f) English name derived
from the name of the month.
Like other first names based on
months of the year, it appears to
have been taken up by English-
speakers early in the 20th century,
often bestowed upon girls born in
June. It became less frequent after
the 1930s.

Junior (m) English name that
developed initially as a nickname
for any young person, derived
from the Latin for 'younger'. Long
used to distinguish a son from a
father with the same name, it does
not appear to have won acceptance as a formal first name until
the early 20th century and is still
rare outside the USA.

Juniper (f) English name derived

from that of the plant, itself from
the Latin *juniperus* (of unknown
meaning). It appears in the Bible
as a translation of the Hebrew
rothem (the name of a desert
shrub). It has never been very
common as a first name.

Juno (f) Roman name derived
from that of the goddess Juno,
wife of Jupiter. It was subsequently taken up by the Irish,
usually in the form UNA. Examples
of its use in relatively modern
times have included the Sean
O'Casey play *Juno and the Paycock*
(1924).

Justie *See* JUSTIN; JUSTINE.

Justin (m) English name
descended from the Roman
Justinus, itself a derivative of
Justus. Borne by several early
saints and by two Byzantine
emperors, it began to appear with
increasing frequency among
English-speakers in the 1970s.
Justie and **Justy** are familiar forms
of the name. Variants include
Justyn and the Welsh **Iestyn**. *See
also* JUSTINE.

Justine (f) French feminine
equivalent of JUSTIN. Borne by a
4th-century Christian martyr of
Padua, it was taken up by English-
speakers in the 19th century and
enjoyed a minor peak in popularity in the 1970s. Sometimes
shortened to **Justie** or **Justy**.

Justy *See* JUSTIN; JUSTINE.

for many years, it was adopted by English-speakers in the USA in the 1920s, after it was imported with Scandinavian settlers. Subsequently it became a favourite choice on both sides of the Atlantic, reaching a peak in the 1960s. Occasionally shortened to **Kar** or **Kaz**. Variant forms include **Karin**, **Karyn**, **Carin**, **Caryn**, CARON, **Caronne**, CARINA, **Karena** and **Karina**. *See also* CARA.

Karenza *See* KERENSA.

Karim (m) Arabic name derived from *karim* ('noble' or 'generous'). A feminine version of the name is **Karima**.

Karin *See* KAREN.

Karina *See* CARINA; CATHERINE.

Karl *See* CARL.

Karyn *See* KAREN.

Kasey *See* CASEY.

Kasia *See* KEZIA.

Kat *See* CATHERINE; KATE; KATRINA.

Kate (f) English name that developed as a diminutive of CATHERINE and its many derivatives, such as KATHLEEN. It was first used by English-speakers during the medieval period. It features twice in the plays of William Shakespeare and became increasingly popular towards the end of the 19th century. Also found as **Katie**, **Kati** and **Katy**.

Kath/Katharine/Katherine *See* CATHERINE.

Kathleen (f) English version of the Irish Caitlin, itself derived

Kaleigh/Kaley *See* KAYLEIGH.

Kane (m) Irish name that developed as an Anglicization of the Gaelic CIAN, or else from the Gaelic words for 'great' or 'head'. Another derivation suggests it can also be traced to a Welsh word meaning 'beautiful'. It was first taken up by English-speakers in the 1950s and is today more common in Australia and the USA than it is in the UK.

Kara *See* CARA.

Karen (f) English name derived from a Danish diminutive of the English CATHERINE. An established favourite among Scandinavians from the English CATHERINE. The name was familiar on both sides of the Atlantic by the 19th century, when it was further promoted in the USA by the 1870s song 'I'll take you home again, Kathleen'. Well-known bearers of the name have included the British contralto Kathleen Ferrier (1912–53) and the US actress Kathleen Turner (b.1954). Variant forms include **Cathleen** and **Kathlyn**. Commonly shortened to **Kath**, **Kathy**, **Kati**, **Katie** or **Katy**.

Kathryn See CATHERINE.

Kathy See CATHERINE; KATHLEEN.

Kati/Katie See KATE; KATHLEEN.

Katrina (f) Scottish variant of CATHERINE, probably descended via CATRIONA from the Italian Caterina. Since the middle of the 20th century the name has been encountered with increasing frequency elsewhere in the English-speaking world. Variants include **Katrine** and **Katriona**. Sometimes shortened to **Treena**.

Katrine/Katriona See KATRINA.

Katy See CATHERINE.

Kay (m/f) English name that as a name for boys probably developed ultimately out of the Roman Gaius (of uncertain meaning). It features in Arthurian legend as the name of Sir Kay, King Arthur's steward. As a name for girls, it probably emerged initially as a simple abbreviation for any longer name beginning with C or K, including CATHERINE and its many derivatives. Also found as **Kaye**, it

made its first appearances among English-speakers towards the end of the 19th century.

Kaye See KAY.

Kayla See KAYLEIGH.

Kayleigh (f) English and Irish first name that is thought to owe its modern popularity to the combination of KELLY or KYLIE and **Leigh** or **LEE**. As **Kayley**, the ultimate source of the name was the Irish O Caollaidhe (meaning 'descendant of Caoladhe'), itself derived from *caol* ('slender'). Also found as **Kaleigh**, **Kaylee**, **Kayly** or **Kayla**.

Kayley/Kayly See KAYLEIGH.

Kaylin (f) Irish name meaning 'slender fair one'. An Anglicization of the original Irish Caoilfhinn or Caoilfhionn, it is also encountered as **Kayline** or **Keelan**.

Kaz See KAREN.

Kean (m) Irish name that developed as an Anglicization of the Gaelic CIAN, meaning 'vast', or of the Gaelic *cean* ('head'). It was once common in Ireland, where it was particularly associated with the O'Hara family. Also rendered as **Keane** or KANE.

Keefe (m) Irish name meaning 'noble'.

Keeley (f) English and Irish name that may have evolved as a variant of the Irish KEELIN. Well-known bearers of the name in recent times have included the British actress Keeley Hawes (b.1976). Also found as **Keely**, **Keeleigh** or KEIGHLEY.

Keelin (f) Irish first name that evolved as an Anglicization of the Gaelic Caoilfhionn, itself derived from *caol* ('slender') and *fionn* ('white'). *See also* KEELEY.

Keenan (m) Irish name derived from the Irish Gaelic for 'little ancient one'.

Kegan (m) Irish name meaning 'son of Egan' or alternatively 'little fiery one'. Sometimes considered an Irish equivalent of HUGH.

Keighley (f) English name (pronounced 'keethly') derived from a place name in Yorkshire, or alternatively treated as an altered form of KEELEY.

Keir (m) Scottish name of uncertain origin, possibly from the Gaelic for 'swarthy'. Largely confined to Scotland, it became widely known through the British trade unionist and politician Keir Hardie (James Keir Hardie; 1856–1915), the Labour Party leader whose mother had borne it as her maiden name.

Keiran *See* KIERAN.

Keith (m) Scottish name derived from a Scottish place name in East Lothian, itself possibly derived from the Celtic word for 'wood' or 'windy place'. As a first name, it made its debut in the 19th century and enjoyed a peak in popularity among English-speakers in the late 1950s. A rare feminine form of the name is **Keitha**.

Keitha *See* KEITH.

Kelan (m) Irish name representing an Anglicization of the Gaelic Caolan, itself derived from *caol* ('slender').

Kelcey *See* KELSEY.

Kelley/Kellie *See* KELLY.

Kelly (m/f) Irish name that was taken up by English-speakers as a first name for both sexes from the late 1950s. The usual Irish Gaelic form of the name is **Ceallagh**, meaning 'strife', 'war' or 'warlike'. Its emergence among English-speakers may have been influenced initially by the popularity of the US film actress Grace Kelly (1928–82), as a result of which it is today usually reserved for girls. Also rendered as **Kelley** or **Kellie**.

Kelsey (m/f) English name derived from the Old English Ceolsige, itself from the Old English *ceol* ('ship') and *sige* ('victory'), that has appeared on an occasional basis as a first name for both sexes, chiefly since the 1870s. Also found as **Kelsie** or **Kelcey**.

Kelvin (m) English name that made its debut in the 1920s, possibly under the influence of such names as CALVIN and MELVIN. It may have had its roots ultimately in the Old English words for 'ship' and 'friend'. The name is more common in Canada than elsewhere in the English-speaking world.

Kemp (m) English name derived from a surname based on the Middle English word *kempe* ('athlete' or 'wrestler'), itself descended from the Old English *kempa* ('warrior' or 'champion').

Ken *See* KENDALL; KENNETH; KENTON; KENYON.

Kena *See* KENINA.

Kendall (m) English name derived from that of Kendal in Cumbria and meaning 'valley of the River Kent'. It has been in occasional use as a first name since the middle of the 19th century. It is also possible that the name evolved from the place name Kendale (in Humberside), itself from the Old Norse *keld* ('spring'), or else from the Old Welsh name Cynnddelw. Also rendered as **Kendal** and commonly shortened to **Ken**.

Kendra *See* KENDRICK.

Kendrick (m) Welsh and Scottish name that was also taken up as a first name among English-speakers around the middle of the 19th century. The original Welsh source was probably the Old Welsh Cynwrig, possibly derived from the Old Celtic for 'high summit'. As used among English-speakers it probably evolved from the Old English Ceneric or Cyneric, itself from *cene* ('keen' or 'bold') and *ric* ('power'). **Kendra** is a rare feminine version.

Kenelm (m) English name descended from the Old English Cenelm, itself from the Old English *cene* ('bold' or 'keen') and *helm* ('helmet' or 'protection') and thus meaning 'bold defender'. It

was fairly common in England during the medieval period.

Kenia *See* KENINA.

Kenina (f) English first name that developed as a feminine version of KENNETH. It was once fairly common in Scotland, but is rarely encountered today. Also found as **Kena**, **Kenna** or **Kenia**.

Kennard (m) English name that evolved from an Old English name derived from *cene* ('keen' or 'bold') or *cyne* ('royal') and *weard* ('guard') or *heard* ('brave' or 'hardy'). It has made occasional reappearances as a first name in the 19th and 20th centuries. A historical variant is **Kenward**.

Kennedy (m) Irish, Scottish and English name that evolved as an Anglicization of the Irish Gaelic Cinneidigh, derived from *ceann* ('head') and *eidigh* ('ugly') and thus meaning 'ugly head', and also as an Anglicized version of the Scottish Gaelic Uarraig. It is occasionally applied to females. It was chosen as a first name by many Americans in the 1960s in tribute to the assassinated President John F. Kennedy (1917–63).

Kenneth (m) Scottish and English name that is thought to have evolved out of the Gaelic names Cinead (meaning 'born of fire') and Cainneach (meaning 'handsome one') and thus interpreted to mean 'fair and fiery'. It was taken up more widely by English-speakers around the middle of the

19th century. The name is commonly shortened to **Ken** or **Kenny**. Variant forms include the Welsh **Cenydd**. *See also* KENINA.

Kenny *See* KENNETH.

Kent (m) English name that may have had its origins in the name of the English county of Kent, itself originally meaning 'border'. It appears to have made its first appearance in the middle of the 20th century and has remained confined largely to Canada and the USA.

Kenton (m) English name possibly inspired by that of the river Kenn or else from an Old English place name derived from *cena* ('keen') or *cyne* ('royal') and *tun* ('settlement'). It is sometimes interpreted to mean 'royal manor'. It has received a boost in modern times as the name of a character in the long-running British radio soap opera *The Archers*.

Kenward *See* KENNARD.

Kenyon (m) English name derived from a place name in Lancashire, itself from the Old English for 'Ennion's mound'. Sometimes shortened to **Ken**.

Keren *See* KAREN.

Kerensa (f) Cornish name meaning 'love' or 'affection'. Variants include **Kerenza** and **Karenza**.

Keri *See* KERRY.

Kermit (m) English version of the Gaelic surname Mac Dhiarmaid (also the source of DERMOT) meaning 'son of Diarmad'. It was taken up by English-speakers in the USA in the 19th century. In modern times the name has become indelibly associated with Kermit the Frog, a puppet character in the 1970s US children's television series *The Muppet Show*.

Kerr (m) English name derived from a place name based on the Old Norse *kjarr* ('rough ground with brushwood').

Kerri/Kerrie *See* KERRY.

Kerry (m/f) English and Irish name probably derived from that of the Irish county of Kerry (meaning 'descendants of Ciar'). Having established itself as a favourite boys' name in Australia, it enjoyed a peak in popularity among English-speakers elsewhere between the 1960s and the 1980s, chiefly as a name for girls. Also found as **Kerrie**, **Kerri**, **Keri** or CERI.

Kerstin *See* KIRSTEN.

Keshia *See* KEZIA.

Kester (m) Scottish version of CHRISTOPHER. Fairly common in medieval times, it enjoyed a substantial revival in the 20th century.

Kestrel (f) English name derived from the Old French *cressele* ('rattle'). Popularly associated with the name of the bird of prey, it enjoyed a minor revival in the 20th century.

Kev/Kevan *See* KEVIN.

Kevin (m) Irish name derived from the Gaelic Caoimhin or

Caoimhinn, itself based on *caomh* ('comely' or 'fair'). The name was confined to Ireland until the early 20th century when it was first taken up by English-speakers on a wider basis. It reached a peak in popularity in the 1960s. Commonly shortened to **Kev**. Also found as **Kevan**.

Kez *See* KEZIA.

Kezia (m) Biblical name derived from the Hebrew Qetsiah, meaning 'cassia' (the name of the tree that produces cinnamon). It appears in the Bible and was consequently among the biblical names taken up by the Puritans in the 17th century. Sometimes shortened to **Kez**, **Kiz**, **Kizzie**, **Kizzy**, **Kissie** or **Kissy**. Also rendered as **Kezlah**, **Keshia**, **Cassia** or **Kasia**.

Keziah *See* KEZIA.

Khalid (m) Arabic name meaning 'eternal'. The name was borne in the 7th century by Khalid ibn al-Walid, who won the praise of Muhammad for his conquests on behalf of Islam. As a result of this association the name has long been one of the most popular of all Arabic names. **Khalida** is a rare feminine form of the name.

Kiaran *See* KIERAN.

Kicki *See* CHRISTINE.

Kid (m) English nickname that has gradually won acceptance as a legitimate first name, especially in the USA. Originally a nickname for any man notable for his youthful good looks, it evokes memories of the Wild West and the various

outlaws who bore the name, such as Billy the Kid. It remains confined largely to Canada and the USA.

Kiera *See* KIERAN.

Kieran (m) English version of the Gaelic **Ciaran**, itself derived from the Irish *ciar* ('black') and usually interpreted to mean 'little dark-haired one'. The name was largely confined to Ireland until the middle of the 20th century. Also rendered as **Kieron**, **Cieran**, **Keiran**, **Kiaran** or **Kyran**. **Kiera**, **Ciera**, **Ciara** and **Kiara** are rare feminine versions of the name.

Kilie *See* KYLIE.

Killian (m) Irish name that represents an Anglicization of the Irish Gaelic **Cillian**, meaning 'church'. Also encountered as **Kilian**.

Kim (m/f) English name that evolved as a diminutive form of KIMBERLEY. It emerged as a name in its own right towards the end of the 19th century, when it was usually given as a masculine name – as evidenced by Rudyard Kipling's novel *Kim* (1901). In Kipling's book it was explained that the full version of his hero's name was **Kimball** – probably derived from the Old English *cynebeald* ('kin bold'). From the 1920s the name became well known as a name for girls. Sometimes rendered as **Kym**. Diminutive forms of the name include **Kimmy** and **Kimmie**.

Kimball *See* KIM.

Kimberley (m/f) English name

derived from that of the South African town of Kimberley. The town was itself named after British statesman John Wodehouse, 1st Earl of Kimberley, whose family came from a place in England called Kimberley (meaning 'Cyneburga's wood'). It was taken up as a first name in celebration of the British army's relief of the South African Kimberley from siege in 1900 during the course of the Boer War. Like KIM, it was initially a boys' name but later came to be used for girls. Also encountered as **Kimberleigh** or **Kimberly**.

Kimmie/Kimmy *See* KIM.

King (m) English name derived from the royal title that has gradually won acceptance since the 19th century, chiefly in the USA. It evolved in parallel with such equivalent names as DUKE and EARL, presumably in the belief that the bearer would thereby be distinguished by aristocratic qualities. Its popularity since the 1960s owes much to the reputation of the US civil rights leader Martin Luther King (1929–68).

Kingsley (m) English name derived from place names in Cheshire, Hampshire and Staffordshire. The original place name meant 'king's wood' in Old English. It was taken up as a first name around the middle of the 19th century. Notable bearers of the name have included the British novelist Kingsley Amis (1922–95).

Kirby (m/f) English name derived from a place name based on the Old Norse *kirkja* ('church'). Its history as a first name dates from the 19th century.

Kirk (m) Scottish and English name derived from the Old Norse *kirkja* ('church') and formerly usually reserved for people living near a church. It enjoyed a peak in popularity in the 1980s. Well-known bearers of the name have included the US film actor Kirk Douglas (Issur Danielovitch Demsky; b.1916).

Kirsten (f) Scandinavian version of CHRISTINE that was taken up as a first name among English-speakers during the 19th century. It became increasingly frequent in the English-speaking world from the 1950s. Commonly shortened to KIRSTY. Also encountered as **Kirstin**.

Kirstie *See* KIRSTY.

Kirstin *See* KIRSTEN.

Kirsty (f) English name that is thought to have developed as a Scottish diminutive of CHRISTINE. Early instances of its appearance in the English-speaking world included its use in the form **Kirstie** in the Robert Louis Stevenson novel *The Weir of Hermiston* (1896). It won wide acceptance as a first name in its own right in the 1960s.

Kissie/Kissy *See* KEZIA.

Kit *See* CHRISTOPHER.

Kitty (f) English name that developed as a diminutive of CATHERINE and its various derivatives, such as KATHLEEN. It emerged as a familiar form of these names among English-speakers in the 18th century and has remained popular ever since (chiefly in the USA).

Kiz/Kizzie/Kizzy *See* KEZIA.

Kodey/Kody *See* CODY.

Korey/Korrie/Kory *See* COREY.

Kris *See* CHRISTOPHER.

Krishna (m) Indian name derived from the Sanskrit *krsna* ('black' or 'dark'). As the name of the most popular and widely venerated of all Hindu gods, it has unique religious significance for Indians. **Kistna**, **Kishen** and **Kannan** are variant forms.

Kurt (m) German name that evolved as a diminutive of Konrad (*see* CONRAD). It was taken up on a limited scale among English-speakers in the 1950s. Famous bearers of the name have included the US rock singer Kurt Cobain (1965–94). Also encountered as **Curt**.

Kyle (m/f) English name derived from a Scottish surname, itself based on a place name from Ayrshire derived from the Gaelic *caol* ('narrow'), as applied to narrow straits or channels. When it was first taken up by English-speakers in the 1940s it was usually bestowed upon boys, but from the 1960s it has appeared with increasing regularity as a name for girls, often being treated as a diminutive of KYLIE.

Kylie (f) Australian name that has become more widely accepted throughout the English-speaking world since the late 1970s. The name is popularly associated with the Aborigine word for 'boomerang' but it probably in fact evolved from KYLE or possibly KELLY. Its popularity in the UK in the 1980s owed much to the success of the Australian television actress and pop singer Kylie Minogue (b.1968). Occasionally rendered in the forms **Kyly**, **Kilie** or **Kyleigh**.

Kym *See* KIM.

Kyran *See* KIERAN.

reserved for settlers from Norway. Another derivation suggests the name came from the Gaelic *laochail* ('warlike'). The name has retained its Scottish associations but is also popular in Australia and Canada. Sometimes shortened to **Lachie** or, in Canada, to **Lockie**. A rare feminine version is **Lachina**.

Lachtna (m) Irish name derived from the Gaelic for 'milk-coloured'. It features in Irish legend as the name of an ancestor of King Brian Boru.

Lacy *See* LACEY.

Laelia (f) Roman name meaning 'cheerful' or 'chatty'. Also found as a variant of AURELIA. It was borne by a 5th-century Irish saint and taken up by English-speakers in the 19th century. Also found as **Lelia** or **Lela**.

Laetitia *See* LETITIA.

Laila *See* LEILA.

Laird (m) Scottish name meaning 'land-owner'. It has made rare appearances as a first name, mostly in the USA.

Lal *See* LALAGE.

Lala *See* HELEN; LALAGE.

Labhrainn/Labhras *See* LAURENCE.

Lacey (m/f) English surname that has made occasional appearances as a first name since medieval times. The original source of the surname was a Norman place name, Lassy in Calvados. When used as a feminine name it is often assumed that there is a link with the ordinary vocabulary word 'lace'. Also found as **Lacy**, usually when adopted as a masculine name.

Lachlan (m) English version of the Scottish **Lachlann** or **Lochlann**, which means 'land of lochs' or 'land of fjords' and was originally

Lalage (f) Greek name derived from *lalagein* ('to chatter' or 'to babble'). Usually pronounced 'lalagee', it featured in the *Odes* of Horace and has appeared sporadically among English-speakers since the 19th century. Diminutive forms include **Lal**, **Lala**, **Lallie** and **Lally**.

Lalla/Lallie/Lally *See* EULALIA; LALAGE.

Lambert (m) English, French, German and Dutch name derived from the Old German *lant* ('land') and *berht* ('famous' or 'bright') and thus meaning 'famous land-owner'. The name came to England with the Normans and was fairly common in medieval times, sometimes as **Lambard**. Notable bearers of the name have included the English imposter Lambert Simnel (1475–1535). Sometimes shortened to BERT.

Lana (f) English name derived either via **Alana** from ALAN, meaning 'shining', or else as an independent name without any particular meaning. It seems to have made its first appearance, in the USA, in the 1920s and became well known in the 1940s as the name of the US actress Lana Turner (Julia Turner; 1920–95).

Lance English name that exists either as a diminutive of LANCELOT or as a name in its own right, derived from the Old German *lant* ('land') or possibly from the French *lance* ('lance'). It was recorded in use in England by the 13th century, when it also appeared as **Launce**, and was revived towards the end of the 19th century.

Lancelot (m) English name possibly derived from the Old French *l'ancelle* ('servant') or else from an unknown Celtic name. Also rendered as **Launcelot**, it became famous as the name of the most prominent of King Arthur's

Knights of the Round Table. It is rare today. Commonly shortened to LANCE or, formerly, to **Launce**.

Lanty *See* LAURENCE.

Laoise *See* LUCY.

Lara (f) English version of the Russian Larissa, which itself is thought to have come from the name of an ancient Greek city (meaning 'citadel') or else from the Latin for 'cheerful'. Also found as a variant of LAURA, the name was popularized by a character called Lara in the film *Doctor Zhivago* (1965), based on the novel (1957) by Boris Pasternak.

Laraine *See* LORRAINE.

Lark (f) English name derived from the name of the songbird. It has made rare appearances among English-speakers since the early 20th century.

Larrie/Larry *See* LAURENCE.

Lars (m) Scandinavian variant of LAURENCE. It emerged as one of the most popular of all masculine names in Scandinavia in the 1960s and has on occasion been imported into the English-speaking world.

Latasha (f) English name apparently resulting from a combination of LATISHA and NATASHA. It first established itself as a favourite within the Black population of the USA in the early 1980s and is just one of several similar names that were created by adding the prefix 'La-' to existing names (others including **Latoya**).

Latisha (f) English name of relatively recent invention, possibly
influenced by LETITIA. Sometimes
shortened to **Tisha**. *See also*
LATASHA.

Latoya *See* LATASHA.

Launce/Launcelot *See* LANCE;
LANCELOT.

Laura (f) English, Spanish and
Italian name derived from the
Latin *laurus* ('laurel' or 'bay'). In
ancient Rome victorious emperors
wore crowns of laurel leaves and
the name thus became associated
with 'victory' or 'triumph'. The
love poetry that the 14th-century
Italian poet Petrarch addressed to
'Laura' helped make the name
popular in medieval Europe. It
made its debut among English-
speakers around the 16th century.
Laurie (or **Lori**) and **Lolly** are
familiar forms of the name. **Lora**,
Loreen, **Laurene**, **Lorena**, **Laurice**,
Laurissa, **Laurina**, **Laurinda**,
Lorelle, **Lorinda** and **Lorita** are
among diminutive versions. *See
also* LAUREN; LAURETTA.

Lauraine *See* LORRAINE.

Laureen *See* LAURA.

Laurel (f) English name, derived
from the name of the tree, that
has emerged since the middle of
the 20th century. The early development of the name is thought to
have been influenced by LAURA
and it is sometimes considered to
be a straightforward variant of
that name. Also found as **Laurelle**.
Laurie can appear as a shortened
form.

Lauren (f) English name that
developed as a variant of LAURA.
It appeared with increasing frequency among English-speakers
from the 1960s, familiar from the
name of the US film actress
Lauren Bacall (Betty Joan Perske;
b.1924). Occasionally encountered
as **Loren** (the usual spelling when
the name is, rarely, given to boys).

Laurence (m) English name
derived from the Roman
Laurentius, which means 'man
from Laurentum' (Laurentum
being a town in Latium). The
name was fairly common in medieval England and Ireland, also
appearing (from the 16th century)
as **Lawrence**, and was revived in
the 19th century. The 'w' spelling
is now usual in the USA and
Canada. Commonly shortened to
Larry (or **Larrie**). Other abbreviated versions include **Lauri**, **Laurie**
and **Lawrie** (or **Lori**) as well as
Loren, **Lorin**, **Lorrin**, **Lol**, **Laz** and
the Irish **Lanty**. Variants in other
languages include the Irish Gaelic
Labhras and the Scottish Gaelic
Labhrainn. **Laurencia** and
Laurentia are rare feminine versions. *See also* LARS.

Laurencia *See* LAURENCE.

Laurene *See* LAURA.

Laurentia *See* LAURENCE.

Lauretta (f) Diminutive form of
LAURA. It made its first appearances
in medieval times but did not
appear with any frequency among
English-speakers until the middle
of the 19th century. Sometimes

shortened to **Laurie** or **Lorrie**. Variants include **Lorette** and **Laurette**.

Laurette See LAURETTA.

Lauri/Laurie See LAURA; LAUREL; LAURENCE; LAURETTA.

Laurina/Laurinda/Laurissa See LAURA.

Lavena See LAVINIA.

Lavender (f) English name derived from that of the scented plant. Like a number of other flower names it was taken up by English-speakers towards the end of the 19th century. It is very rare today.

Laverne (f) English name that resulted from the addition of the prefix 'La-' to the established **Verne** (*see* VERNON). This was one of a series of names that appeared by a similar process in the middle of the 20th century, chiefly in the USA. The fact that there was an ancient Italian goddess of thieves called Laverna is almost certainly coincidental.

Lavina See LAVINIA.

Lavinia (f) Roman name derived from that of the ancient Roman town of Lavinium (itself of unknown origin). According to legend, Lavinia was the name of the wife of Aeneas, and thus that of the mother of the Roman people. Long considered an aristocratic name, it was revived among English-speakers in the 18th century. Sometimes shortened to

Vinnie or **Vinny**. **Lavina** and **Lavena** are variant forms.

Lawrence/Lawrie See LAURENCE.

Lawson (m) English surname that was adopted as a first name around the middle of the 19th century. The surname itself evolved from Law, a nickname derived from Lawrence.

Layla (f) Arabic name meaning 'wine' or 'intoxication'. The name became widely familiar throughout the Arabic world through the poetry of Qays ibn-al-Mulawwah (d.688), whose works were often addressed to his cousin Layla. Centuries later the name enjoyed a new lease of life through the Eric Clapton hit single 'Layla' (1970). *See also* LEILA.

Layton See LEIGHTON.

Laz See LAURENCE.

Lazarus (m) Biblical name derived via the Greek Lazaros and the Aramaic Lazar from the Hebrew Eleazar (meaning 'God has helped' or 'God is my help'). It appears in the Bible and made sporadic appearances among English-speakers from the 17th century but is rare today outside the Jewish community.

Lea See LEAH; LEE.

Leah (f) Hebrew name meaning 'antelope', 'gazelle' or even 'cow' – although another derivation suggests it means 'languid' or 'weary'. It appears in the Bible as the name of Jacob's first wife and was taken up by English Puritans in the 17th century. It has continued in irregular use ever since. Variants include **Lea**, LEE and LIA.

Leander (m) Roman version of the Greek Leandros, itself derived from *leon* ('lion') and *andros* ('man') and thus meaning 'strong brave man'. The name is famous from the Greek myth of Hero and Leander, in which the youthful Leander drowns while swimming the Hellespont in order to visit his lover Hero. The name has enjoyed a limited revival in the 20th century, chiefly among Black Americans.

Leanna/Leanne See LIANNE.

Leanora/Leanore See LEONORA.

Leda (f) Greek name possibly derived from the Lycian for 'woman'. The name is best known from the Greek myth of Leda and the Swan, in which Leda is seduced by Zeus in the guise of a swan.

Lee (m/f) English name derived from the Old English *leah* ('wood', 'meadow' or 'clearing'). It has been employed as a first name for boys since the 19th century and for girls since the early 20th century. In the USA the name was promoted by association with the Confederate general Robert E. Lee (1807–70). Also found as **Lea** or **Leigh** (usually treated as a feminine version of the name, although Australians tend to treat it as a masculine form). *See also* LEAH.

Lee-Ann See LIANNE.

Leesa See LISA.

Leigh See LEE.

Leighton (m) English name derived from a place name meaning 'herb garden'. Pronounced 'layton', it has been in use since the late 19th century. Also found as **Layton** or **Leyton**.

Leila (f) Arabic name meaning 'dark-haired', 'swarthy' or 'dark-eyed'. As **Leilah** it features in Persian legend. Lord Byron and Edward Bulwer-Lytton both made use of the name in their writings, promoting its use from the 19th century. Also found as **Laila**, **Lela** or **Lila**. *See also* LAYLA.

Lela See LEILA; LAELIA.

Leland (m) English surname derived from the Old English *laege* ('fallow') and *land* ('land') that has also been in use as a first name, particularly in the USA, since the 19th century.

Lelia See LAELIA.

Lemmy See LEMUEL.

Lemuel (m) Hebrew name meaning 'devoted to God'. It features in the Bible and was taken up by English-speakers in the middle of the 19th century. The most famous bearer of the name is Lemuel Gulliver in Jonathan Swift's *Gulliver's Travels* (1725). Commonly shortened to **Lemmy**.

Len See LENNOX; LEONARD; LIONEL.

Lena (f) English, Scottish, German, Dutch and Scandinavian name that exists as a diminutive of various longer names ending

'-lena' or '-lina', such as HELENA. It was taken up by English-speakers in the middle of the 19th century. Also found as LINA.

Lenda See LINDA.

Lennard/Lennie See LEONARD.

Lennox (m) Scottish and English surname that has also been taken up as an occasional first name. Also found as **Lenox**, it is particularly associated with Scotland, where there is an earldom of the same name, referring to a district near Loch Lomond. Sometimes shortened to **Len** or **Lenny**.

Lenny See LENNOX; LEONARD; LIONEL.

Lenora See LEONORA.

Lenore See ELEANOR.

Lenox See LENNOX.

Leo (m) English name derived from the Latin *leo* ('lion'). It made its first appearances among English-speakers in the medieval period and enjoyed a peak in popularity in the late 19th and early 20th centuries. Feminine versions of the name include **Lea** and **Leola**. See also LEON; LEOPOLD.

Leolin/Leoline See LLEWELLYN.

Leon (m) English, German and Irish Gaelic name derived from LEO and thus meaning 'lion'. It became fairly common among English-speakers in the 19th century but is today rare outside the Jewish community, where it is used in remembrance of the dying words of Jacob, in which he likened the kingdom of Judah to a lion. **Leonie** and **Leona** are femi-

nine forms. See also LEONTINE; LIONEL.

Leona See LEON.

Leonard (m) English name derived via Old French from the Old German *leon* ('lion') and *hard* ('strong' or 'brave') and thus meaning 'brave as a lion'. It came to England with the Normans and was revived in the 19th century. Also encountered as **Lennard**. Common abbreviations of the name are **Len**, **Lennie** and **Lenny**.

Leonie See LEON.

Leonora (f) English name that developed via **Eleanora** as a variant of ELEANOR. It made its first appearances among English-speakers in the 19th century, promoted by characters of the same name in three celebrated operas – Beethoven's *Fidelio* (1806, 1814), Donizetti's *La Favorita* (1840) and Verdi's *Il Trovatore* (1853). Sometimes shortened to **Nora** or **Norah**. Variants include **Leanora**, **Leanore**, **Lenore** and **Lenora**.

Leontine (f) English version of the French Léontine, itself derived ultimately from the Roman Leontius – a derivation of the Latin *leo* ('lion'). Alternatively, the name is considered to have resulted from the combination of LEONORA and **Clementine** (*see* CLEMENTINA). Also found as **Leontyne**, it was taken up by English-speakers in the 19th century.

Leontyne See LEONTINE.

Leopold (m) German and English

Leroy

name derived from the Old German Liutpold, meaning 'of a bold people'. Popular among European royal families, it was irregularly taken up by English-speakers around the middle of the 19th century but is now usually considered to be a non-English name. Commonly shortened to **Leo** or, more rarely, to **Poldie**.

Leroy (m) English name derived from the Old French *le roy* ('the king'). Used initially as a nickname, it is thought to have been given initially to royal servants. It was taken up as a first name in the USA in the 19th century and in the UK in the 1960s, chiefly among the Black population. Variant forms include **LeRoy** and **LeRoi**. *See also* DELROY; ELROY.

Les *See* LESLIE; LESTER.

Lesley *See* LESLIE.

Leslie (m/f) Scottish name derived from a place name (Lesslyn in Aberdeenshire) possibly based on the Gaelic *leas cuilinn* ('garden of hollies'). Also encountered as **Lesley**, it was first recorded as a first name in the 18th century, promoted by the Robert Burns poem 'Bonnie Lesley'. It reached a peak in the 1950s and 1960s, since when it has held its own as a name for girls but gone into decline as a boys' name. Although the spelling Lesley is now chiefly reserved for girls, Leslie is still used for both sexes. Commonly shortened to **Les**.

Lester (m) English name derived

from a place name (now Leicester), itself a combination of a tribal name of unknown meaning and *caester* ('Roman fort'). It appears to have made its debut as a first name around the middle of the 19th century.

Leta (f) English name derived from the Latin *letus* ('glad').

Letitia (f) English name derived from the Latin *laetitia* ('gladness' or 'joy'). Also rendered as **Lecia**, **Laetitia** or **Leticia**, it was taken up by English-speakers during the medieval period and has continued in use into relatively modern times. Commonly shortened to **Lettie**, **Letty**, **Tish** or **Tisha**. *See also* LETTICE.

Lettice (f) English name derived from LETITIA. This diminutive form of the name has medieval roots and was the more popular form of the name between the 12th and 17th centuries. It is now rare. Sometimes shortened to **Lettie** or **Letty**.

Lettie/Letty *See* ALETHEA; LETITIA; LETTICE.

Levi (m) Jewish name derived from the Hebrew *lewi* ('associated', 'attached' or 'pledged'). It features in the Bible and was in use among English Jews as early as the 17th century. Also rendered as **Levy**.

Levy *See* LEVI.

Lew *See* LEWIS.

Lewella *See* LLEWELLYN.

Lewin (m) English name derived

from the Old English for 'beloved friend'.

Lewis (m) English version of the French LOUIS, also encountered in Wales as an Anglicization of LLEWELLYN. First recorded among English-speakers during the medieval period, it enjoyed a peak in popularity in the 1990s. Commonly shortened to **Lew**.

Lex (m) English name that is thought to have evolved as a diminutive of ALEXANDER, influenced perhaps by REX. The name made its first appearances among English-speakers in the 19th century. **Lexie** and **Lexy** are familiar versions of the name. A rare feminine variant is the English and Scottish **Lexine**.

Lexie/Lexine/Lexy *See* LEX.

Leyton *See* LEIGHTON.

Lia (f) Variant form of LEAH. Since the 1950s the name has also been encountered among English-speakers as a diminutive of various longer names, such as AMELIA and DELIA.

Liam (m) Irish variant of WILLIAM, via the Gaelic **Uilliam**. Long popular among the Irish, it has appeared with increasing frequency elsewhere in the English-speaking world since the 1930s. Notable bearers of the name have included the Northern Ireland actor Liam Neeson (b.1952) and the British rock musician Liam Gallagher (b.1972).

Liana (f) French name derived from JULIANA or from various other names ending in '-liana'. It is rare among English-speakers, who generally prefer the related name LIANNE.

Lianne (f) English name that evolved either out of the French Julianne (*see* JULIAN) or through the combination of LEE and ANNE. It was taken up by English-speakers in the 1940s and has since become fairly popular in Australia. **Leanne** is a common variant form. **Leanna**, **Lee-Ann** and **Leigh-Ann** are less common versions.

Lib/Libby *See* ELIZABETH; OLIVIA.

Liddy *See* LYDIA.

Lil *See* LILIAN; LILY.

Lilac (f) English name derived from that of the scented shrub. The name of the plant came ultimately via French and Spanish from the Arabic *lilak*, itself derived from the Persian *nilak* ('bluish').

Lilian (f) English name that is thought to have developed from ELIZABETH or else through the combination of LILY and ANNE. It was first recorded among English-speakers towards the end of the 16th century and enjoyed a peak in popularity towards the end of the 19th century. Also found (especially in the USA) as **Lillian**. Commonly shortened to **Lil** or **Lily**. Variants include the Scottish **Lilias** or **Lillias**.

Lilias *See* LILIAN.

Lilith (f) Hebrew name variously interpreted to mean 'night monster', 'storm goddess' or 'screech owl'. In medieval times it was commonly believed that Adam had had a wife called Lilith before Eve but that she had been turned into a hideous demon for refusing to obey her husband. As a result of its biblical history, the name was not taken up as a first name until the 20th century, by which time Lilith was being taken up as a variant of LILY.

Lilla/Lillah *See* LILY.

Lillian/Lillias *See* LILIAN.

Lily (f) English name derived from the flower, itself a symbol of purity. Also encountered occasionally as a diminutive form of ELIZABETH. It was taken up around the middle of the 19th century. Familiar forms of the name include **Lil**, **Lilly** and **Lillie**. Other variants include **Lilla**, **Lillah**, **Lila** and **Tiger Lily** – borrowed from a character in J. M. Barrie's *Peter Pan* (1904). *See also* LILIAN.

Lin *See* LINDA; LINDSAY; LYNN.

Lina (f) English name that developed as a diminutive of **Adelina**, **Carolina** and other names ending '-lina' around the middle of the 19th century. It is sometimes also encountered as a variant of LENA.

Lincoln (m) English name derived from that of the city of Lincoln (meaning 'lake settlement'). It is more common in the USA than elsewhere, being bestowed in many cases in honour of President Abraham Lincoln (1809–65).

Linda (f) English name that

appears to have developed in the late 19th century as a diminutive form of BELINDA and other names with similar '-linda' endings. During the 1950s and 1960s it ranked among the top five favourite names across the English-speaking world. Occasionally rendered as **Lynda** or **Lenda** and sometimes shortened to **Lin**, **Lynn** or **Lynne**. **Lindie**, **Lyndi** and **Lindy** are diminutive forms of the name.

Linden (f) English name that appears to have developed as a 20th-century variant of LINDA. It is often assumed that it came from the Old English *lind* ('lime tree') and *dun* ('hill'), but this is probably a later derivation (*see* LYNDON). Also found as **Lindon**.

Lindon *See* LINDEN; LYNDON.

Lindsay (m/f) English name derived from that of Lindsey in Lincolnshire, meaning 'island of Lincoln' or 'wetland belonging to Lincoln'. Also rendered as **Lindsey**, it was taken up as a first name in the 19th century, reserved initially for males. Since the 1930s it has been used with increasing frequency as a name for girls rather than boys. Sometimes shortened to **Lin** or **Lyn**. Also rendered as **Linsay**, **Linsey**, **Linzi**, **Lyndsay**, **Lynsay**, **Lindsie** or **Lynsey**.

Lindsey *See* LINDSAY.

Lindy *See* LINDA.

Linette *See* LYNETTE.

Linford (m) English name derived from a place name in Berkshire, itself from the Old English *lin* ('flax') or *lind* ('lime tree') and *ford* ('ford'). Well-known bearers of the name have included the British athlete Linford Christie (b.1960).

Linnet (f) English name derived from that of the songbird, or else encountered as a variant form of LYNETTE or of the Welsh **Eiluned**. The bird name came ultimately from the Old French *linotte*, itself from *lin* ('flax'), the seeds of which are the bird's usual food.

Linnette *See* LYNETTE.

Linton (m) English name derived from a place name based on the Old English *lin* ('flax' or 'cotton') or *lind* ('lime tree') and *tun* ('enclosure'). It is commonest within the Black community in the UK.

Linus (m) English name derived from the Greek Linos, itself possibly derived from *lineos* ('blond' or 'flaxen-haired'). The name features in the Bible and today is more familiar in the USA than elsewhere in the English-speaking world. Notable bearers of the name in real life have included the US chemist Linus Pauling (1901–94).

Linzi *See* LINDSAY.

Lionel (m) English name derived via French from LEON and meaning 'little lion'. It was first recorded in use among English-speakers in the medieval period but remained relatively unknown until the early 20th century. Sometimes shortened to **Len** or **Lenny**.

Lis *See* FELICITY.

Lisa (f) English name that developed as a diminutive of ELIZABETH. It emerged as a popular first name in its own right in the 1960s. Also found as **Liza** and, rarely, **Leesa**. Notable bearers of the name in its various forms have included the US actress and singer Liza Minnelli (b.1946). Diminutive forms include **Liz**, **Lizzie**, **Lisette** and **Lysette**.

Lisbet/Lisbeth *See* ELIZABETH.

Lisette *See* ELIZABETH; LISA.

Lisha (f) English name that developed as a diminutive form of such names as DELICIA and **Felicia**.

Liss *See* FELICITY.

Lissa *See* MELISSA.

Lissie *See* FELICITY.

Lita *See* LOLITA.

Livia (f) Roman name possibly derived from the Latin *lividus* ('leaden-coloured' or 'bluish'). It is also encountered as a diminutive form of OLIVIA. It featured in William Shakespeare's *Romeo and Juliet* (1595) and made further appearances in English literature from the 16th century onwards. **Livy** and **Livvy** are familiar forms of the name.

Livvy/Livy *See* LIVIA.

Liz/Liza *See* ELIZABETH; LISA.

Lizbeth *See* ELIZABETH.

Lizzie/Lizzy *See* ELIZABETH; LISA.

Lleu (m) Welsh name meaning 'bright' or 'shining'. It was borne by a Celtic Irish god and appears in the *Mabinogion*. It was revived among Welsh-speakers in the 20th century.

Llew/Llewella *See* LLEWELLYN.

Llewellyn (m) Welsh name often thought to mean 'leader' or else to be derived from the Welsh *llyw* ('lion') and *eilun* ('likeness') but probably, in fact, descended from the much older Old Celtic name Lugobelinos (of uncertain meaning). Rendered originally as **Llywelyn**, it has retained its strong association with Wales. Sometimes shortened to **Lew**, **Lyn** or **Llew**. **Lewella** and **Llewella** are feminine versions of the name. Variant forms include **Leolin** and **Leoline**.

Lloyd (m) English name derived from a Welsh surname that in turn evolved as a nickname meaning 'grey' or 'grey-haired'. It was taken up by English-speakers in the early 20th century, when it became widely known from the name of Prime Minister David Lloyd George (1863–1945). Occasionally rendered as **Loyd**. *See also* FLOYD.

Llywelyn *See* LLEWELLYN.

Lo *See* LOIS; LOLA; LOLITA.

Lochlann/Lockie *See* LACHLAN.

Logan (m) Scottish name derived from a place name (from Ayrshire), possibly from the Gaelic for 'hollow'. It remains confined largely to Scotland.

Lois (f) Biblical name possibly derived from the Greek *loion* ('better' or 'good') but also encountered as a diminutive form of LOUISA or LOUISE. The name features in the Bible and was taken up by English-speakers in the 17th century. Since the early 20th century the name has been found more frequently in Canada and the USA than elsewhere. Sometimes shortened to **Lo**.

Lol *See* LAURENCE.

Lola (f) Spanish and English name that developed alongside LOLITA as a diminutive of DOLORES. Long established across the Spanish-speaking world, it has made occasional appearances among English-speakers since the 19th century. Sometimes shortened to **Lo**. Variants include the rare **Lolicia**.

Lolicia *See* LOLA.

Lolita (f) Spanish name that developed alongside LOLA as a diminutive of DOLORES. It first entered English-speaking use in the USA in the 19th century. Today it is closely associated with Vladimir Nabokov's novel *Lolita* (1955). Commonly shortened to **Lo** or **Lita**.

Lolly *See* LAURA.

Loman (m) Irish name derived from *lomm* ('bare'). It was borne by several early Irish saints.

Lonan (m) Irish name derived from *lon* ('blackbird'). It was borne by a number of little-known Irish saints.

Lonnie (m) English name that variously developed as an Anglicized diminutive of Alonzo and as a variant of **Lennie** (*see* LEONARD). Also found as **Lonny**, it appears to have been a 20th-century invention. Famous bearers of the name have included the Scottish pop musician Lonnie Donegan (1931–2002). Sometimes shortened to **Lon**.

Lora *See* LAURA.

Loraine *See* LORRAINE.

Lorcan *See* LAURENCE.

Loreen/Lorelle *See* LAURA.

Loren *See* LAUREN; LAURENCE.

Lorena *See* LAURA.

Loreto (f) English and Irish name derived ultimately from an Italian place name. It was to Loreto in central Italy that angels were supposed to have carried the Holy House of the Virgin from Nazareth – hence the popularity of the name among Roman Catholics.

Loretta/Lorette *See* LAURETTA.

Lori *See* LAURA; LORRAINE.

Lorin *See* LAURENCE.

Lorinda *See* LAURA.

Loris (f) English name of obscure origins, but possibly a diminutive form of LAURA. It seems to have made its first appearance in the latter half of the 20th century, winning particular approval in Australia.

Lorn *See* LORNE.

Lorna (f) English name that is thought to have been invented by the British novelist R. D. Blackmore in his romantic novel *Lorna Doone* (1869). According to Blackmore, the name was based on the Scottish place name Lorn (in Argyll). *See also* LORNE.

Lorne (m) English name that may have developed out of LORNA or may simply share the same origin in the Scottish place name Lorn (in Argyll). It is particularly popular in Canada and other countries with strong Scottish connections. Also found as **Lorn**.

Lorraine (f) English name derived from a Scottish surname that may in turn have been borrowed from the eastern French province of Lorraine. It is often assumed to be a variant of LAURA. The name may have become familiar to English-speakers in the 16th century through Mary Queen of Scots' mother, Mary of Lorraine. Also rendered as **Lauraine**, **Laraine**, **Lorain**, **Loraine** or **Lorayne**. Familiar forms of the name are **Lori** and **Lorri**.

Lorri *See* LORRAINE.

Lorrie *See* LAURETTA.

Lorrin *See* LAURENCE.

Lotta/Lottie/Lotty *See* CHARLOTTE.

Lotus (f) English name referring to the lotus fruit of Greek mythology, which was reputed to induce a state of indolent forgetfulness in those who ate it.

Lou *See* LOUIS; LOUISA; LOUISE.

Louella (f) English name derived from the combination of Lou (from LOUISA or LOUISE) and the feminine suffix '-ella' (*see* ELLA). It was taken up by English-speakers in the 19th century and remains in circulation chiefly in the USA. Notable bearers of the name have included the US Hollywood gossip columnist Louella Parsons (1880–1972). Also rendered as **Luella**.

Louie *See* LOUIS; LOUISA; LOUISE.

Louis (m) French name derived from the German Ludwig, itself from the Old German *hlut* ('famous') and *wig* ('warrior'). The name was Anglicized as LEWIS after it came to England in the medieval period. The French form of the name, however, made a comeback among English-speakers from the 18th century. When spelt Louis, the name is still usually pronounced in the French manner, without the final 's' being sounded. Commonly shortened to **Lou** or **Louie**. *See also* ALOYSIUS; LOUISA; LOUISE.

Louisa (f) Feminine form of LOUIS, adopted by English-speakers in the 18th century. A popular name in the late 19th century, it has been eclipsed since the early 20th century by LOUISE. Also found as **Louiza** or **Luisa**. Commonly shortened to **Lou** or **Louie**. LULU is a familiar form of the name, of German origin. *See also* LOIS.

Louise (f) Feminine variant of LOUIS that has largely replaced LOUISA among English-speakers since the early 20th century. This French version of the name seems to have made its first appearance among English-speakers in the 17th century. At a peak in the USA in the 1920s, it increased in frequency in the UK from the 1950s. Commonly shortened to **Lou** or **Louie** and occasionally to LULU. **Luise** is a variant of German origin.

Loveday (f) English name referring to the medieval 'lovedays' on which disputes were traditionally settled. First recorded in use during the early 13th century, the name was usually reserved for children born on one of these days. Its modern use is largely confined to Cornwall (where it may also be found as **Lowdy**).

Lovell (m) English name derived from an Old French nickname Louvel ('wolf-cub' or 'little wolf'). Its use among English-speakers dates back to at least the 11th century. Shortened to **Love**, it enjoyed some popularity among English Puritans during the 17th century. It has strong Scottish connections. Sometimes rendered as **Lowell**, **Lovel** or **Lovet**.

Lowell *See* LOVELL.

Lowri (f) Welsh name representing a regional variant of LAURA. Also encountered as **Lowry**.

Loyd *See* LLOYD.

Lu *See* LULU.

Luana *See* LUANNE.

Luanne (f) English and Italian first name apparently without any specific meaning. Also found as **Luana** (or **Luanna**), it was taken up as a first name by English- and Italian-speakers after it was used (as the name of a Polynesian maiden) in the King Vidor film *The Bird of Paradise* (1932), for which it appears to have been invented.

Lucan (m) Irish name derived from a place name meaning 'place of elms'.

Lucas (m) English name derived either from the surname or else from the Roman Lucas, also the source of LUKE. It may have come ultimately from the Roman place name Lucania. During the medieval period it appeared in the Authorized Version of the New Testament as a formal version of Luke. It came into vogue among English-speakers in the 1930s.

Lucasta (f) English name invented by the English poet Richard Lovelace (1618–57). It is thought that the original Lucasta of Lovelace's poem 'Lucasta' (1649) was probably called LUCY or else bore the surname LUCAS.

Luce *See* LUCIA; LUCY.

Lucetta (f) English name that developed as a diminutive form of LUCIA or LUCY. It would appear to be of mainly historical interest, with records of its use among English-speakers going back to the 16th century but with relatively

few appearances since then. A variant form is the French **Lucette**.

Lucette *See* LUCETTA.

Lucia (f) Roman name (variously pronounced 'loocheea' or 'loosia') that developed as a feminine version of LUCIUS. Because of its meaning it is thought that the name was originally reserved for children born at dawn. It was taken up by English-speakers towards the end of the 19th century, often as an alternative to LUCY. Sometimes shortened to **Luce**.

Lucian (m) English version of the French Lucien and the Italian Luciano, both descendants of the Roman LUCIUS. As Lucianus, the name appeared among English-speakers as early as the 12th century. **Luciana** and **Lucienne** are rare feminine forms.

Luciana *See* LUCIAN.

Lucie *See* LUCY.

Lucienne *See* LUCIAN.

Lucille (f) French variant of the Roman Lucilla, itself a derivative of LUCIA. The name was in use among English-speakers as early as the 16th century. The modern form of the name, Lucille, took over in the 19th century. Occasionally rendered as **Lucile**. The usual abbreviated form of the name is LUCY.

Lucinda (f) English name that developed as a variant of LUCIA or LUCY. The earliest records of the name go back to Cervantes' classic work *Don Quixote* (1605). It became a popular choice of first name among English-speakers in the 18th century. It has always been considered an aristocratic name. Sometimes shortened to Lucy or to CINDY, **Cindi** or **Sindy**.

Lucius (m) Roman name derived from the Latin *lux* ('light'). It appears in the Bible and made its first appearances in English in the 16th century. LUCKY is a familiar diminutive variant. In Ireland the name is sometimes used as an Anglicized form of the Irish LACHTNA. *See also* LUCIA.

Lucky (m/f) English name that developed either as a nickname or else as a familiar derivative of such names as FELICITY, LUCIUS, LUCY or LUKE. It has made irregular appearances as a first name since the early 20th century, chiefly in the USA. One well-known bearer of the name was the notorious US gangster Charles 'Lucky' Luciano (1897–1962).

Lucretia (f) Roman name that developed as a feminine form of the masculine Lucretius, itself possibly derived from LUCIUS but otherwise of unknown origin. Notable bearers of the name have included the notorious Lucretia Borgia (1480–1519). The name appeared irregularly among English-speakers between the 16th and 18th centuries.

Lucy (f) English version of the Roman LUCIA. It also exists as a diminutive of LUCILLE or LUCINDA. It was taken up by English-speakers during the medieval period and

became increasingly popular from the 18th century. Familiar forms of the name include **Luce**, LUCKY and LULU. Variants include LUCETTA, **Lucette**, the French **Lucie** and the Irish Gaelic **Laoise**.

Ludo *See* LUDOVIC.

Ludovic (m) English version of the Roman Ludovicus, also found in Scotland as an Anglicization of the Gaelic Maol Domhnaich, meaning 'devotee of the Lord'. It was taken up by English-speakers in the 19th century, becoming commonest in Scotland, where it is particularly associated with the Grant clan. Commonly abbreviated to **Ludo**.

Luella *See* LOUELLA.

Luise *See* LOUISE.

Luke (m) English name derived ultimately from the Greek Loukas, meaning 'man from Lucania' (Lucania being an area in southern Italy). It features in the Bible as the name of the author of the third gospel. The name came to England with the Normans, emerging in its modern form around the 12th century. LUCKY is a familiar form of the name.

Lulu (f) German name that developed as a diminutive form of Luise, the German version of LOUISE. Also found in use among English-speakers as a familiar form of LUCY, it is a relatively recent introduction to the English-speaking world, of 20th-century origin. It is best known in the UK from the pop singer Lulu (Marie Lawrie; b.1948). **Lu** is a diminutive form.

Luther (m) German name derived from the Old German *liut* ('people') and *heri* ('warrior') and thus meaning 'people's warrior' that was adopted among English-speakers from the 19th century. As the surname of the German religious reformer Martin Luther (1483–1546) it has always had a special significance for Protestants. Following the assassination of the Black US civil rights leader Martin Luther King (1929–68) the name was taken up by many Black Americans.

Lyall (m) Scottish name derived from the Old Norse name Liulfr (possibly meaning 'wolf') that has also made occasional appearances as a first name, chiefly among Scots. *See also* LYLE.

Lydia (f) English name derived ultimately from a Greek name meaning 'woman of Lydia' (a region in Asia Minor). It features in the Bible as the name of one of St Paul's converts. **Liddy** is a familiar form of the name.

Lyle (m) English name derived from the French *de l'isle* ('of the island'). As a surname it was originally used to refer to someone who came from any raised area of land, not just islands. Its popularity in Scotland may have been influenced by confusion with the otherwise unconnected Scottish name LYALL.

Lyn *See* LINDSAY; LLEWELLYN; LYNN.

Lynda *See* LINDA.

Lyndon (m) English name derived from a place name (from Rutland) based on the Old English *lind* ('linden' or 'lime tree') and *dun* ('hill'). Awareness of the name in modern times is due in part to US President Lyndon Baines Johnson (1908–73). Also found as **Lindon**. *See also* LINDEN.

Lynette (f) English name that developed as a diminutive of LYNN. The addition of the '-ette' ending suggests a French influence. Also found as **Lynnette**, it was taken up by English-speakers during the 19th century and was promoted by Alfred, Lord Tennyson's poem 'Gareth and Lynette' from *The Idylls of the King* (1859–85). The name is popularly linked with the French *lune* ('moon') and the songbird called the linnet – hence such variants as LINNET, **Linette** and **Linnette**.

Lynn (m/f) English name that developed variously as a diminutive of the masculine names LLEWELLYN or LYNN or else from the feminine names LINDA, LINDEN or **Lynda**. As a masculine name it is rarely used outside Wales, where it seems to have made early appearances in the 19th century. It is better known as a name for females, having made its first appearance around the same time. Also found as **Lin**, **Lyn** or **Lynne**.

Lynne *See* LYNN.

Lynnette *See* LYNETTE.

Lynsey *See* LINDSAY.

Lynton (m) English name derived from a place name meaning 'place on the torrent'. Also rendered as LINTON.

Lysette *See* LISA.

Lyssa *See* ALICIA.

Lytton (m) English name meaning 'loud torrent'. Also found as **Litton**, it is best known through the English biographer Lytton Strachey (1880–1932).

Mab *See* MABEL; MAEVE.

Mabel (f) English name derived from the Old French *amabel* or *amable* ('lovely'). Pronounced originally with a short 'a' (as in 'gabble'), as Mabel the name was found fairly frequently between the 12th and 15th centuries. It was revived in the 19th century, when the pronunciation of the name was changed to rhyme with 'table'. Also found as **Mable** or **Mabelle** (although this version is sometimes alternatively derived from the French *ma belle*, meaning 'my lovely'). Other variants are **Maybelle** and **Maybelline**. Common diminutive forms include **Mab**, **Mabs** and MAY.

Mabelle/Mable *See* MABEL.

Mabon (m) Welsh name derived from the Old Celtic *mab* ('son'). It probably began as the name of a Celtic god. Like other ancient Celtic names it was revived in the 20th century.

Mackenzie (m/f) Scottish name meaning 'son of Kenneth'. It is particularly associated with Canada, where it is chiefly applied to girls and is understood to be a reference to the Mackenzie River.

Maddie *See* MADELEINE; MADONNA.

Maddison *See* MADISON.

Maddy *See* MADELEINE; MADONNA.

Madeleine (f) French and English name derived from the Hebrew Magdalene, meaning 'of Magdala' (Magdala being a town on the Sea of Galilee). Mary Magdalene was the New Testament figure who supposedly washed Christ's feet with her tears. As **Magdalen**, **Madeline** or **Madlin**, the name was imported to England from France in the 13th century. The name became significantly popular among English-speakers in the mid 19th century, with Madeleine becoming the usual spelling. Also found occasionally as **Madolina**, **Madoline**, **Madelaine** or **Madlyn**. Sometimes shortened to **Mad**, **Madge**, **Maddie**, **Maddy** or LENA.

Madelina/Madeline *See* MADELEINE.

Madge *See* MADELEINE; MARGARET.

Madison (m/f) English name either derived from Magdalen or meaning 'son of Maud'. Also encountered as **Maddison**, it is largely confined to the USA, where it was promoted as a first name through James Madison (1751–1836), the country's fourth president (New York's Madison Avenue and Madison Square were named after him).

Madoc (m) Welsh name meaning 'fortunate', or else derived from the Celtic *aodh* ('fire'). Recorded as early as the 11th century, it remains rare outside Wales. Also found as **Madog**.

Madonna (f) English name derived from the Italian title for the Virgin Mary, meaning 'my lady'. As a first name it appears to have been a 20th-century introduction, being taken up initially by American Italians. The name is famous as that of the US pop singer and film actress Madonna (Madonna Louise Veronica Ciccone; b.1958). Diminutive forms of the name include DONNA and **Maddy**.

Mae *See* MARY; MAY.

Mael (m) Welsh name (pronounced 'mile') derived from the Gaelic for 'prince'.

Maeve (f) English version (pronounced 'mave') of the Irish **Meadhbh**, possibly derived from the Irish *meadhbhan* ('intoxication') and thus meaning 'she who intoxicates'. It is the name of a legendary queen of Connacht and is still largely confined to Ireland today. Famous bearers of the name have included the Irish novelist Maeve Binchy (b.1940). Also found as **Maev**, **Mave**, **Meave**, **Meaveen**, **Medbh** or **Mab**.

Maggie *See* MARGARET.

Magnolia (f) English flower name that like many other flower names made its first appearance among English-speakers in the late 19th century. It has never been common.

Magnus (m) Roman name meaning 'great'. The name is usually traced back to the 9th-century Holy Roman Emperor Charlemagne, who was also known as *Carolus Magnus* ('Charles the Great'). The name subsequently reached Scotland and Ireland via the Shetlands, where it remains common. It became more widespread among English-speakers from the 1960s. Variant forms include the Irish **Manus**.

Mahalia (f) English name derived from the Hebrew for 'tenderness' (although other suggestions are that it was based on a musical term or on an ordinary vocabulary word meaning 'barren'). A biblical name, it seems to have made its first appearances among English-speakers in the 17th century and is now commonest in the USA. A famous bearer of the name was the US gospel singer Mahalia Jackson (1911–72). Variants of the name include **Mahala**, **Mehala**, **Mehalah** and **Mehalia**.

Mahmud (m) Arabic name derived from *hamida* ('to praise') and thus meaning 'praiseworthy'. The name was popularized at an early date by Mahmud of Ghazna (971–1030), a Muslim commander of Turkish origin. Also found as **Mahmood**, **Mehmud** or **Mehmood**. *See also* MUHAMMAD.

Mahon (m) English version of the Irish Mathuin, itself descended from Mathghambain, meaning 'bear'. In its earliest form it was borne by a brother of Brian Boru, a king of Ireland in the 11th century.

Maia *See* MAYA.

Maidie (f) Scottish and Irish name apparently derived from the ordinary vocabulary word 'maid', possibly influenced by MAISIE. It may also be encountered as a rare diminutive form of MARY (probably because the Virgin Mary is sometimes referred to as a 'maid of God' or 'Maid Mary' etc). It enjoyed a minor vogue among English-speakers in the late 19th and early 20th centuries. Occasionally found as **Maidy**.

Maire *See* MARY.

Mairead *See* MARGARET.

Mairi *See* MARY.

Mairin *See* MAUREEN.

Mairwen (f) Welsh name derived from MARY and *gwyn* ('white' or 'blessed').

Maisie (f) Diminutive form of the Scottish **Mairead**, a variant of MARGARET. It came into fashion among English-speakers in the late 19th century, reached a peak in the 1920s, but fell from favour again after the 1930s. Also found as **Mysie**.

Maitland (m) English name of uncertain meaning. The original surname from which the first name came is of Norman French origin.

Maja *See* MAYA.

Mal *See* MALCOLM; MALDWYN.

Malachi (m) Hebrew name meaning 'my messenger'. It features in the Bible as the name of the last of the 12 minor Old Testament prophets and was taken up by Puritans in the 17th century. Also found as **Malachy**, although this version of the name (as borne by an early Irish king) can also be interpreted to mean 'devotee of St Seachnall'.

Malandra (f) English name apparently devised through the combination of ALEXANDRA and MELANIE. It received a boost in the UK in the 1990s through the British television actress Malandra Burrows (b.1965), although in her case the name resulted from the combination of her parents' names Malcolm and Sandra.

Malcolm (m) English version of the Gaelic Mael Colum ('disciple of St Columba'). It is also found in Scotland as an Anglicized version of COLUM. The name Columba itself means 'dove' in Latin. St Columba's conversion of the Scots to Christianity in the 6th century ensured the name's lasting popularity in Scotland. The name was taken up elsewhere in the English-speaking world on a significant scale in the 1920s and 1930s. Diminutive forms of the name include **Mal** and **Malc**. **Malcolmina** and **Malina** are rare feminine versions.

Maldwyn (m) Welsh variant of the English BALDWIN. The name is relatively unknown outside Wales, where it is also a county name. **Mal** is a diminutive form of the name.

Malina *See* MALCOLM.

Malinda *See* MELINDA.

Malise (f) Gaelic name meaning 'servant of Jesus'. In Scotland it is traditionally associated with the Gordon family.

Mallory (m/f) English name derived from a surname that evolved from a Norman French nickname meaning 'unfortunate', from the Old French *malheure* ('unhappy' or 'unlucky'). It is usually encountered as a masculine name, but is occasionally also given to girls, most often in the alternative spelling **Malory**.

Malone (m) Irish name meaning 'follower of St John'.

Malory *See* MALLORY.

Malvina (f) First name devised by the Scottish poet James Macpherson (1736–96) for a character in the celebrated poetry he claimed was the work of the legendary Gaelic bard Ossian.

Macpherson may have based the name on the Gaelic *mala mhin* ('smooth brow'). Modern bearers of the name have included the US singer-songwriter Malvina Reynolds (1900–1978). **Malvin** is a masculine version of the name.

Mamie (f) English name that developed as a diminutive of several different names, including MARGARET, MARY and MAY, although it is often assumed to be based on 'mammy' or 'mummy'. It made its first appearances in the USA during the 19th century but is rarely heard today. Also found as **Mame**.

Man *See* EMANUEL.

Manasseh (m) Hebrew name meaning 'causing to forget'. It appears in the Bible and was recorded in use in England in the 11th and 12th centuries before being taken up by Puritans on both sides of the Atlantic. Instances of the name in subsequent centuries have included a character in William Makepeace Thackeray's *Vanity Fair* (1847–8). Also found as **Manasses**.

Mandy *See* AMANDA; MIRANDA.

Manette *See* MARY.

Manfred (m) English, German and Dutch name derived from the Old German *mana* ('man') or *magin* ('strength') and *fridu* ('peace') and usually taken to mean 'man of peace'. The name was brought to Britain by the Normans but subsequently fell into disuse until revived on an occasional basis after being reintroduced from Germany in the 19th century.

Manley (m) English name possibly derived from 'manly' or else from an English place name based on the Old English *maene* ('common') and *leah* ('wood' or 'clearing'). It made an early appearance in William Wycherley's comedy *The Plain-Dealer* (1676) but has never been very common. Well-known bearers of the name have included the British poet Gerard Manley Hopkins (1844–89).

Manny *See* EMANUEL.

Mansel (m) English name that may have come originally from the French place name Le Mans. Also found as **Mansell**.

Manus *See* MAGNUS.

Mara (f) Hebrew name supposedly meaning 'bitter', although it is often assumed to be a variant of MARY. The name appears in the Bible as the name that Ruth's mother-in-law Naomi (meaning 'sweetness') gives herself when she complains that God has treated her badly. It has made occasional appearances in the English-speaking world since the 17th century. Also found as **Marah**.

Maralyn *See* MARILYN.

Marc *See* MARCUS; MARK.

Marcel (m) French name derived from the Roman Marcellus, itself a diminutive of MARCUS. It was popularized in France through a 3rd-century martyr of the name and was adopted on an occasional

basis by English-speakers in the late 19th century. **Marcella** (or, in France, **Marcelle**) is a feminine version of the name also found in English-speaking countries, especially Ireland.

Marcella/Marcelle *See* MARCEL.

Marcia (f) English feminine variant of the Roman Marcius (or MARIUS). The name became current in the English-speaking world in the late 19th century, notably in the USA (where the usual spelling since the 1920s has been **Marsha**). **Marcine** is a variant. Familiar forms of the name include **Marcie** and **Marcy**.

Marcie *See* MARCIA.

Marco *See* MARK.

Marcus (m) Roman name possibly (though probably incorrectly) derived like MARIUS from that of Mars, the Roman god of war. Common in ancient Rome, it was taken up by English-speakers around the middle of the 19th century. Sometimes shortened to **Marc**. *See also* MARK.

Marcy *See* MARCIA.

Mared *See* MARGARET.

Maredudd *See* MEREDITH.

Margaret (f) English and Scottish version of the Roman **Margarita**, which was itself descended from the Greek *margaron* ('pearl'). The name was taken up first in Scotland in the 11th century and was adopted by English-speakers in medieval times, becoming one of the most lastingly popular of all girls' names – although, as a saint's name, it suffered a temporary decline after the Reformation. Diminutive forms of the name include **Madge**, **Maggie** (or **Maggi**), **Marge**, **Margi**, **Margie**, **Meg**, **Meggie**, **Megs**, **Meta**, **Moggy**, MAY, PEGGY and RITA. As well as Margarita, variants include **Margareta**, **Margaretta**, **Marghanita**, MARJORIE, the Welsh MEGAN and **Mared**, the Scottish MAISIE, the Gaelic **Mairead** and the French **Marguerite** and MARGOT (Anglicized as **Margo**). *See also* DAISY; PEARL.

Margareta/Margaretta/ Margarita *See* MARGARET.

Margaux *See* MARGOT.

Marge *See* MARGARET; MARJORIE.

Margery *See* MARJORIE.

Marghanita/Margi/Margie *See* MARGARET.

Margot (f) French diminutive (pronounced 'margo') of **Marguerite** (*see* MARGARET). It was adopted from the French by English-speakers in medieval times but remained rare until the 19th century. Also found as **Margo**. The unusual spelling **Margaux** was invented by US actress Margaux Hemingway (Margot Hemingway; 1955–96), who wished to honour the bottle of Margaux red wine that her mother and father (novelist Ernest Hemingway) drank on the night she was conceived.

Marguerita/Marguerite *See* MARGARET.

Mari *See* MARIE.

Maria (f) Roman name descended from the Greek Mariam, which was itself derived from the Hebrew Miryam. The original meaning may possibly have been 'to swell' (as in pregnancy). Maria owes its international popularity across the Christian world to the Virgin Mary and was taken up by English-speakers by the 16th century, but has always been less popular than the alternative MARY. The usual pronunciation of the name has changed since the 19th century from 'marigha' to 'mareea', probably under the influence of the Spanish and Portuguese pronunciation. Variants include **Mariah** and the abbreviated forms MIA, **Mitzi** and **Ria**. Among the name's diminutive forms are **Mariel**, **Mariella** (or **Marielle**), **Marietta** (or **Mariette**) and the Irish **Moya**. *See also* MARIE; MARIUS.

Mariah *See* MARIA.

Mariam/Mariamne *See* MIRIAM.

Marian (f) Feminine version of MARION, which was itself derived from the French MARIE. It is sometimes also considered to be a combined form of MARY and ANN. The name was in use in England in medieval times and was subsequently popularized through Maid Marian, a character in the Robin Hood legend. *See also* MARIANNE.

Mariana/Marianna *See* MARIANNE.

Marianne (f) Variant of MARIAN,

also assumed to be a combination of MARY and ANNE. It was first taken up by English-speakers in the 18th century, when it existed alongside **Mary-Ann**. In France the name has been adopted for the symbolic woman representing the Republic itself. Also found as **Mariane**, **Maryanne**, **Mariana** and **Marianna**.

Marie (f) French equivalent of MARY, derived from the Roman MARIA. It was taken up by English-speakers in the 19th century, initially in the USA, and reached a peak in popularity in the 1960s and 1970s. Also found as **Maree** or **Mari**. **Mimi** is a diminutive form, famous from Giacomo Puccini's opera *La Bohème* (1896). It may also appear in combination with other names, as in **Anne-Marie**.

Mariel *See* MARIA; MURIEL.

Mariella/Marielle/Marietta/ Mariette *See* MARIA.

Marigold (f) English flower name taken up by English-speakers towards the end of the 19th century. The flower itself was originally named *golde* (after the precious metal, because of its colour) but was renamed in the medieval period in honour of the Virgin Mary, with whom the flower was associated. GOLDIE is an accepted diminutive form of the name.

Marilyn (f) English name based on a combination of MARY and LYNN (or ELLEN), or simply an elaboration of Mary with the suffix

'-lyn'. Occasionally found as **Maralyn** or **Marolyn**, it is a relatively recent introduction dating from the early 20th century. Its early history was mostly confined to the USA, but it was taken up increasingly elsewhere from the 1950s in response to the international popularity of the US film actress Marilyn Monroe (Norma Jean Baker; 1926–62). Other variants include **Marilene**, **Marylin**, **Marylyn**, **Merilyn** and **Merrilyn**.

Marina (f) Italian, Spanish, German and English name representing a feminine equivalent of the Roman family name Marinus, itself derived from MARIUS. Because of its similarity to the Latin *marinus* ('of the sea') it has always had maritime associations – as evidenced by Shakespeare's use of it for Pericles' daughter in *Pericles* (1607–8), with the explanation that she was born at sea. The earliest records of the name among English-speakers date from the 14th century. Sometimes shortened to **Rena**. *See also* MARNIE.

Marion (m) English name derived via Marianus from the Roman MARIUS. It also exists as an alternative spelling of MARIAN. The most famous bearer of the name to date has been the US film actor John Wayne (Marion Michael Morrison; 1907–79).

Maris (f) English name of uncertain origin. It is thought that it may have had its roots in the Latin *stella maris* ('star of the sea').

Marisa (f) Italian, Spanish and

English first name that evolved through the combination of MARIA or MARINA and LISA. Also found as **Marissa**, it is a relatively recent introduction to the English-speaking world, dating from the 1950s, and is uncommon outside the USA.

Marius (m) Roman name that may have come from that of Mars, the Roman god of war, or else possibly from the Latin *maris* ('male' or 'manly'). A suggestion that it comes from the Latin *mare* ('sea') is usually discounted. Common to several other European languages, it has made occasional appearances as a first name among English-speakers since the 19th century. *See also* MARCIA; MARCUS.

Marje/Marji *See* MARJORIE.

Marjorie (f) English version of the French **Marguerite** (*see* MARGARET), regarded as a separate name since at least the 13th century. A derivation from the 17th century suggests it comes from the name of the herb marjoram. The earliest record of the name in England dates back to 1194, when it was given as **Margerie** or **Margery**. The spelling Marjorie was adopted initially in Scotland at the end of the 13th century. Abbreviated versions of the name include **Marje**, **Marji**, **Marge**, **Margy** and **Margie**.

Mark (m) English version of the Roman MARCUS, coming ultimately from the name of the Roman god of war, Mars, and thus meaning 'warlike'. The name appears in the Bible and enjoyed some currency among English Puritans from the 17th century, although it was not until the 1960s that it suddenly emerged as one of the most popular choices of boys' names. Variant forms include the French **Marc** and the Italian and Spanish **Marco**. Among familiar versions of the name are **Markie** and **Marky**.

Marla *See* MARLENE.

Marlene (f) German diminutive form of Maria Magdalene that was taken up by English-speakers in the 1930s. Its acceptance throughout the English-speaking world was a reflection of the international fame enjoyed by the German-born US actress Marlene Dietrich (Maria Magdalene von Losch; 1904–92), whose greatest hit song was 'Lili Marlene'. Also found as **Marlena**, **Marleen** or **Marline**. Sometimes shortened to **Marla** or **Marley**.

Marley (m) English name derived from a place name meaning 'pleasant wood'. It has appeared more frequently in recent decades in tribute to the Jamaican reggae musician Bob Marley (1945–81). *See also* MARLENE.

Marlin *See* MARLON; MERLIN.

Marlon (m) English name of uncertain origin, possibly derived either from **Marc** (*see* MARK) or else from MARION or MERLIN. It made its first appearance among English-speakers in the 1950s, when it received a huge boost through the massive popularity of the US film actor Marlon Brando (1924–2004), who inherited the name from his father. Also found as **Marlo** or **Marlin**.

Marmaduke (m) English and Irish name of uncertain origin. Attempts have been made to trace the name back to the Celtic name Mael Maedoc, meaning 'disciple of Maedoc' (Maedoc, or Madoc, being the name of several early Irish saints). Records of its use among English-speakers date back to the 12th century. Always considered an aristocratic name, it is associated traditionally with Yorkshire. Sometimes abbreviated to **Duke**.

Marna See MARNIE.

Marnie (f) English name of uncertain origin. Also found as **Marni**, it may have developed, via **Marna**, as a variant of MARINA. Alfred Hitchcock's film *Marnie* (1964) helped to promote the name, particularly in the USA.

Marsha See MARCIA.

Marshal See MARSHALL.

Marshall (m/f) English name derived from the Old French *marechal* ('marshal') that has been in occasional use as a masculine name since the 19th century and as a name for girls since the 1940s. The name was ultimately Germanic in origin, coming from *marah* ('horse') and *scalc* ('servant'), and was originally reserved for people connected with looking after horses. Also found as

Marshal, it is more common in Canada and the USA than in the UK.

Martha (f) English name derived from the Aramaic for 'lady'. It appears in the Bible and was among the biblical names taken up by Puritans in the 16th century. It later enjoyed a marked resurgence in popularity in the USA in the 19th century in tribute to Martha Washington (1732–1802), the wife of President George Washington. It is sometimes shortened to **Marti**, **Martie**, **Marty**, **Mattie** or **Matty** as well as to **Patty** or **Pattie**.

Martin (m) English, French and German name derived from the Roman Martinus, itself probably from the name of the Roman god of war, Mars, and interpreted to mean 'warlike'. It became a popular choice of name throughout medieval Europe and has remained in currency among English-speakers since the 12th century. Notable bearers of the name have included the German Protestant theologian Martin Luther (1483–1546) and US Black activist Martin Luther King (1929–68). Variant spellings include **Martyn**, originally a Welsh version of the name. Commonly abbreviated to **Marty**. *See also* MARTINA.

Martina (f) Feminine equivalent of MARTIN, first used by the Romans and subsequently taken up by English-speakers around the middle of the 19th century.

Customarily abbreviated to **Marti**. Variants include **Martine**.

Martine *See* MARTINA.

Marty *See* MARTHA; MARTIN.

Martyn *See* MARTIN.

Marvin (m) English name of uncertain origin that has been in use as a first name since the 19th century. It may have emerged as a variant of MERVYN, although another theory traces it back to the Old English name Maerwine, which meant 'famous friend'. The name is more frequent in Canada and the USA, where it made its first appearances. Also found as **Marvyn**, it reached a peak in popularity in the 1920s. Sometimes shortened to **Marv**.

Mary (f) English version of the French MARIE, derived from the Roman MARIA. The ultimate source of the name is thought to have been the Hebrew Miryam, which may have meant 'to swell', thus evoking pregnancy and motherhood. As the name of Christ's mother, Mary was considered unsuitable for secular use for several centuries. Attitudes eventually changed, however, and the name became well established throughout Europe around the 12th century. By the middle of the 18th century around one-fifth of all female children born in England were being given the name. The many variant and diminutive forms include **Mae**, MAY, MAIDIE, **Maisie**, MAMIE, MOLLY, **Mimi**, **Minnie**, **Poll** (or POLLY), **Marietta**,

Mariella, **Mitzi** and MIA. It also appears in combination with a variety of other names, as in **Mary Ann**, **Mary Jane** and **Marylou**. Variants in other languages include the Irish Gaelic **Maire** and **Maura**, the Scottish **Mairi** and MOIRA and the Welsh **Mair** and **Mari**.

Maryann/Maryanne *See* MARIANNE.

Marylou *See* MARY.

Marylyn *See* MARILYN.

Mason (m) English name, originally an occupational name for anyone working with stone. It is more common in the USA than elsewhere.

Masterman (m) Scottish and English name meaning 'master's man' or 'servant' that has made occasional appearances as a first name. Traditionally considered an aristocratic name sometimes given by barons to their first sons, it has never been very common.

Mat *See* MATILDA; MATTHEW.

Mathew *See* MATTHEW.

Mathias *See* MATTHIAS.

Matilda (f) English name derived via Norman French from the Old German Mahthildis, itself from *macht* ('might') and *hiltja* ('battle') and thus meaning 'mighty in battle'. It came to England with the Normans, being borne by William the Conqueror's wife Matilda (d.1083). It fell from favour after the medieval period and it was not until the 18th century that it was substantially revived. Sometimes shortened to **Mat**, **Mattie** (or **Matty**), **Pattie** (or **Patty**), **Tilda** or **Tilly**. *See also* MAUD.

Matt *See* MATTHEW.

Matthew (m) English name derived from the Hebrew Mattathiah, meaning 'gift of God'. The name features in the Bible as the author of the first Gospel. It came to England with the Normans and was relatively common in medieval times. It received a boost after the Reformation, but it was not until the 1960s that the name claimed a position among the most frequent names in use. A common diminutive form is **Mat** or **Matt**. *See also* MATTHIAS.

Matthias (m) Greek version of the Hebrew Mattathiah (also the source of MATTHEW). It appears in the Bible as the name of the apostle who took the place of Judas Iscariot and was subsequently among the biblical names taken up by the Puritans in the 17th century. Also found as **Mathias**.

Mattie/Matty *See* MARTHA; MATILDA.

Maud (f) English, French, German and Dutch diminutive form of MATILDA. It came to England as the name of William the Conqueror's granddaughter and was subsequently well known as that of Henry I's daughter Maud or Matilda (1102–67). Throughout the medieval period Maud was the

usual vernacular version of the more formal Matilda. Also found as **Maude** or **Maudie**.

Maude/Maudie *See* MAUD.

Maura *See* MARY; MOIRA.

Maureen (f) English version of the Irish **Mairin**, itself derived from MARY and meaning 'little Mary'. It was taken up by English-speakers towards the end of the 19th century and enjoyed a peak in popularity in the 1930s, since when it has been largely out of favour – although it is still fairly common in Scotland and Ireland. Also found as **Maurene**, **Maurine** or **Moreen**. Sometimes shortened to **Mo**.

Maurice (m) English and French version (pronounced 'morris') of the Roman Mauricius, itself derived from the Latin *maurus* ('moor', 'dark-skinned' or 'swarthy'). It may also be encountered in Ireland as an Anglicized version of **Muirgheas**, from *muir* ('sea') and *gus* ('choice'). The name was popular in medieval times, usually as **Morris**, but subsequently appeared irregularly until the mid 19th century, when it enjoyed a minor vogue. Sometimes shortened to **Mo**, **Moss**, **Maurie** or **Morrie**. Variants in other languages include the Welsh **Meuric** or **Meurig** and the Irish **Muiris**.

Maurine *See* MAUREEN.

Mave *See* MAEVE; MAVIS.

Mavis (f) English and Scottish name derived from a traditional name for the song thrush, itself originally from the Old French *mauvis*. It made its first appearance among English-speakers towards the end of the 19th century after it was used by the novelist Marie Corelli for her character Mavis Clare in *The Sorrows of Satan* (1895). **Mave** is a shortened form of the name.

Mavourneen (f) Irish first name derived from the Irish Gaelic for 'darling little one'. Also found in the form **Mavourna**.

Max *See* MAXIMILIAN; MAXINE; MAXWELL.

Maxene *See* MAXINE.

Maxie *See* MAXIMILIAN; MAXINE; MAXWELL.

Maxim (m) Russian name derived from the Latin *maximus* ('greatest'), in fairly common use among English-speakers. Its modern adoption was promoted by its use for the romantic central character of Daphne du Maurier's novel *Rebecca* (1938). Variants include the Welsh **Macsen**.

Maximilian (m) English and German version of the Roman Maximilianus, derived from the Latin *maximus* ('greatest'). The name became a favourite choice of the Habsburgs and also, from the 16th century, of the royal house of Bavaria. It was in use among English-speakers in the early 17th century, although it has always been rare. The diminutive form **Max** appeared towards the end of the 19th century. It is also shortened to **Maxie**.

Maxine (f) Feminine version of **Max** (*see* MAXIMILIAN). It emerged as a popular girls' name among English-speakers in the 1930s and remained a fairly frequent choice until the 1960s. Also found as **Maxene**. Sometimes shortened to **Maxie** (or **Maxy**) or **Micki** (or **Mickie**).

Maxwell (m) Scottish name derived from a place name either meaning 'Magnus' well' or 'large spring'. Its history as a first name dates from the 19th century. Often shortened to **Max** or **Maxie**.

May (f) Diminutive form of MARGARET and MARY that is now often treated as a name in its own right, invoking either the name of the plant and its blossom or else the name of the month. It was taken up by English-speakers towards the end of the 19th century. It is also found as **Mae** – a variant popularized by the US film actress Mae West (1892–1980).

Maya (f) English name (pronounced 'miya') of ancient Greek and Roman origin, possibly meaning 'nurse' or else derived from the Latin root *mai-* ('great'). It is also possible to derive it from the Sanskrit for 'illusion'. Also found as **Maia** or **Maja**, it was borne in Greek mythology by the mother of Hermes by Zeus. The name made its first appearances among English-speakers in the early 20th century.

Maybelle/Maybelline *See* MABEL.

Maynard (m) English name

derived via Norman French from the Old German *magin* ('strength') and *hard* ('brave' or 'hardy'), that has been in occasional use as a first name since the Norman Conquest. Notable bearers of the name have included the British economist John Maynard Keynes (1883–1946).

Meadhbh/Meave/Meaveen/ Medbh *See* MAEVE.

Meg *See* MARGARET.

Megan (f) Welsh variant via Meg of MARGARET. It was largely confined to Wales until the late 20th century, when it began to appear throughout the English-speaking world. Commonly shortened to **Meg** or **Meggie** (or **Meggy**). Variants include **Meghan**, **Meaghan** and **Meagan** – forms that have been taken up in Australia and Canada as a result of a mistaken belief that the name has Irish roots.

Meggie *See* MARGARET; MEGAN.

Meghan *See* MEGAN.

Megs *See* MARGARET; MEGAN.

Mehalia *See* MAHALIA.

Mehmud *See* MAHMUD.

Meical *See* MICHAEL.

Meinwen (f) Welsh name meaning 'white' or 'fair'.

Meir (m) Jewish name derived from the Hebrew for 'giving light'. Variants include **Meyer**.

Meirion (m) Welsh name that may have its roots ultimately in the Roman Marianus, itself

derived from MARIUS. Also found as **Merrion**. Relatively recent feminine versions of the name are **Meiriona** and **Meirionwen**.

Mel *See* IMELDA; MELANIE; MELINDA; MELISSA; MELVILLE; MELVIN.

Melanie (f) French, English and Dutch name adapted via Old French from the Roman Melania, which itself was derived from the Greek *melas* ('black' or 'dark'). The name was originally reserved for children with dark hair, dark eyes or a swarthy complexion. It made its first appearance among English-speakers in medieval times, perhaps introduced by French Huguenot immigrants. It remained relatively rare outside south-western England until the 1960s, since when it has become frequent throughout the English-speaking world. Often shortened to **Mel**. Variants include **Melany**, **Mellony** and the French **Mélanie**.

Melba (f) English first name of Australian origin. The name appears to have been taken up initially in tribute to the celebrated Australian opera singer Dame Nellie Melba (Helen Mitchell; 1861–1931), who adopted the name from her home city, Melbourne.

Melesina/Melicent *See* MILLICENT.

Melina (f) Diminutive version of several different names, such as EMMELINE, MELINDA and MELISSA. It has made rare appearances among English-speakers since the 19th century.

Melinda (f) English name that is thought to have developed as a variant form of BELINDA and other similar names. A link with the Latin *mel* ('honey') has been suggested. Also found as **Malinda**, it was first taken up by English-speakers in the 18th century. Today it is heard most frequently in Australia and the USA. Sometimes shortened to **Mel**.

Meliora (f) English name derived from the Latin *melior* ('better'). It has made rare appearances in Britain since medieval times, confined chiefly to Cornwall.

Melissa (f) Greek name derived from *melissa* ('bee'), itself from *meli* ('honey'). It has been in use among English-speakers since the 16th century and became widely popular in the latter half of the 20th century, especially in the USA and Australia. Occasionally shortened to **Mel**, **Missie** or **Lissa**.

Mellony *See* MELANIE.

Melody (f) English name derived from the ordinary vocabulary word 'melody', itself descended from the Greek *melodia* ('singing of songs'). It made its first appearances among English-speakers in the late 18th century and became increasingly popular in the 1920s, perhaps inspired by the Irving Berlin song 'A pretty girl is like a melody' (1919). Also found as **Melodie**.

Melva (f) English name of uncertain origin, sometimes encountered as a diminutive form of

Melvina (*see* MELVIN). It has been suggested that the name may have developed from a Celtic word for 'chief'.

Melville (m) English and Scottish name derived ultimately from the Norman French place name Malville, meaning 'bad settlement'. It appeared as a surname in Scotland as early as the 12th century and was taken up as a first name from the 19th century. Often shortened to **Mel**.

Melvin (m) Scottish name that was taken up among English-speakers towards the end of the 19th century. Its roots are obscure, but it may be descended in part from the Old English *wine* ('friend'). Another theory links the name with the Gaelic **Malvin** ('smooth brow'). Also found as **Melvyn**. **Melvina** is a rarely encountered feminine version. All forms of the name are commonly shortened to **Mel**.

Melvyn *See* MELVIN.

Meraud (f) English name of uncertain origin. It is often assumed that the name was originally derived from 'emerald', but others suggest that it is more likely to have evolved from an earlier Celtic name, perhaps based on *mur* ('the sea'). It is confined largely to Cornwall, where records of it go back to the 13th century.

Mercedes (f) Spanish and French name derived from the Spanish *merced* ('mercy'), itself descended from the Latin *mercedes* ('wages' or 'ransom'). Christ's crucifixion was sometimes interpreted as a form of ransom for the sins of mankind and it was this notion that linked 'ransom' with 'mercy'. Today the name is often associated with the Mercedes Benz motor car, which was named after the daughter of the company's top executive. Familiar forms of the name include MERCY and **Sadie**.

Mercia *See* MERCY.

Mercy (f) English virtue name also encountered as a diminutive form of MERCEDES. It was one of the many virtue names adopted by English Puritans in the 17th century, and like several of the others it has long since fallen from favour. MERRY is a diminutive form of the name. A rare Latinate variant is **Mercia**.

Meredith (m/f) English version of the Welsh **Maredudd** or **Meredydd**, meaning 'great chief'. The Welsh form of the name is little known outside Wales itself, although the English form can be found across the English-speaking world. Today the name is perhaps commoner among females than it is among men, especially in the USA. Sometimes shortened to MERRY.

Merfyn *See* MERVYN.

Meriel *See* MURIEL.

Merilyn *See* MARILYN.

Merle (m/f) English name that probably developed initially as a variant of MERYL or MURIEL. It is often related to the French *merle*

('blackbird'). As a first name for girls it was taken up towards the end of the 19th century. It made its first appearances as a boys' name early in the 20th century, largely confined to the USA.

Merlin (m) English version of the Welsh **Myrddin**, meaning 'sea-hill fort'. It is most famous as the name of the magician of Arthurian legend. Also found as **Marlin** or **Merlyn** – as borne by the Welsh politician Merlyn Rees (b.1920). Merlyn is occasionally found as a girls' name.

Merrilyn *See* MARILYN.

Merrion *See* MEIRION.

Merry (m/f) English name that exists as a diminutive form of various other names, including MARY, MERCY and MEREDITH. It first won acceptance among English-speakers in the 19th century and today is usually found in the USA employed as a variant of Mary, from which it is indistinguishable in normal US pronunciation.

Merton (m) English name derived from a place name meaning 'settlement by a lake'.

Merv *See* MERVYN.

Mervyn (m) English version of the Welsh **Merfyn**, probably from the Old Celtic for 'sea ruler'. It was largely confined to Wales until the 1930s, when it began to be heard more widely among English-speakers. Also found as **Mervin**. Often shortened to **Merv**. *See also* MARVIN.

Meryl (f) Diminutive form of MURIEL that has emerged as an independent name among English-speakers since the early 20th century. The most well-known bearer of the name to date has been the US film actress Meryl Streep (Mary Louise Streep; b.1949).

Mia (f) Italian and Spanish name adopted by English-speakers in the early 20th century. It may come from the Italian and Spanish *mia* ('mine') but is also often treated as a diminutive form of MARIA. The most famous bearer of the name to date has been the US film actress Mia Farrow (b.1945).

Micah (m) Hebrew equivalent of MICHAEL, meaning 'who is like Yah?' (Yah being an alternative name for Jehovah, or God). It appears in the Bible as the name of one of the prophets and subsequently made occasional appearances among English Puritans from the 17th century.

Michael (m) English and German name derived from the Hebrew for 'who is like God?'. St Michael was the archangel who led the angels against Satan. The name was taken up by English-speakers in the 12th century and has since remained one of the most frequently encountered of all English names. As well as the Irish **Mick**, the name is commonly shortened to **Mickey** (or **Micky**), **Mike**, **Mikey** or **Midge**. Variants include the English **Mitchell** (or **Mitch**) and

the Welsh **Meical**. A feminine version of the name is **Michaela** or **Mikaela** (pronounced 'mikayla'). *See also* MICAH; MICHELLE; MILES.

Michaela *See* MICHAEL.

Michelle (f) English version of the French Michèle, itself a feminine equivalent of Michel (*see* MICHAEL). The French Michèle was taken up by English-speakers in the 1940s, but was soon eclipsed by its Anglicized form Michelle. Often shortened to **Chelle**, **Shell** or **Shelley**. **Micheline** is a rare variant form.

Mick/Mickey *See* MICHAEL.

Micki/Mickie *See* MAXINE.

Micky/Midge/Mikaela/Mike/ Mikey *See* MICHAEL.

Milborough (f) English name derived from the Old English *milde* ('mild') and *burg* ('borough' or 'fortress'). The name of a 7th-century English saint, it made occasional reappearances among English-speakers from medieval times until the 18th century.

Milburn (m) English name derived from a place name meaning 'mill stream'.

Mildred (f) English name derived from the Old English Mildthryth, itself from *milde* ('mild') and *thryth* ('strength') and thus meaning 'gentle strength'. It was borne by a 7th-century saint and was revived by English-speakers in the 17th century and again in the 19th century, but is now rare.

Commonly shortened to **Millie** or **Milly**.

Miles (m) English name of uncertain origin. Attempts have been made to trace it back to the Roman Milo, itself possibly from the Latin *miles* ('soldier'), although a link has also been suggested with the Slavonic *mil* ('dear' or 'beloved') or with the Old German for 'merciful' or 'generous'. The name came to England with the Normans and often appeared as **Milo** in medieval times. It has long been a popular name in Ireland, where it may be considered a translation of **Maoileas** ('servant of Jesus'), **Maolmuire** ('servant of Mary') or **Maelmore** ('majestic chief'). Also found as **Myles**.

Milford (m) English name derived from a place name meaning 'mill ford'.

Miller (m) English name derived from the ordinary vocabulary word, originally a surname.

Millicent (f) English version of the French Mélisande, itself derived from the Old German for 'hard worker'. It came to England from France in the late 12th century (as Melisende or Melisenda) and was revived in the 19th century but is rare today. Commonly shortened to **Millie** or **Milly**. Variants include **Melicent**, **Melisent** and **Melesina**.

Millie/Milly See AMELIA; CAMILLA; EMILY; MILDRED; MILLICENT.

Milo See MILES.

Milton (m) English name derived from a place name meaning 'settlement with a mill'. The name's popularity was greatly influenced by respect for the English poet John Milton (1608–74). Today it is more common in the USA than elsewhere. Sometimes shortened to **Milt**.

Mima See JEMIMA.

Mimi See MARIE.

Mina See WILHELMINA.

Mindy (f) English name that appears to have developed under the influence of **Mandy** (see AMANDA) and CINDY.

Minerva (f) Roman name, borne by the goddess of wisdom and possibly derived from the Latin *mens* ('mind') or else from an unknown Etruscan source. Records of its use as a first name date from the Renaissance. It has continued to make rare appearances among English-speakers since the 19th century. Sometimes shortened to **Minnie**.

Minna (f) English name derived either from the Old German *minna* ('memory' or 'love') or else from the Old German *min* ('small'). Also adopted as a diminutive of WILHELMINA. Its use among English-speakers was for many years confined largely to Scotland.

Minnie See MINERVA; WILHELMINA.

Minta/Minty See ARAMINTA.

Mira See MYRA.

Mirabel (f) English name derived from the Latin *mirabilis* ('wonderful'). It was taken up by English-speakers in the 12th century and was often employed as a masculine name until the 18th century. Also found as **Mirabelle** or **Mirabella**.

Mirabella/Mirabelle *See* MIRABEL.

Miranda (f) English name derived from the Latin *mirari* ('to wonder at') and thus meaning 'adorable' or 'fit to be loved'. The name was invented by William Shakespeare for Prospero's daughter in his play *The Tempest* (1611) and has appeared with increasing frequency since the middle of the 19th century. Sometimes shortened to **Mira**, **Mandy** or **Randy**.

Miriam (f) Hebrew name, originally Maryam, usually interpreted as meaning 'good' or 'full' and possibly descended ultimately from an unknown Egyptian root. Closely related to MARY, the name features in the Bible and has always been a favourite within the Jewish community. It was taken up by English-speakers during the 17th century. Also encountered as **Myriam**, **Mariam** or **Marianne**. A familiar form of the name is **Mitzi**.

Missie *See* MELISSA.

Misty (f) English name derived from the ordinary English vocabulary word. The name made its debut among English-speakers in the 1970s, inspired by the Clint Eastwood film *Play Misty for Me* (1971) – 'Misty' being the name of a song (1954) that features centrally in the plot.

Mitch/Mitchell *See* MICHAEL.

Mitzi *See* MARIA; MIRIAM.

Mo *See* MAUREEN; MAURICE; MOSES.

Moreen *See* MAUREEN.

Modesty (f) English virtue name that appears to have made its debut only in the 20th century. It appears to be a modern equivalent of the Late Latin name Modestus, which had much the same meaning. Notable bearers of the name have included the 1960s British cartoon character Modesty Blaise.

Moggy *See* MARGARET.

Mohammed *See* MUHAMMAD.

Moina (f) Irish and Scottish name possibly derived from the Gaelic for 'girl of the peat-moss'.

Moira (f) English version of the Irish **Maire**, itself a variant of MARY. It probably evolved through the usual pronunciation of Mary in Irish. As **Maura**, the name was borne by a 5th-century martyr. English-speakers took up Moira in the 19th century, since when it has established itself as a particular favourite in Scotland. Also found in the USA as **Moyra**.

Mollie *See* MOLLY.

Molly (f) English name that had emerged as a diminutive of MARY by the 18th century. The change of 'r' to 'll' is a standard evolution shared with several other names. Also found as **Moll**, best known from Daniel Defoe's novel *Moll Flanders* (1722), and **Mollie**.

Mona (f) English version of the

Irish Muadhnait, itself derived from *muadh* ('noble' or 'good'). Occasionally also encountered as a diminutive form of MONICA. It took root initially in Ireland and was taken up by English-speakers elsewhere towards the end of the 19th century, when Irish names were in vogue. Also found as **Moyna**.

Monday (f) English name usually reserved for girls born on a Monday. Little used since medieval times.

Monica (f) English name of uncertain origin. Attempts have been made to trace it back to the Greek *monos* ('alone') or the Latin *monere* ('to warn' or 'to advise'). Having been taken up by English-speakers in the 19th century, it increased in frequency in the 1930s, since when it has remained moderately popular. Sometimes shortened to MONA. Variant forms include the French **Monique** and the familiar form **Monny**.

Monique/Monny *See* MONICA.

Monroe (m) English and Scottish name that is thought to have had its roots in a Scottish place name meaning 'mouth of the Roe' (a reference to the River Roe in Ireland's County Derry, from which the Scottish Munro clan are supposed to have come). The name is especially popular in the USA, promoted by the US President James Monroe (1758–1831). Also found as **Monro**, **Munroe** or **Munro**.

Montague (m) English surname adopted as a first name in the early 19th century. It began as a Norman place name, Mont Aigu near Caen, itself derived from the Old French *mont* ('hill') and *aigu* ('pointed'). The name has strong aristocratic associations, being the surname of a celebrated noble family of England. Also found as **Montagu**. Often shortened, like MONTGOMERY, to **Monty**.

Montgomery (m) English surname that has appeared occasionally as a first name among English-speakers since the 1920s. It began life as a Norman place name, Mont Goumeril, meaning something like 'mountain of the powerful one'. Postwar appearances of the name owed more to the popularity of Field Marshal Bernard Montgomery (1887–1976), who was widely known by the usual diminutive form of the name, **Monty**.

Montmorency (m) French surname that made occasional appearances as a first name among English-speakers in the 19th century. The surname came originally from a Norman place name derived from the Old French *mont* ('hill') and the Gallo-Roman name Maurentius. Sometimes shortened to **Monty**.

Monty *See* MONTAGUE; MONTGOMERY; MONTMORENCY.

Mor (f) Scottish and Irish name derived from the Gaelic for 'large' or 'great'. In late medieval times this was the most popular of all

Irish girls' names and it has remained in regular use in Scotland and Ireland into modern times. Variants include MORAG and **Moreen** (*see* MAUREEN).

Morag (f) Scottish name derived from *mor* ('great'). Another derivation suggests it comes from the Gaelic for 'sun'. Some authorities have also described it as a Scottish equivalent of MARY or SARAH. It is still thought of as a predominantly Scottish name.

Moray *See* MURRAY.

Morcant *See* MORGAN.

Mordecai (m) Hebrew name probably derived from Persian and meaning 'devotee of Marduk' (Marduk being the most important of the gods of ancient Babylon). It features in the Bible and was taken up by English Puritans in the 17th century. Today it is rare outside the Jewish community. Sometimes shortened to **Mordy** or **Morty**. Among Jews it is sometimes abbreviated to **Motke** or **Motl**.

Mordy *See* MORDECAI.

Moreen *See* MAUREEN.

Morgan (m/f) English name derived from the Welsh **Morcant**, which may have come from the words *mor* ('sea') and *cant* ('circle' or 'edge') but is otherwise of unknown origin. It is sometimes suggested that the name means 'sea-bright'. The name has a long history among the Welsh but is now found throughout the English-speaking world. Its use as

a girls' name was promoted by Arthurian legend, in which it is borne by Morgan le Fay. A feminine variant is **Morgana**.

Morley (m) English name derived from a place name based on the Old English *mor* ('moor' or 'marsh') and *leah* ('wood' or 'clearing').

Morna *See* MYRNA.

Morrie/Morris *See* MAURICE.

Mort *See* MORTIMER; MORTON.

Mortimer (m) English surname that was taken up as a first name among English-speakers in the 19th century. It probably had its roots in a Norman place name derived from the Old French for 'dead sea' (referring to a stagnant lake or marsh). Another suggestion is that it is of Celtic origin, meaning 'sea warrior'. Sometimes shortened to **Mort**.

Morton (m) English name derived from a place name based on the Old English *mortun* ('settlement on a moor'). Having made its debut as a first name in the mid 19th century, it is most frequently found today within the Jewish community as an Anglicized version of MOSES. **Mort** and **Morty** are familiar forms of the name.

Morty *See* MORDECAI; MORTON.

Morven (f) English name of uncertain Scottish derivation. It may have been taken from the name of the Morvern district in north Argyll, Scotland, itself based on the Gaelic for 'great gap', or else from the Gaelic *mor bheinn* ('great peak'). Its use as a first name was promoted by its identification as Fingal's kingdom in the unauthentic but much admired Ossianic poems of James Macpherson published in the 18th century.

Morwenna (f) Cornish and Welsh name derived either from the Welsh *morwyn* ('maiden') or else from the Welsh *mor* ('sea') and *gwaneg* ('wave'). Several Cornish churches are named after the Celtic St Morwenna, who lived in the 5th century. The name was revived around the middle of the 20th century. Also rendered as **Morwen**.

Moses (m) Hebrew name of uncertain origin. It may have evolved, via the Hebrew Moshel, from the Egyptian *mes* ('child' or 'born of'). The story of the biblical Moses established the name as a favourite among Jews. Early records of the name in English, dating from the 11th century, give it as **Moyses**. Also found as **Moyse** or **Moss**, it was adopted by English Puritans in the 17th century, but is rare today. Abbreviated forms of the name include **Mo**, **Mose** and **Moy**. **Moshe** (or **Moishe**) is a Yiddish variant.

Moshe See MOSES.

Moss See MAURICE; MOSES; MOSTYN.

Mostyn (m) Welsh name derived from a place name in Clwyd, itself derived from the Old English *mos* ('moss') and *tun* ('settlement'). Sometimes abbreviated to **Moss**.

Motke/Motl See MORDECAI.

Moy See MOSES.

Moya See MARIA.

Moyna See MONA.

Moyra See MOIRA.

Muhammad (m) Arabic name derived from *hamida* ('to praise') and thus meaning 'praiseworthy'. As the name of the founder of Islam, it has long been one of the most popular masculine names among Muslims around the world. Also found as **Mahomet**, **Mohammad** or **Mohammed**.

Muir (m) Scottish name derived from a place name meaning 'moor'. Notable bearers of the name have included the Scottish film music director Muir Mathieson (1911–72).

Muireann (f) Irish name derived from the Irish Gaelic *muir* ('sea') and *fionn* ('white' or 'fair'). Also found as **Muirinn** or **Morann** and frequently equated with MAUREEN.

Muiris See MAURICE.

Muirne See MYRNA.

Mungo (m) Scottish name possibly derived from the Welsh *mwyn* ('dear', 'gentle' or 'kind'). It was borne as a nickname meaning 'most dear' by a 6th-century Scottish saint, otherwise known as St Kentigern, and to this day is rare outside Scotland itself.

Munro/Munroe See MONROE.

Murdo See MURDOCH.

Murdoch (m) English name derived from the Scottish Gaelic

Murdo or **Muireadhach**, itself based on the Gaelic *muir* ('sea') and usually interpreted to mean 'seaman' or 'mariner'. Sometimes shortened to **Murdy** or **Murdie**. Rare feminine forms include **Murdag** and **Murdina**. **Murtagh** is an Irish equivalent.

Murgatroyd (m) English name derived from a place name (in Yorkshire). The original place of that name – unlocated – was derived from the first name MARGARET and the Yorkshire dialect *royd* ('clearing') and the name thus means 'Margaret's clearing'.

Muriel (f) English version of the Irish Gaelic **Muirgheal** and the Scottish Gaelic **Muireall**, meaning 'sea-bright'. The earliest records of the name come from Brittany, Scotland and Ireland, although it also appears to have been in use in England by medieval times. It became more frequent in the 19th century and won particular favour in Scotland. Also found as **Mariel**, **Meriel**, **Merrill** or MERYL.

Murphy (m) Irish name derived from the Irish Gaelic for 'sea hound'.

Murray (m) Scottish surname that made its debut as a first name in the 19th century. Borne by the Dukes of Atholl among others, it came originally from the Scottish place name Moray, derived from *mor* ('sea'). As a first name Murray may also be found as an Anglicized version of the Gaelic **Muireach**. Also found as **Moray** or **Murry**.

Murtagh *See* MURDOCH.

Mustafa (m) Arabic name meaning 'chosen'. As a title of MUHAMMAD, it has long been one of the most popular names among Muslims. Notable bearers of the name have included Mustafa Kamal (1881–1938), the founder of the modern Turkish state. Also found as **Mostafa**.

Myf *See* MYFANWY.

Myfanwy (f) Welsh name derived from the Welsh *my* ('my dear') and *manwy* ('fine' or 'precious') and thus meaning 'my fine one' or 'my dear precious one'. Alternatively, the name may have developed from *menyw* ('woman'). Pronounced 'muvanwee', it is largely confined to Wales and was little known before the 20th century. Sometimes shortened to **Myf** (pronounced 'muv'), **Myfi** or FANNY.

Myles *See* MILES.

Myra (f) English name possibly derived from the Greek *muron* ('myrrh') or the Latin *mirari* ('to wonder at'), or else as an anagram of MARY or as a variant of MOIRA. In Scotland it is sometimes used as an Anglicization of **Mairead**. The name appears to have been invented by the English poet Fulke Greville (1554–1628) for the subject of his love poems. It was taken up as a first name by English-speakers in the 19th century and became particularly popular in Scotland. Also found as **Mira**.

Myriam *See* MIRIAM.

Myrna (f) English version of the Irish **Muirne**, a name derived from the Gaelic *muirne* ('affection' or 'tenderness'). The name of the mother of the legendary Irish hero Fion Mac Cumhaill, it was taken up by English-speakers in the 19th century. Well-known bearers of the name have included the US film actress Myrna Loy (1905–93). Also found as **Morna**.

Myron (m) Greek name meaning 'myrrh' that was taken up as a first name by English-speakers in the 20th century. Sometimes today interpreted to mean 'fragrant'. It was popular among early Christians because of its link with myrrh, one of the gifts presented to the baby Jesus.

Myrtill/Myrtilla *See* MYRTLE.

Myrtle (f) English plant name derived from the name of the garden shrub, which was a symbol of victory in ancient Greece. Like many other flower names, it was adopted as a first name among English-speakers in the middle of the 19th century. It has fallen out of favour since the middle of the 20th century. Variants of the name include **Myrtill** and **Myrtilla**.

Mysie *See* MAISIE.

Nadia (f) Diminutive of the Russian Nadezhda, meaning 'hope' (or, alternatively, from Arabic words meaning 'moist with dew'). The name became popular among English- and French-speakers in the early 20th century, when the hugely successful tours of Sergei Diaghilev's Ballets Russes did much to promote Russian names in Europe. Variant forms of the name include the French **Nadine**.

Nadim (m) Arab name meaning 'drinking companion' or 'confidant'. The name derives from the verb *nadama* ('to drink') and is also commonly used in Indian communities, where variants include the feminine **Nadeem**.

Nadine *See* NADIA.

Nahum (m) Hebrew name meaning 'comforter'. The name of an Old Testament prophet who lived in the 7th century BC, it was among the biblical names taken up by the Puritans in the 17th century. Notable bearers of the name have included the English playwright Nahum Tate (1652–1715).

Nan *See* ANN; NANCY; NANETTE.

Nana *See* ANNA; HANNAH.

Nance *See* NANCY.

Nancy (f) English name that probably evolved as a familiar form of ANN. It emerged as an independent name in its own right during the 18th century. Notable bearers of the name have included a character in Charles Dickens's *Oliver Twist* (1837–8). Diminutive forms include **Nan** and **Nance**.

Nandy *See* FERDINAND.

Nanette (f) English and French name that probably evolved from ANN, via **Nan**. It seems to have made its first appearance in the early years of the 20th century. Its popularity was much promoted by the success of Vincent Youmans's operetta *No, No, Nanette* (1925).

Nanny *See* ANN; NANCY.

Naoise (m) Irish Gaelic name of uncertain meaning, pronounced 'neesha'. It is best known as the name of the lover of Deidre in ancient Irish legend: on Naoise's death at the hands of Conchobar, king of Ulster, Deidre died of grief.

Naomi (f) Hebrew name meaning 'pleasantness', 'pleasure' or 'my delight'. In the Old Testament Book of Ruth, Naomi is Ruth's mother-in-law. It was among the many biblical names adopted by the Puritans in the 17th century and has enjoyed renewed popularity in non-Jewish communities (especially in Australia) since the 1970s.

Napier (m) English and French name derived from the Greek for 'of the new city'.

Napoleon (m) French name based on the Italian Napoleone, which was probably derived originally from the name of the city of Naples, combined with the Italian *leone* ('lion'). A relatively rare name in Italy, as the first name of the Corsican-born French emperor Napoleon Bonaparte (1769–1821) it became one of the best-known, and feared, names in Europe. It has occasionally been adopted as a first name in English-speaking countries since the early 19th century.

Narcissus (m) English version of the Greek name Narkissos, which may have been derived from the Greek word *narke* ('numbness'). The name is indelibly associated with the Greek legend of Narcissus, the beautiful youth who fell in love with his own reflection and was eventually transformed into the flower bearing his name. A rare feminine form is **Narcissa**.

Narelle (f) Australian name of obscure meaning. A relatively recent introduction, it ranked among the most popular girls' names in Australia in the 1970s.

Nat *See* NATHAN; NATHANIEL.

Natalia *See* NATALIE.

Natalie (f) English and French name derived from the Russian Natalya, itself from the Latin *natale domini* ('birthday of the Lord'). The name is often given to girls born on or near Christmas Day. The earliest records of the name's introduction to Britain date from the late 19th century. **Tally** is a common diminutive form. *See also* NATASHA.

Natasha (f) Russian name that evolved initially as a familiar variant of Natalya (*see* NATALIE). It has since won acceptance as a distinct name in its own right not only in Russia but also in French-, German- and English-speaking cultures. Notable instances of the name in literature have included Natasha Rostova in Leo Tolstoy's epic novel *War and Peace* (1863–9). Diminutive forms include **Tasha**.

Nathan (m) Hebrew name meaning 'gift' or 'he has given'. Borne by an Old Testament prophet, it was among the biblical names adopted by Puritans in England and America in the 17th century. It is sometimes treated as a diminutive form of NATHANIEL and JONATHAN. **Nat** is a common diminutive form.

Nathanael *See* NATHANIEL.

Nathaniel (m) Hebrew name meaning 'gift of God' or 'God has given'. In the New Testament it is the personal name of the apostle Bartholomew. The name was first adopted in English-speaking countries after the Reformation. It is commoner today in the USA than it is on the British side of the Atlantic. Famous bearers of the name have included the American writer Nathaniel Hawthorne (1804–64). Sometimes found as **Nathanael**. **Nat** and **Natty** are the most common diminutive forms. *See also* NATHAN.

Natty *See* NATHANIEL.

Neal *See* NEIL.

Neassa (f) Irish Gaelic name of uncertain but undoubtedly ancient origin. It was borne by the mother of King Conchobar of Ulster.

Ned *See* EDMUND; EDWARD.

Neil (m) English name derived from the Irish Gaelic *niadh* (variously thought to mean 'champion', 'cloud' or 'passionate'). Also found as **Neal**, **Neale**, **Niall** (the Irish Gaelic version of the name) and the Scottish **Neilie** or **Neillie**, it predated the Norman Conquest and is thought to have spread to the rest of Britain via Scandinavia. *See also* NIGEL.

Neirin *See* ANEURIN.

Nell (f) Diminutive form of various girls' names, including ELEANOR, ELLEN and HELEN. The initial 'N' was probably adopted through the repeated use of such everyday phrases as 'mine Ell'. Now considered a name in its own right, it is rarely found in the older variant forms **Nelly** and **Nellie**.

Nellie/Nelly *See* FENELLA; NELL.

Nelson (m) English name meaning 'son of Neil' or 'son of Nell'. It was adopted as a first name in tribute to the great naval hero Admiral Horatio Nelson (1758–1805) after his death in victory at the Battle of Trafalgar. Notable bearers of the name since then have included the South African President Nelson Mandela (b.1918).

Nena *See* NINA.

Nerissa (f) English name that was probably originally derived from the Greek *nereis* ('sea-nymph'). It is thought to have been coined by the English playwright William Shakespeare as a name for Portia's sharp-witted maidservant in *The Merchant of Venice* (1596–8).

Nerys (f) Welsh name of uncertain derivation but possibly meaning 'lady' (derived from the Welsh *ner*, meaning 'lord'). Alternatively, it may be a development of NERISSA. A relatively modern invention, it is little heard outside Wales.

Nessa *See* VANESSA.

Nessie/Nesta *See* AGNES.

Netta/Nettie *See* ANNETTE; HENRIETTA; JANET; JEANETTE.

Nev *See* NEVILLE.

Neville (m) English name derived from the French place name

Neuville, meaning 'new town'. It was adopted as a first name in English-speaking countries after the Norman Conquest. The name has strong aristocratic associations and appeared as a first name in English-speaking countries from the 17th century. **Nev** is a common diminutive of the name.

Newt *See* NEWTON.

Newton (m) English name derived from a place name meaning 'new town'. Its history as a first name dates from the 19th century. It is rare outside the USA. The usual abbreviated form is **Newt**.

Ngaio (f) New Zealand name (pronounced 'nayo' or 'nigh-o') derived from a Maori tree name (or, alternatively, meaning 'clever'). The most famous bearer of the name to date has been the New Zealand crime novelist Dame Ngaio Marsh (1899–1982).

Nia *See* NIAMH.

Niall *See* NEIL.

Niamh (f) Irish name meaning 'radiance' or 'brightness'. Pronounced 'neev' or 'nee-av', it is popular within Ireland but little encountered elsewhere in the English-speaking world. The name was borne by a pagan goddess. Sometimes abbreviated to **Nia** in Wales.

Nichol *See* NICHOLAS.

Nichola *See* NICOLA.

Nicholas (m) First name common to many cultures that was derived

from the Greek Nikolaos, meaning 'victory of the people'. The name was borne by a 4th-century bishop of Myra, who later achieved sainthood and immortality as the original 'Father Christmas' or 'Santa Claus'. The name became popular in England from the 12th century. Variants include **Nicolas**, **Nichol** and **Nicol** (a popular form of the name in Scotland). Among the name's diminutive forms are **Nick**, **Nik** and **Nicky**. *See also* COLIN.

Nick/Nicky *See* NICHOLAS; NICOLA.

Nicol *See* NICHOLAS.

Nicola (f) English and Italian name representing a feminine equivalent of NICHOLAS. It is fairly common in English-speaking countries, where it has been used since the 12th century, and, as **Nicole**, in France. Variants include **Nichola**. **Nick**, **Nickie**, **Nicky** and **Nikki** are among common diminutive forms.

Nicolas *See* NICHOLAS.

Nicole *See* NICOLA.

Nigel (m) English name that is thought to have been adopted as the Latin version of NEIL soon after the Norman Conquest. The name can be found in the *Domesday Book* and enjoyed renewed popularity from the 19th century, when Nigel became the usual form of the name. Sometimes shortened to **Nige**. **Nigella** and **Nigelia** are relatively uncommon feminine versions of the name.

Nigelia/Nigella *See* NIGEL.

Nikita (f) Russian first name derived from the Greek name Aniketos, meaning 'unconquerable'. It has made infrequent appearances in the English-speaking world in recent years.

Nikki See NICOLA.

Nina (f) Russian first name that may have evolved from ANN or simply as a diminutive form of various longer Russian names ending in '-nina', such as Antonina. An alternative derivation suggests the name developed from the Spanish for 'little girl'. It was first adopted in English-speaking countries in the 19th century. Famous bearers of the name have included the US jazz singer Nina Simone (Eunice Kathleen Wayman; 1933–2003). Variant forms include **Nena**, **Ninette** and **Ninita**.

Ninette See NINA.

Ninian (m) Scottish and Irish name of uncertain origin. It may possibly be related to VIVIAN, itself based on the Latin *vivus* ('alive'). It was borne by a 5th-century saint who was responsible for bringing Christianity to the Picts of southern Scotland.

Nita See ANITA.

Noah (m) Hebrew name meaning 'long-lived' or, alternatively, 'rest' or 'comfort'. Best known as the name of the Old Testament builder of the Ark at the time of the Great Flood, the name was taken up by Puritans on both sides of the Atlantic during the 17th century. Notable bearers of the name

have included the American lexicographer Noah Webster (1758–1843).

Noam (m) Hebrew name meaning 'pleasantness', 'delight' or 'joy'. The name is popular chiefly among American Jewish families. Famous bearers have included the US linguist Noam Chomsky (b.1928).

Noble (m) English name of medieval origin inspired by the ordinary vocabulary word. The intention behind the name was presumably the same as that behind such equivalents as DUKE and EARL, meant to convey a notion of social status and nobility of character.

Noel (m) French and English name based on the French *Noël* ('Christmas'). Variously given with or without the diaeresis, the name has been reserved traditionally for children born on Christmas Day or during the Christmas period. Feminine equivalents include **Noele**, **Noelle** and **Noelene** (or **Noeleen**). Variants of the masculine name include **Nowell**.

Noele/Noeleen/Noelene/Noelle See NOEL.

Nola See FENELLA.

Nolan (m) Irish name meaning 'descendant of a noble' or simply 'famous'. A feminine version of the name popular in Australia is **Nolene** (or **Noleen**).

Noleen/Nolene See NOLAN.

Noll *See* OLIVER.

Nonie *See* NORA.

Nora (f) Irish name derived from HONOR, which has since been adopted in England, Scotland and other English-speaking countries. Also found as **Norah**, it is sometimes treated as an abbreviation of ELEANOR and LEONORA or as a feminine version of NORMAN. It began to appear in England from the 19th century and enjoyed a peak in popularity in the first half of the 20th century. Familiar variants of the name in Ireland include **Nonie** and **Noreen**.

Norbert (m) English name derived from the Old German for 'famous northman' (from words meaning 'north' and 'bright'). The name came to Britain with the Normans and was subsequently revived in the late Victorian era, when many medieval names came back into vogue. Familiar forms of the name include BERT, BERTIE and **Norrie**.

Noreen *See* NORA.

Norm *See* NORMAN.

Norma (f) English and Italian first name possibly derived from the Latin *norma* ('rule', 'pattern' or 'standard'). It is also sometimes considered (especially in Scotland) to be a feminine version of NORMAN. The name became popular in the wake of the great success enjoyed by Vincenzo Bellini's opera *Norma* (1831).

Norman (m) English name derived from the Old English for 'Northman' (first applied to the Vikings). It also exists as an Anglicization of the Norse name Tormod (from the name of the god Thor and Norse for 'wrath'). The name remained common until the 14th century and was among the many medieval names that were later revived by the Victorians. **Norm** and **Norrie** are common diminutive forms. Feminine versions of the name include NORMA, NORA and MONA.

Nornie *See* LEONORA.

Norrie *See* NORBERT; NORMAN.

Norris (m) English name that developed as a variant of NORMAN. It was fairly popular during the 19th century but has since become rare.

Norton (m) English name derived from a place name combining the Old English words for 'north' and 'settlement'. Its history as a first name dates from the 19th century.

Nowell *See* NOEL.

Nuala *See* FENELLA.

Nye *See* ANEURIN.

Nyree (f) Anglicized version of the Maori name **Ngaire** (of unknown origin). The popularity of the New Zealand-born actress Nyree Dawn Porter (1940–2001) in the popular British television series *The Forsyte Saga* did much to promote use of the name throughout the English-speaking world from the 1970s, though curiously it remains relatively uncommon in New Zealand.

Originally reserved for eighth-born children, it was adopted in the English-speaking world from the 19th century. **Octavian** and **Octavius** are masculine versions of the name.

Octavian/Octavius *See* OCTAVIA.

Odell (m) English name derived from the Old English for 'hill of woad'. Rare feminine forms of the name are **Odella**, **Odelyn** and ODILE.

Odette (f) French name derived via the Old French masculine name Oda from the Old German *od* ('riches'). First adopted by English-speakers towards the end of the 19th century, it is best known from the Second World War French Resistance heroine Odette Churchill (1912–95).

Odile (f) French name (pronounced 'ohdeel') that may have been derived from the German OTTO, meaning 'riches', or otherwise descended from the Old German *othal* ('fatherland'). It is sometimes employed as a feminine version of ODELL. **Odilia** is a variant form.

Ofra *See* OPRAH.

Ogden (m) English name derived from the Old English for 'valley of oak'. It has been in occasional use as a first name since the 19th century. Notable bearers of the name have included the US humorous poet Ogden Nash (1902–71).

Ogilvie (m) Celtic name meaning 'high peak'. Also encountered as **Ogilvy**.

Obadiah (m) English name derived from the Hebrew for 'servant of the Lord'. The name is borne by several biblical characters and was among those adopted by the Puritans in the 17th century, as a result of which it became a slang term for anyone with Puritan leanings.

Oberon *See* AUBERON.

Ocean (m/f) English name derived from the ordinary vocabulary word 'ocean'. Oceanus was the name of a Greek sea-god.

Ocky *See* OSCAR.

Octavia (f) Roman name derived from the Latin *octavus* ('eighth').

Ol *See* OLIVER.

Olaf (m) Scandinavian name derived from the Old Norse *anleifr* ('family descendant'). Borne by several Scandinavian kings, it came to Britain with the Vikings, but remains relatively rare in the English-speaking world. Variant forms include the Scottish **Aulay**.

Oleg (m) Russian variant of the Scandinavian Helge (*see* HELGA).

Olga (f) Russian variant of the Scandinavian HELGA. The name was adopted in England in the late 19th century. Also found as **Olya**.

Olive (f) English name derived from the Latin *oliva* ('olive tree'). As **Oliva**, it was first adopted by English-speakers in the 13th century. It was revived in the 19th century, probably inspired by the olive's reputation as a symbol of peace. It has since been eclipsed by the related OLIVIA. Variants include **Olivette**.

Oliver (m) English name that is thought to have developed either from the Scandinavian OLAF or alternatively from the Old German *alfihar* ('elf host'). It was in common use among English-speakers in medieval times. Notable bearers of the name have included Oliver Cromwell (1599–1658) and the fictional hero of Charles Dickens's *Oliver Twist* (1837). Among variants are the French **Olivier** and the Welsh HAVELOCK. **Ol**, **Ollie**, **Nol** and **Nollie** are diminutive forms.

Olivette *See* OLIVE.

Olivia (f) English and Italian name derived ultimately from the Latin *oliva* ('olive tree'). It became popular among English-speakers in imitation of William Shakespeare's Olivia in *Twelfth Night* (1601). It has enjoyed a revival in popularity since the 1970s. Diminutive forms include **Libby** and **Livvy**.

Olivier/Ollie *See* OLIVER.

Olwen (f) Welsh name derived from the Welsh *ol* ('footprint') and *gwyn* ('white' or 'blessed'). In Welsh legend, as related in the *Mabinogion*, Olwen was a beautiful woman whose footprints sprouted white clover. Also found as **Olwin** and **Olwyn**.

Olya *See* OLGA.

Olympia (f) Greek name derived from Olympus (the home of the gods in ancient Greek mythology). It is best known as the title of a frankly realistic portrait of a reclining nude woman painted by Édouard Manet in 1865.

Omar *See* UMAR.

Omega (f) Greek name derived from the last letter of the Greek alphabet. It has tended to be reserved for last-born children, just as ALPHA has been employed on occasion for the first-born.

Ona *See* UNA.

Oona/Oonagh *See* UNA.

Opal (f) Indian name derived from the Sanskrit for 'precious stone'. It was adopted in the

English-speaking world towards the end of the 19th century, often being bestowed upon girls born in October (opal being the birthstone for that month). Variants include the rare **Opaline**.

Opaline *See* OPAL.

Ophelia (f) English and Italian name derived from the Greek Ophelos, meaning 'help' or 'profit'. It may have been a 16th-century invention, appearing for the first time in the works of Jacopo Sannazzaro (1458–1530). It is indelibly associated with the doomed heroine in William Shakespeare's tragedy *Hamlet* (1599). Formerly very rare, it has enjoyed a resurgence in popularity since the 1980s.

Oprah (f) Hebrew name of obscure meaning (possibly 'she who turns her back' or 'fawn'). The similar **Orpah** appears in the Bible, though as a man's name. Made famous through the US chat show host Oprah Winfrey (b.1954), it may also be encountered in such variant forms as **Ofra** or **Ophrah**.

Ora (f) English name of obscure origin, possibly derived from the Latin *orare* ('to pray'). It may also have developed as a diminutive of CORA or DORA.

Oralie (f) English name of obscure origin, sometimes assumed to be a variant of AURELIA. Also found as **Oralee**.

Oran (m) Irish name, originally Odhran, derived from the Gaelic *odhar* ('green' or 'sallow'). Notable bearers of the name have included one of St Columba's most loyal followers.

Oriana (f) English name derived from the Latin *oriri* ('to rise') and thus interpreted as meaning 'dawn' or 'sunrise'. It was popular during the 16th century, when it was among the poetic names bestowed by admirers upon Elizabeth I. Variant forms include **Ariane**.

Oriel (m) English name derived either from the Latin for 'porch' or from the Old German for 'battle heat'. Introduced to Britain by the Normans in the 11th century, it has never been very common. Variants include **Auriel** and **Oriole**.

Orinthia (f) Greek name derived from *orinein* ('to excite'). In the variant form **Orinda**, it was well known in the 17th century as the pseudonym of the English writer Katherine Philips (1631–64), popularly dubbed 'The Matchless Orinda'. The central character in George Bernard Shaw's play *The Apple Cart* (1929) is called Orinthia.

Orla (f) Irish name derived from the Gaelic for 'golden princess'. Also found as **Orlagh** or **Orlaidh**.

Orlagh/Orlaidh *See* ORLA.

Orlando (m) Italian version of ROLAND, meaning 'famous land'. It has been in occasional use among English-speakers since medieval times. It appears in Shakespeare and as the title of Virginia Woolf's novel *Orlando* (1928).

Orpah *See* OPRAH.

Orsina *See* ORSON.

Orson (m) English and French first name derived via the Old French *ourson* ('bearcub') from the Latin *ursus* ('bear'). In medieval legend, Orson was a small child carried off and raised by a family of bears. Notable bearers of the name have included the US film director Orson Welles (1915–85). A rare feminine version is **Orsina**. *See also* URSULA.

Ortho (m) Cornish name derived from the Greek *ortho* ('straight').

Orval *See* ORVILLE.

Orville (m) English name invented by Fanny Burney for one of the central characters in her book *Evelina* (1778), but also possibly derived from a French place name. Famous as the name of the US flight pioneer Orville Wright (1871–1948), it remains relatively rare outside the USA.

Osbert (m) English name derived from the Old English *os* ('god') and *beorht* ('famous') and thus interpreted as meaning 'famous as a god'. It was in use in Northumberland prior to the Norman Conquest but has been relatively rare since the 15th century. Notable bearers of the name in relatively recent times have included the British writer Osbert Sitwell (1892–1969). Diminutive forms include **Oz** and **Ozzie**.

Osborne (m) English name derived from the Old English *os* ('god') and *beorn* ('bear' or 'warrior') and thus interpreted as meaning 'god-like warrior'. It is more popular in the USA than elsewhere in the English-speaking world. Occasionally found as **Osborn** or **Osbourne** and shortened to **Oz** or **Ozzie**.

Oscar (m) English and Irish name derived either from the Gaelic *os* ('deer') and *cara* ('friend'), and thus interpreted as meaning 'gentle friend', or from the Old English *ansfar* ('god-spear'). It became popular towards the end of the 18th century but grew less common in the early 20th century after the scandal involving the Irish playwright and wit Oscar Wilde (1854–1900). It has since enjoyed something of a revival. Occasionally shortened to **Ocky**, **Os** or **Ossie**.

Osmond (m) English name derived from the Old English *os* ('god') and *mund* ('protection'). It was in use prior to the Norman Conquest and was subsequently revived in the 19th century, but is very rare today. **Osmund** is a rare variant form, and **Ossie** a diminutive.

Ossie *See* OSCAR; OSMOND.

Oswald (m) English name derived from the Old English *os* ('god') and *weald* ('rule') and thus interpreted as meaning 'rule of god' or 'divine power'. It was common in Anglo-Saxon England but later fell into disuse before being revived in the 19th century. The notoriety of the British fascist leader Oswald Mosley (1896–1980) did little to promote the name during and after the Second World War. Diminutive forms are **Oz** and **Ozzie**.

Otis (m) English name derived via the German OTTO from the Old German *ot* ('riches'). It is rare outside the USA, where notable bearers of the name have included the soul singer Otis Redding (1941–67).

Ottilie (f) French and German name equivalent to ODILE. A variant form is **Ottoline**, as borne by the British literary figure Lady Ottoline Morrell (1873–1938).

Otto (m) German name derived from the Old German *ot* ('riches'). It was brought to Britain by the Normans in the 11th century but became less frequent after the medieval period. Like many other German names it became virtually extinct among English-speakers after the outbreak of the First World War.

Ottoline *See* OTTILIE.

Owain *See* OWEN.

Owen (m) Welsh name that may have developed from EUGENE, meaning 'well-born', or else from the Welsh *oen* ('lamb'). Occasionally encountered in its original form **Owain**, it was famously borne by the great Welsh rebel leader Owen Glendower (1359–1416). **Owena** is a rare feminine version.

Owena *See* OWEN.

Oz/Ozzie *See* OSBERT; OSBORNE; OSWALD.

Pacifica *See* PEACE.

Paddy *See* PATRICIA; PATRICK.

Padraic/Padraig *See* PATRICK.

Page/Paget *See* PAIGE.

Paige (f) English name meaning 'page' or 'servant'. Medieval pages were young men serving in the households of the rich noble families of England and were always male, although curiously in modern times the name has been reserved exclusively for girls. Also encountered as **Page** and **Paget**, the name is especially popular in the USA.

Palmer (m) English name mean-

ing 'pilgrim'. It is thought that the name began as 'palm-bearer' and thus referred to palm-bearing pilgrims to the Holy Land.

Pam/Pamala *See* PAMELA.

Pamela (f) English name that was invented by the English poet and soldier Sir Philip Sidney in his pastoral romance *Arcadia* (1590). Sidney (who put the stress on the second syllable) apparently derived the name from the Greek words *pan* ('all') and *meli* ('honey'), thus creating a name meaning 'all sweetness'. The use of the name by the British novelist Samuel Richardson in his hugely successful *Pamela* (1740) did much to promote the name from the mid 18th century. Variant forms include **Pamala**, **Pamelia** and **Pamella**. **Pam** is a common diminutive form of the name. It may also be shortened to **Pammy**, chiefly in Australia.

Pamelia/Pamella/Pammy *See* PAMELA.

Pandora (f) English and Greek first name derived from the Greek words *pan* ('all') and *doron* ('gift') and thus meaning 'all-gifted' or 'many-gifted'. According to Greek legend, Pandora was offered to Prometheus' brother Epimetheus as a wife, together with a mysterious box that Pandora was forbidden to open. Pandora, however, opened the box and out flew all the woes that mankind has been subject to ever since. All that remained in the box was hope. The name does not appear to have been taken up by English-speakers before the 20th century.

Pansy (f) English flower name that was first introduced in the 19th century. It is sometimes derived from the French *pensée* ('thought'). Notable bearers of the name have included the fictional Pansy Osmond in *The Portrait of a Lady* (1881) by Henry James.

Paris (m) Greek name borne by the son of King Priam of Troy, a central character in the story of the Trojan War. It was Paris' abduction of the beautiful Helen from Sparta that provoked the start of the epic conflict between the Greeks and the Trojans. Also found as **Parris**, the name has been popular chiefly in the USA. Traditionally a boys' name, in recent years it has also been employed for girls.

Parker (m) English name meaning 'park keeper' that has been in occasional use (chiefly in the USA) as a first name since the 19th century. There is a Dr Parker Peps in the novel *Dombey and Son* (1848) by Charles Dickens.

Parry (m) Welsh name derived from *ap Harry* (meaning 'son of Harry'). It is rarely encountered outside the principality of Wales itself.

Parthenia (f) Greek name derived from the Greek *parthenos* ('virgin'). Popularly associated with the Parthenon in Athens, which was dedicated to the goddess Athena Parthenos (Athena the

Maid), the name has made sporadic reappearances among English-speakers since the late 19th century.

Parthenope (f) Greek name (pronounced 'parthenopee') derived from the Greek *parthenos* ('virgin') and *ops* ('face') and thus meaning 'maiden-faced'. In Greek legend, Parthenope was a siren who drowned herself in despair after she failed to lure Odysseus with her singing because he had had himself tied to the mast of his ship. The name was taken up by English-speakers in the 19th century.

Pascal (m) French name derived from the Latin *Paschalis* ('of Easter'). It was taken up as a first name by the early Christians, usually reserved for boys born in the Easter season. Subsequently it became especially popular in medieval Cornwall. Occasionally found as **Paschal**. Another variant form (for boys) is **Pascoe**. In France the name is found as **Pascale**, in which form it has sometimes been given to girls in English-speaking countries since the 1960s.

Pascoe *See* PASCAL.

Pat *See* PATIENCE; PATRICIA; PATRICK.

Patience (f) English 'virtue' name derived ultimately from the Latin *pati* ('to suffer'). It was popular with the early Christians and was revived by Puritans in the 16th and 17th centuries. At first it was given to boys as well as girls but it has long since been reserved exclusively for females. Gilbert and Sullivan used the name for the title and central character of their comic opera *Patience; or, Bunthorne's Bride* (1881), thus promoting its use at the end of the century. Sometimes shortened to **Pat** or **Patty**.

Patricia (f) Feminine version of PATRICK, derived from the Latin *patricius* ('nobleman'). The name was introduced in written records of the Romans to distinguish female members of noble families from males. It was accepted as a first name among English-speakers only from the 18th century, especially in Scotland. It became more widespread after it was bestowed upon Queen Victoria's granddaughter Princess Victoria Patricia Helena Elizabeth of Connaught (1886–1974). Familiar diminutive forms include **Pat**, **Patsy**, **Patty**, **Patti**, **Pattie**, **Paddy**, **Tricia** and **Trisha**.

Patrick (m) English and Irish first name derived from the Latin *patricius* ('nobleman'). The name is particularly popular in Ireland in tribute to St Patrick (c.385–461), the patron saint of Ireland. Such was the reverence the Irish had for St Patrick that initially his name was thought too holy for general use and it was left to the Scottish and subsequently people living in northern England to be the first to take the name up on a significant scale. However, since the 17th century it has been thought of as a primarily Irish name. Variants

include the Irish **Padraic**, **Padraig**, **Patric** and **Patraic**. Often shortened to **Pat** or **Paddy**.

Patsy *See* HYPATIA; PATRICIA.

Patti/Pattie/Patty *See* MARTHA; MATILDA; PATIENCE; PATRICIA.

Paul (m) Roman name derived from the Latin *paulus* ('little' or 'small'). The name started life as a nickname but was subsequently borne by several saints and by the apostle St Paul (who changed his name from Saul on his conversion to Christianity), thus guaranteeing its lasting popularity with Christians. It was recorded in Britain before the Norman Conquest but only became significantly popular from the 17th century. *See also* PAULA; PAULETTE; PAULINE.

Paula (f) English name, a feminine version of PAUL. It was first taken up by English-speakers in medieval times but emerged as a significantly popular choice only from the 1950s. POLLY is sometimes treated as a familiar variant of the name.

Pauleen/Paulene *See* PAULINE.

Paulette (f) French name, a feminine version of PAUL. Although French in origin this version of the name may now be encountered in many English-speaking countries. It became fairly popular in the 1920s and in the 1960s tended to eclipse the longer-established PAULINE. Famous bearers of the name have included the US actress Paulette Goddard

(Pauline Marion Goddard Levy; 1911–90). Also found as **Pauletta**.

Paulina *See* PAULINE.

Pauline (f) French name, a feminine version of PAUL. Although **Paulina**, the original Roman version of the name, became the traditional English version (popular from the 19th century onwards) the French spelling is now much more common among English-speakers. The name became popular in the USA before it was taken up on a significant scale elsewhere in the English-speaking world. Also found as **Paulene, Pauleen** or **Paulanne**. *See also* PAULETTE.

Peace (f) English name that was among the names celebrating a variety of abstract qualities favoured by the Puritans on both sides of the Atlantic in the 17th century. It is now found only infrequently. A rare feminine equivalent of the name is **Pacifica**.

Peadar *See* PETER.

Pearce *See* PIERS.

Pearl (f) English jewel name, which was adopted as a first name among English-speakers in the late 19th century. The jewel itself represents tears and unhappiness, but this has not affected the popularity of the name. It is also encountered occasionally as a diminutive of MARGARET, which was itself derived from the Greek for 'pearl'. The name has occasionally been applied to males, especially in the USA. Also found as **Pearle**.

Familiar forms include **Pearlie, Pearly** and **Perlie**.

Peers *See* PIERS.

Pegeen (f) Irish name that evolved as a diminutive form of MARGARET. There is a character of the name in J. M. Synge's *The Playboy of the Western World* (1907).

Peg *See* PEGGY.

Peggy (f) Diminutive form of MARGARET. Also found as **Peg** or **Peggie**, this has long been treated as an independent name in its own right as well as an abbreviation of Margaret. It probably arose originally as a rhyming version of **Meggy**. Records of its use date back at least to the 16th century. Famous bearers of the name have included the British actress Peggy Ashcroft (1907–91).

Pelham (m) English name derived from a place name meaning 'Peola's place'. Notable bearers of the name have included the British/US novelist P. G. Wodehouse (Pelham Grenville Wodehouse; 1881–1975), the creator of Jeeves and Bertie Wooster and known as 'Plum'.

Pen *See* PENELOPE.

Penelope (f) English name of uncertain origin, probably derived from the Greek *pene* (meaning 'thread' or 'bobbin'), or else just possibly from the Greek *penelops* (the name of a species of duck). According to Greek legend, Penelope was the loving wife of the great hero Odysseus, who waited faithfully at home for her long-absent husband. The name was taken up by English-speakers in the 16th century. In Ireland it is sometimes considered to be an Anglicization of the Gaelic Fionnghuala (*see* FENELLA). The name is often shortened to **Pen** or **Penny**.

Penny *See* PENELOPE.

Peony (f) English flower name that made its debut as a first name in the 19th century. Unlike some of the other flower names, this one has never enjoyed significant popularity. The flower may have got its original (Greek) name from Paion, physician to the gods.

Peppi *See* PERPETUA.

Perce *See* PERCIVAL; PERCY.

Percival (m) English and French name, apparently invented by the 12th-century French poet Chrétien de Troyes for the hero of his poem *Percevale, a knight of King Arthur* (c.1175). Chrétien himself indicated that the name came from the Old French *perce-val* ('one who pierces the valley'), although some people seem to have borne it as a surname derived from the place name Percheval in Normandy and another theory links the name to the Celtic *Peredur* ('hard steel'). In Arthurian legend, Sir Percival was the purest of the knights of the Round Table. Often shortened to PERCY, **Perce** or **Val**.

Percy (m) English name derived from a French place name. It also exists as a diminutive form of PERCIVAL, although the two names have different origins. The source place name, Perci in Normandy, appears to have had its roots in the Roman personal name Persius. The name has strong aristocratic connections, as the Percy family were one of the most powerful baronial houses of England. As a first name Percy was first adopted by members of the aristocratic Seymour family, who married into the Percy line in the early 18th century. Like Percival, the name is sometimes shortened to **Perce**.

Perdita (f) English name derived from the Latin *perditus* ('lost') William Shakespeare is thought to have invented the name for the castaway heroine in his play *The Winter's Tale* (1611). **Purdie** (or **Purdy**) is an accepted diminutive form.

Peregrine (m) English name ultimately derived via Italian from the Latin *peregrinus* ('stranger' or 'foreigner'). The name was recorded in use among early Christians, apparently selected to emphasize the transitory nature of man's existence on earth. Its use in England dates from the 13th century. Notable bearers of the name have included the central character in Tobias Smollett's *Peregrine Pickle* (1751). Sometimes shortened to PERRY.

Perlie *See* PEARL.

Peronel/Peronelle *See* PETRONELLA.

Perpetua (f) Roman name derived from the Latin *perpetuus* ('perpetual'). The name was borne by a 3rd-century Christian martyr and since then has been largely confined to members of the Roman Catholic community. Sometimes shortened to **Peppi**.

Perrine *See* PETER.

Perry (m) English name derived from the Old English *pirige* ('man who lives by a pear tree'). It is also encountered as a diminutive of PEREGRINE or PETER. The name is especially popular in Canada and the USA, partly in tribute to two 19th-century American admirals of the name who respectively beat the British in battle on the high seas and opened up trade with Japan.

Persephone (f) Greek first name derived from the Greek *pherein* ('to bring') and *phone* ('death') and thus meaning 'bringing death'. According to Greek legend, Persephone was the beautiful daughter of Zeus and Demeter who was carried off to the Underworld by Hades and had to be rescued from there by her mother. Unfortunately Persephone had eaten six pomegranate seeds while in the Underworld and was therefore doomed to spend six months of each year with Hades as goddess of the dead (which is how winter came about).

Pet *See* PETRA; PETRONELLA; PETULA.

Peta/Pete/Petena *See* PETER.

Peter (m) English, German and Scandinavian first name derived via the Roman name Petrus from the Greek *petros* ('rock' or 'stone'). The lasting popularity of the name owes much to the apostle St Peter. Originally named Simon, he was given the name by Christ himself, who chose it to reflect the fact that he would be the 'rock' on which the Christian Church would be built. The name was very common during medieval times, often rendered as PIERS or in other variant forms before the modern version of the name became generally accepted in the 14th century. The name was boosted in the early 20th century through the huge popularity of Peter Rabbit in the children's stories of Beatrix Potter and Peter Pan in J. M. Barrie's novel and play *Peter Pan: or the Boy Who Would Not Grow Up* (1904). Commonly shortened to **Pete**. Rare feminine versions of the name are **Peta** (apparently a modern Australian invention), **Petena**, **Peterina**, **Peternella** and **Perrine**. Variants in other languages include the Scottish and Irish Gaelic **Peadar**. *See also* PETERKIN; PETRA.

Peterina *See* PETER.

Peterkin (m) English name that evolved as a variant of PETER. Of chiefly historical interest today, it was borne by a character in R. M. Ballantyne's adventure novel *The Coral Island* (1857).

Peternella *See* PETER.

Petra (f) Feminine equivalent of the boys' name PETER, derived from the Latin *petros* ('rock'). As a first name it seems to have been first adopted by English-speakers in the 1940s. Variants include **Petrina** and **Petrona**.

Petrina/Petrona See PETRA.

Petronella (f) Roman family name (originally *Petronius*) of uncertain meaning that has been used as a first name in the English-speaking world since the 12th century. It was supposedly borne by an early Christian martyr, said by some to be the daughter of the apostle Peter, and as such enjoyed some popularity in medieval times. Also found as **Petranella**, **Petronilla**, **Petronel** or **Peronelle**, it is treated sometimes as a feminine version of PETER. Sometimes shortened to **Pet**.

Petula (f) English name of uncertain origin, though possibly inspired by the flower name *petunia*. Apparently a 20th-century invention, it is more frequently assumed to be a feminine equivalent of the boys' name PETER. Notable bearers of the name have included the British pop singer Petula Clark (Sally Owen; b.1932). Sometimes shortened to **Pet**.

Peyton (m) English name derived from a place name meaning 'farm of Paega'. The name is more frequent in the USA than elsewhere in the English-speaking world, promoted perhaps by the popularity of the US television drama series *Peyton Place* in the 1960s.

Phebe See PHOEBE.

Phelan (m) Irish name derived from the Irish Gaelic for 'wolf'.

Phemie See EUPHEMIA.

Pheobe See PHOEBE.

Phil See FELICITY; PHILIP; PHILIPPA; PHILOMENA; PHYLLIDA; PHYLLIS.

Philadelphia (f) Greek name meaning 'brotherly love'. The name was borne by an ancient city in Asia Minor and was subsequently taken up as a first name by the Puritans. It is popular chiefly in the USA, perhaps because it was chosen by William Penn as the name of the city of Philadelphia, Pennsylvania.

Philip (m) English name derived from the Greek Philippos, itself derived from the Greek words *philein* ('to love') and *hippos* ('horse'), and thus meaning 'lover of horses'. Alexander the Great's father was Philip II of Macedonia (382–336 BC) and the name was also borne by one of the 12 apostles. In medieval times the name was shared by both sexes, although distinct feminine versions of the name – such as PHILIPPA – were introduced in written records. It suffered a decline among English-speakers in the 16th century through association with England's enemy Philip II of Spain, but was revived in the 19th century. Common diminutives include **Phil**, **Pip** and **Flip**. Variants include **Phillip** (the usual spelling in Australia and when it is found as a surname).

Philippa (f) Feminine version of PHILIP meaning 'lover of horses'. It was introduced originally for use in medieval written records to distinguish male and female bearers of the name Philip, which was formerly common to members of both sexes. Also found as **Phillipa** or **Philipa**. *See also* PHILIPPINA; PIPPA.

Philippina (f) English and German name that emerged as a diminutive of PHILIPPA. In medieval times it was sometimes suggested that the name came from the Greek words *philein* ('to love') and *poine* ('pain') and referred to the Christian practices of self-flagellation and the wearing of hairshirts etc as methods of purging sin.

Philis *See* PHYLLIS.

Phillida *See* PHYLLIDA.

Phillie *See* PHILOMENA; PHYLLIDA; PHYLLIS.

Phillip *See* PHILIP.

Phillipa *See* PHILIPPA.

Phillis *See* PHYLLIS.

Philly *See* PHILOMENA; PHYLLIDA; PHYLLIS.

Philo (m) English and German rendering (pronounced 'fighlo') of the ancient Greek name Philon, derived from the Greek prefix *phil-* ('love') and meaning 'loved'. The name was adopted by English-speakers in the 18th century, enjoying widest acceptance in the USA. Well-known bearers of the name have included the US typewriter and sewing-machine

manufacturer Philo Remington (1816–89).

Philomela (f) Greek name derived from the Greek words *philos* ('dear' or 'sweet') and *melos* ('song'), and thus meaning 'sweet singer'. Another derivation suggests the word means 'nightingale', a theory that is supported by the ancient Greek myth of King Pandion's daughter Philomela, who was transformed into a nightingale. The name was taken up by English-speakers in the 16th century. Also found as **Philomel**.

Philomena (f) English and German name derived from the Greek words *philein* ('to love') and *menos* ('strength') and thus meaning 'strongly beloved' or 'strength-loving'. The name was formerly popular in Italy and in Ireland, where it was associated with two early saints. Variants include **Philomene**, **Philomina** and **Filomena**. Sometimes shortened to **Phil** and **Phillie** (or **Philly**).

Phineas (m) Biblical name possibly derived from the Hebrew Phinehas ('serpent's mouth' or 'oracle'), but more likely descended from the Egyptian Panhsj ('the black'), a name used for Nubians. It appears in the Old Testament and was adopted as a first name among English-speakers in the 16th century. Notable bearers of the name have included the central character in Anthony Trollope's novels *Phineas Finn* (1869) and *Phineas Redux* (1874) and the US showman Phineas T. Barnum (1810–91).

Phoebe (f) Roman version of a Greek name derived from the Greek *phoibe* ('bright' or 'shining'). According to Greek legend, Phoebe was a daughter of Uranus and Gaia. Artemis and the Roman moon goddess Diana were also sometimes known by the name. It also features in the New Testament, which was why the name was adopted with some enthusiasm in post-Reformation England. The name also features in Shakespeare, as the name of a shepherdess. Sometimes encountered in the forms **Phebe** and **Pheobe** and occasionally as a diminutive form of EUPHEMIA.

Phoenix (f) English name that alludes to the legendary bird of Arabian mythology, which was believed to burst periodically into flames and rise renewed from its own ashes.

Phyllida (f) Variant form of PHYLLIS, which emerged as a distinct name in its own right in the 15th century. Also encountered in the variant form **Phillida**, it was particularly popular among English-speakers in the 17th century. Sometimes shortened to **Phil** and **Phillie** (or **Philly**).

Phyllis (f) English and German first name derived from the Greek *phullis* ('foliage' or 'green branch'). In Greek legend, Phyllis was a beautiful country girl who hanged herself when she was disappointed in love. The gods took pity on her and transformed her into an almond tree. The name was borne by several beautiful rustic heroines in classical poetry. In the 16th century it appears to have become confused with **Felicia** to produce such variants as **Felis** and **Phillice**. Also found as **Phillis**, **Philis** or **Phyliss**. Sometimes shortened to **Phil** or **Phillie** (or **Philly**). *See also* PHYLLIDA.

Pia (f) Italian name derived from the Latin *pia* ('pious', 'dutiful' or 'godly'), a feminine equivalent of the now effectively defunct masculine Pius. It has made occasional appearances among English-speakers in the 20th century, especially since the 1970s.

Piaras/Pierce *See* PIERS.

Piers (m) French equivalent of PETER that has long since been adopted among English-speakers as an alternative to the English form of the name. The name became familiar in England after the Norman Conquest and quickly established its place, as evidenced by William Langland's poem *Piers Plowman* (c.1362). Variant forms include **Pearce**, **Pierce** and **Peers**. The Irish also have the less common Gaelic variant **Piaras**.

Piety (f) English 'virtue' name that was adopted by the Puritans in the 17th century. Piety was one of the characters representing different virtues depicted in John Bunyan's *The Pilgrim's Progress* (1678, 1684). It is now rare.

Pip *See* PHILIP; PIPPA.

Pippa (f) Diminutive form of PHILIPPA, now also used as a name in its own right. It became popular with English-speakers after the publication of Robert Browning's poetic drama *Pippa Passes* (1841), in which Pippa is a naive young Italian silk worker. Ironically, although Browning clearly believed the name had Italian roots, the name is not actually used in Italy. Sometimes shortened to **Pip**.

Piran (m) Cornish name derived from a place name of unknown meaning. It is suggested that the original place name was itself derived from the name PETER. Also found as **Perran**, the name was borne by the Celtic abbot St Piran, the patron saint of Cornish miners.

Plaxy (m) Cornish name supposedly descended from the Greek name Praxedes, which was itself derived from the Greek *praxis* ('action' or 'doing') and is usually taken to mean 'active'. It has been encountered occasionally outside Cornwall since the 20th century.

Pleasance (f) English name derived from the Old French *plaisance* ('pleasure'). The name was introduced to England by the Normans. **Pleasant** is a rare variant – as borne by Pleasant Riderhood, a character in Charles Dickens's novel *Our Mutual Friend* (1865).

Pleasant *See* PLEASANCE.

Pol *See* POLLY.

Poldie *See* LEOPOLD.

Poll *See* POLLY.

Polly (f) Variant form of MARY, influenced by MOLLY. This familiar form of Mary has been known for several centuries, as illustrated by its use in 'Polly put the kettle on' and other traditional nursery rhymes, and there have been suggestions that it is not in fact dependent upon Mary for its existence but came from a distinct forgotten source. Notable bearers of the name have included the fictional Polly Peachum in John Gay's hugely successful *The Beggar's Opera* (1728). Also found as **Pollie**. Sometimes shortened to **Pol** or **Poll**.

Pollyanna (f) English first name combining POLLY and ANNA that is popular chiefly in the USA. It appears to have been invented by Eleanor Hodgman Porter in her novel *Pollyanna* (1913), in which the central character Pollyanna Whittier is an irrepressibly optimistic girl of the same name.

Poppy (f) English flower name derived from Old English *popaeg* that was first introduced towards the end of the 19th century. The name was very popular in Edwardian England and reached a peak in the 1920s, despite the association between the flower and the thousands who died on the poppy fields of north-eastern France during the First World War

– commemorated ever since on 'Poppy Day'.

Portia (f) Anglicization of the Roman name Porcia, a feminine form of the family name Porcius, which was itself probably derived from the Latin *porcus* ('hog' or 'pig'). Another theory suggests it could mean 'safe harbour'. Borne by a famous Roman family, it was selected by William Shakespeare for the heroine of *The Merchant of Venice* (1598). Like many other Shakespearean names it has made occasional reappearances as a first name ever since.

Posie *See* POSY.

Posy (f) English flower name that seems to have made its first appearance among English-speakers in the 1920s. Sometimes treated as a diminutive of JOSEPHINE. Notable bearers of the name have included the British newspaper cartoonist Posy Simmonds (b.1945). Also found as **Posie**.

Presley (m) English name meaning 'priest's meadow'.

Preston (m) English name derived from a place name based on the Old English *preost* ('priest') and *tun* ('enclosure'), thus meaning 'priest's farm' or 'priest's place'. It made its debut as a first name in the 19th century. Notable bearers of the name have included the US film director and screenwriter Preston Sturges (Edmund Preston Biden; 1898–1959).

Price (m) Welsh name meaning 'son of Rhys'. Also found as **Pryce**.

Primrose (f) English flower name derived from the Latin *prima rose* ('first rose') that made its debut as a first name towards the end of the 19th century and reached a peak in popularity during the 1920s. In Scotland the name appeared as a surname before being adopted as a first name. It is the family name of the earls of Rosebery.

Primula (f) English flower name derived from the Latin *primus* ('first') that made its debut as a first name towards the end of the 19th century.

Prince (m) English name derived from the royal title (itself from the Latin *princeps*, 'one who takes first place'). It was used originally as a surname by families with royal connections and by those who were in the service of a prince. Notable bearers of the name have included the US pop star Prince (Prince Rogers Nelson; b.1958), who in the 1990s dropped the name in favour of an unpronounceable symbol – prompting the media to dub him 'the artist formerly known as Prince' for the sake of convenience.

Princess (f) Feminine equivalent of the boys' name PRINCE. Similarly derived from the royal title, it tends to be used more often as an informal term of endearment rather than as a formal first name.

Pris *See* PRISCILLA.

Priscilla (f) Roman name derived from the Latin *priscus* ('ancient' or 'old'). The intention behind the name seems to have been to suggest that the bearer will enjoy a very long life. The name features variously as Priscilla or Prisca in the New Testament as that of one of St Paul's companions. The name also appears in Edmund Spenser's *The Faerie Queene* (1590, 1596) and in the 17th century was taken up by the Puritans. It came back into fashion in the 19th century. Diminutive forms include CILLA – as borne by the British singer and television presenter Cilla Black (Priscilla White; b.1943) – and the less common **Pris**, **Prissy** and **Scilla**.

Prissy *See* PRISCILLA.

Proserpine (f) Roman version of the Greek PERSEPHONE. It has been suggested that the name may be linked to the Latin *proserpere* ('to creep forth'), evoking the idea of spring flowers emerging after winter. The name was taken up on an occasional basis by English-speakers in the 19th century. There is a character of the name in George Bernard Shaw's play *Candida* (1894). Sometimes shortened to **Pross** or **Prossy**.

Prosper (m) French and English name derived from the Latin *prosper* ('fortunate' or 'prosperous'), which itself came from *pro spe* ('according to one's wishes'). It was commonly found among the saints of the early Christian Church and was later adopted by the Puritans.

Pross/Prossy *See* PROSERPINE.

Pru *See* PRUDENCE; PRUNELLA.

Prudence (f) English name derived from the Roman name Prudentia, itself from the Latin *prudens* ('provident'). It made occasional appearances in medieval England before establishing itself as one of the most popular 'virtue' names espoused by the Puritans in the 17th century. Unlike some of the other virtue names, Prudence has retained its appeal into modern times. Sometimes shortened to **Pru**, **Prue** or **Purdy** (or **Purdie**).

Prue *See* PRUDENCE; PRUNELLA.

Prunella (f) English name probably derived from the Latin *pruna* ('little plum'). The name was first adopted by English-speakers in the 19th century, although the word was already familiar as the name of a smooth woollen silk used for clerical and academic gowns and also of the wild flower selfheal (*Prunella vulgaris*), and furthermore as an alternative name for the hedge sparrow or dunnock. The most widely known bearer of the name in modern times has been the British actress Prunella Scales (b.1932). Sometimes shortened to **Pru** or **Prue**.

Pryce *See* PRICE.

Pryderi (m) Welsh name meaning 'caring for' or 'anxiety'. There is a character of the name in the *Mabinogion*.

Psyche (f) Greek name (pronounced 'sighkee') derived from the Greek *psukhe* ('soul'). In Greek mythology, Psyche represented the human soul, falling in love with Eros (or Cupid). English-speakers adopted the name in the 19th century. There are characters named Psyche in Alfred, Lord Tennyson's poem 'The Princess' (1847) and in Gilbert and Sullivan's comic opera *Princess Ida* (1884), which was based on Tennyson's work.

Pugh (m) Welsh name meaning 'son of Hugh'.

Purdie/Purdy *See* PERDITA; PRUDENCE.

Quintin or **Quinton**. *See also* QUINN.

Quincey *See* QUINCY.

Quincy (m) English name of French origin, derived (like QUENTIN) ultimately from the Roman *quintus* ('fifth') and often given to fifth sons. It is particularly popular in the USA, inspired by admiration for President John Quincy Adams (1767–1848). **Quincey** is a variant form.

Quinn Irish name derived from a Gaelic surname meaning 'counsel'. It may also be encountered as a diminutive form of QUENTIN.

Quintin/Quinton *See* QUENTIN.

Queenie (f) English name derived either from REGINA ('queen' in Latin) or from the Old English *cwene* ('woman'). Sometimes used as a nickname for anyone called VICTORIA (a reference to Queen Victoria). Also found as **Queeny**.

Queeny *See* QUEENIE.

Quentin (m) English name of French origin, derived ultimately from the Latin *quintus* ('fifth') and formerly reserved for fifth sons. Roman versions of the name were Quintus and Quintinus. The name came to Britain with the Normans and was subsequently revived in the 19th century. Also found as

Rab/Rabbie *See* ROBERT.

Rachael *See* RACHEL.

Rachel (f) Hebrew name meaning 'ewe' (symbolizing innocence and gentleness). As Rahel it appears in the Old Testament as the name of Jacob's beautiful second wife, the mother of Joseph and Benjamin. It was subsequently taken up as a first name by Christians, Jews and Muslims alike. Also found as **Rachael** (and occasionally **Rachelle**), it was adopted in England after the Reformation. A popular variant is **Raquel**, originally the Spanish incarnation of the name. It may be shortened to

Rach, Rachie, Rae, Ray or Shelley. *See also* ROCHELLE.

Rachelle *See* RACHEL.

Radcliff (m) English name derived from an Old English place name meaning 'red cliff'. **Radcliffe** and **Radclyffe** are feminine versions of the name – as borne by the British novelist Marguerite Radclyffe Hall (1886–1943), author of *The Well of Loneliness* (1928).

Rae *See* RACHEL.

Raelene (f) Australian compound name combining **Rae** (a diminutive of RACHEL) with the standard feminine suffix '-lene'. A relatively recent introduction dating from the middle of the 20th century, it was probably inspired by such parallel names as DARLENE. It is rarely found outside Australia.

Rafe *See* RALPH.

Raina/Raine *See* REGINA.

Rainer/Rainier *See* RAYNER.

Raleigh (m) English name derived from an Old English place name meaning 'clearing with roe deer'. The name evokes the memory of the celebrated English seafarer, writer and explorer Sir Walter Raleigh (c.1552–1618).

Ralph (m) English name derived via Norman French from the Old Norse Rathulfr, from *raed* ('counsel') and *wulf* ('wolf') and thus meaning 'wise and strong'. As **Ralf** or **Rauf** it was popular in medieval times. **Rafe** was the usual form of the name in the 17th century, reflecting its contemporary pronunciation, but it eventually gave way to Ralph in the 18th century. The modern pronunciation of the name with a short 'a' and with the 'l' sounded dates only from the early 20th century (although the older pronunciation is still heard occasionally). A familiar version of the name is **Ralphie**. **Ralphina** is a rare feminine variant.

Ralston (m) English name derived from an identical place name. Its history as a first name goes back to the 19th century.

Ramona *See* RAYMOND.

Ramsay (m) English and Scottish name derived from a place name based on the Old English *hramsa* ('wild garlic' or 'ram') and *eg* ('island'). The name's Scottish connections date back to the 12th century, when courtiers at the Scottish court included one called Ramsay. Notable bearers of the name have included the British Labour Prime Minister James Ramsay MacDonald (1866–1937). Also encountered as **Ramsey**.

Ramsden (m) English name meaning 'ram's valley'.

Ran *See* RANDOLPH; RANULPH.

Randa *See* MIRANDA.

Randal/Randall *See* RANDOLPH.

Randolph (m) English name derived from the Old English *rand* ('shield edge') and *wulf* ('wolf') and thus meaning, roughly, 'strong defender'. Historical versions of the name included

Randal, Randall, Randel, Randle and **Randalf**, though the '-f' ending had largely given way to '-ph' by the 19th century. It is more common in Canada and the USA than elsewhere in the English-speaking world. Sometimes shortened to **Ran** or **Randy** (or **Randi**).

Randy *See* ANDREW; MIRANDA; RANDOLPH.

Ranulf *See* RANULPH.

Ranulph (m) English version of the Old Norse Reginulfr, which was itself derived from *regin* ('advice' or 'decision') and *ulfr* (wolf) thus meaning 'well-counselled and strong'. The original English form of the name was **Ranulf**. Notable bearers of the name in recent times have included the British explorer Sir Ranulph Fiennes (b.1944). Sometimes shortened to **Ran**.

Raphael (m) Hebrew name meaning 'God has healed'. As the name of a biblical archangel it became very popular among early Christians and was taken up by English-speakers in the 16th and 17th centuries, though frowned upon by the Puritans. Notable bearers of the name have included the celebrated Italian Renaissance painter Raphael (Raffaello Santi; 1483–1520).

Raquel *See* RACHEL.

Rastus *See* ERASTUS.

Ray *See* RACHEL; RAYMOND.

Raymond (m) English name

derived via the French Raimont from an Old German name combining *ragin* ('advice' or 'decision') and *mund* ('protection') and thus meaning 'well-advised protector'. The name came to England with the Normans and re-emerged among English-speakers in the middle of the 19th century. Often shortened to **Ray**. **Redmond** and **Redmund** are Irish versions of the name. Feminine versions of the name include the Spanish **Ramona**, which became popular in Canada and the USA after the publication of Helen Hunt Jackson's novel *Ramona* in 1884.

Rayner (m) English name derived from the Old German *ragin* ('advice' or 'protection') and *hari* ('army' or 'warrior'). The name was introduced to England by the Normans and remained in fairly frequent use until the 14th century. Also found as **Raynor** and **Rainier** (a French version), as borne by Prince Rainier III of Monaco (b.1923). **Raina** and **Raine** are feminine variants.

Read *See* REID.

Reanna (f) English name of obscure origins. A recent introduction, it may have evolved from RHEA and was probably influenced by DEANNA and the Welsh RHIANNON. Also found as **Reanne** or **Rheanna**.

Rearden *See* RIORDAN.

Reba *See* REBECCA.

Rebecca (f) Hebrew name possibly meaning 'heifer' or, according to another theory, 'binding', 'knotted cord' or 'noose' (perhaps in reference to the marriage bond). In fact, the name probably has an older lost Aramaic source. It appears (as Rebekah) in the Old Testament and was among the many biblical names favoured by the Puritans in the 16th and 17th centuries. The name enjoyed a new lease of life in the wake of the publication of Daphne du Maurier's novel *Rebecca* (1938). Commonly shortened to **Becky**, **Becca** or, less frequently, to **Reba**.

Red (m) English name that began life as a nickname for any person with red hair, or alternatively as a derivative of EDWARD or RICHARD. Also found as **Redd**, it is more common in the USA than elsewhere.

Redmond/Redmund *See* RAYMOND.

Redvers (m) English name with strong aristocratic associations. It appears to have made its debut as a first name in the 19th century, when notable bearers of it included the British general Sir Redvers Buller (1839–1908).

Reece *See* RHYS.

Reed *See* REID.

Reenie *See* DOREEN; MAUREEN; RENÉ.

Rees *See* RHYS.

Reg *See* REGINALD.

Regan (f) English name of unknown origin, though conceivably derived from REGINA. Possibly linked with the Irish surname

Regan or Reagan, it was most famously employed by William Shakespeare for one of the king's three daughters in his tragedy *King Lear* (1605).

Reggie *See* REGINA; REGINALD.

Regina (f) English name derived from the Latin *regina* ('queen'). Regina was a fairly popular choice of girls' name in medieval times, when it was also encountered occasionally as **Reina**, an Anglicization of the French Reine. It fell from favour after the Reformation, only to be revived in the 18th century. Today it is mostly confined to the USA. Sometimes shortened to **Reggie**. A relatively recent variant form, possibly derived from a surname, is **Raine**. Another variant, of Russian origin, is **Raina**. *See also* GINA; QUEENIE; REGAN; REX.

Reginald (m) English name derived from the Old English *regen* ('counsel') and *weald* ('power') and thus meaning 'well-counselled ruler'. The name became more popular after the Norman Conquest through its French equivalents Reinald and Reynaud. Anglicized originally as REYNOLD until the 15th century. Reginald came back into fashion during the 19th century as a result of its appearance in Sir Walter Scott's *Ivanhoe* (1820). Commonly shortened to **Reg**, **Reggie** or **Rex**.

Reid (m) English name derived from the Old English *read* ('red'), usually reserved for children with red hair or a ruddy complexion.

Today it is more common in the USA than elsewhere. Occasionally encountered as **Reed** or **Read**.

Reina *See* REGINA.

Remus (m) English name possibly derived from the Latin *remus* ('oar') or else from Romulus' brother Remus, legendary founder of Rome. It made sporadic appearances as a first name among English-speakers in the 19th century. The most famous bearer of the name is the fictional former black slave Remus in Joel Chandler Harris's *Uncle Remus* tales (1880–1910).

Rena/Renata *See* RENÉ.

René (m) French name derived from the Latin *renatus* ('reborn'). As **Renatus** it was popular among the early Christians and was later taken up by the Puritans in the 17th century. Its frequency in Canada and the USA reflects the influence of the French missionary St René Goupil (d.1642). Both René and the feminine version **Renée** (or **Reenie**) have been adopted among English-speakers in the 20th century, becoming especially popular in Australia. The name may or may not appear with an accent. Other variants include the feminine **Rena** (or **Rina**) and **Renata**.

Renée *See* RENÉ.

Renie *See* IRENE.

Reuben (m) Hebrew name meaning 'behold, a son'. The name appears in the Bible as that of Jacob's eldest son. Also found as

Ruben, it was among the many biblical names adopted by English-speaking Puritans in the 17th century. **Rube** and **Ruby** are common abbreviations of the name.

Rex (m) English name derived from the Latin *rex* ('king'). It is largely a 20th-century introduction, although it is also sometimes considered to be a shortened form of REGINALD. Famous bearers of the name have included the British actor Rex Harrison (Reginald Carey Harrison; 1908–90). *See also* REGINA.

Rexanne (f) English first name derived from REX, probably influenced by **Roxanne** (*see* ROXANA).

Reynold (m) English name derived via Norman French from the Old German *ragin* ('advice' or 'decision') and *wald* ('ruler') and thus meaning 'well-counselled ruler'. Also encountered as a variant form of REGINALD, in its current form it has been in irregular use among English-speakers since the 19th century. Variants in other languages include the Welsh **Rheinallt**.

Rhea (f) Greek name meaning 'flow', originally borne by an earth goddess identified as the mother of Zeus. Another legend names Rhea Silva as the mother of Romulus and Remus, founders of Rome. *See also* MARY.

Rheanna *See* REANNA.

Rhett (m) English name of uncertain origin, possibly derived from the older BRETT or else from the Dutch surname de Raedt, itself derived from the Middle Dutch *raet* ('advice'). A more fanciful suggestion traces the name back rather tentatively to the Greek *rhetor* ('speaker' or 'orator'). It became popular from the 1940s through Rhett Butler in Margaret Mitchell's novel *Gone with the Wind* (1936). A relatively recent feminine version of the name is **Rhetta**. *See also* SCARLETT.

Rhian (f) Welsh name meaning 'maiden'. This appears to be a modern innovation. A variant is **Rhianu**.

Rhiannon (f) Welsh name meaning 'nymph' or 'goddess', probably derived from *rigantona*, a Celtic royal title meaning 'great queen'. The name is thought to have been borne by a Celtic goddess associated with horses and was later carried by the legendary Celtic Princess Rhiannon. In modern times it has been taken up by many English-speakers without Welsh connections. Older forms of the name include **Riannon**. A recently introduced variant is **Rhianna**.

Rhianu *See* RHIAN.

Rhoda (f) Hebrew name derived from the Greek *rhodon* ('rose'), or alternatively possibly meaning 'a woman from Rhodes' (the name of the island of Rhodes having itself been taken from the Greek *rhodon*). It appears in the New Testament as the name of a servant girl in the house of Mary, mother of John. The name was adopted by Puritans in England in the 17th century. In Scotland the name is often treated as a feminine equivalent of RODERICK.

Rhodri (m) Welsh name derived from the Old Welsh *rhod* ('wheel') and *rhi* ('ruler'), or alternatively treated as a Welsh variant of RODERICK. Notable bearers of the name have included a 9th-century Welsh king.

Rhona (f) Scottish name that developed either from a place name (from Rona, an island in the Hebrides) or as a feminine variant of RONALD or **Raghnaid**. It seems to have made its debut as a first name around 1870. Although also found as **Rona**, the usual variant spelling of the name may have resulted from the influence of RHODA. Its use is still largely confined to Scotland. *See also* ROWENA.

Rhonda (f) Welsh name derived from the Welsh *rhon* ('pike' or 'lance') and *da* ('good'). It was probably influenced by RHODA and RONA and acquired extra significance through the link with the Rhondda valley (named after a local river) in south Wales.

Rhonwen *See* ROWENA.

Rhydderch *See* RODERICK.

Rhys (m) Welsh name meaning 'ardour' or 'rashness'. Also found as **Reece** and in the Anglicized form **Rees**, the name was borne by an 11th-century King of Wales, Rhys ap Tewdwr (d.1093), and by his grandson Rhys ap Gruffud

(1132–97) but remains little used today outside the Welsh community around the world.

Ria *See* MARIA; MARY.

Rian *See* RYAN.

Riannon *See* RHIANNON.

Rica *See* ERICA; FREDERICA.

Rich *See* RICHARD.

Richard (m) English name derived via French from the Old German Ricohard, a combination of the German words *ric* ('power') and *hard* ('strong') and thus meaning 'powerful ruler'. Introduced in its modern form by the Normans, it appears in the traditional 'Tom, Dick and Harry' list of common English names, DICK (or **Dickie**) being a common diminutive form. Other common diminutive forms include **Rich**, **Richie** (or **Ritchie**), **Rick** (or **Rik**) and **Ricky** (or **Rikki**). Rare feminine versions of the name include **Ricarda**, **Richelle** and **Richenda**, an 18th-century coinage possibly modelled on such names as BRENDA and GLENDA. *See also* RICHMAL.

Richenda/Richie *See* RICHARD.

Richmal (f) English combination of MICHAEL and RICHARD. A relatively recent introduction, it is known chiefly from the British children's author Richmal Crompton (1890–1969), writer of the *Just William* stories.

Rick *See* ERIC; RICHARD.

Rickie *See* FREDERICA.

Ricky *See* ERIC; FREDERICA; RICHARD.

Rider (m) English name derived from the ordinary vocabulary word. Its most famous bearer to date has been the English novelist Sir Henry Rider Haggard (1856–1925).

Ridley (m) English name derived from a place name based on the Old English *hreod* ('reeds') and *leah* ('wood' or 'clearing'). The name enjoyed some popularity among Protestants in 16th-century England after the burning of the Protestant Bishop Nicholas Ridley (c.1500–1555) during the reign of Mary Tudor.

Rik/Rikki *See* RICHARD.

Riley (m) English name derived from a place name based on the Old English *ryge* ('rye') and *leah* ('clearing' or 'meadow'). In Ireland it may also represent a development of the surname Reilly or be descended from the Irish first name Raghallach (of obscure meaning).

Rina *See* RENÉ.

Riona *See* CATRIONA.

Riordan (m) English version of the Irish Gaelic name **Rordan**, derived from *riogh* ('king') and *bard* ('poet'). Also encountered as **Rearden**.

Rita (f) English and Scandinavian name that developed originally as an Italian and Spanish variant of **Margarita** (*see* MARGARET) and is now considered to exist as a name in its own right. Since being adopted by English-speakers around the beginning of the 20th

century it has become much more common than the fuller version of the name. It was further boosted by the popularity of the US film star Rita Hayworth (Margarita Carmen Cansino; 1918–87).

Ritchie *See* RICHARD.

Rob/Robb/Robbie/Robby *See* ROBERT.

Robert (m) English, Scottish and French name derived via Norman French from the Old German Hrodebert, from *hrod* ('fame') and *berht* ('bright' or 'famous') and thus meaning 'bright famous one' or simply 'famously famous'. In its modern form it arrived in England with the Normans. The Scottish king Robert the Bruce (1274–1329) made the name especially popular in Scotland. Common diminutive forms of the name include **Rob** (or **Robb**), **Robbie** (or **Robby**), BOB (or BOBBY) and BERT (or BERTIE). Long-established Scottish diminutives are **Rab** and **Rabbie**. *See also* ROBERTA; ROBIN; RUPERT.

Roberta (f) Feminine equivalent of ROBERT. It was introduced in the 1870s and became especially popular in Scotland and the USA, where it was further popularized by the Jerome Kern musical *Roberta* (1933). Often shortened to **Bobbie** or **Berta**. **Robertina** is a rare variant form.

Robin (m/f) English name that developed as a diminutive form of ROBERT but has long had its own independent existence. The name came to England from France in medieval times and subsequently emerged as a separate boys' name in its own right. It has been bestowed upon members of both sexes only since the 1950s. The exclusively feminine versions of the name **Robyn**, **Robynne** and **Robina** (also found as **Robena** and **Robinia**) go back to the 15th century or earlier.

Robina/Robyn *See* ROBIN.

Rocco (m) Italian name derived from the Old German *hrok* ('repose'). Variant forms of the name include the US **Rocky**, which evokes the idea of physical toughness or strength of character. It is particularly associated with boxers – in tribute to the US boxer Rocky Marciano (Rocco Marciano; 1923–69).

Rochelle (f) French name that is alternatively a feminine diminutive form of the French Roch, a variant of RACHEL, or else derived from a place name (from the French port of La Rochelle) meaning 'little rock'.

Rocky *See* ROCCO.

Rod/Roddie/Roddy *See* RODERICK; RODNEY.

Roderick (m) English name derived from the Old German Hrodic, from the words *hrod* ('fame') and *ric* ('power') and thus meaning 'famously powerful'. It was first brought to England by the Normans and was subsequently revived following the publication of Sir Walter Scott's poem 'The Vision of Don

Roderick' (1811). The name was originally considered to be Scottish rather than English. Also found as **Rodrick** and **Roderic** and commonly shortened to **Rod** or **Roddy**. **Rodina** and RHODA are feminine versions of the name. *See also* RHODRI; RORY.

Rodge/Rodger *See* ROGER.

Rodney (m) English name derived from a place name (from Somerset) meaning 'reed island'. Its popularity in England dates from the 19th century when it was associated with the naval exploits of Admiral Lord George Rodney (1719–92). Commonly shortened to **Rod**, **Roddie** or **Roddy**.

Roger (m) English and French name derived via Norman French from the Old German *hrod* ('fame') and *gar* ('spear') and thus meaning 'famous warrior'. The modern form of the name was introduced to England by the Normans and became a popular choice in medieval times. The name is occasionally encountered as **Rodger**, which is sometimes shortened to **Rodge**.

Roisin *See* ROSE.

Roland (m) English name derived via Norman French from the Old German *hrod* ('fame') and *land* ('land' or 'territory') and thus meaning 'famous landowner'. It was introduced to England by the Normans in the 11th century. In medieval legend, Roland was the most gallant of all the knights in the court of the Emperor

Charlemagne. Also found as **Rowland**. Diminutive forms include **Roly**, **Rowley** and **Rollo**.

Rolf (m) English, German and Scandinavian variant of RUDOLPH, derived from *hrod* ('fame') and *wulf* ('wolf'). In the Latinized form **Rollo** the name dates at least as far back as the Vikings. As Rolf, it reached England at the time of the Norman Conquest. Well-known bearers of the name in recent times have included the Australian artist and television presenter Rolf Harris (b.1930). Rarely found in the variant form **Rolph**.

Rollo *See* ROLAND; ROLF.

Rolph *See* ROLF.

Roly *See* ROLAND.

Roma (f) Roman name derived from that of the city of Rome. The Emperor Hadrian built a temple in Rome to the goddess Roma and she was worshipped throughout Roman territories. It has appeared sporadically as a first name since the 19th century.

Romaine (f) French first name meaning 'Roman woman'. The French equivalent of the masculine ROMAN, it was first adopted by English-speakers in the 19th century and is also encountered as **Romayne**. The Latinate **Romana** is a variant form.

Roman (m) Russian, Polish and Czech first name derived from the Latin Romanus ('man from Rome'). It remains rare among English-speakers, but is occasionally imported from other lan-

guages. Notable bearers of the name have included the Polish-born film director Roman Polanski (b.1933).

Romayne *See* ROMAINE.

Romeo (m) Italian first name meaning 'pilgrim to Rome'. It became widely known among English-speakers through William Shakespeare's character of the name in his tragedy *Romeo and Juliet* (1595). It enjoyed new prominence in 2002 when the English footballer David Beckham and his popstar wife Victoria Beckham chose it for their second son.

Romey/Romy *See* ROSEMARY.

Ron *See* RONALD; ROWENA; VERONICA.

Rona *See* RHONA.

Ronald (m) English and Scottish equivalent of REGINALD that developed from the Old Norse Rognvaldr. Also found in Scotland as **Ranald** or **Raghnall**, the name is no longer thought of as uniquely Scottish. Often shortened to **Ron** or **Ronnie** (or **Ronni**). Rare feminine variants include **Ronalda**, **Ronna** and **Ronnette**.

Ronalda *See* RONALD.

Ronan (m) Irish name derived from the Irish Gaelic *ron* ('little seal'). The most famous of several Irish saints to bear the name was a 5th-century Irish missionary working in Cornwall and Brittany. Notable bearers of the name have included the Irish pop singer Ronan Keating (b.1977).

Ronna/Ronnette *See* RONALD.

Ronnie *See* RONALD; ROWENA; VERONICA.

Roo *See* RUE; RUTH.

Rory (m) Irish and Scottish name derived from the Gaelic name Ruairi (or Ruaidhri), from the Gaelic *ruadh* ('red' or 'red-haired') and *ri* ('king') and thus meaning 'great king'. It is sometimes considered to be an equivalent of ROGER and is also used as a diminutive form of RODERICK. Sometimes found as **Rorie** or in the Gaelic forms **Ruari** or **Ruaridh**.

Ros *See* ROSALIND; ROSAMUND.

Rosa/Rosabel/Rosabella *See* ROSE.

Rosaleen *See* ROSALIND.

Rosalie (f) French name that developed from the older Latin Rosalia, the name of a Roman festival in which people decorated the tombs of the dead with garlands of roses. The Latin form of the name is encountered only rarely in English-speaking communities, having been replaced fairly comprehensively by the French form in the middle of the 19th century. The success of the Hollywood musical *Rosalie* in the 1930s, starring Nelson Eddy, did much to popularize the name in the mid 20th century.

Rosalind (f) English name that had its origins in the Old German Roslindis, derived from *hros* ('horse') and either *lind* ('tender' or 'soft') or *linta* ('lime'), in which case it means 'horse shield made of lime wood'. The Goths intro-duced the name to Spain, where it acquired a much more attractive new derivation from *rosa* and *linda*, meaning 'pretty rose'. The name came to England with the Normans in the 11th century. Variants include **Rosalyn**, **Rosalynne**, **Rosalin**, **Rosalinda**, **Roseline**, **Roslyn**, **Rosslyn** and **Rosaleen**. Often shortened to **Ros** or **Roz**.

Rosalinda/Rosaline/Rosalyn *See* ROSALIND.

Rosamund (f) English name combining the Old German *hros* ('horse') and *mund* ('protection'), although a more popular derivation of medieval origin suggests that it comes from the Latin *rosa mundi* ('rose of the world') or *rosa munda* ('pure rose'). It was introduced to England by the Normans in the 11th century. Also found as **Rosamond**. Sometimes shortened to **Ros** or **Roz**.

Rosanna (f) English name combining ROSE and ANNA. It was first adopted in the 18th century and has remained popular ever since, often appearing as **Rosanne**, **Rozanne** or **Roseanne**. Other variants include **Roseanna** and **Rosannah** (suggesting a combination of Rose with HANNAH).

Roscoe (m) English name derived from a place name based on the Old Norse *ra* ('roe-deer') and *skogr* ('wood' or 'copse').

Rose (f) English name derived from the Old German *hros* ('horse') or *hrod* ('fame'). Now associated universally with the flower, from the Latin *rosa*, the name came to England with the Normans and has remained consistently popular, in part because the flower is a symbol of the Virgin Mary. Sometimes rendered as **Rosie** or **Rosy**. Other variants include **Rosa**, **Rosabel** and **Rosabella** ('beautiful rose'), **Rosetta** ('little rose'), **Roselle**, **Rosette** and the Spanish **Rosita**. An Irish variant of the name, meaning 'little rose', is **Roisin** (alternatively rendered as **Rosheen**, reflecting its pronunciation). Sometimes encountered as an abbreviation of ROSEMARY and other names beginning with 'Rose-'.

Roseanna/Roseanne *See* ROSANNA.

Roseline *See* ROSALIND.

Roselle *See* ROSE.

Roselyn *See* ROSALIND.

Rosemarie *See* ROSEMARY.

Rosemary (f) English flower name derived from the Latin *ros marinus* ('sea dew'), a reference to the plant's blue-green foliage. It is sometimes also considered to be a simple combined form of ROSE and MARY. Like other flower names, it became an increasingly popular choice of first name from the late 19th century. Sometimes encountered as **Rosemarie**. Diminutive forms of the name include **Rose**, **Rosie** and the rare **Romey** and **Romy**.

Rosetta *See* ROSE.

Rosheen *See* ROSE.

Rosie *See* ROSE; ROSEMARY.

Rosita *See* ROSE.

Roslyn *See* ROSALIND.

Ross (m) English and Scottish name derived from a Scottish place name, itself from the Gaelic *ros* ('peninsula' or 'promontory'). Other derivations suggest that it came from the Old German *hrod* ('fame'), the French *roux* ('red') or the Anglo-Saxon *hros* ('horse'). It has become increasingly popular since the 1970s.

Rosslyn *See* ROSALIND.

Rosy *See* ROSE.

Rowan (m/f) English version of the Irish Gaelic Ruadhan, meaning 'little red-haired one'. It is sometimes derived instead from the alternate name of the mountain ash, which bears red berries. A traditional Irish favourite, it seems to have made its first appearances among English-speakers in the middle of the 20th century. It used to be an exclusively boys' name but is now used for both sexes, although it is sometimes altered to **Rowanne** when applied to girls.

Rowena (f) English name derived from the Old English *hrod* ('fame') and *wynn* ('joy') or, alternatively, a Celtic first name derived from the Welsh Rhonwen, based on *rhon* ('pike' or 'lance') and *gwyn* ('white' or 'fair') and thus meaning 'slender and fair'. In the legend of Vortigern and Rowena, the beautiful Rowena was the cause of the great 5th-century British king's downfall. Sometimes encountered as **Rowina**. Diminutive forms of the name include **Ron**, **Ronnie**, **Rona** and **Rhona**.

Rowland/Rowley *See* ROLAND.

Roxana (f) Latinized version of the Persian first name **Roschana**, meaning 'dawn' or 'light'. The most famous Persian bearer of the name was Roxana, the wife of Alexander the Great, who lived in the 4th century BC. The popularity of the name was boosted among English-speakers by the publication of Daniel Defoe's novel *Roxana* (1724). **Roxane** or **Roxanne** are now the most common English and French versions of the name. Commonly shortened to **Roxie** or **Roxy**.

Roxane/Roxanne/Roxie/Roxy *See* ROXANA.

Roy (m) English name of uncertain derivation. According to one theory the name comes from the French *roi* ('king'); according to another it developed as an Anglicization of the Gaelic RORY, coming ultimately from the Gaelic *ruadh* ('red') and thus being reserved primarily for children with red hair or a ruddy complexion. Sir Walter Scott's novel *Rob Roy* (1817) did much to familiarize the name in the 19th century, particularly in Scotland. *See also* LEROY.

Royal (m) English name alterna-

tively derived from the adjective 'royal' or from a surname meaning 'rye hill'. Its use as a first name is largely restricted to the USA. *See also* ROYLE.

Royce (m) English name that has been in occasional use since the late 19th century.

Royle (m) English name derived from a place name (from Lancashire), itself based on the Old English *ryge* ('rye') and *hyll* ('hill'). It probably developed under the influence of such similar-sounding names as **Doyle** (*see* DOUGAL) and because of the link with the ordinary vocabulary word 'royal'. *See also* ROYAL.

Royston (m) English name derived from a place name (from Hertfordshire) meaning 'settlement of Royce'. It appears to have made its debut as a first name in the 18th century and today is popular chiefly in England and Australia.

Roz *See* ROSALIND; ROSAMUND.

Rozanne *See* ROSANNA.

Ruari/Ruaridh *See* RORY.

Rube *See* REUBEN; RUBY.

Rubina *See* RUBY.

Ruby (f) English jewel name derived from the Latin *rubeus* ('red') that was taken up as a first name in the late 19th century. Notable bearers of the name have included the Canadian-born US singer and dancer Ruby Keeler (Ethel Keeler; 1909–93) and the US television comedienne Ruby Wax (b.1953). Variant forms include **Rubie** and **Rubina**.

Rudi/Rudolf *See* RUDOLPH.

Rudolph (m) English name derived from the Old German Hrodulf, from *hrod* ('fame') and *wulf* ('wolf') and thus meaning 'famous warrior'. The name has made occasional appearances among English-speakers since the 19th century, occasionally appearing in the modern Germanic form **Rudolf**. It subsequently received further boosts through public adulation for the US film star Rudolph Valentino (Rodolfo di Valentina d'Antonguolla; 1895–1926). Commonly shortened to **Rudy**.

Rudy *See* RUDOLPH.

Rudyard (m) English name derived from that of Rudyard Lake in Staffordshire. It was made lastingly famous by the British writer Rudyard Kipling (1865–1936).

Rue (f) English name inspired by the plant name, but also sometimes considered to be a diminutive form of RUTH. Also encountered as **Roo**, it did not emerge as a first name among English-speakers until the 20th century.

Rufus (m) English name derived from the Latin for 'red-haired'. A biblical name, it was later borne by William Rufus (1056–1100), who as William II succeeded his father William the Conqueror as king of England. It is unclear whether William acquired the name through the colour of his hair or through the colour of his complexion.

Rupert (m) English version of the Dutch Rupprecht, which like ROBERT comes ultimately from the Old German for 'bright fame'. The name came to England with Prince Rupert of the Rhine (1619–92), the nephew of Charles I who fought on behalf of his uncle in the English Civil War. **Ruperta** is a rare feminine version of the name.

Ruperta *See* RUPERT.

Russ *See* RUSSELL.

Russell (m) English name derived from the French nickname *rousel* ('little red one'). It was originally reserved for children with red hair or a ruddy complexion. Also found as **Russel**, it has strong aristocratic connections and is the family name of the dukes of Bedford. As a first name its history dates from the 19th century. Sometimes shortened to **Russ** or **Rusty**.

Rusty *See* RUSSELL.

Ruth (f) Hebrew name of uncertain origin, variously interpreted as meaning 'companion', 'friend' or 'vision of beauty'. The name appears in the Old Testament and was among the biblical names taken up by Puritans in England after the Reformation, perhaps because in its otherwise unrelated ordinary vocabulary sense it also evoked the concepts of pity and compassion. Also encountered in the familiar forms **Roo** and **Ruthie**.

Ruthie *See* RUTH.

Rutland (m) English name derived from the name of the English county. It has been in occasional use as a first name since the 19th century.

Ryan (m) Irish name of uncertain origin. The original Gaelic sur-name meant 'descendant of Rian', Rian probably coming from *ri*, meaning 'king'. An alternative derivation links the name with that of an ancient sea or river god (also the inspiration behind the name of the River Rhine). The name reached a peak in popularity in the 1990s. Occasionally found in the form **Rian**.

who was drowned in the River Severn (subsequently named after her) on the orders of Locrine's widow Gwendolen.

Sacha *See* SASHA.

Sacheverell (m) English name that is thought to have come from a place name in Normandy, Saute-Chevreuil (meaning 'roebuck leap'). The name was popularized in the 18th century by the celebrated English political preacher Henry Sacheverell (c.1674–1724). Other famous bearers of the name have included the British writer Sacheverell Sitwell (1897–1985). Sometimes shortened to **Sachie**.

Sachie *See* SACHEVERELL.

Sadhbh (f) Irish name derived from the Gaelic for 'sweet'. It was commonly given to girls in medieval Ireland. Today it is more likely to be found in such Anglicized forms as SABIA, **Sabina** and **Sive**.

Sadie (f) English name that developed as a diminutive form of SARAH. It emerged from the shadow of Sarah in the late 19th century and enjoyed a peak in popularity in the 1970s, notably in the USA. *See also* MERCEDES.

Saffie/Saffrey *See* SAFFRON.

Saffron (f) English name that has been in occasional use among English-speakers since the 1960s. The origin of the name lies in the golden-yellow crocus pollen long used as a spice. Diminutive forms include **Saffie** and **Saffrey**.

Sabella (f) English name that is thought to have developed from ISABELLA. This is a relatively recent introduction, of 20th-century invention.

Sabia (f) Irish name that developed as a Latinized version of the Gaelic SADHBH. The earliest records of the name go back to the medieval period.

Sabina *See* SADHBH.

Sabrina (f) Welsh name that has been in occasional use among English-speakers since the 19th century. The name features in Welsh legend as that of an illegitimate daughter of King Locrine

Said (m) Arabic name meaning 'happy' or 'lucky'.

Sal See SALLY; SARAH.

Salah (m) Arabic name meaning 'goodness' or 'righteousness'. Also found as **Saleh**, it is one of the most popular of all Arab names today. **Salih** or **Salha** is a feminine equivalent.

Salena See SELINA.

Salim (m) Arabic name meaning 'safe' or 'secure'. Also found as **Saleem** or **Selim**. **Salma** is a feminine equivalent.

Salina See SELINA.

Sally (f) English name that began life as a diminutive form of SARAH. The process by which the 'r' in the name became 'll' is fairly standard among English first names. The name was well established by the 18th century and received another boost in the 1930s with the Gracie Fields song 'Sally'. Also found as **Sallie** or **Salley**. Commonly shortened to **Sal**. The name may also be combined with other names, as in **Sallyann** (or **Sally-Anne**) and **Sally-Jane**.

Sallyann/Sally-Anne/Sally-Jane See SALLY.

Salome (f) Greek version of an Aramaic name of unknown meaning, possibly linked to the Hebrew *shalom* ('peace'). The name's association with Herod's grand-daughter, whose demand for the head of John the Baptist brought about his execution, has stopped it becoming a popular choice. It was occasionally taken up by the Puritans in the 16th and 17th centuries, probably because it was also borne in the New Testament by the mother of the apostles James and John.

Sam See SAMANTHA; SAMSON; SAMUEL.

Samantha (f) English variant of SAMUEL. It appears to have first entered use in the southern USA, perhaps under the influence of ANTHEA, during the 18th century, but it was not until the 1960s that the name became widespread throughout the English-speaking world. Its popularity was boosted in 1956 by the Cole Porter song 'I love you, Samantha' from the film *High Society*. Sometimes shortened to **Sam** or **Sammy** (or **Sammie**).

Sammy See SAMANTHA; SAMSON; SAMUEL.

Sampson See SAMSON.

Samson (m) English version of the Hebrew Shimshon, which was itself derived from *shemesh* ('sun'), thus meaning 'sun child'. It features in the Bible as the name of the immensely powerful leader of the Israelites who was deceived by Delilah but got his revenge by pulling down the temple of the Philistines on their heads. Sometimes found as **Sampson**, it was revived by the Puritans in the 17th century. **Sam** and **Sammy** are common familiar forms of the name.

Samuel (m) English version of the Hebrew Shemuel or Shmuel, variously meaning 'name of God' or

'He has hearkened'. Another derivation suggests the name comes from the Hebrew *shaul meel* ('asked of God'). It features in the Bible as the name of an Old Testament prophet and as a result was taken up by Puritans in the 17th century. In Scotland and Ireland it is sometimes considered to be an Anglicized version of the Gaelic Somhairle, derived from the Old Norse for 'summer wanderer' or 'Viking'. The diminutive form **Sam** is in common use. Another familiar variant is **Sammy**.

Sandford *See* SANFORD.

Sandie *See* SANDRA.

Sandor *See* ALEXANDER.

Sandra (f) English name derived from the Italian Alessandra (*see* ALEXANDRA). It made early appearances in the English-speaking world in the 19th century, notably in George Meredith's novel *Sandra Belloni* (1886), and enjoyed a peak in popularity in the 1950s. Also found in the form **Zandra** – as borne by the British fashion designer Zandra Rhodes (b.1940). Variants include the Scottish **Saundra** and the chiefly US **Sondra**. Familiar versions of the name are **Sandy** and **Sandie**. *See also* CASSANDRA.

Sandy *See* ALEXANDER; SANDRA; SAWNEY.

Sanford (m) English name derived from a place name, originally **Sandford**, from Old English *sand* ('sand') and *ford* ('ford'). It is more common in the USA than elsewhere, sometimes appearing in tribute to an early governor of Rhode Island called Peleg Sanford.

Sanjay (m) Indian name derived from the Sanskrit *samjaya* ('triumphant'). It is borne by several characters in Indian mythology and figures in the *Mahabharata*. Bearers of the name in more recent times have included Indira Gandhi's son Sanjay Gandhi (1948–80).

Sanna *See* SUSANNAH.

Sapphira *See* SAPPHIRE.

Sapphire (f) English jewel name derived from the Hebrew *sappir* ('sapphire' or 'lapis lazuli'). It was first taken up by English-speakers along with other jewel names in the 19th century, but has never been common. A variant of the name, in which form it may be found in the New Testament, is **Sapphira**.

Sara *See* SARAH.

Sarah (f) Hebrew name meaning 'princess'. It appears in the Bible as the name of the 90-year-old wife of Abraham, and as a result of its religious associations was taken up by English-speaking Puritans in the 16th century, when it often appeared as **Sarey**, **Sarra** or **Sara** (a variant of Greek origin). It reached a peak in popularity in Britain in the late 19th century. Familiar forms of the name include SALLY, **Sal** and **Sassie**. Among rarer variants are **Sarina** and **Sarita**. In Ireland the name is sometimes used as an equivalent of **Saraid** (meaning 'excellent') or SORCHA. *See also* SADIE; ZARA.

Saraid *See* SARAH.

Saranna (f) English first name, a combined form of SARAH and ANNA. It seems to have made its first appearance among English-speakers in the 18th century, but remains rare.

Sarey/Sarina/Sarita/Sarra *See* SARAH.

Sasha (m/f) Diminutive form of ALEXANDER or ALEXANDRA. Originally a Russian variant, it was introduced to the English-speaking world in the early 20th century through the international tours of Sergei Diaghilev's Ballets Russes. **Sacha** – as borne by the French singer Sacha Distel (1933–2004) – is a common French version. Occasionally shortened to **Sy**.

Saskia (f) Dutch first name of obscure origin that was taken up by English-speakers in the 1950s. Recorded in use among the Dutch in medieval times, the name may have evolved from the Old German *sachs* ('Saxon'). Notable bearers of the name have included the Dutch artist Rembrandt's wife, the subject of several of his paintings.

Sassa/Sassie *See* SARAH.

Saul (m) Hebrew name meaning 'asked for' or 'desired'. It features in the Bible as the name of one of the first kings of Israel and as the Jewish name of St Paul (Paul being his Roman name). Revived by the Puritans in the 17th century, it has been encountered only sporadically among English-speakers since the 19th century, almost exclusively within the Jewish community.

Saundra *See* SANDRA.

Savanna (f) English name derived from the Spanish *zavana* ('grassland' or 'plain'). Popular chiefly in the USA, where it is also the name of a port in Georgia. Also found as **Savannah** or **Zavanna**.

Sawney (m) Scottish variant of **Sandy** (*see* ALEXANDER). The name has lost ground since the 19th century, perhaps because it acquired a new vocabulary sense meaning 'fool'.

Saxon (m) English name derived from the name of the 5th-century Germanic invaders of Britain, the Saxons. The Old German *sachs* originally meant 'dagger' or 'short sword'. It was taken up as a first name during the 19th century, when there was a considerable enthusiasm for archaic names from the medieval period or earlier.

Scarlett (f) English name that was taken up in the middle of the 20th century. It was originally reserved for (chiefly male) dealers in scarlet cloth or for people habitually wearing scarlet-coloured clothing. As a first name for girls it was popularized by the US novelist Margaret Mitchell, who gave it to her heroine Scarlett O'Hara in her novel *Gone with the Wind* (1936).

The name has also appeared as **Scarlet**. *See also* ASHLEY; RHETT.

Scilla *See* PRISCILLA.

Scott (m) Scottish and English name meaning 'Scotsman' or 'Scottish' that was formerly commonly applied to anyone from Scotland. Also found as **Scot**, the name increased in popularity as a choice of first name around the middle of the 20th century, perhaps in tribute to the US novelist F. Scott Fitzgerald (1896–1940). Familiar variants include **Scottie** and **Scotty**.

Seaghdh (m) Scottish first name derived from the Gaelic for 'fine' or 'hawk-like'. **Seaghdha** is an Irish Gaelic variant. Anglicized versions of the name include SETH and SHAW.

Seamus (m) English version of the Irish **Seamas**, itself an equivalent of the English JAMES. Commonly encountered in Ireland, it remains rare elsewhere in the English-speaking world, although it has made occasional appearances among people with no Irish links since the middle of the 20th century. Also found as **Seumas** or **Shamus**, a variant reflecting the usual pronunciation of the name. *See also* HAMISH.

Sean (m) Irish name that is an equivalent of the English JOHN. Pronounced 'shawn', it retains its position as a typically Irish name but since the 1920s has also been found fairly frequently outside the Irish community. Also encountered in the variant forms **Shane** (from the Northern Irish pronunciation of the name), **Shaun** and **Shawn**. Rare feminine versions of the name are **Shauna** and **Shani**, although the variant Shane has been given to girls with increasing frequency since the 1950s, chiefly in Australia.

Seaton (m) English name derived from a place name meaning 'farmstead at the sea'. Also found as **Seton**.

Seb *See* SEBASTIAN.

Sebastian (m) English form of the Roman Sebastianus, meaning 'of Sebasta' (a town in Asia Minor). Another derivation suggests the name comes from the Greek *sebastos* ('respected' or 'august'). As the name of the 3rd-century Christian martyr St Sebastian, who was shot with arrows and then beaten to death, it was widely known to English-speakers in medieval times and later. **Seb**, **Sebbie**, **Bastian**, **Baz** and **Bazza** are diminutive forms of the name.

Sefton (m) English name derived from a place name meaning 'settlement in the rushes'. Its history as a first name began in the 19th century.

Seirian (f) Welsh name meaning 'bright one'. It is pronounced 'sighreean'. A masculine equivalent is **Seiriol**.

Selby (m) English name derived from a place name meaning 'willow farm'. It was taken up as a first name in the 19th century.

Selena *See* SELINA.

Selima (f) Arabic name meaning 'peace', also sometimes treated as a variant of SELINA. The earliest records of its use among English-speakers date from the 18th century. A modern variant of the name is SELMA, probably a contracted version that emerged in the 18th century under the influence of THELMA.

Selina (f) English version of the Greek Selene, derived either from the Greek *selene* ('moon') or possibly from the Latin *caelum* ('heaven'). **Salena**, **Selena** and **Salina** are variant forms. *See also* CÉLINE.

Selma (f) English name of uncertain origin, probably a contracted form of SELIMA. Also found as **Zelma**.

Selwyn (m) English name of uncertain origin that has been in occasional use as a first name since medieval times. The name may originally have come from the Old English *sele* ('prosperity') or *sele* ('hall') and *wine* ('friend') or else, via Old French, from the Roman Silvanus, derived from *silva* ('wood'). A third derivation links the name to Welsh words meaning 'ardour' and 'fair'. Also found as **Selwin**.

Senan (m) English version of the Irish **Seanan**, from the Gaelic *sean* ('old' or 'wise'). The name was borne by several early Irish saints.

Senga (f) Scottish name that probably evolved from the Gaelic *seang*

('slender'). Another theory links the name with AGNES, which it spells when read backwards.

Septimus (m) Roman name meaning 'seventh'. It was taken up by English-speakers in the 19th century, when it was often reserved for seventh-born male children. **Septima** is a relatively infrequent feminine version of the name.

Seraphina (f) Latin name derived from the Hebrew *seraphim* ('fiery' or 'burning ones'). In the Bible the name is borne by an order of angels. Sometimes found as **Serafina** and shortened to **Fina**.

Serena (f) English name derived from the Latin *serenus* ('calm' or 'serene'). It is sometimes considered to be an aristocratic name and in recent times has become a royal name, as borne by Serena Stanhope, Viscountess Linley (b.1970). Rare variant forms include **Serina**, **Serenah** and **Serenna**.

Seth (m) English name derived from the Hebrew *sheth* ('appointed' or 'set'). It appears in the Bible as the name of the third son of Adam and Eve and is sometimes interpreted to mean 'compensation' – the birth of Seth compensating to some extent for the loss of their murdered second son, Abel. It was taken up by English-speakers in the 17th century and came to be considered a traditional rural name. The name is also used by Indian peoples, who trace it back to the Sanskrit *setu* ('bridge') or *sveta* ('white').

Seton See SEATON.

Seumas See SEAMUS.

Seward (m) English name derived from the Old English for 'sea' or 'victory' and 'guard'. It was first used as a first name in the 19th century.

Sexton (m) English name derived from the Old French for 'sacristan'. It is most familiar from Harry Blyth's fictional radio detective Sexton Blake.

Sextus (f) Roman name meaning 'sixth'. It was revived by English-speakers in the 19th century, when it was reserved chiefly for sixth-born male children.

Seymour (m) English name that has been in occasional use as a first name since the 19th century. The surname came originally from a Norman French place name, Saint-Maur in Normandy, which itself took its name from the little-known 6th-century North African St Maurus (Maurus meaning 'Moor'). Occasionally found as **Seamor**, **Seamore** or **Seamour**.

Shamus See SEAMUS.

Shane See SEAN; SHANNON.

Shannah See SUSANNAH.

Shannon (f) English name that probably developed as a combination of **Shane** and SHARON, although it is often assumed that it comes from the name – meaning 'the old one' – of the Irish river (despite the fact that the name is little used in Ireland). It seems to have made its debut as a first name in the 1950s and is today commoner in Canada and the USA than elsewhere.

Shantel/Shantelle See CHANTAL.

Shari See SHARON.

Sharlene See CHARLENE.

Sharlott See CHARLOTTE.

Sharmain/Sharmaine See CHARMAINE.

Sharon (f) English name derived ultimately from the Hebrew Saron, from sar ('to sing' or 'singer'). The name features in the Bible as the name of a valley in Palestine, famed for its natural beauty, and is sometimes interpreted to mean 'the plain'. It was taken up by English-speakers in the 1930s and reached a peak in popularity in the 1960s and 1970s. Variant forms of the name include **Sharron**, **Sharona**, **Sharonda** and **Sharyn**. Sometimes shortened to **Shari**.

Sharona/Sharonda/Sharron/ Sharyn See SHARON.

Shaun/Shauna See SEAN.

Shaw (m) English name derived from the Old English sceaga ('wood' or 'copse') and used as a first name since the 19th century. It can also be found in Scotland as an Anglicized equivalent of SEAGHDH.

Shawn See SEAN.

Sheba See BATHSHEBA.

Sheelagh See SHEILA.

Sheena (f) English version of the Scottish and Irish Gaelic **Sine**, itself an equivalent of the English JANE. It was taken up by English-speakers in the 1930s, chiefly in Scotland. Also found in the forms **Shena**, **Sheenagh**, **Sheona** or **Shona**.

Sheila (f) English version of the Irish Gaelic Sile, an equivalent of the English CELIA. It made its debut among English-speakers in the late 19th century and reached a peak in the UK in the 1930s, by which time it was no longer thought of as distinctly Irish. Also found as **Sheela**, **Sheelah** or **Shelagh**.

Shelagh/Sheelah *See* SHEILA.

Sheldon (m) English name derived from a place name (from Derbyshire, Devon and the West Midlands) meaning 'steep-sided valley' or 'flat-topped hill'. It appears to have made its debut as a first name in the early 20th century, initially in the USA.

Shell *See* MICHELLE.

Shelley (f) English name derived from a place name (from Essex, Suffolk and Yorkshire) meaning 'wood on a slope'. It may also be encountered as a familiar form of MICHELLE or RACHEL. As a first name it emerged in the mid 19th century under the influence of the British Romantic poet Percy Bysshe Shelley (1792–1822). The fact that it is now reserved almost exclusively for girls reflects the influence of SHIRLEY. Also found as **Shelly**.

Shena/Sheona *See* SHEENA.

Sherborne (m) English name meaning 'clear stream'. Also encountered as **Sherbourne**.

Sheree/Sheri *See* CHERIE.

Sheridan (m) Irish name of uncertain meaning, possibly from the Gaelic *sirim* ('to seek'). It made its debut as a first name in the middle of the 19th century, boosted by the popularity of the works of the Irish playwright Richard Brinsley Sheridan (1751–1816). Sometimes shortened to **Sherry**.

Sherie *See* CHERIE.

Sherill/Sherilyn *See* CHERYL.

Sherley *See* SHIRLEY.

Sherlock (m) English name derived from the Middle English for 'shear lock' (possibly reserved for people with closely cropped hair). The name is strongly associated with Sherlock Holmes, the fictional detective created by Sir Arthur Conan Doyle in the late 19th century.

Sherman (m) English name derived from the Old English *sce-ara* ('shears') and *mann* ('man'). It began as a medieval trade name reserved for those whose job it was to trim the nap of woollen cloth after weaving. Its popularity in the USA was boosted by the exploits of the US general William Tecumseh Sherman (1820–91) in the US Civil War.

Sherri/Sherry *See* CHERIE; SHERIDAN; SHIRLEY.

Sherwin (m) English name meaning 'loyal friend' or 'fast-footed'.

Sheryl *See* CHERYL.

Shevaun *See* SIOBHAN.

Shirl *See* SHIRLEY.

Shirley (f) English name derived from a place name (from Derbyshire, Hampshire, Surrey and the West Midlands), in use since the 1860s. The name came originally from the Old English *scir* ('county' or 'bright') and *leah* ('wood' or 'clearing') and was formerly reserved for boys. It was transferred to girls after the publication of Charlotte Brontë's novel *Shirley* (1849), in which the heroine's parents chose the name for their unborn son and kept to their choice even when the baby turned out to be a girl. Variant forms include **Sherley** and **Shirlee**. **Shelley**, **Sherry**, **Sherri** and **Shirl** are diminutive forms.

Sholto (m) English version of the Scottish Gaelic **Sioltach** (meaning 'sower' or 'fruitful'). It is largely confined to Scotland, where it first emerged in the 19th century and is traditionally associated with the Douglas family.

Shona *See* SHEENA.

Shug/Shuggie *See* HUGH.

Shula (f) Diminutive form of the Jewish Shulamit, derived ultimately from *shalom* ('peace'). The name Shulamit features in the biblical Song of Solomon and is today a common Hebrew name. The name has been promoted in recent years as that of a leading character in the BBC radio soap opera *The Archers*.

Si *See* SIMON.

Siân (f) Welsh version of JANE, also in existence as a feminine variant of SEAN. Pronounced 'sharn', it was taken up in Wales in the 1940s and has since made occasional appearances elsewhere in the English-speaking world. It may appear with or without the accent. **Siana** is a recognized diminutive form.

Sib/Sibb *See* ISABEL; SYBIL.

Sid *See* SIDNEY.

Sidney (m/f) English name that may have begun as a Norman French place name, Saint-Denis, or, more likely, came from the Old English *sidan* ('wide') and *eg* ('river island' or 'wide island'). Also found from the 19th century as **Sydney**, a form of the name that is now usually reserved for females. Commonly shortened to **Syd** or **Sid**.

Sidonie (f) French version of the Roman Sidonia (meaning 'of Sidon', Sidon being the capital of Phoenicia). Another derivation suggests it comes from the Greek *sindon* ('linen'), probably in reference to the linen shroud of Jesus Christ. The French version of the name was taken up by English-speakers in the 19th century. Also found as **Sidony**.

Siegfried (m) German name derived from the Old Germanic *sige* ('victory') and *frid* ('peace'). It has made rare appearances among English-speakers, being borne by, among others, the British war poet Siegfried Sassoon (1886–1967). Sometimes shortened to **Sigi**.

Siena (f) Italian name derived from that of the city. As a first name it appears to have made its debut in the 19th century.

Sierra (f) Spanish name meaning 'mountain range'. Its history as a first name among English-speakers is a relatively recent phenomenon.

Sigi *See* SIEGFRIED; SIGMUND.

Sigmund (m) German and English name derived from the Old German *sige* ('victory') and *mund* ('defender') and thus meaning 'victorious defender'. Famous as the name of a legendary German hero and as the name of the Austrian psychiatrist Sigmund Freud (1856–1939), it has made occasional appearances among English-speakers since before the Norman Conquest. Sometimes shortened to **Sigi**.

Sigourney (f) English name that appeared in the 1920s. The name seems to have been introduced by the US novelist F. Scott Fitzgerald via his character Sigourney Howard in *The Great Gatsby* (1925). In due course the name was adopted by the US film actress Sigourney Weaver (Susan Alexandra Weaver; b.1949).

Silas (m) English name derived via Hebrew from the Latin Silvanus, from *silva* ('wood'). Silvanus was the Roman god of trees. The name was originally applied to people who lived in wooded areas or who

worked with wood in some way. It features in the New Testament as the name of a prophet and was taken up by the Puritans in the 17th century.

Silver (m) English name derived from the Old English *siolfor* ('silver'). It was reserved originally for children with silvery hair.

Silvester *See* SYLVESTER.

Silvia (f) Italian and English name derived from the Latin Silvius, itself from *silva* ('wood'). According to Roman legend, Rhea Silvia was the mother of Romulus and Remus, the founders of Rome. It was not until the 19th century that the name was taken up by English-speakers on a significant scale. The variant form **Sylvia** is now the more common spelling of the name. **Sylvie** is a French version of the name. Sometimes shortened to **Syl**.

Sim/Simeon *See* SIMON.

Simon (m) English version of the Hebrew **Simeon** or **Shimon**, meaning 'hearkening' or 'he who hears' (although another derivation traces it back to the Greek *simos*, meaning 'snub-nosed'). The name is borne by several biblical figures and was in use among English-speakers in medieval times. After falling from use, Simon returned to favour early in the 20th century. Often shortened to **Si** or **Sim**. *See also* SIMONE.

Simone (f) French variant of SIMON that has also won acceptance among English-speakers. It was first taken up in the English-speaking world in the 1940s. Celebrated bearers of the name have included the French writer Simone de Beauvoir (1908–86) and the French actress Simone Signoret (1921–85). Also encountered in the form **Simona**.

Sinclair (m) Scottish name that has also made sporadic appearances throughout the English-speaking world. The name itself came from a Norman French place name, Saint-Clair, which in turn may have been named after the French St Clair. It appears to have made its debut as a first name towards the end of the 19th century.

Sindy See CINDY.

Sinead (f) Irish version (pronounced 'shinnayd') of the English JANET. It retains its identification as an essentially Irish name. Famous bearers of the name have included the Irish actress Sinead Cusack (b.1948) and the Irish singer-songwriter Sinead O'Connor (b.1966).

Siobhan (f) Irish version (pronounced 'shivorn') of the English JOAN. The name is more common in Ireland than elsewhere. Notable bearers of the name have included the Irish actress Siobhan McKenna (1923–86). Also found as **Shevaun** and the modern form **Chevonne**.

Sis/Sissy See CECILIA; CISSIE.

Skeeter (m/f) English name that began as a nickname for any small or energetic person. It may have

come from 'mosquito' or else from 'skeets' or 'scoots'. It is a 20th-century introduction of US origin. A well-known bearer of the name is the US country singer Skeeter Davis (Mary Frances Penick; b.1931).

Skip (m) English name adopted as a diminutive of **Skipper**. It may have come ultimately from a Dutch word meaning 'ship's captain'.

Sly See SYLVESTER.

Sofia/Sofie See SOPHIA.

Sol/Solly See SOLOMON.

Solomon (m) Hebrew name derived from *shalom* ('peace') and meaning 'man of peace'. It appears in the Bible as the name of the son of David and Beersheba, whose wise rule over Israel brought about a lengthy peace. Almost exclusively a Jewish name, it was first adopted by English-speakers in the 16th century. Commonly abbreviated to **Sol** or **Solly**.

Somerset (m) English name derived from the name of the county, meaning 'summer farmstead'. The most notable bearer of the name to date has been the English novelist William Somerset Maugham (1874–1965).

Sondra See SANDRA.

Sonia (f) Russian diminutive of Sofiya, an equivalent of the English SOPHIA. It was taken up by English-speakers in the early 20th century and it now exists as an independent name. Also found as **Sonya** and **Sonja**.

Sonja *See* SONYA.

Sonny (m) English diminutive of SAUL, SOLOMON and several other names. Largely a 20th-century introduction, it was promoted by the song 'Sonny Boy' in the Al Jolson film *The Singing Fool* (1928). Notable bearers of the name have included the US boxer Sonny Liston (Charles Liston; 1932–70). Also found as **Sonnie**.

Sonya *See* SONIA.

Sophia (f) Greek name meaning 'wisdom'. The original St Sophia was probably not a real person but the result of a misinterpretation of the phrase *hagia sophia* ('holy wisdom'). The name was taken up by English-speakers in the 17th century, promoted by Sophia, Electress of Hanover (1630–1714), mother of George I. Variant forms include **Sofia** and **Sophie** (or **Sophy**), a French version of the name that since the 1960s has become the more common form. *See also* SONIA.

Sophie *See* SOPHIA; SOPHRONIA.

Sophronia (f) Greek name derived from *sophron* ('prudent' or 'sensible'). The name was taken up by English-speakers in the 19th century. Sometimes shortened to **Sophie** or **Sophy**.

Sophy *See* SOPHIA; SOPHRONIA.

Sorcha (f) Irish and Scottish Gaelic name meaning 'brightness'. In Ireland it is often treated as a Gaelic variant of SARAH. In Scotland it is sometimes assumed to be a variant of CLARA.

Sorrel (f) English plant name adopted as a first name in the 1940s. The plant name is thought to have come originally from the German *sur* ('sour'), a reference to the sour taste of its leaves. Also found as **Sorrell**, **Sorell** and **Sorel**.

Spencer (m) English name meaning 'dispenser' that was originally reserved for the stewards who dispensed supplies in English manor houses. The name is closely identified with the Churchill family and also with Diana, Princess of Wales (1961–97), whose maiden name was Spencer. It was taken up as a first name in the 19th century.

Spike (m) English name that began life as a nickname for anyone with tufty or spiky hair. It has also been used traditionally as a nickname for anyone whose real name is not known. Of early 20th-century origin, it is rarely given at birth but adopted later. Famous bearers of the name have included the Irish comedian Spike Milligan (Terence Alan Milligan; 1918–2002) and the US film director Spike Lee (Shelton Jackson; b.1956).

Spring (f) English name derived either from the name of the spring season or from natural springs or wells. A 19th-century introduction, it remains relatively rare.

Stacey (f) English name that evolved as a feminine equivalent of STACY. It may also be found as a diminutive form of ANASTASIA. It enjoyed a minor vogue among English-speakers from the 1960s. Also found as **Stacy**, **Stacie** or **Staci**. Commonly shortened to **Stace**.

Stacy (m) English name derived from EUSTACE that was taken up as a first name in the 19th century. Well-known bearers of the name have included the US actor Stacy Keach (Walter Stacy Keach; b.1941). Also found as **Stacey**.

Stafford (m) English name derived from a place name based on the Old English *staeth* ('landing place') and *ford* ('ford'). In the 15th and 16th centuries it was famous primarily as the surname of the dukes of Buckingham. Notable bearers of the name have included the British politician Sir Stafford Cripps (Richard Stafford Cripps; 1889–1952).

Stamford *See* STANFORD.

Stan *See* STANLEY.

Stanford (m) English name derived from an Old English place name meaning 'stony ford'. Occasionally found as **Stamford**.

Stanhope (m) English name meaning 'stony hollow'.

Stanley (m) English name derived from the Old English *stan* ('stone') and *leah* ('wood' or 'clearing') and thus meaning 'stony field'. As a surname it was strongly associated with the earls of Derby. As a first name it enjoyed a peak in popularity between 1880 and 1930.

Interest in the name was much boosted by the exploits of the British journalist and explorer Sir Henry Morton Stanley (John Rowlands; 1841–1904), discoverer of the 'lost' Dr Livingstone in 1869. Commonly shortened to **Stan**.

Star *See* STELLA.

Steenie *See* STEPHEN.

Stef/Stefanie/Steffie *See* STEPHANIE.

Stella (f) English name derived from the Latin *stella* ('star'). The name was first used as a title for the Virgin Mary, *Stella Maris* ('star of the sea'). It made its debut as a first name among English-speakers in medieval times but it was not until the 18th century that it started to be used on a significant scale. Modern diminutive forms of the name include **Star**. *See also* ESTELLE.

Steph *See* STEPHANIE.

Stephanie (f) English version of the French Stéphanie, itself derived from the Latin Stephania or Stephana, an equivalent of the English STEPHEN. It was taken up by English-speakers in the late 19th century and enjoyed a peak in popularity in the 1990s. Also found as **Stefanie** or **Steffany**. Diminutive forms of the name include **Steph**, **Stef**, **Steffie**, **Stevi** and **Stevie**.

Stephen (m) English version of the Greek name Stephanos, meaning 'garland', 'wreath' or 'crown', and the Latin Stefanus. The name features in the Bible as that of the first Christian martyr, who was stoned to death on false charges. It was borne by England's King Stephen (c.1097–1154) and has been consistently popular since medieval times. Also found as **Steven**. It is commonly abbreviated to **Steve** or **Stevie**. Variants of the name include **Stephan**, the Welsh **Steffan**, the Irish **Steafan** and the Scottish **Steenie**.

Sterling *See* STIRLING.

Steve/Steven *See* STEPHEN.

Stevie *See* STEPHANIE; STEPHEN.

Stew *See* STEWART; STUART.

Stewart (m) English name that developed either from a Scottish surname, derived from the Old English *stigweard* ('steward'), or as a variant of STUART. It emerged as a first name in the early 19th century and enjoyed a minor vogue in the 1950s. Well-known bearers of the name have included the British film actor Stewart Granger (James Lablanche Stewart; 1913–93). **Stew**, **Stu** and **Stewie** are common diminutive forms.

Stirling (m) English and Scottish name that can be variously derived from the place name Stirling (of uncertain meaning) or from the ordinary vocabulary word 'sterling', itself from the Middle English *sterrling* ('little star'). The term 'sterling' became linked with money in Norman times when coins sometimes bore a small star pattern and the word thus came to mean 'valuable' or

'excellent'. As a first name Stirling (or **Sterling**) is a relatively recent introduction.

St John (m) English name derived from the French place name Saint-Jean, and ultimately from the name of John the Baptist. Usually pronounced 'sinjun' and confined to the Roman Catholic English-speaking world, it has been in occasional use since the late 19th century.

Storm (f) English name derived from the ordinary vocabulary word, suggesting perhaps a passionate, lively nature. The name does not seem to have been used before the early 20th century.

Strachan (m) Scottish name derived from a place name meaning 'little valley'. Also rendered in the form **Strahan**.

Stratford (m) English name derived from a place name meaning 'ford on a Roman road'.

Struan (m) Scottish name derived from the Scottish Gaelic *sruthan*, meaning 'streams'.

Stu *See* STEWART; STUART.

Stuart (m) Scottish name that developed as a French version of STEWART and has been in use as a first name throughout the English-speaking world since the early 19th century. It came to Scotland in the 16th century with Mary Stuart, Queen of Scots, who had spent her childhood in France, and among the Scottish is still closely identified with the royal house of Stuart. **Stew**, **Stu**

and **Stewie** are common diminutive forms.

Su/Sue *See* SUSAN; SUSANNAH.

Sukie/Suky *See* SUSAN.

Summer (f) English name inspired by the name of the season, itself originally a Sanskrit word.

Sunday (f) English name derived from the day of the week. Never common, this appears to be a 20th-century invention, confined to children born on a Sunday.

Sunny (m) English name derived from the ordinary vocabulary word 'sunny', suggesting that the bearer has a cheerful, optimistic personality. Clearly influenced by SONNY, this does not appear to date from earlier than the beginning of the 20th century. It may have evolved from 'Sunny Jim', a familiar form of address.

Susan (f) English name derived originally from SUSANNAH but now accepted as a name in its own right. It made its first appearances in the 17th century but did not enjoy great popularity until the middle of the 20th century, when it suddenly became very frequent. Occasionally found as **Suzan**. Common diminutives include **Sue** and **Su** as well as **Susie** (or **Suzie**), **Suzy** and **Sukie** (or **Suky**).

Susanna *See* SUSANNAH.

Susannah (f) English version of the Hebrew Shushannah, derived from *shoshan* ('lily'). In the Bible Susannah is the wife of Joachim, wrongly suspected of adultery. It was taken up by English-speakers as early as the 13th century and remained in currency until the 18th century, when it was largely replaced by SUSAN. The name also appears as **Susanna** or **Suzanna**. Other variants include **Suzanne** and **Suzette** (both originally French) as well as **Susanne**. Among diminutives of the name are **Sue** (or **Su**), **Susie**, **Suzie** (or **Suzy**) and the more unusual **Sanna** and **Shanna**.

Susie *See* SUSAN; SUSANNAH.

Suzanne/Suzette *See* SUSANNAH.

Suzie/Suzy *See* SUSAN; SUSANNAH.

Swithin (m) English name derived from the Old English *swith* ('strong' or 'mighty'). It dates back to before the Norman Conquest but is rare today. The most famous bearer of the name was St Swithin (or Swithun), the 9th-century bishop of Winchester whose feast day falls on 15 July: according to tradition, if it rains on St Swithin's Day then it will continue to rain for another 40 days.

Sy *See* CYRUS; SASHA.

Sybil (f) English version of the Roman Sibilla, Sibylla, Sybella or Sybilla, derived ultimately from the Greek for 'prophetess'. The name was borne by the prophetesses who were guardians of the sibylline oracles in the ancient world. The name was later taken up by the Normans and William the Conqueror himself had a daughter-in-law called Sibylla. Benjamin Disraeli's novel *Sybil* (1845) did much to revive the name in the 19th century. Variant spellings include **Sybille** and **Cybill** – a form popularized by the US actress Cybill Shepherd (b.1949). Diminutive forms include **Sib** and **Sibb**.

Syd/Sydney *See* SIDNEY.

Sylvester (m) English and German name derived from the Latin for 'wood-dweller' or 'of the woods'. It was first taken up by English-speakers in medieval times and has remained in sporadic use ever since. Notable bearers of the name have included the US film actor Sylvester Stallone (b.1946). Also found as **Silvester**. **Silvestra** is a rare feminine form. It is occasionally shortened to **Syl** or **Sly**.

Sylvia/Sylvie *See* SILVIA.

Tad *See* THADDEUS.

Taffy (m) Welsh version of DAVID that has made occasional appearances as a name in its own right. Also widely known as a nickname for anyone with Welsh ancestry, the name evolved from David and its Welsh equivalent **Dafydd** in the 19th century. Also found as **Taff**.

Talbot (m) English name possibly derived from the Old French *taillebotte* ('cleave faggot' or 'cut bundle') or else from obscure Germanic roots. It has strong aristocratic connections, being the family name of the earls of Shrewsbury.

Talfryn (m) Welsh name derived from a place name meaning 'high hill'. Its use as a first name is a relatively recent phenomenon.

Tallulah (f) American Indian name meaning 'running water'. The most famous bearer of the name was Tallulah Bankhead (1903–68), the beautiful and outrageous US actress and wit who inherited it from her grandmother. The name may also sometimes be treated as a variant of the Irish Gaelic **Tallula**, from words meaning 'abundance' and 'lady' or 'princess'.

Tally *See* NATALIE.

Tam *See* THOMAS.

Tamara (f) Russian version of the Hebrew Tamar, meaning 'palm tree' or 'date palm'. It was introduced to the English-speaking world by the Puritans in the 17th

Tabitha (f) Aramaic name meaning 'doe' or 'gazelle'. It was revived in 17th-century England by the Puritans, inspired by the story of the biblical Tabitha, a worthy and charitable Christian woman of Joppa who was brought back to life by the prayers of St Peter. Also found as **Tabatha**. A Greek equivalent of the name is DORCAS. **Tabbie** and **Tabby** are common diminutive forms.

Tacey (f) English first name derived from the Latin *tacere* ('to be silent'). The Puritans adopted the name in the form Tace (meaning 'hush'). Variant forms today include **Tacy** and **Tacita**.

century and was revived in the 20th century. Perhaps the most influential biblical bearer of the name was Absalom's daughter Tamar, who was praised for her 'fair countenance'. *See also* TAMMY.

Tammy (f) Diminutive form of TAMARA and TAMSIN that is now often considered a name in its own right. Its popularity was much boosted in 1957 when the pop song 'Tammy' (sung by Debbie Reynolds in the film *Tammy and the Bachelor*) topped the US charts for three weeks. Well-known bearers of the name have included US country singer Tammy Wynette (Virginia Wynette Pugh; 1942–98). Also found as **Tammie**. *See also* THOMAS.

Tamsin (f) Cornish version of the medieval Thomasin, Thomasina or Thomasine (a feminine form of THOMAS) that has enjoyed a considerable vogue in popularity since the 1950s. **Tasmin** is a modern variant of the name, probably influenced by JASMINE. TAMMY is a common diminutive form.

Tania *See* TANYA.

Tanisha (f) English name derived ultimately from the Hausa for 'born on Monday'.

Tansy (f) English name taken from that of the strongly perfumed colourful yellow garden flower. The original source of the plant name is the Greek *athanasia* ('immortality'). Also found as a diminutive form of ANASTASIA, its

use as a first name dates only from the late 19th century.

Tanya (f) Anglicization of the Russian TATIANA, which has emerged as a name in its own right since the 1940s. The name has increased steadily in popularity since then. Also found as **Tania** or **Tonya** (also an abbreviated form of ANTONIA).

Tara (f) English name derived from an Irish place name meaning 'hill'. It was adopted as a first name by English-speakers in the late 19th century. An alternative derivation suggests a link with the earth goddess Temair, meaning 'dark one'. The castle on the hill of Tara in County Meath was until the 6th century the site of coronations and the location features prominently in Irish legend.

Tariq (m) Arabic name meaning 'one who knocks at the door at night'. The name is borne by the morning star and also by a celebrated 8th-century Berber leader, Tariq ibn Ziyad (d. c.720). Sometimes found as **Tari**.

Tarquin (m) Roman family name of obscure Etruscan origin which remains in occasional use as a first name among English-speakers. Two early Roman kings bore the name. In Arthurian legend, Tarquin makes an appearance as the name of a 'recreant knight'.

Tasgall (m) Scottish Gaelic name derived from Old Norse words meaning 'god' and 'sacrificial cauldron'. The name is particularly associated with the MacAskill clan and is sometimes rendered as **Taskill** by English-speakers.

Tasha *See* NATASHA.

Taskill *See* TASGALL.

Tate (m) English name derived ultimately from the Old Norse for 'cheerful'. Also encountered as **Tait** or **Teyte**.

Tatiana (f) Russian name of uncertain origins that has been in use among English-speakers since the early 20th century. It may have Asian roots, although another derivation suggests it comes ultimately from the Roman family name Tatius or from the Greek *tatto* ('I arrange'). It appears in William Shakespeare's *A Midsummer Night's Dream* (c.1594). Familiar shortened versions of the name include TANYA.

Tawny (f) English name derived from Old French *tané* ('tanned'). Like GINGER and **Sandy** it was traditionally reserved for people with a certain hair colour – in this case brown. Also found as **Tawney**.

Taylor (m/f) English name derived from a surname originally reserved for those engaged in the business of tailoring. It was formerly given only to boys but is now more common among girls. Notable bearers of the name have included the British poet Samuel Taylor Coleridge (1772–1834). Also found as **Tayler**.

Ted/Teddy *See* EDMUND; EDWARD; THEODORE.

Teena *See* TINA.

Tegan *See* TEGWEN.

Tegwen (f) Welsh name combining words meaning 'beautiful' and 'fair' or 'holy'. It appears to be a relatively modern invention. Also encountered as **Tegan**.

Tel *See* TERENCE; TERRY.

Temperance (f) English name that was among the 'virtue' names adopted by the Puritans in the 17th century. It has become rare since the late 19th century.

Tempest (f) English name derived from the ordinary vocabulary word meaning 'severe storm'.

Terence (m) English name derived ultimately from the Roman Terentius, itself of obscure origin. In Ireland it is used as an Anglicization of the Gaelic Turlough (meaning 'instigator' or 'one who initiates an idea'). It was widely adopted as a first name among English-speakers in the late 19th century and reached a peak in popularity in the 1950s. Also found as **Terance**, **Terrance**, **Terrence** and **Terrell**. Common diminutive forms are **Tel** and TERRY.

Teresa (f) English, Italian and Spanish name possibly derived ultimately from one of two Greek words variously meaning 'reaper' or 'harvest' and 'guarding' or 'watching' – or else conceivably derived from the name of the Greek island of Thera. Alternatively spelt **Theresa**, it was confined chiefly to Italy and Spain until the 16th century, but later spread throughout the Roman Catholic world in response to the popularity of two saints bearing the name. English-speakers adopted the name in the 18th century. Common diminutives of the name are **Teri**, TERRY, **Tess**, **Tessie** and TESSA, all of which are sometimes considered to be distinct names in their own right. *See also* TRACY.

Teri *See* TERESA.

Terrell/Terrence *See* TERENCE.

Terry (m/f) English name of Germanic origin, from words meaning 'tribe' and 'power'. It is also a diminutive form of several other names, including TERENCE, THEODORE and the feminine TERESA. Variant spellings of the name for girls include **Terri** and **Teri**. The masculine form of the name is sometimes shortened to **Tel**.

Tess *See* TERESA; TESSA.

Tessa (f) English name that exists both as a diminutive form of TERESA and as an independent name of obscure European origins. It made its first appearance among English-speakers in the late Victorian era. Notable bearers of the name and its variant forms **Tess** and **Tessie** have included the fictional heroine of Thomas Hardy's novel *Tess of the D'Urbervilles* (1891).

Tetty *See* ELIZABETH.

Tex (m) American name derived from an abbreviation of the state name Texas and originally

reserved for inhabitants of that state. It is confined largely to the USA, where notable bearers of the name have included the US cartoon director Tex Avery (Frederick Bean; 1908–80).

Teyve (m) Jewish name representing a Yiddish version of the Hebrew Tuvia, which is itself a version of Tobias (*see* TOBY). The most famous bearer of the name is the fictional milkman who is the central character in the musical *Fiddler on the Roof* (1967). Also found as **Teive**.

Thaddeus (m) Hebrew first name possibly meaning 'valiant' or 'wise' or else derived from THEODORE. The name occurs in the New Testament as the name of one of the apostles and has consequently been adopted in various parts of the English-speaking world since the 19th century. **Tad** and **Thad** are common diminutive forms.

Thea *See* DOROTHY; THEODORA.

Theda *See* THEODORA.

Thel *See* ETHEL; THELMA.

Thelma (f) English name invented by the British popular novelist Marie Corelli (1855–1924) for the Norwegian central character in her novel *Thelma* (1887). It is speculated that Corelli may have based the name on the Greek *thelema* ('will' or 'wish'). The name enjoyed a vogue in the 1920s and 1930s but has since lost ground. Sometimes shortened to **Thel**.

Thelonius (m) English name of Roman origins. It is also found as **Thelonious**, in which form it was borne by the celebrated US jazz musician Thelonious Monk (1920–82).

Theo *See* THEOBALD; THEODORA; THEODORE.

Theobald (m) German name descended from the Old German Theudobald, which was itself derived from words meaning 'people' or 'race' and 'bold' or 'brave'. The name featured in the *Domesday Book* and continued to be found fairly regularly among English-speakers through medieval times, often in such variant forms as Tebald and Tybalt. Diminutive forms include **Theo**, **Tibby** and **Tibs**.

Theodora (f) Feminine version of THEODORE, derived from the Greek for 'God's gift'. It shares the same roots as **Dorothea** (*see* DOROTHY), with the two parts of the name put in reverse order. It was first adopted by English-speakers in the 17th century, and is sometimes abbreviated to **Thea**, DORA or **Theda**.

Theodore (m) English first name derived from the Greek for 'God's gift'. The name was popular with early Christians and was borne by no fewer than 28 saints. Because it was so closely associated with saints, the name was not favoured by the Puritans in the 17th century, but it enjoyed a resurgence in popularity in the 19th century, often in the abbreviated form

Theo. In the USA the name is often shortened to **Ted** or **Teddy**. *See also* THEODORA; TUDOR.

Theophilus (m) Greek first name derived from the Greek words *theos* ('god') and *philos* ('loving' or 'friend') and thus meaning 'loved by God' or 'one who loves God'. It features in the New Testament and was taken up by the Puritans in the 16th century. A rare feminine version of the name is **Theophila**. Often shortened to **Theo**.

Theresa *See* TERESA.

Thirsa *See* THIRZA.

Thirza (f) English first name descended from the Hebrew Tirzah, which may have had its origins in a place name or else in Hebrew words meaning 'acceptance' or 'pleasantness'. The name was taken up by the Puritans in the 17th century. Also found as **Thirsa**.

Thom *See* THOMAS.

Thomas (m) English first name derived from the Aramaic for 'twin'. The name appears several times in the Bible, notably as the name of one of the twelve apostles. The name, often shortened to **Tom** (or more unusually **Thom**) or to **Tommy**, has always been popular among English-speakers and has long been one of the most typical English forenames (as evidenced by its inclusion in the proverbial 'Tom, Dick and Harry' list of commonplace boys' names). Scottish variants include **Tam**, TAMMY and **Tomas**.

Thomasina *See* TAMSIN.

Thora (f) Scandinavian name derived from that of Thor, the Norse god of thunder. In Britain it became widely familiar as the name of the film and television actress Thora Hird (1913–2003).

Thorley (m) English name derived from a place name meaning 'thorn wood'. It has been in occasional use as a first name since the Victorian era.

Thornton (m) English name derived from a place name meaning 'settlement among the thorns'. A notable bearer of the name was the US writer Thornton Wilder (1897–1975).

Thurstan (m) English name derived from an Old Norse place name meaning 'Thor's stone'. Also found as **Thurston**, the name came to England with the Vikings. It appeared as a first name in the 19th century. *See also* DUSTIN.

Tia (f) English name that has evolved as a diminutive of various longer names, such as **Laetitia**.

Tiarnan (m) Irish name derived from the Gaelic for 'lord'. Also found in the forms **Tiernan** and **Tierney**.

Tibbie *See* ISABEL.

Tibby/Tibs *See* THEOBALD.

Tiernan/Tierney *See* TIARNAN.

Tiffany (f) English first name derived from the Greek Theophania (meaning 'manifestation of God') via the French variant Tifainé. It was traditionally reserved for girls born on the feast of Epiphany (6 January), which celebrates the arrival of the Magi. Subsequently it enjoyed a resurgence in popularity in the wake of the film *Breakfast at Tiffany's* (1961) – Tiffany's being the name of a select real-life jewellery shop in New York. Sometimes shortened to **Tiff**, **Tiffy** or **Tiffie**.

Tiger Lily *See* LILY.

Tilda/Tilly *See* MATILDA.

Tim *See* TIMOTHY.

Timothy (m) Hebrew first name derived from the Greek Timotheos (meaning 'honouring God' or 'honoured by God'). The name was apparently unknown in England prior to the Reformation. A rare feminine version of the name is **Timothea**. Common diminutives are **Tim** and **Timmy**.

Tina (f) Diminutive form of CHRISTINA and other names ending '-tina', now accepted as a name in its own right. First heard among English-speakers in the 19th century, it reached a peak in popularity in the 1960s and 1970s. Famous bearers of the name have included US rock singer Tina Turner (Annie Mae Bullock; b.1939). Occasionally found as **Teena**.

Tisha/Titty *See* LETITIA.

Titus (m) Roman first name of uncertain origin (possibly meaning 'honoured' from Latin *titulus*,

'title of honour'). St Titus was a
disciple of St Paul. The name was
adopted by English-speakers after
the Reformation and was borne
by, among others, the 17th-
century English conspirator Titus
Oates (1649–1705).

Tobias/Tobin *See* TOBY.

Toby (m) English version of the
Hebrew **Tobias** (meaning 'the
Lord is good'). The name features
in William Langland's poem *Piers
Plowman* (late 14th century) but
does not appear to have become
widely popular until after the
Reformation. Variants include
Tobin.

Todd (m) English name meaning
'fox'. The name enjoyed a considerable vogue during the 1970s,
especially in Canada and the USA
where it ranked among the 50
most popular boys' names. Also
found as **Tod**.

Tolly *See* BARTHOLOMEW.

Tom/Tomas/Tommy *See* THOMAS.

Toni *See* ANTOINETTE; ANTONIA.

Tony *See* ANTHONY.

Tonya *See* ANTONIA; TANYA.

Topaz (f) English jewel name that
has made occasional appearances
since the late 19th century. During
medieval times the name was
sometimes encountered as a variant of the boys' name Tobias. Also
found as **Topaze**.

Topsy (f) English name of obscure
origin. One derivation suggests it
evolved from the word 'topsail'
and thus became associated with

the black slaves brought to the
Americas in sailing ships. Harriet
Beecher Stowe's use of it for the
black orphan slave girl in her
novel *Uncle Tom's Cabin* (1852) has
tended to limit its attractiveness
for subsequent generations
unhappy about the book's senti-
mental and patronizing attitude
towards race relations.

Torcall *See* TORQUIL.

Toria *See* VICTORIA.

Torkel *See* TORQUIL.

Torquil (m) Scottish version of
the Old Norse name Thorketill
(meaning 'Thor's cauldron'). The
name came to Britain with the
Danes and also entered Gaelic cul-
ture as **Torcall**, **Torcul** or **Torcail**,
being adopted in the Outer
Hebrides and especially by
members of the Scottish Macleod
clan, who claim descent from a
man named Torquil. **Torkel** is
another variant.

Tory *See* VICTORIA.

Totty *See* CHARLOTTE.

Tracey *See* TRACY.

Tracy (f) English and French
name ultimately derived from a
Greek place name meaning 'place
of Thracius' (although an alternative derivation identifies it as a
diminutive of TERESA). It was
formerly given to boys as well as
girls, but is now virtually
unknown as a boys' name. The
name enjoyed a considerable
boost in popularity in the 1940s
and 1950s following the release of

the films *The Philadelphia Story* (1940) and *High Society* (1956), both featuring the heiress Tracy Samantha Lord. Also found as **Tracey** or **Tracie** and shortened to **Trace**.

Trafford (m/f) English first name of Germanic origin meaning 'dweller beyond the ford'.

Trahearn (m) Welsh first name meaning 'iron'. Also found as **Traherne**.

Travers *See* TRAVIS.

Travis (m) English name meaning 'toll-keeper' or 'crossing', originally from the French *traverser* ('to cross'). Also found as **Travers**, the name figured among lists of the 50 most popular boys' names by the 1970s.

Treena *See* KATRINA.

Trefor *See* TREVOR.

Tremaine (m) Cornish name meaning 'homestead on the rock'. Also encountered as **Tremayne**.

Trent (m) English name derived from that of the River Trent in north-west England. It is more commonly encountered in the USA than it is on the British side of the Atlantic.

Trev *See* TREVOR.

Trevelyan (m) Cornish name derived from a place name meaning 'place of Elian'.

Trevor (m) English and Welsh name derived from a place name meaning 'great homestead'. Rendered in Welsh as **Trefor**, it

has been in use as a first name since the 1860s. The success of the British actor Trevor Howard (1916–88) in the popular romantic film *Brief Encounter* (1945) did much to popularize the name in the post-war years. The usual diminutive form of the name is **Trev**.

Tricia *See* PATRICIA.

Trina *See* CATRIONA.

Tris *See* BEATRICE; TRISTRAM.

Trish/Trisha *See* PATRICIA.

Trissie *See* BEATRICE.

Tristan *See* TRISTRAM.

Tristram (m) English version of the Celtic Drystan, which may have been derived from the Celtic *drest* or *drust* (meaning 'din' or 'tumult') or alternatively from the Latin *tristis* ('sad'). As Tristram the name made its first appearance in England in the 12th century. In recent years **Tristan** has replaced Tristram as the usual version of the name. **Tris** is a common diminutive form.

Trix/Trixie *See* BEATRICE.

Troy (m) English and Irish name derived from that of the French city of Troyes. Another derivation suggests the name comes from the Irish for 'foot soldier' or else from a phrase meaning 'from the place of the people with curly hair'. The romantic association of the name with that of the ancient city besieged by the Greeks for 10 years, as celebrated by Homer, has undoubtedly done much to keep the name in use.

Trudy (f) Diminutive form of GERTRUDE, meaning 'ruler of the spear', or alternatively of ERMINTRUDE ('wholly beloved'), that is now widely accepted as a first name in its own right. Also found as **Trudi** or **Trudie**.

Truman (m) English name derived from the Old English for 'trusty man'. It is uncommon outside the USA, where notable bearers of the name have included the writer Truman Capote (1924–84). Also found as **Trueman**.

Tryphena (f) English first name derived from the Greek for 'daintiness' or 'delicacy'. It features in the New Testament and has made occasional appearances among English-speakers since the Reformation.

Trystan *See* TRISTRAM.

Tudor (m) Welsh first name that

evolved from the Celtic Teutorix (meaning 'people's ruler'). Also found in Wales as **Tudur**, the name has strong royal connections, being borne by monarchs of the royal house of Tudor.

Tuesday (f) English name usually reserved for children born on a Tuesday.

Turlough *See* TERENCE.

Ty/Tye *See* TYRONE.

Tyler (m) English name that was originally an occupational surname given to workers employed to tile roofs. Also found as **Tylar**.

Tyrone (m) Irish name derived from the county name, meaning 'Eoghan's (or Owen's) land'. Celebrated bearers of the name have included the US film star Tyrone Power (1913–58) and the British theatre director and critic Tyrone Guthrie (1900–1971). Sometimes shortened to **Ty** or **Tye**.

from the Roman equivalent of the Greek Odysseus, famous as the name of the legendary hero of Homer's *Odyssey*. Possibly meaning 'hater' in the original Greek, it has sometimes been taken up as a first name in Ireland and the USA, where it is best known from the name of the US President Ulysses S. Grant (1822–85). **Ulick** is a diminutive form of the name.

Uma (f) English name that appears to have been invented towards the end of the 19th century by the Scottish novelist Robert Louis Stevenson in his story 'The Beach of Falesa'. Well-known bearers of the name in recent times have included the US film actress Uma Thurman (b.1970).

Umar (m) Arabic name meaning 'populous' or 'flourishing'. Also rendered as **Omar**, it ranks among the most common first names in the Arab world. Its popularity reflects its history as the name of one of Muhammad's most loyal followers, Umar ibn-al-Khattab (c.581–644).

Una (f) Irish and Scottish name possibly derived from the Irish *uan* ('lamb') or else from the Latin *unus* ('one'). Variant forms include **Ona**, **Oonagh** and **Oona**, in which incarnation it appears prominently in Edmund Spenser's epic poem *The Faerie Queene* (1596), representing the unity of religion. Well-known bearers of the name in recent times have included the

Uilleam *See* WILLIAM.

Ulick *See* ULYSSES; WILLIAM.

Ulla *See* ULRICA.

Ulrica (f) Scandinavian name that has been in occasional use among English-speakers in recent times. Also rendered as **Ulrika**, it developed as a feminine version of the masculine Ulric, itself derived from the Norse Wulfric ('wolf ruler'). Well-known bearers of the name in modern times have included the Swedish-born British television personality Ulrika Jonsson (b.1967). The name is sometimes shortened to **Ulla**.

Ulysses (m) Irish name derived

British television personality Una Stubbs (b.1937).

Undine (f) Roman name (pronounced 'undeen') derived from the Latin for 'of the waves'. Roman legend identified Undine as a water-sprite who sought to win a soul by bearing a child by a human husband and thus became acquainted with all the perils of a mortal existence.

Unice *See* EUNICE.

Unity (f) English name derived ultimately from the Latin *unus* ('one'). It was among the various 'virtue' names enthusiastically taken up by English Puritans in the 16th and 17th centuries. Notable bearers of the name have included the infamous Unity Mitford (1914–48), who became notorious for her links with top German Nazis before the Second World War.

Upton (m) English name derived from a place name meaning 'upper settlement' or 'town on the heights' in Old English. Its history as a first name dates from the 19th century. Notable bearers of the name over the years have included the US novelist Upton Sinclair (1878–1968).

Urse/Ursie *See* URSULA.

Ursula (f) English, German and Scandinavian name derived from the Latin *ursa* ('little she-bear'). It became popular among English-speakers in medieval times through admiration of the legendary 4th-century Cornish St Ursula, who is said to have led 11,000 female companions to martyrdom in Germany while on a crusade to the Holy Land. Other notable Ursulas have included Ursula Brangwen in D. H. Lawrence's novel *The Rainbow* (1915). Diminutive forms of the name include **Urse** and **Ursie**.

Usha (f) Indian name derived from the Sanskrit for 'dawn'. Pronounced 'oosher', it appears in classical Indian legend, notably in the *Rig-Veda* as the name of the beautiful daughter of heaven.

the variant **Valentina** is reserved for girls. A diminutive form (also used of both sexes) is **Val**.

Valerie (f) English and French name descended ultimately from the Latin Valeria (from the Latin for 'strong' or 'healthy'). It was introduced to the English-speaking world in the 17th century, initially in the form Valeria before it was replaced by the French version, Valerie. It enjoyed a peak in popularity between the two world wars. The usual diminutive form is **Val**.

Van *See* IVAN; VANCE.

Vance (m) English name derived from the Old English for 'fen-dweller'. It is sometimes abbreviated to **Van**.

Vanda *See* WANDA.

Vanessa (f) English name that began life as an invention of the poet and satirist Jonathan Swift (1667–1745). Swift devised the name when writing to his close friend Esther Vanhomrigh, taking 'Van' from Vanhomrigh and 'Essa' from Esther. Notable bearers of the name in recent times have included the British actress Vanessa Redgrave (b.1937). Common diminutives of the name are **Nessa** and **Nessie**.

Val *See* PERCIVAL; VALENTINE; VALERIE.

Valentina *See* VALENTINE.

Valentine (m/f) English and French name derived ultimately from the Latin *valens* ('strong' or 'healthy'). The link with St Valentine's Day (14 February) has long given the name romantic associations, although the link between the historical St Valentine (martyred for opposing the Roman emperor Claudius II) and romance is very tenuous. Its use among English-speaking people dates from the 13th century. Valentine has always been used for both sexes, though

Vaughan (m/f) English and Welsh name (pronounced 'vorn') derived from the Welsh *fychan* ('little one'). Also encountered as **Vaughn**, it is usually reserved for male children, although it is sometimes chosen for girls in the USA.

Famous bearers of the name have included the British composer Ralph Vaughan Williams (1872–1958).

Vaughn *See* VAUGHAN.

Velma (f) English name of uncertain origin, possibly inspired by such similar names as SELMA and THELMA. It is largely confined to the USA, where it first appeared towards the end of the 19th century.

Velvet (f) English name inspired by the luxurious soft cloth of the same name.

Venetia (f) English name derived from the Latin title for the city of Venice. First introduced in the 16th century, the name enjoyed a resurgence in popularity after the publication of the novel *Venetia* (1837) by Benjamin Disraeli.

Venus (f) Roman name for the goddess of love. It has occasionally been taken up as a first name ever since its first appearance in the 16th century. Famous bearers of the name in modern times have included the US tennis player Venus Williams (b.1980).

Vera (f) English name derived either from the Russian *viera* ('faith') or else from the Latin *verus* ('true'). Sometimes treated as a diminutive of VERONICA, it was first taken up in the English-speaking world in the 19th century. It enjoyed a peak in popularity in the 1920s. Notable bearers of the name have included the

British wartime singer Dame Vera Lynn (b.1917).

Vere (m) French name derived from the Old French *ver* ('alder'). Introduced to Britain from France at the time of the Norman Conquest, it has been in occasional use as a first name in the English-speaking world since the 17th century.

Verena (f) Swiss name of unknown meaning, though possibly sharing the same roots as VERA. There was a 3rd-century St Verena, who is supposed to have been Egyptian in origin. Its use among English-speakers was promoted by its appearance in the Henry James novel *The Bostonians* (1886).

Vergil *See* VIRGIL.

Verily *See* VERITY.

Verity (f) English name derived from the Latin *verus* ('truth'). It was among the 'virtue' names adopted by English Puritans in the 17th century and has remained in occasional use ever since. A relatively rare variant is **Verily** (meaning 'truly').

Vern *See* VERNON.

Verna (f) English first name of uncertain origin. It may have evolved as a feminine version of VERNON or else out of the Latin *vernus* ('spring'). It was first adopted in English-speaking countries in the 1880s.

Verne *See* VERNON.

Vernon (m) English name derived

from a French place name meaning 'place of alders' or 'alder grove'. As a surname, it was introduced to Britain by the Normans and appears to have made its initial appearances as a first name in the 19th century, by which time it had strong aristocratic associations. **Vern** and **Verne** are common diminutive forms.

Verona (f) English name derived from that of the Italian city (itself of uncertain origin). It is sometimes considered to be a variant of VERONICA.

Veronica (f) English first name probably derived from the Latin *vera icon* ('true image'), or else from the Greek Pherenike ('victory bringer'). The name was bestowed upon the otherwise unidentified saint who is said to have wiped Christ's face with a cloth on his way to the Crucifixion and eventually found its way via France to Scotland in the 17th century. **Verona** is a variant form, while **Ron**, **Ronnie** and **Vera** are diminutive forms.

Vesta (f) English name derived from that of the Roman goddess of the hearth and fire, itself ultimately from the Greek *hestia* ('hearth'). It was adopted as a first name in the English-speaking world in the 19th century.

Veva *See* GENEVIEVE.

Vi *See* VIOLET.

Vic *See* VICTOR; VICTORIA.

Vickie/Vicky *See* VICTORIA.

Victor (m) English name derived from the Roman Victorius, itself from the Latin for 'conqueror'. Commemorating Christ's victory over sin and death, the name was fairly common among early Christians. It re-emerged in the English-speaking world in the 19th century in tribute to Queen Victoria. The usual diminutive form is **Vic**.

Victoria (f) English and Spanish name derived from the Latin *victoria* ('victory'). It was more or less unknown in the English-speaking world before the accession to the British throne of Queen Victoria (1819–1901) in 1839. The queen had inherited the name from her German mother, Princess Maria Louisa Victoria of Saxe-Coburg-Gotha. Diminutives include **Tory**, **Vic**, **Vickie**, **Vicky**, **Vikki** and **Viti**. *See also* QUEENIE; VITA.

Vijay (m) Indian name (pronounced 'veejay') derived from the Sanskrit *vijaya* ('victory' or 'booty'). The name of one of Krishna's grandchildren, it has been popular as a first name for many centuries and is the base of many longer names. Variants include the Bengali **Bijay**.

Vikki *See* VICTORIA.

Vikram (m) Indian name derived from the Sanskrit *vikrama* ('stride' or 'pace', but later interpreted as meaning 'heroism' or 'strength'). It was borne by Vishnu in the *Mahabharata* and was also the name of a celebrated king of Ujjain, who expelled the

Scythians from India and ushered in the Vikrama era in 58 BC.

Vilma *See* WILHELMINA.

Vin *See* VINCENT.

Vina *See* DAVINA.

Vince *See* VINCENT.

Vincent (m) English, French, Dutch and Scandinavian name derived from the Latin *vincens* ('conquering'). It was borne by several saints and has remained in regular use ever since. Notable bearers of the name have included the Dutch painter Vincent Van Gogh (1853–90) and US film actor Vincent Price (1911–93). **Vin**, **Vince**, **Vinnie** and **Vinny** are diminutive forms. Feminine equivalents include **Vincentia** and **Vincetta**.

Vincentia/Vincetta *See* VINCENT.

Vinnie/Vinny *See* LAVINIA; VINCENT; VIRGINIA.

Viola (f) English name derived from the Latin *viola* ('violet'). The popularity of the name in the English-speaking world was largely the result of the influence of the character Viola in William Shakespeare's *Twelfth Night* (1601). It enjoyed a peak in popularity in the early 20th century. *See also* YOLANDA.

Violet (f) English name derived from the Latin plant name (a traditional symbol of modesty). It was introduced to Britain in medieval times, sometimes in the form Violante. Variants include **Violetta** and **Violette**. A common diminutive is **Vi**.

Violetta/Violette *See* VIOLET.

Virgil (m) Roman name of obscure meaning that has been in occasional use among English-speakers since medieval times. Also found as **Vergil**, it appears to have been taken up at an early date more often in tribute to a revered French bishop or a celebrated Irish monk of the same name than to the great 1st-century Roman poet Publius Vergilius Maro (or Virgil) with whom the name is usually associated today. In modern times it is encountered more frequently in the USA than elsewhere in the English-speaking world.

Virginia (f) English name derived from the Roman name Verginius, itself from the Latin for 'maiden'. Roman legend identified Verginius as a beautiful young woman who was murdered by her father to save her from seduction by the unsuitable Appius Claudius. Sir Walter Raleigh called the first English possessions in America Virginia in tribute to England's 'Virgin Queen', Elizabeth I. Notable bearers of the name since then have included the British novelist Virginia Woolf (1882–1941) and the British tennis player Virginia Wade (b.1945). Diminutive forms include GINGER; **Ginny**; **Jinny**; **Vinnie** and **Vinny**.

Vita (f) English and Scandinavian name derived from the Latin *vitus* ('life'), or alternatively from the Sanskrit for 'desire' or 'wish'. It is also sometimes regarded as a diminutive of VICTORIA. Notable bearers of the name have included the British writer Vita Sackville-West (1892–1962). **Vitus** is the less commonly encountered masculine form.

Viti *See* VICTORIA.

Vitus *See* VITA.

Viv *See* VIVIAN.

Vivian (m/f) English name derived ultimately from the Latin *vivus* ('alive' or 'lively'). It was borne by a little-known 5th-century Christian martyr called St Vivianus and appears to have been first taken up in the English-speaking world in the 12th century, when it was rendered as **Vivyan** or **Vyvyan**. It was originally reserved for males, but later came to be used for both sexes. The variant forms **Viviana**, **Vivianne**, **Vivien**, **Vivienne** and **Viviette** are all feminine versions of the name. The most common diminutive is **Viv**.

Viviana/Vivianne/Vivien/Vivienne/Viviette/Vivyan *See* VIVIAN.

Vonda *See* WANDA.

Vonnie *See* YVONNE.

Vyvyan *See* VIVIAN.

Wade (m) English name meaning 'ford' or 'dweller by the ford'. Long established as a surname, its history as a first name is relatively short and generally confined to the USA, where it was popularized as the name of one of the characters in Margaret Mitchell's novel *Gone with the Wind* (1936).

Wal *See* WALLACE; WALTER.

Waldo (m) English name that developed as a diminutive of the German Waldemar, meaning 'rule' or 'power'. Borne by the celebrated US writer and philosopher Ralph Waldo Emerson (1803–82), it remains rare outside the USA.

Walid (m) Arab name meaning 'newborn baby'. Its use was much promoted by the military successes of Arab armies during the reign of Walid I (d.715).

Walker (m) English name, originally a surname meaning 'fuller'.

Wallace (m) English name that began life as a Scottish surname meaning 'Welsh' or 'Welshman' or (from Old French *waleis*) simply 'foreign' or 'stranger'. It became popular among Scots in the 19th century in tribute to the Scottish patriot Sir William Wallace (1274–1305). Diminutive forms include **Wal** and **Wally**. *See also* WALLIS.

Wallis (m/f) Variant of WALLACE. More common in the USA than elsewhere in the English-speaking world, it is particularly associated with Wallis Simpson (1896–1986), the US divorcee for whom Edward VIII gave up the British throne in 1936.

Wally *See* WALLACE; WALTER.

Walt *See* WALTER.

Walter (m) English, German and Scandinavian name derived from the Old German *waldhar* ('army ruler' or 'folk ruler'). It came to England in its modern form with the Normans in the 11th century but was originally pronounced with a silent 'l' (as 'water'), thus giving rise to such variants as **Watkin** and its diminutives **Wat** and the Scottish **Wattie**. Other diminutives include **Wal**, **Wally** and **Walt**.

Wanda (f) English name of

obscure origin, possibly from the Old German for 'young shoot'. It was adopted by English-speakers in the 19th century and is sometimes treated as a variant of WENDY. The release of the film *A Fish Called Wanda* (1988) greatly promoted familiarity with the name, which is also found in such variant forms as **Vanda** and **Vonda**.

Ward (m) English name derived from the Old English *weard* ('guard' or 'watchman'). Originally a surname, it began to be taken up as a first name around the middle of the 19th century.

Warner (m) English name equivalent to the German Werner, itself derived from the German tribal name Warin (meaning 'to protect') and the Old German *harja* (meaning 'people'). Adopted as a surname after the Norman Conquest, Warner has been in use as a first name among English-speakers since the 19th century.

Warren (m) English name that may have been introduced originally as a Norman surname from the Norman French La Varenne ('game park') or else came from the Old German tribal name Warin (meaning 'to protect'). It was adopted as a first name in the 19th century, since when it has enjoyed particular popularity in the USA.

Warrie *See* WARWICK.

Warwick (m) English name (pronounced 'worrik') derived from

that of the county town of Warwickshire, which itself means 'farm by the weir'. It was adopted as a first name in the 19th century. **Warrie** is a diminutive form.

Washington (m) English name derived from an Old English place name meaning 'settlement of Wassa's people'. It is particularly popular in the USA, where it evokes the memory of the country's first president, George Washington (1732–99). **Wash** is a diminutive form.

Wasim (m) Arab and Indian name meaning 'handsome' or 'good-looking'. An Indian variant is **Waseem**.

Wat/Watkin/Wattie *See* WALTER.

Wayne (m) English name derived from a surname meaning 'carter' or 'cart-maker'. It became a popular choice of first name in the 1940s, inspired by the films of the US film actor John Wayne (Marion Michael Morrison; 1907–79), who based his stage name on that of Anthony Wayne (1745–96), a general in the American War of Independence. It enjoyed a peak in popularity in the 1970s, but has since become less frequent.

Webster (m) English name derived from a surname meaning 'weaver'. It is more common in the USA than elsewhere in the English-speaking world.

Wendell (m) English name derived from a Germanic surname usually interpreted as meaning 'wanderer'. It has been in occasional use as a first name since the 19th century.

Wendy (f) English name invented by the Scottish playwright J. M. Barrie in his classic children's story *Peter Pan* (1904). It is said to have been inspired by the young daughter of one of Barrie's friends, who called the writer her 'fwendy-wendy'. Alternatively, it may have been in circulation before then as a diminutive form of GWENDA or GWENDOLEN.

Wenonah *See* WINONA.

Wes *See* WESLEY.

Wesley (m) English name derived from an Old English place name meaning 'west meadow'. Originally in use as a surname, it was taken up as an occasional first name in tribute to John Wesley (1703–91), the founder of the Methodist movement. **Wes** is a diminutive form.

Whitney (m/f) English name derived from a place name meaning 'at the white island'. Originally a surname, it has been used as a first name for babies of both sexes since the early 20th century. Notable bearers of the name have included the US singer and film actress Whitney Houston (b.1964).

Wilberforce (m) English name derived from a place name in North Yorkshire, meaning 'Wilbur's ditch'. It became popular in tribute to the English politician William Wilberforce (1759–1833), who led the campaign to end the slave trade.

Wilbert (m) English name derived from the Old English *will* ('will') and *beorht* ('bright'). Its use is largely confined to the USA.

Wilbur (m) English name derived from a surname of obscure origins, possibly from the Old English *will* ('will') and *burh* ('defence'). It is more common in the USA than elsewhere in the English-speaking world, having been taken there (probably) by Dutch settlers.

Wilf *See* WILFRED.

Wilfred (m) English name derived from the Old German *wil* ('will' or 'desire') and *frid* ('peace') and thus interpreted as meaning 'desiring peace'. Also encountered as **Wilfrid**, it largely disappeared after the Norman Conquest but was revived in the 19th century. Diminutive forms include **Wilf** and **Wilfie**. **Wilfreda** and **Wilfrida** are rare feminine forms. *See also* WILKIE.

Wilfreda/Wilfrida *See* WILFRED.

Wilhelmina (f) German name occasionally taken up by English-speakers. A feminine equivalent of Wilhelm, the German form of WILLIAM, it has tended to be restricted in the English-speaking world to Scotland, Canada and the USA. It may also be found as **Williamina**. Diminutive forms include **Velma**, **Vilma**, **Wilma**, **Ilma**, **Mina**, MINNA, **Minnie** and ELMA.

Wilkie (m) English name derived from WILFRED or WILLIAM. It has been in occasional use as a first name since the 19th century. Notable bearers of the name have included the British novelist Wilkie Collins (1824–89).

Will *See* WILLIAM.

Willard (m) English name derived from the Old German *wil* ('will') and *heard* ('hardy'). It is largely confined to the USA. Notable bearers of the name have included the Jamaican-born opera singer Willard White (b.1946).

William (m) English name derived from the Old German *wil* ('will') and *helm* ('helmet' or 'protection'). It came to Britain with the Normans under William the Conqueror and for several centuries remained among the most popular of all English names. Notable bearers of the name have included William Shakespeare (1564–1616), William Gladstone (1809–98) and several members of the royal family. Variant forms include the Scottish Gaelic **Uilleam**, the Irish Gaelic **Ulick** and the Welsh **Gwilym**. Among the name's diminutive forms are **Bill**, **Billy**, **Will** and **Willy** (or **Willie**). *See also* LIAM.

Williamina *See* WILHELMINA.

Willie *See* WILLIAM.

Willis (m) English name meaning 'son of Will'. It has been in occasional use as a first name since the 19th century.

Willoughby (m) English name derived from a place name meaning 'farm among the willows'. It

was taken up as a first name in the 19th century.

Willow (f) English name derived from that of the tree. Its use as a first name is a relatively recent phenomenon.

Willy *See* WILLIAM.

Wilma *See* WILHELMINA.

Wilmer (m) English name that evolved either as a masculine version of Wilma (*see* WILHELMINA) or from the Old German *wil* ('will' or 'desire') and *meri* ('famous').

Wilmot (m) English name derived either from WILLIAM or else from the Old German *wil* ('will' or 'desire') and *muot* ('mind' or 'courage'). Its use as a first name dates from the 19th century.

Wilson (m) English name meaning 'son of Will'. Also encountered as **Willson**.

Win *See* WINIFRED; WINSTON; WINTHROP.

Windsor (m) English name derived from an Old English place name meaning 'river bank with a windlass (for hauling boats)'. Famous for its royal connections, it has been employed as an occasional first name since the 19th century.

Winifred (f) English and Welsh name derived from the Old English *wynn* ('joy') and *frith* ('peace'). Also encountered as **Winifrid** or **Winnifred**, it became common from the 16th century, enjoying a peak in popularity around the early 20th century.

Diminutive forms include **Win**, **Winn** and **Winnie**.

Winnie *See* WINIFRED; WINSTON.

Winnifred *See* WINIFRED.

Winona (f) Sioux Indian name meaning 'eldest daughter'. Borne by a legendary American Indian princess, it is also the name of a city in Minnesota. Variant forms include **Wenonah** and **Wynona**. It is best known today from the name of the US film actress Winona Ryder (b.1971).

Winston (m) English name derived from that of the village of Winston in Gloucestershire, itself meaning either 'boundary stone of a man called Wynna' or 'friend's settlement'. It is indelibly associated with the British wartime leader Sir Winston Churchill (1874–1965), whose mother's family came from Winston. **Win** and **Winnie** are diminutive forms of the name.

Winthrop (m) English name derived from a place name meaning 'village of Wynna'. More familiar as a surname, it has been employed occasionally as a first name, chiefly in the USA. Sometimes shortened to **Win**.

Winton (m) English name derived from a place name found in both Cumbria and North Yorkshire, meaning 'pasture enclosure' or 'willow enclosure'.

Wolf (m) German and Jewish name (pronounced 'volf') that probably evolved as a diminutive of WOLFGANG. Variant forms

include **Wolfe**, as born by the Irish nationalist Wolfe Tone (1763–98).

Wolfgang (m) German name (pronounced 'volfgang') derived from the Old German *wolf* ('wolf') and *gang* ('going'). Its occasional use as a first name in the English-speaking world owes much to the enduring fame of the German composer Wolfgang Amadeus Mozart (1756–91).

Woodrow (m) English name derived from an Old English place name meaning 'row of houses by a wood'. Its popularity in the USA was boosted through President Thomas Woodrow Wilson (1856–1924). The most usual diminutive form is WOODY.

Woody (m) Diminutive form of WOODROW. Notable bearers of the name have included US folk singer Woody Guthrie (1912–67) and the US comedian and film director Woody Allen (Allen Stewart Konigsberg; b.1935).

Wyatt (m) English name derived from the Old German *wido* ('wood' or 'wide'). More familiar as a surname, it has been used as an occasional first name (chiefly in the USA) since the 19th century. Notable bearers of the name have included the US lawman Wyatt Earp (1848–1929).

Wyn *See* WYNN.

Wyndham (m) English name derived from a place name from Norfolk meaning 'Wyman's homestead'. Famous bearers of the name have included the British novelist Percy Wyndham Lewis (1882–1957).

Wynfor *See* GWYNFOR.

Wynford (m) Welsh name derived from a place name meaning 'white stream' or 'holy stream'. Its use as a first name dates from the early 20th century.

Wynn (m) English name variously derived from the Welsh *gwyn* ('white' or 'blessed') or else from an Old English surname meaning 'friend'. Also found as **Wyn** or in the feminine form **Wynne**, it may also be encountered as a variant of GWYN.

Wynne *See* WYNN.

Wynona *See* WINONA.

Wystan (m) English name derived from the Old English *wig* ('battle') and *stan* ('stone'). The name of a murdered 9th-century boy saint of Mercia, it is rare today, though it became more widely familiar in the mid 20th century through the name of the British poet Wystan Hugh Auden (1907–73).

Xavier (1506–52). Feminine versions of the name include **Xavia**, **Xaviera**, **Xaverine** and **Zavia**.

Xaviera/Xaverine *See* XAVIER.

Xenia (f) English name (pronounced 'zeeneea') derived from the Greek *xenia* ('hospitable'). Sometimes encountered in the form **Xena**, **Zenia** or **Zina**. *See also* ZENA.

Xanthe (f) Greek name (pronounced 'zanthee') derived from *xanthos* ('golden' or 'yellow'). It appears several times as the name of minor characters in Greek mythology.

Xara *See* ZARA.

Xavia *See* XAVIER.

Xavier (m) Spanish name (pronounced 'zayveea' or 'zavveea' in English) derived either from a Basque word meaning 'new house' or from the Arabic word for 'bright'. Also found as **Javier** or **Zavier**, it became popular originally through the fame of the Basque Jesuit missionary St Francis deceased court jester in William Shakespeare's *Hamlet* (1599).

Ysabel *See* ISABEL.

Yseult/Ysolde *See* ISOLDE.

Yves *See* IVES.

Yvette *See* YVONNE.

Yvonne (f) English name of French origin that was originally taken up as a feminine equivalent of Yves, itself from the Old Norse *yr* ('yew'). It has been widely taken up in English-speaking countries since 1900, with a peak in popularity in the 1950s and 1960s. Variant forms include **Evonne** and **Yvette**. A diminutive form is **Vonnie**.

Yasmin/Yasmina/Yasmine *See* JASMINE.

Yehudi *See* JUDAH.

Yola *See* YOLANDA.

Yolanda (f) French name of Germanic origin, derived ultimately from the Greek for 'violet flower'. Alternatively, it may have developed originally from VIOLA. Variant forms include IOLANTHE, **Jolanda**, **Jolana**, **Yalinda** and **Yolette**. **Jola** and **Yola** are diminutive forms of the name.

Yorick (m) Danish equivalent of the English GEORGE. It is best known as the name of the

Zac *See* ZACHARY.

Zachary (m) English name derived from the Hebrew Zachariah or Zechariah, meaning 'Jehovah has remembered'. It appears in the Bible as the name of John the Baptist's father as well as of around thirty other people and was subsequently taken up by Puritans in the 17th century. It is commonly shortened to **Zac**, **Zack**, **Zak** or **Zakki**.

Zack/Zak/Zakki *See* ISAAC; ZACHARY.

Zandra *See* ALEXANDRA; SANDRA.

Zane (m) English name derived either from JOHN or possibly of Danish origin or otherwise inspired by an unidentified surname or place name. It is confined largely to the USA.

Zara (f) Arabic name meaning 'splendour' or 'flower', but also in use as a variant of SARAH. The name has become more popular in the English-speaking world since 1981, when it was chosen for Princess Anne's daughter Zara Phillips. Also found in the form **Xara**.

Zavia/Zavier *See* XAVIER.

Zeb (m) Hebrew name that is sometimes treated as a shortened form of the Hebrew name Zebulun (meaning 'exaltation') but more often is assumed to be a diminutive of the biblical name Zebedee (meaning 'my gift'). As Zebedee, it was taken up by English-speaking Puritans in the 17th century.

Zed (m) Hebrew name that is a shortened form of Zedekiah (meaning 'the Lord is just'). The full form of the name appears in the Old Testament as the name of a king of Judaea and of three other characters. It was among the biblical names taken up by English-speaking Puritans in the 17th century.

Zeke *See* EZEKIEL.

Zelda (f) English name that may have been derived originally from the Yiddish for 'happiness' but is otherwise treated as a shortened form of the Germanic GRISELDA. It is best known from Zelda Fitzgerald (1900–1947), the schizophrenic wife of the US novelist F. Scott Fitzgerald.

Zelma *See* SELMA.

Zena (f) Persian name meaning 'woman'. Also found in the form **Zina**, it may have developed as a familiar form of **Zinaida**, but is sometimes treated as a variant of **Rosina** or XENIA.

Zenia *See* XENIA.

Zenobia (f) Greek name meaning 'power of Zeus' or 'life from Zeus'. It was the name of the beautiful but ruthless Queen of Palmyra who opposed Rome in the 3rd century. Since the 16th century it has become particularly associated (for now obscure reasons) with Cornwall and other parts of southwestern Britain.

Zeta *See* ZITA.

Zillah (f) Hebrew name meaning 'shade' or 'shadow'. Appearing in the Bible as Zilla, it enjoyed a peak in popularity in the English-speaking world after the Reformation, but has since appeared only irregularly (although it remains a traditional choice of name among Romany families).

Zina *See* XENIA; ZENA.

Zinaida *See* ZENA.

Zinnia (f) English flower name that it appears began to be taken up as a first name in the 20th century.

Zita (f) English and Italian name derived from the medieval Tuscan *zita* ('little girl'). Also found as **Zeta**, it was the name of a popular 13th-century saint who became the patron of domestic servants. Well-known bearers of the name in its various forms in modern times have included the Welsh film actress Catherine Zeta Jones (b.1969).

Zoë (f) Greek name meaning 'life'. It became popular among Alexandrian Jews and early Christians after it appeared in Greek translations of the Bible as the nearest equivalent to the Hebrew EVE. It was subsequently taken up as a name among English-speakers in the 19th century and may be rendered with or without a diaeresis on the final letter. It enjoyed a recent peak in popularity in the 1970s. Variant forms include **Zoey**.

Zoey *See* ZOË.

Zola (f) English name of obscure origins that is possibly derived from an Italian surname or else developed as a variant of ZOË. It is particularly associated with the celebrated French novelist Emile Zola (1840–1902). Notable bearers of the name in modern times have included the South African runner Zola Budd (b.1966).

Zuleika (f) Persian name meaning 'brilliant beauty' that has been in occasional use among English-speakers since the early 19th century. Variously pronounced 'zooliker' or 'zooleeker', it appears in the Bible as the name of Potiphar's wife and is also well known from the Max Beerbohm novel *Zuleika Dobson* (1911), which is about a young woman whose beauty drives her lovers to kill themselves.

Saints' Days

January

1 Basil, Fulgentius, Justin, Telemachus
2 Abel, Basil, Caspar, Gregory, Macarius, Seraphim
3 Daniel, Frances, Geneviève
4 Angela, Benedicta, Roger
5 Paula, Simeon
6 Balthasar, Gaspar, Raphaela
7 Cedda, Crispin, Lucian, Raymond, Reynold, Valentine
8 Atticus, Gudule, Lucian, Severinus
9 Adrian, Alix, Hadrian, Peter
10 Agatho, Marcian, William
11 Brandan
12 Ailred, Benedict, Tatiana
13 Godfrey, Hilary
14 Felix, Hilary, Kentigern, Malachi
15 Isidore, Ita, Macarius, Maurus, Micah, Paul
16 Henry, Honoratus, Marcellus, Otto, Priscilla
17 Antony, Roseline
18 Dermot, Faustina, Priscilla, Susanna
19 Gerontius, Henry, Marius, Martha, Pia, Wulfstan
20 Euthymius, Fabian, Sebastian
21 Agnes, Fructuosus, Josepha, Maximus, Meinrad
22 Dominic, Timothy, Vincent
23 Aquila, Bernard, Ildefonsus, Raymond
24 Babylas, Francis, Timothy
25 Artemas, Gregory, Joel
26 Aubrey, Conan, Paula, Timothy, Titus, Xenophon
27 Angela, Candida, John, Julian, Marius, Theodoric
28 Ephraem, Paulinus, Peter, Thomas

29 Francis, Gildas
30 Hyacintha, Martina, Matthias
31 Adamnan, Aidan, Cyrus, John, Julius, Marcella, Tryphena

February

1 Bridget, Ignatius, Pionius
2 Joan, Theodoric
3 Anskar, Blaise, Ives, Laurence, Margaret, Oliver, Simeon, Werburga
4 Andrew, Gilbert, Isidore, Joan, Joseph, Nicholas, Phileas, Theophilus
5 Adelaide, Agatha, Avitus, Caius, Joachim, Matthias
6 Dorothy, Gerald, Luke, Mel, Paul, Silvanus, Titus, Vedast
7 Juliana, Luke, Moses, Richard, Theodore
8 Isaiah, Jerome, Sebastian, Stephen, Theodore
9 Apollonia, Cyril, Teilo
10 Hyacinth, Scholastica, Silvanus
11 Benedict, Blaise, Caedmon, Gregory, Jonas, Lazarus, Lucius, Theodore, Victoria
12 Alexis, Eulalia, Julian, Marina, Meletius
13 Agabus, Beatrice, Catherine, Priscilla
14 Abraham, Adolf, Cyril, Methodius, Valentine
15 Claud, Georgia, Jordan, Sigfrid
16 Elias, Flavian, Gilbert, Jeremy, Juliana, Pamphilus, Philippa, Samuel, Valentine
17 Reginald
18 Bernadette, Colman, Flavian, Leo, Simeon
19 Boniface, Conrad
20 Amata, Wulfric
21 George, Peter
22 Margaret
23 Lazarus, Martha, Mildburga, Milo, Polycarp
24 Adela, Lucius, Matthias
25 Ethelbert, Tarasius, Walburga
26 Alexander, Isabel, Porphyrius, Victor
27 Gabriel, Leander
28 Antonia, Hedwig, Hilary, Louisa, Oswald

March

1 Albinus, David, Felix, Roger
2 Agnes, Chad, Simplicius
3 Ailred, Anselm, Camilla, Marcia, Owen
4 Adrian, Casimir, Humbert, Lucius, Peter
5 Kieran, Piran, Virgil
6 Chrodegang, Colette, Cyril, Felicity, Jordan, Perpetua
7 Felicity, Paul, Perpetua, Thomas
8 Beata, Felix, Humphrey, John, Julian, Philemon, Pontius, Stephen
9 Catherine, Dominic, Frances, Gregory, Pacian
10 Anastasia, Caius, John, Macarius, Simplicius
11 Alberta, Aurea, Constantine, Oengus, Sophronius, Teresa
12 Bernard, Gregory, Maximilian, Paul, Seraphina
13 Gerald, Nicephorus, Patricia, Roderick, Solomon
14 Benedict, Eustace, Matilda
15 Clement, Louise, Lucretia, Zachary
16 Abraham, Julian, René
17 Gertrude, Joseph, Patrick, Paul
18 Alexander, Anselm, Christian, Cyril, Edward, Egbert, Narcissus, Salvator
19 Joseph
20 Alexandra, Claudia, Cuthbert, Euphemia, Herbert, Hippolytus, John, Martin, Sebastian, Theodosia
21 Benedict, Clementia, Serapion
22 Basil, Catherine, Nicholas, Octavian
23 Aquila, Theodosia, Turibius
24 Catherine, Gabriel, Simon
25 Harold, Humbert, Lucy, Richard
26 Basil, Emmanuel
27 Augusta, John, Lydia, Matthew
28 Gwendoline, John
29 Berthold, Gladys, Jonas, Mark, Rupert
30 John
31 Aldo, Amos, Benjamin, Cornelia, Guy

April

1 Gilbert, Hugh, Ludovic, Mary, Melito
2 Constantine, Drogo, Francis, Leopold, Mary, Theodosia, Urban
3 Alexandrina, Irene, Richard

4   Benedict, Isidore
5   Gerald, Juliana, Vincent
6   Celestine, William
7   George, Hegesippus, Herman, John, Llewellyn
8   Agabus, Dionysius, Walter
9   Hugh, Mary, Reginald
10 Ezekiel, Fulbert, Hedda, Michael, Terence
11 Gemma, Guthlac, Hildebrand, Isaac, Leo, Stanislaus
12 Damian, Julius, Zeno
13 Ida, Martin
14 Bernard, Caradoc, Eustace, Justin, Lambert
15 Anastasia, Aristarchus, Pudus, Silvester, Trophimus
16 Benedict, Bernadette, Drogo, Hervé, Lambert, Magnus
17 Agapetus, Elias, Robert, Stephen
18 Andrew, James
19 Alphege, Leo
20 Agnes
21 Anastasius, Anselm, Beuno, Conrad, Januarius, Simeon
22 Alexander, Caius, Theodore
23 Fortunatus, George, Gerard, Giles, Helen
24 Egbert, Fidelis, Ives, Mellitus
25 Mark, Phaebadius
26 Alda, Franca, Stephen
27 Zita
28 Louis, Patrick, Paul, Peter, Theodora, Valeria, Vitalis
29 Antonia, Ava, Catherine, Hugh, Peter, Robert, Wilfrid
30 Catherine, Hildegard, James, Miles, Pius, Sophia

May

1   Asaph, Bertha, Isidora, Joseph, Peregrine, Sigismund, Walburga
2   Athanasius, Zoë
3   Antonina, James, Maura, Philip, Timothy
4   Ethelrad, Florian, Gotthard, Monica, Silvanus
5   Angelo, Hilary
6   Benedicta, Prudence
7   Augustus, Flavia, Gisela, John, Stanislas
8   Benedict, Boniface, John, Michael, Peter, Victor
9   Gerontius
10 Antoninus, Aurelian, Beatrice, Comgall, Job, John, Simon
11 Aloysius, Cyril, Ignatius, James, Mamertus, Methodius, Philip,
    Walter

12   Achilleus, Dominic, Epiphanius, Gemma, Nereus, Pancras
13   Robert
14   Carthage, Giles, Mary, Matthias, Michael, Petronilla
15   Bertha, Dionysia, Dympna, Hilary, Isidore, Magdalen, Rupert,
     Silvanus
16   Brendan, John, Peregrine, Simon
17   Basilla, Paschal, Robert
18   Alexandra, Camilla, Claudia, Eric, John, Julitta
19   Celestine, Dunstan, Pudens, Pudentia, Yves
20   Aquila, Basilissa, Bernardino, Ethelbert, Orlando
21   Helena, Theobald, Theophilus
22   Julia, Rita
23   Ivo, William
24   David, Joanna, Patrick, Susanna, Vincent
25   Aldhelm, Bede, Dionysius, Gregory, Madeleine, Urban
26   Augustine, Lambert, Philip, Quadratus, Zachary
27   Augustine, Frederick, John, Julius
28   Augustine, Bernard
29   Theodosia, William
30   Felix, Ferdinand, Hubert, Isaac, Joan
31   Camilla, Petronilla

June

1   Angela, Justin, Pamphilus, Simeon, Theobald
2   Erasmus, Eugene, Marcellinus, Nicephorus, Nicholas, Peter,
    Pothinus
3   Charles, Clotilda, Isaac, Kevin, Matthias, Paula
4   Cornelius, Francis, Optatus, Petrock, Vincentia, Walter
5   Boniface, Ferdinand, Franco, Marcia, Valeria
6   Claud, Felicia, Martha, Norbert, Philip
7   Paul, Robert, Willibald
8   Melania, William
9   Amata, Cecilia, Columba, Cyril, Diana, Ephraem, Richard
10 Margaret, Olive, Zachary
11 Barnabas, Bartholomew, Fortunatus
12 Antonia, Christian, Humphrey, Leo
13 Anthony, Lucian
14 Basil
15 Alice, Germaine, Guy, Orsisius, Vitus, Yolanda
16 Aurelian, Julitta
17 Alban, Botolph, Emily, Harvey, Manuel, Sanchia, Teresa

18 Elizabeth, Fortunatus, Guy, Marina, Mark
19 Bruno, Gervase, Jude, Juliana, Odo, Protasius, Romuald
20 Alban, John
21 Alban, Aloysius, Lazarus, Ralph, Terence
22 Alban, Ederhard, John, Niceta, Pantaenus, Paulinus, Thomas
23 Audrey
24 Bartholomew, Ivan, John
25 Prosper, Solomon, William
26 John
27 Cyril, Ferdinand, Ladislaus, Madeleine, Samson
28 Irenaeus, Marcella, Paul
29 Emma, Judith, Paul, Peter, Salome
30 Bertrand, Lucina, Theobald

July

1   Aaron, Cosmas, Damian, Oliver, Simeon, Theodoric
2   Marcia, Otto, Reginald
3   Aaron, Anatolius, Julius, Leo, Thomas
4   Andrew, Aurelian, Bertha, Elizabeth, Odo, Ulrich
5   Anthony, Blanche, Grace, Gwen, Philomena, Zoë
6   Isaiah, Mary
7   Cyril, Hedda, Palladius, Pantaenus
8   Adrian, Aquila, Arnold, Edgar, Elizabeth, Kilian, Morwenna, Priscilla, Raymund
9   Alberic, Barnabas, Cornelius, Everild, Godfrey, Jerome, Nicholas, Thomas, Veronica
10 Amelia, Emmanuel, Maurice
11 Benedict, Olga, Oliver, Pius
12 Fortunatus, Jason, John, Monica, Veronica
13 Eugene, Henry, Joel, Mildred, Silas
14 Camillus, Deusdedit, Humbert, Nicholas, Ulric
15 Baldwin, Bonaventure, David, Donald, Edith, Henry, Jacob, Swithin, Vladimir
16 Eustace, Milo, Valentine
17 Alexis, Antoinette, Ennodius, Kenelm, Leo, Marcellina, Margaret, Nahum
18 Arnulf, Bruno, Camillus, Edith, Frederick, Marina, Philastrius
19 Ambrose, Aurea, Jerome, Symmachus, Vincent
20 Aurelius, Elias, Elijah, Jerome, Margaret, Marina
21 Angelina, Constantine, Daniel, Julia, Laurence, Praxedes, Victor
22 Joseph, Mary, Theophilus

23 Anne, Apollinaris, Balthasar, Bridget, Gaspar, Susanna
24 Boris, Christiana, Christina, Declan, Felicia
25 Anne, Christopher, James, Joachim, Thea, Valentina
26 Anne, Joachim
27 Berthold, Celestine, Natalia, Pantaleon, Rudolph, Theobald
28 Innocent, Samson, Victor
29 Beatrice, Felix, Flora, Lucilla, Lupus, Martha, Olaf, Urban
30 Everard, Julitta, Peter, Silas
31 Giovanni, Helen, Ignatius, Joseph

August

1   Alphonsus, Charity, Eiluned, Ethelwold, Faith, Hope, Justin, Kenneth
2   Alphonsus, Eusebius, Stephen
3   Gamaliel, Lydia, Nicodemus
4   Dominic, Jean-Baptiste, Perpetua
5   Afra, Oswald
6   Hormisdas, Octavian
7   Albert, Cajetan, Claudia, Sixtus
8   Dominic, Myron
9   Matthias, Oswald, Samuel
10 Geraint, Laurence, Oswald, Philomena
11 Alexander, Blane, Clare, Lelia, Susanna
12 Clare, Murtagh
13 Hippolytus, Maximus, Pontian, Radegunde
14 Marcellus, Maximilian
15 Arnulf, Mary, Napoleon, Stanislaus, Tarsicius
16 Joachim, Roch, Serena, Simplicianus, Stephen, Titus
17 Benedicta, Cecilia, Clare, Hyacinth, Myron, Septimus
18 Evan, Helena, Milo
19 John, Louis, Magnus, Sebaldus, Thecla, Timothy
20 Bernard, Herbert, Oswin, Philibert, Ronald, Samuel
21 Abraham, Jane, Pius
22 Andrew, Hippolytus, Sigfrid, Timothy
23 Claudius, Eleazar, Eugene, Philip, Rose, Sidonius, Zacchaeus
24 Alice, Bartholomew, Emily, Jane, Joan, Nathanael, Ouen
25 Joseph, Louis, Lucilla, Menas, Patricia
26 Dominic, Elias, Elizabeth, Zephyrinus
27 Caesarius, Gabriel, Hugh, Margaret, Monica, Rufus
28 Adelina, Alexander, Augustine, Julian, Moses, Vivian
29 Basilla, John, Merry, Sabina

30 Felix, Pammachius, Rose
31 Aidan, Paulinus, Raymund

September

1 Anna, Augustus, Gideon, Giles, Joshua, Simeon, Verena
2 John, René, Stephen, William
3 Dorothy, Euphemia, Gabriel, Gregory, Phoebe, Simeon
4 Babylas, Boniface, Candida, Hermione, Ida, Marcellus, Moses, Rosalia, Rose
5 Laurence, Urban, Vitus, Zacharias
6 Beata, Magnus, Zechariah
7 Eustace, Regina
8 Adrian, Natalia, Sergius
9 Isaac, Kieran, Louise, Peter, Seraphina, Sergius, Wilfrida
10 Aubert, Candida, Finnian, Isabel, Nicholas, Pulcheria
11 Daniel, Ethelburga, Hyacinth, Paphnutius, Theodora
12 Guy
13 Amatus, John
14 Cormac
15 Albinus, Catherine, Roland
16 Cornelius, Cyprian, Edith, Eugenia, Euphemia, Lucy, Ninian, Victor
17 Ariadne, Columba, Hildegard, Justin, Lambert, Narcissus, Robert, Satyrus, Theodora
18 Irene, Sophia
19 Constantia, Emily, Januarius, Susanna, Theodore
20 Candida, Eustace, Philippa, Vincent
21 Jonah, Matthew, Maura
22 Felix, Jonas, Maurice, Thomas
23 Adamnan, Helen, Linus, Thecla
24 Gerard
25 Albert, Aurelia, Herman, Sergius
26 Cosmas, Cyprian, John, Justina, René
27 Adolphus, Caius, Cosmas, Damian, Frumentius, Terence, Vincent
28 Exuperius, Solomon, Wenceslas
29 Gabriel, Michael, Raphael
30 Jerome, Otto, Simon, Sophia

October

1   Francis, Nicholas, Remigius, Romanos, Teresa
2   Leodegar, Theophilus
3   Gerard, Thérèse, Thomas
4   Ammon, Aurea, Berenice, Francis, Petronius
5   Flavia, Flora
6   Aurea, Bruno, Faith, Magnus, Mary, Thomas
7   Augustus, Julia, Justina, Mark
8   Bridget, Laurentia, Sergius, Simeon
9   Abraham, Demetrius, Denis, Dionysius, Gunther, James, John, Louis
10 Daniel, Francis, Paulinus, Samuel
11 Atticus, Bruno, Juliana, Kenneth, Nectarius
12 Cyprian, Edwin, Maximilian, Wilfrid
13 Edward, Gerald, Magdalen, Maurice, Theophilus
14 Callistus, Cosmas, Dominic
15 Aurelia, Leonard, Lucian, Teresa, Thecla, Willa
16 Baldwin, Bertrand, Gall, Gerard, Hedwig, Lullus, Margaret
17 Ignatius, Margaret, Rudolph, Victor
18 Blanche, Candida, Gwen, Gwendoline, Luke
19 Cleopatra, Isaac, John, Laura, Lucius, Paul, Peter
20 Adelina, Andrew, Irene, Martha
21 Hilarion, Ursula
22 Abercius, Philip
23 Bartholomew, Ignatius, James, John, Josephine
24 Anthony, Martin, Raphael, Septimus
25 Balthasar, Crispin, Crispinian, Dorcas, Gaudentius, George, Tabitha, Thaddeus, Theodoric
26 Albinus, Cuthbert, Damian, Demetrius, Lucian
27 Antonia, Sabina
28 Anastasias, Firmilian, Godwin, Jude, Simon, Thaddaeus
29 Narcissus, Terence
30 Alphonsus, Artemas, Dorothy, Marcellus, Serapion, Zenobia
31 Quentin, Wolfgang

November

1   Cledwyn, Cosmas, Damian, Mary
2   Eustace, Maura, Tobias, Victorinus
3   Hubert, Malachy, Martin, Pirminius, Sylvia, Valentine, Winifred

4 Agricola, Charles, Frances, Vitalis
5 Cosmo, Elizabeth, Martin, Zacharias
6 Illtyd, Leonard, Paul
7 Carina, Florentius, Gertrude, Rufus, Willibrord
8 Elizabeth, Godfrey, Willehad
9 Simeon, Theodore
10 Florence, Justus, Leo, Tryphena
11 Bartholomew, Martin, Menas, Theodore
12 Josaphat, Martin, Matthew, Nilus, René
13 Abbo, Brice, Eugene, John, Nicholas, Stanislaus
14 Dubricius, Gregory, Laurence
15 Albert, Leopold, Machutus
16 Agnes, Edmund, Eucherius, Gertrude, Margaret, Matthew
17 Dionysius, Elizabeth, Gregory, Hilda, Hugh, Victoria, Zacchaeus
18 Constant, Odo, Romanus
19 Crispin, Elizabeth, Mechtild, Nerses
20 Edmund, Octavius, Silvester
21 Albert, Gelasius, Rufus
22 Cecilia, Philemon
23 Amphilochius, Clement, Columban, Felicity, Gregory, Lucretia
24 Flora, John, Thaddeus
25 Catherine, Clement, Mercurius, Mesrob, Moses
26 Conrad, Leonard, Peter, Silvester, Siricius
27 Barlam, Fergus, James, Josaphat, Virgil
28 James, Simeon, Stephen
29 Blaise, Brendan, Cuthbert, Frederick
30 Andrew, Frumentius, Maura

December

1 Eligius, Nahum, Natalia, Ralph
2 Aurelia, Chromatius, Viviana
3 Claudius, Francis Xavier, Jason, Lucius
4 Ada, Barbara, Bernard, John, Osmond
5 Bartholomew, Clement, Sabas
6 Abraham, Dionysia, Gertrude, Nicholas, Tertius
7 Ambrose, Josepha
8 Mary
9 Peter
10 Brian, Eulalia, Gregory, Julia, Miltiades, Sidney
11 Damasus, Daniel, Franco
12 Agatha, Cormac, Dionysia, Jane Frances, Spyridon, Vicelin

13 Aubert, Judoc, Lucy, Ottilia
14 Conrad, John, Spyridon
15 Christiana, Mary
16 Adelaide, Albina, Azariah, Eusebius
17 Florian, Lazarus, Olympias
18 Frumentius, Rufus
19 Thea, Urban
20 Dominic, Ignatius
21 Peter, Thomas
22 Adam, Anastasia, Chrysogonus
23 John, Victoria
24 Adam, Adela, Eve
25 Anastasia, Eugenia
26 Christina, Dionysius, Stephen, Vincentia
27 Fabiola, John, Stephen, Theodore
28 Theophila
29 David, Marcellus, Thomas, Trophimus
30 Sabinus
31 Columba, Cornelius, Fabian, Melania, Sextus, Silvester

Popular First Names

England and Wales

Boys

	1700		1800		1900
1	John	1	William	1	William
2	William	2	John	2	John
3	Thomas	3	Thomas	3	George
4	Richard	4	James	4	Thomas
5	James	5	George	5	Charles
6	Robert	6	Joseph	6	Frederick
7	Joseph	7	Richard	7	Arthur
8	Edward	8	Henry	8	James
9	Henry	9	Robert	9	Albert
10	George	10	Charles	10	Ernest

	1920s		1950s		1960s
1	John	1	David	1	Paul
2	William	2	John	2	David
3	George	3	Peter	3	Andrew
4	James	4	Michael	4	Stephen
5	Ronald	5	Alan	5	Mark
6	Robert	6	Robert	6	Michael
7	Kenneth	7	Stephen	7	Ian
8	Frederick	8	Paul	8	Gary
9	Thomas	9	Brian	9	Robert
10	Albert	10	Graham	10	Richard

1970s		1980s		1990s	
1	Stephen	1	Christopher	1	Daniel
2	Mark	2	Matthew	2	Matthew
3	Paul	3	David	3	James
4	Andrew	4	James	4	Christopher
5	David	5	Daniel	5	Adam
6	Richard	6	Andrew	6	Thomas
7	Matthew	7	Steven	7	David
8	Daniel	8	Michael	8	Luke
9	Christopher	9	Mark	9	Jamie
10	Darren	10	Paul	10	Robert

2002		2003		2004	
1	Jack	1	Jack	1	Jack
2	Joshua	2	Joshua	2	Joshua
3	Thomas	3	Thomas	3	Thomas
4	James	4	James	4	James
5	Daniel	5	Daniel	5	Daniel
6	Benjamin	6	Oliver	6	Samuel
7	William	7	Benjamin	7	Oliver
8	Samuel	8	Samuel	8	William
9	Joseph	9	William	9	Benjamin
10	Oliver	10	Joseph	10	Joseph

Girls

1700		1800		1900	
1	Mary	1	Mary	1	Florence
2	Elizabeth	2	Ann	2	Mary
3	Ann	3	Elizabeth	3	Alice
4	Sarah	4	Sarah	4	Annie
5	Jane	5	Jane	5	Elsie
6	Margaret	6	Hannah	6	Edith
7	Susan	7	Susan	7	Elizabeth
8	Martha	8	Martha	8	Doris
9	Hannah	9	Margaret	9	Dorothy
10	Catherine	10	Charlotte	10	Ethel

1920s

1 Joan
2 Mary
3 Joyce
4 Margaret
5 Dorothy
6 Doris
7 Kathleen
8 Irene
9 Betty
10 Eileen

1950s

1 Susan
2 Linda
3 Christine
4 Margaret
5 Carol
6 Jennifer
7 Janet
8 Patricia
9 Barbara
10 Ann

1960s

1 Tracey
2 Deborah
3 Julie
4 Karen
5 Susan
6 Alison
7 Jacqueline
8 Helen
9 Amanda
10 Sharon

1970s

1 Claire
2 Sarah
3 Nicola
4 Emma
5 Joanne
6 Helen
7 Rachel
8 Lisa
9 Rebecca
10 { Karen / Michelle }

1980s

1 Sarah
2 Claire
3 Emma
4 Laura
5 Rebecca
6 Gemma
7 Rachel
8 Kelly
9 Victoria
10 Katharine

1990s

1 Emma
2 Sarah
3 Laura
4 Charlotte
5 Amy
6 Rebecca
7 Gemma
8 Katharine
9 Lauren
10 Hayley

2002

1 Chloe
2 Emily
3 Jessica
4 Ellie
5 Sophie
6 Megan
7 Charlotte
8 Lucy
9 Hannah
10 Olivia

2003

1 Emily
2 Ellie
3 Chloe
4 Jessica
5 Sophie
6 Megan
7 Lucy
8 Olivia
9 Charlotte
10 Hannah

2004

1 Emily
2 Ellie
3 Jessica
4 Sophie
5 Chloe
6 Lucy
7 Olivia
8 Charlotte
9 Katie
10 Megan

Scotland

Boys		Girls	
2004		2004	
1	Lewis	1	Emma
2	Jack	2	Sophie
3	James	3	Ellie
4	Cameron	4	Amy
5	Ryan	5	Chloe
6	Liam	6	Katie
7	Jamie	7	Erin
8	Ben	8	Emily
9	Kyle	9	Lucy
10	Callum	10	Hannah

USA

Boys

1900		1920s		1940s	
1	John	1	Robert	1	Robert
2	William	2	John	2	James
3	Charles	3	William	3	John
4	Robert	4	James	4	William
5	Joseph	5	Charles	5	Richard
6	James	6	Richard	6	Thomas
7	George	7	George	7	David
8	Samuel	8	Donald	8	Ronald
9	Thomas	9	Joseph	9	Donald
10	Arthur	10	Edward	10	Michael

1950s	1960s	1970s
1 Robert	1 Michael	1 Michael
2 Michael	2 David	2 Robert
3 James	3 Robert	3 David
4 John	4 James	4 James
5 David	5 John	5 John
6 William	6 Mark	6 Jeffrey
7 Thomas	7 Steven	7 Steven
8 Richard	8 Thomas	8 Christopher
9 Gary	9 William	9 Brian
10 Charles	10 Joseph	10 Mark

1990s	2001	2002
1 Michael	1 Jacob	1 Matthew
2 Christopher	2 Michael	2 Tyler
3 Matthew	3 Matthew	3 Joshua
4 Joshua	4 Joshua	4 Michael
5 Jacob	5 Christopher	5 Nicholas
6 Andrew	6 Nicholas	6 Alex
7 Daniel	7 Andrew	7 Jacob
8 Nicholas	8 Joseph	8 Andrew
9 Tyler	9 Daniel	9 Brandon
10 Joseph	10 William	10 Taylor

2003

1 Jacob
2 Michael
3 Joshua
4 Matthew
5 Ethan
6 Joseph
7 Andrew
8 Christopher
9 Daniel
10 Nicholas

Girls

1900		1920s		1940s	
1	Mary	1	Mary	1	Mary
2	Ruth	2	Barbara	2	Patricia
3	Helen	3	Dorothy	3	Barbara
4	Margaret	4	Betty	4	Judith
5	Elizabeth	5	Ruth	5	Carol
6	Dorothy	6	Margaret	6	Sharon
7	Catherine	7	Helen	7	Nancy
8	Mildred	8	Elizabeth	8	Joan
9	Frances	9	Jean	9	Sandra
10	Alice / Marion	10	Ann	10	Margaret

1950s		1960s		1970s	
1	Linda	1	Mary	1	Michelle
2	Mary	2	Deborah	2	Jennifer
3	Patricia	3	Karen	3	Kimberly
4	Susan	4	Susan	4	Lisa
5	Deborah	5	Linda	5	Tracy
6	Kathleen	6	Patricia	6	Kelly
7	Barbara	7	Kimberly	7	Nicole
8	Nancy	8	Catherine	8	Angela
9	Sharon	9	Cynthia	9	Pamela
10	Karen	10	Lori	10	Christine

1990s		2001		2002	
1	Ashley	1	Emily	1	Emily
2	Jessica	2	Madison	2	Jessica
3	Emily	3	Hannah	3	Hannah
4	Sarah	4	Ashley	4	Alyssa
5	Samantha	5	Alexis	5	Amanda
6	Brittany	6	Samantha	6	Samantha
7	Amanda	7	Sarah	7	Madison
8	Elizabeth	8	Abigail	8	Megan
9	Taylor	9	Elizabeth	9	Katie
10	Megan	10	Jessica	10	Alexis

2003

1 Emily
2 Madison
3 Hannah
4 Emma
5 Alexis
6 Ashley
7 Abigail
8 Sarah
9 Samantha
10 Olivia

Australia

Boys

1950s		1970s		1990s	
1	John	1	Matthew	1	Matthew
2	Peter	2	Andrew	2	Daniel
3	Michael	3	David	3	Michael
4	David	4	Michael	4	Thomas
5	Robert	5	Paul	5	Benjamin
6	Stephen	6	Adam	6	James
7	Paul	7	Christopher	7	Samuel
8	Phillip	8	Daniel	8	Nicholas
9	Christopher	9	Mark	9	Joshua
10	Ian	10	Scott	10	Christopher

2001	2002	2003
1 Jack	1 Jack	1 Joshua
2 Lachlan	2 Joshua	2 Jack
3 Joshua	3 Lachlan	3 Thomas
4 James	4 Thomas	4 Ethan
5 Benjamin	5 William	5 Liam
6 Matthew	6 Liam	6 Jacob
7 Thomas	7 Ethan	7 Matthew
8 Nicholas	8 James	8 Mitchell
9 William	9 Benjamin	9 Lachlan
10 Samuel	10 Matthew	10 Daniel

Girls

1950s	1970s	1990s
1 Susan	1 Michelle	1 Jessica
2 Margaret	2 Catherine	2 Sarah
3 Anne	3 Kylie	3 Emma
4 Elizabeth	4 Nicole	4 Lauren
5 Christine	5 Rebecca	5 Rebecca
6 Jennifer	6 Melissa	6 Ashleigh
7 Judith	7 Lisa	7 Amy
8 Patricia	8 Belinda	8 Emily
9 Catherine	9 Rachel	9 Kate
10 Helen	10 Sarah	10 Katherine

2001	2002	2003
1 Emily	1 Emily	1 Chloe
2 Georgia	2 Chloe	2 Jessica
3 Jessica	3 Georgia	3 Emma
4 Chloe	4 Jessica	4 Grace
5 Olivia	5 Olivia	5 Sarah
6 Sophie	6 Ella	6 Shakira
7 Hannah	7 Sophie	7 Emily
8 Grace	8 Charlotte	8 Amy
9 Sarah	9 Isabella	9 Hannah
10 Ella	10 Hannah	10 Hayley